Mormons in Early Victorian Britain

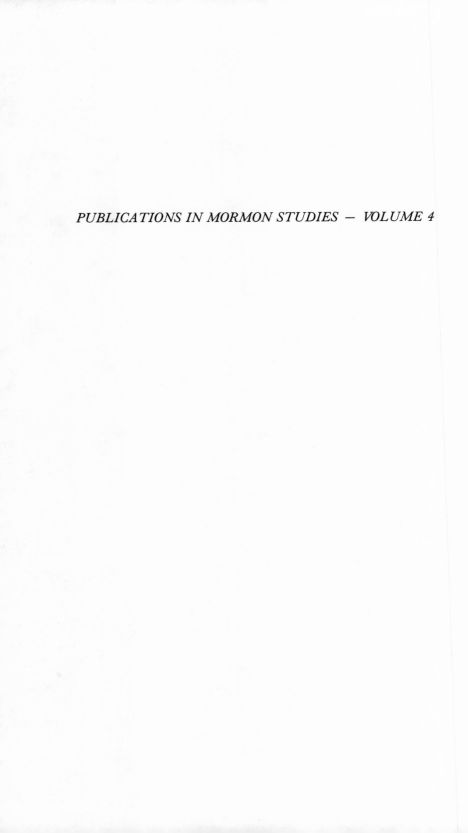

PUBLICATIONS IN MORMON STUDIES — VOLUME 4

Mormons in Early Victorian Britain

EDITED BY

RICHARD L. JENSEN AND MALCOLM R. THORP

University of Utah Press

Salt Lake City

1989

Publications in Mormon Studies
Linda King Newell, editor

Publications in Mormon Studies was established to encourage creation and submission of work on Mormon-related topics that would be of interest to scholars and the general public. The initiation of the series represents an acknowledgment by the Press and the editor of the region's rich historical and literary heritage and of the quality of work being done in various areas of Mormon studies today.
ISSN 0893-4916

The editors wish to express appreciation to Brigham Young University for assistance in their work.

Library of Congress Cataloging-in-Publication Data

Mormons in early Victorian Britain / edited by Richard L. Jensen and
    Malcolm R. Thorp.
        p.   cm. — (Publications in Mormon studies ; v. 4)
    Bibliography: p.
    Includes index.
    ISBN 0-87480-322-5
    1. Church of Jesus Christ of Latter-Day Saints — Great Britain —
History — 19th century.   2. Mormon Church — Great Britain —
History — 19th century.   3. Great Britain — Church history — 19th
century.   I. Jensen, Richard L.   II. Thorp, Malcolm R., 1943-
III. Series.
BX8617.G7M67   1989
289.3'41 — dc19   89-4808
                                               CIP

Contents

Illustrations

Tables

Figures

Contributors

Bernard Aspinwall is Visitor to Colleges and Universities in North America, University of Glasgow Office for International Programmes.

The late John B. Cotterill obtained his Ph.D. degree from Keele University in 1985.

D. L. Davies, of Cwmaman, Aberdare, Wales, is a teacher of the Welsh language at Merthyr Tydfil, Wales.

Ray Jay Davis is professor of law, J. Reuben Clark Law School, Brigham Young University.

Ronald K. Esplin is director and research associate professor with the Joseph Fielding Smith Institute for Church History, Brigham Young University, and associate professor of Church History and Doctrine, Brigham Young University.

Susan L. Fales is chairperson of the history/religion department, Harold B. Lee Library, Brigham Young University.

John F. C. Harrison is emeritus professor of history at the University of Sussex, England.

William G. Hartley is research assistant professor with the Joseph Fielding Smith Institute for Church History, Brigham Young University, and research assistant professor of history, Brigham Young University.

Richard L. Jensen is a research historian with the Joseph Fielding Smith Institute, Brigham Young University.

Robert L. Lively, Jr., teaches religion at the University of Maine at Farmington, where he is also the Director of Continuing Education.

Paul H. Peterson is assistant professor of Church History and Doctrine, Brigham Young University.

Andrew Phillips is lecturer in history, Colchester Institute, Colchester, Essex, England.

Richard D. Poll, is professor of history, emeritus, Western Illinois University.

Malcolm R. Thorp is professor of history, Brigham Young University.

Grant Underwood is director of the Latter-day Saint Institute of Religion located at the University of Southern California.

David J. Whittaker is university archivist and curator of the Archives of the Mormon Experience, Archives and Manuscripts, Brigham Young University.

Introduction

RICHARD L. JENSEN AND MALCOLM R. THORP

The flowering of Mormon studies in the past three decades has provided the basis for a wealth of insights not only into the Latter-day Saint Church itself but also into the societies and environments within which its history has transpired. Crucial to the early survival and development of Mormonism was its British Mission. However, surprisingly little has been written until recently on this significant topic.[1] Conspicuously absent in studies by Latter-day Saints was critical analysis of events and any attempt to relate the Mormon experience to the broader spectrum of religious and social history in early Victorian Britian. This omission is particularly regrettable because Latter-day Saint missionary work among the working classes is an important theme that transcends the narrow bounds of denominational history.[2] Indeed, the successes of missionaries among common people was so significant that no other sect in the 1840s matched the Mormons in terms of rapidity of growth. Thus, beginning with the modest successes of the first missionaries, led by the Apostle Heber C. Kimball, the church grew by the addition of 51,000 converts in the British Isles by 1851. The reasons for this impressive growth deserve more attention than has thus far

---

[1] Richard L. Evans, *A Century of "Mormonism" in Great Britain* (Salt Lake City: Deseret News Press, 1937, reprint Salt Lake City: Publishers Press, 1984), was primarily a celebration of the beginnings of the British Mission, published in the mission's centennial year. It has been largely superceded by V. Ben Bloxham, James R. Moss, and Larry R. Porter, eds., *Truth Will Prevail* (Solihull, England: The Church of Jesus Christ of Latter-day Saints, 1987), a general study for Latter-day Saints.

[2] James B. Allen and Malcolm R. Thorp, "The Mission of the Twelve to England, 1840–41: Mormon Apostles and the Working Classes," *Brigham Young University Studies* 15 (1975): 499–526.

been given to this theme, from both historical and sociological perspectives.[3]

A new approach was taken with the publication of P. A. M. Taylor's pioneering study of Mormon emigration from the British Isles in 1968.[4] Written by a reputable social historian, this book was the first concerted attempt to place Mormonism within the context of the times. Taylor's analysis of the social composition of Latter-day Saint converts, largely from maritime sources, has been confirmed by subsequent scholars.[5] Not only did he demonstrate the working-class character of the movement, but he was the first historian to relate the social origins of Mormonism to the religious climate of the times. While Taylor's thesis that the Mormons came predominantly from "splinter groups," especially offshoots from Methodism, might well be questioned,[6] his sociological approach to the subject has been suggestive to historians. At the same time, however, it can be said that Taylor relied heavily on printed sources for his understanding of Mormonism, and his study does not reflect the wealth of archival materials available on this topic.

The 150th anniversary of the British Mission in 1987 intensified interest in the scholarly investigation of its history. New studies probed many topics that had not heretofore been examined in depth. For the present volume we have chosen what we consider to be some of the most significant recent essays on Mormonism in the British Isles during the critical decades of the early Victorian period. Many of these originated as papers presented at a conference of the Mormon History Association at Oxford in July 1987. In selecting this material it has been the purpose of the editors to create a balance between administrative history, focusing on the role of church leaders overseeing the operation of the British Mission, and on local developments. We have also chosen for this collection essays which,

---

[3] There has been considerable interest in popular religion from scholars delving into the early Victorian period. See, for example, the most recent effort by Hugh McLeod, *Religion and the Working Class in Nineteenth-Century Britain* (London: Macmillan, 1984), which presents a useful summary of what has thus far been done. Because of the relative remoteness of sources in Utah, however, mainline scholars of religion have virtually ignored the Mormon experience in the British Isles in their studies.

[4] P. A. M. Taylor, *Expectations Westward: The Mormons and the Emigration of their British Converts in the Nineteenth Century* (Edinburgh and London: Oliver & Boyd, 1965).

[5] Malcolm R. Thorp, "The Religious Backgrounds of Mormon Converts in Britain, 1837–52," *Journal of Mormon History* 4 (1977):51–66. Richard L. Jensen and Gordon I. Irving, "British Mormon Emigrants on the Ship *Amazon*, 1863: A Computer-assisted Study," paper presented at annual meeting of Pacific Coast Branch, American Historical Association, San Francisco, 19 August 1978.

[6] See Thorp, "Religious Backgrounds."

we hope, will contribute to an understanding of varying factors that help account for church growth in England, Wales, and Scotland. In addition, it is hoped that by demonstrating the development of the church in local communities such as Leeds, Essex, and Birmingham, readers will begin to see how, in a diverse country such as Britain, regional factors played a role not only in church successes, but also in the failure of the movement to establish itself in certain areas. Given the working-class character of this movement, we have also included a seminal study that for the first time, utilizing LDS autobiographical sources, probes into the fascinating and diverse elements of plebian culture within the British Mission.

Elements of working-class culture in the Mormon movement deserve even more attention than they receive here. While the general religious milieu was undoubtedly important to understanding the Mormon successes, it is likewise important to establish the linkage between religious ideas and the actual conversions. In this regard the Sunday School movement probably exerted a more profound effect on the minds of those who eventually converted than many of the essentially middle-class religious formulations that were commonplace during this time.[7] Many working-class Mormon journals allude to the experience of the Sunday School, although they do not reveal much about the ideas that were discussed. Notions of self-help and the converts' desire for the improvement of their lives were the product of such influences. In addition, as the study on Leeds suggests, negative attitudes toward social class would preclude much religious influence from middle-class sources on the lives of working people. Hugh McLeod has stated, "the working man, conscious of an inferior status in the eyes of his social superiors, was far more likely than a clerk enjoying a similar standard of living to behave in ways condemned by these superiors, and far less likely to identify himself with the social system."[8] In significant ways, the desire to commune with the Saints and to seek the building of Zion in an American New Jerusalem was the working-class Mormon response to a class society that offered only limited opportunities for self-improvement.

The inception of the Mormon mission to Britain is well known, but here we consider this event in a new light, from the perspective of sectarian leaders whose congregations were affected by the faith, as well as LDS missionary accounts. The British Mission played a significant role in the

---

[7] See Thomas Walter Laqueur, *Religion and Respectability: Sunday Schools and Working Class Culture 1780–1850* (New Haven and London: Yale University Press, 1976).

[8] Hugh McLeod, "Class, Community and Region: The Religious Geography of Nineteenth-Century England," in Michael Hill, ed., *A Sociological Yearbook of Religion in Britain* (London: SMC, 1973) 6:34–35.

development and growth of the Latter-day Saint Church as a whole. Considered here are the ways in which the 1840–41 mission of the Quorum of the Twelve Apostles became a major turning point in church administrative history.

Many of these essays examine developments in the 1850s, a watershed decade for Mormonism in several respects. Throughout the period under consideration, millennialistic expectations gave urgency to British Mission preparations for the holocaust which was forecast to precede the imminent Second Coming. Rapid growth was followed by years of intensive focus on recommitment and of weeding out individuals whose dedication to the cause flagged. Culminating in the reformation of 1857, this may have revitalized the remaining membership, but it also accelerated the numerical decline of mission membership—partly a result of the church's highly successful emigration policy. Meanwhile, the 1853 announcement that polygamy was indeed being practiced in Utah curtailed proselytizing success and challenged the faith of many British Latter-day Saints. Proselytizing absorbed a further blow during the so-called Utah War with the withdrawal of most U.S. missionaries, although the mission used the opportunity to regroup and pursue administrative reform. By the late 1850s, conversions were no longer keeping pace with defections and emigration. Thus, by the end of our period (1870), Mormonism in the British Isles was clearly in decline, and this withering process continued until by 1914 the church was a numerically obscure sect known principally for its polygamist past. It was not until after 1950, when the church developed a more positive public image, that significant numbers of Britishers were attracted to this now conservative faith.

While much remains to be done, this modest contribution explores some of the major themes that have so far captured the attention of Mormon historians. Like any collection of essays, it leaves numerous gaps in the narrative that must be filled by further historical research. Still, it is hoped that the essays will collectively suggest historical trends and fruitful areas of inquiry for the early Victorian years and provide the basis for dialogue that will promote further understanding.

1

The Popular History of Early Victorian Britain: A Mormon Contribution

*JOHN F. C. HARRISON**

For some time now I have been interested in exploring the history of the common people of Britain. This is a type of history that presents peculiar problems, among them the difficulty of sources. Imagine therefore my delight when I came upon the rich collection of Mormon journals and autobiographies and found that they contained a great deal of material relevant to my purposes. Here is a source, scarcely known outside Mormon circles, just waiting to be exploited by historians of nineteenth-century Britain. I would like to suggest some ways in which these sources might be used for purposes wider than strictly Mormon history.

The writing of histories of the common people is not new.[1] Indeed, the tradition stretches from J. R. Green and Thorold Rogers in the later nineteenth century, through Cole and Postgate, and Mitchell and Leys, to the present.[2] Most of this work, however, has been either primarily economic history or social history of the "men and manners" variety. My concern is

---

*This essay was presented as the annual Tanner Lecture at the Twenty-third Annual Meeting of the Mormon History Association at Oxford, July 6, 1987, and was published first in *Journal of Mormon History* 14 (1988): 3-15. Its preparation was made possible through the generosity of Obert C. and Grace A. Tanner. The essay is republished here with the permission of Professor Harrison and the board of editors of *Journal of Mormon History*.

[1] *Common people* is the term by which the great majority of ordinary people who had to work for their living were known in Britain. I have used the words *common* and *popular* throughout the paper despite their slightly different usage in British and American English.

[2] See J. R. Green, *Short History of the English People* (London, 1874); James E. Thorold Rogers, *Six Centuries of Work and Wages: The History of English Labour*, 2 vols. (London: Swan Sonnenschein, 1884); G. D. H. Cole and Raymond Postgate, *The Common People, 1746-1938* (London: Methuen, 1938); R. J. Mitchell and M. D. R. Leys, *A History of the English People* (London: Longmans, Green, 1950).

somewhat different. It is to write history from below as it were, to start from the perceptions of the people themselves, rather than accept the views of what others, whether contemporary reformers and sympathizers or later historians, thought about working people. These are the people who have usually been left out of history, and to write their history is to encounter formidable problems of chronology, theme, and sources.[3]

We cannot, for instance, ignore the historian's basic requirement of chronology, for history is essentially the study of change over time. But the chronology of popular history will not necessarily be the same as is appropriate for other types of history. Probably the traditional chronology and periodization of English history, being based on the political and economic decisions of the ruling classes, distorts or confuses the history of the common people, whose lives were largely determined by other considerations. We need an alternative periodization based on changes in popular experience and perceptions. Unfortunately, the danger of forcing popular history into a procrustean bed of traditional historiography cannot be entirely avoided. Until we have much more evidence to work on, we have to take some of the accepted historian's categories and periods, even though they may not be truly relevant. Moreover, although the history of the common people should not be submerged in general history, the two are obviously interrelated. The common people have always been faced with the problem of living in a world they did not create.

History of the common people is also different in its selection of themes. All history is a pattern made by interweaving chronological and thematic evidence from the records of the past; and for the common people, the themes will be those which seem to show most closely how they lived and what they made of their lives. This means (at least ideally) that the history of the common people will not be simply traditional history with highlights on the contributions of ordinary men and women, but a completely different pattern, starting from different assumptions and ideas of what is important and what is not. Historians will never be able to re-create, no matter how sympathetic or imaginative they are, anything more than a tiny fragment of the experiences and sentiments of that infinite host of men and women "which have no memorial, who are perished as though they had never been born." But if we start by asking the right questions and looking for answers in new directions, we may at least stand a chance of uncovering more than has been discovered about the common people in

---

[3] These problems are discussed at greater length in the introduction to J. F. C. Harrison, *The Common People of Great Britain* (Bloomington: Indiana University Press, 1985); also published in the United Kingdom as *The Common People* (London: Fontana, 1984).

the past. The starting point must be those things which were central in the life of laboring people.

Here we come up against one of the greatest problems in writing the history of the common people: the scarcity of sources. We are dealing with that part of the community which was largely inarticulate. They did not, for the most part, leave written records in which they described their thoughts and feelings and the events in which they were involved. The literary sources upon which historians rely so heavily do not at present exist in the same form and quantity for the common people as for their social superiors. This, more than any other, has been the argument advanced by professional historians against the possibility of writing a history of the common people. The historian is bound by evidence, and if it is not there, he or she can make no headway. This, of course, is correct; but it is not the whole story. Known sources can be reworked. Oral testimony, folklore, the work of men's hands, and the comparative researches of archaeologists and anthropologists can be used to escape the tyranny of literary evidence. Most relevant here, many hitherto unknown autobiographies of working men and women have come to light in the past fifteen years, when scholars have deliberately gone out to look for them.[4] No truth is greater for the historian than that he who seeketh, findeth.

Mormon historians have been aware for some time of the great wealth of autobiographical material that exists among LDS records. Ten years ago Malcolm Thorp, James B. Allen, Thomas G. Alexander, and others made good use of it.[5] And we are all immensely indebted to Davis Bitton for his magnificent *Guide to Mormon Diaries and Autobiographies* published in 1977 and surely a model of its kind.[6] Naturally these historians were interested in using the material to explore aspects of Mormon history. My pur-

---

[4] Notably in John Burnett, David Vincent, and David Mayall, *The Autobiography of the Working Class: An Annotated, Critical Bibliography*, vol. 1, 1790–1900 (Brighton: Harvester Press, 1984). See also David Vincent, *Bread, Knowledge and Freedom: A Study of Nineteenth-Century Working Class Autobiography* (London: Europa, 1981); and the introduction to *Robert Lowery: Radical and Chartist*, ed. Brian Harrison and Patricia Hollis (London: Europa, 1979). A valuable recent study is Regenia Gagnier, "Social Atoms: Working-Class Autobiography, Subjectivity, and Gender," *Victorian Studies* 30 (Spring 1987).

[5] See Malcolm R. Thorp, "The Religious Backgrounds of Mormon Converts in Britain, 1837–52," *Journal of Mormon History* 4 (1977), to which I am much indebted. Also James B. Allen and Malcolm R. Thorp, "The Mission of the Twelve to England, 1840–41: Mormon Apostles and the Working Classes," *Brigham Young University Studies* 15 (Summer 1975); Thomas G. Alexander, "Wilford Woodruff and the Changing Nature of Mormon Religious Experience," *Church History* 45 (March 1976).

[6] Davis Bitton, *Guide to Mormon Diaries and Autobiographies* (Provo, Utah: Brigham Young University Press, 1977), on which I have relied heavily.

pose is somewhat different. It is to suggest that we should examine the autobiographies, diaries, and journals as products of the common people of early Victorian England as part of a popular culture, the evidence of which is still all too scarce. It is not primarily as a record of events that the autobiography is to be evaluated, but as a statement by and about the author. Fascinating (often compelling) as are the accounts of missionary endeavor in the 1840s, or the hardships endured in the handcart companies of the 1850s, it is the type of perception and quality of the testimony that is of primary concern here. The autobiography is to be used as a key, or way, into the mental world of laboring men and women. As an offshoot of this, it is possible that some aspects of early Mormon history may appear in a slightly new context — though that is hardly within my competence to determine.

The writing of autobiography, however, is an extremely complex activity, and its use as historical evidence is by no means straightforward. At the risk of getting embroiled in current literary debates about the nature of autobiography, the historian cannot avoid certain problems. If it is used simply as a record, we have to make allowances for the fallibility of memory, especially as autobiographies were often written many years after the events they purport to describe. Even greater are the difficulties when we try to squeeze out more complex matter. Autobiography, even of the simplest and most naive kind, is in fact an art form, closely akin to fiction. The selection of memories is made in the light of the author's present conception of himself or herself. A coherence and pattern have been imposed as the author looks back; a process of smoothing out and tying up has gone on; some things have been deliberately left out and others overemphasized; self-justification and explanation have been added. The result is a curious tangle with which the historian has to wrestle. Yet this is the challenge. Documents, as Marc Bloch reminded us, are witnesses, and our task is to force them to speak, even against their will.[7] To probe into the motives of the autobiographer, to examine the use of language and concepts of time, to try to disentangle the sense of self, opens up new vistas for the social historian. And nowhere are such opportunities greater than in a sample of early Mormon autobiographies.

Patience Loader, born in 1827, was a domestic servant from an Oxfordshire village, where her father was "head gardener to an English Nobler Man for twenty-three years."[8] There were thirteen children in the family,

---

[7] See Marc Bloch, *The Historian's Craft* (Manchester: Manchester University Press, 1954), 63, 64, and quoted in Alan Macfarlane, *The Origins of English Individualism* (Oxford: Blackwell, 1978), 190.

[8] Patience Loader Rozsa Archer (1827–1921), Autobiography, Brigham Young University Library (hereafter BYU Library). In this and all following quotations

and at the age of seventeen she went into service, first in a neighboring village and afterward in London. Following her parents' conversion to Mormonism, she too was baptized, although at first she had been uninterested. She emigrated to Utah in 1856, and in 1858 she married John Rozsa, a sergeant in the 10th Infantry, U.S. Army. Her autobiography, entitled "Recollections of Past Days," is a marvelously vivid document. Through her oral speech style, phonetic spelling, and unpunctuated sentences, there shines the personality of a laboring woman. Unlike most such journal writers, she includes a great deal of how she felt about events and people. Now this is the very stuff of social history; for, as a great social historian once wrote, "the real, central theme of History is not what happened, but what people felt about it when it was happening."[9]

Patience's thoughts on leaving home for the first time, her observations on life in London in the late 1840s, the realities of life as a hotel housemaid — all make her so much more than the usual cardboard figure describing external events. Her natural powers of narration are perhaps shown at their best in her description of the journey by handcart to Utah in 1856. Terrified by hostile Indians, and with her sister giving birth in a tent, she writes an emotional and moving account of her father's sufferings and death on the plains. In this remarkable tour de force, told so simply and with such deep feeling, we are reminded of some of the qualities to be found in the common people. This is not to say that Patience Loader's autobiography is all on this level. At times she gives way to sentimentality. Looking back on her early days, she describes a romantic mist arising around "the old home" in England, where she had, she writes, "sweet recollections of childhood and girlhood when I think of the old home whare I was born and raised it fills my heart with joy and pleasure the dear old house with thatched roof and old fashion casements windows with dimant cut glass and verada in front with wood-bines roses and honeysuckles twing up to the upstairs windows a beautifull flower garden on each side of the walk from the street." The reality of a gardener's cottage in the 1830s was, alas, somewhat different.

The oral tones of the popular culture also come through in other autobiographies. Edwin Smout, born in 1825, was a foreman tailor from Dudley, and his Black Country speech can be heard when the following passage from his unpunctuated and phonetically spelled journal[10] is read aloud:

---

the original spelling, punctuation (or lack of it), and grammar have been retained, without the use of the infuriating sic.

[9] G. M. Young, *Victorian England: Portrait of an Age* (Oxford: Oxford University Press, 1936), vi.

[10] Edwin Ward Smout (1823–1900), Journal, BYU Library.

I was rease and Brought up in the Town of Dudley Worcestershire England in my fourteen (14) year I was Bownd Apprentice to William Stokes in Said Town of Dudley I severed 18 mounth and then I when to the Taylors Cuting Bord for to learn to be a foreman in a Taylors Shop which traide I like in my 17 years I became acquainted with Leah Oakley She was born May 5th 1826 in Dudley Worcestershire England She was the Daughter of Samuel Oakley and Mary Adlington in my 17 year I got made a odd Fellow in the love and Unity Lodge I was then Choosen Secretary of the Lodge which office I held for 18 mounths when I was elected Vice Grand of the Lodge After keeping Company with Leah Oakley for upwards of four years we got Married. . . . we Spent 2 months at Mothers and then we when to house Keeping I did at my trade firstrate I furnish a house good I Rented a pew in the Methodist Church from them and other Churchs I got my trade we appeared in the world firstrate and in good order On the 3 day of October 1847 my wife Brought my first Son Felix She had a Bad time with her first Child it was a Seven months Child We had hard work to keep life in him for two months then he did very well in December I Received invitation from John Wever a Master Shoe Maker to go and hear the Later Day Saints Preach.

He was baptized in 1848 and resigned from the Oddfellows: "I went to my Lodge as I was Vicegrand of the Same and give up my office and gave them adress I tould them I had nothing against the Order of odd Fellows I love the Order But I was a Latter day Saint I was in a member of a Church that was truth I Sould hold to that and give up the odd Fellows."

This autobiography is significant for its priorities: occupation, marriage and family, respectability, friendly society, and religion; but it tells us little about the author's thoughts and feelings.

An autobiography of a different type is that of John Freeman.[11] Born in 1807, probably illegitimate and soon orphaned, Freeman spent his childhood in the parish school of industry of St. James, Westminster. Twelve months after being apprenticed by the parish as a shoemaker, he ran away "owing to ill usage" and worked in a brickyard at Hammersmith for ten years. In 1832 (the year of the Great Reform Bill), he became a farm worker in Bedfordshire, Warwickshire, and the Midland counties; and in between reaping times, he sang reform songs, with a companion, in marketplaces and at fairs. This arrangement, however, soon came to an end, and the two singers parted after "having a few words." Freeman was then

followed by a young woman of the name of Hannah Whiting, who had followed me for some months, but I not wanting to have anything to do with her, evaded her as much as possible, until at last she found me out where I was reaping, and then I could not get rid of her, so we two went together, to Birmingham, then back to Alcester, Evesham, Cheltenham and Banbury,

[11] John Freeman (1807–?), Reminiscences and Diary, Archives, The Church of Jesus Christ of Latter-day Saints (hereafter LDS Church Archives).

where we took lodgings and I commenced to make cloth slippers and she sold them, I singing in the markets and fairs at intervals. We next took a furnished house, and after a bit we bought some goods of our own and took a house to ourselves where we continued until December 18, 1834, when her temper being so bad and so quarrelsome I at length resolved to leave her, which I did on the above day, leaving her and goods altogether and travelled on to Stratford on Avon where I arrived the same evening and took lodgings at Thomas Heritage's and went on with my shoe making, having to bind them myself and likewise sell them.

Then in February 1835 he got a young woman, Esther Smith, to bind shoes for him. After her father died, and she was being pressured by her family to leave home and go into service, he decided to marry her. "After some equivocations" she agreed, and they were married in Stratford parish church in April 1835. Their first child was born in November 1836 and died the following March. Freeman seems to have been very unsettled during the next few years and was constantly moving back and forth between Stratford and Birmingham, living first in the one place and then in the other. He joined the Independents and attended their chapels, but was soon attracted to the Chartists after hearing them speak in the Bull Ring, Birmingham, in 1839. He joined the Christian Chartists, their discourses being "as nigh the Truth as most of them inasmuch as they advocated the Golden Rule of our Saviour and the Rights of their fellow creatures—so I joined with them and we opened a new place of worship, thus starting another [of] the numerous sects already upon the earth." This last phrase has a distinctly LDS ring about it; and indeed, in 1844 Freeman was converted to Mormonism, convinced that it was what he was looking for: "on the evening of the 6th March I was so foolish as to follow Christ through the water of regeneration and thus become a Son of God by being born of the Water."

Freeman's autobiography is one of those that is important not only for what it says but also for what it does not say. We sense something that is not wholly revealed. Why, for instance, does he tell us so little about his childhood and those ten years when he was working in the brickyard? We learn nothing about his schooling or level of educational attainment, though the journal is competently written and full of lively domestic detail. Nor does he fully explain his radical sympathies, although he was ready to sing songs supporting reform in 1832 and to join the Chartists in 1841. His views on marriage and the relation between the sexes, if deduced from his actions, are interesting, to say the least. He did not marry until he was twenty-eight, and then only because he feared he was about to lose the girl's services as a helpmate in his trade. Previously he had set up house with her predecessor, although (he would have us believe) only reluctantly. The contrast with the respectability and concern for worldly success manifested by the previous autobiographer, Edwin Smout, is marked.

Nevertheless, it is pointless for the historian to regret what he or she sees as the inadequacies and limitations of such evidence. Rather, we have to accept the autobiographies of common people as statements of how things appeared to them. Otherwise we fall into that "enormous condescension of posterity" against which we have been warned.[12] The things left out or treated only perfunctorily, the priorities accorded to different themes, the foreshortened chronology are themselves the evidence for which we are looking. They are part of the consciousness of the common people. George Morris, a farm laborer, explained how it was: "This scrapbook is an index to my life and caracter as the scraps are arranged in it so it has been with me. If I got anything I had to take it as I could catch it running, standing up, sitting or laying down. I was born in Hanley, Cheshire, England—of poore parents in a poor country—in August 1816."[13]

And there in pencil, in large, unformed handwriting, written as he spoke, is his testimony of what it was like to work on the land. As soon as he could walk, he was employed in bird scaring, armed with a set of clappers and "hollering" to scare off the rooks from early morning to late at night. His account of how he learned all the jobs required of a farm laborer is reminiscent of William Cobbett, though without any touch of romanticism. The detailed descriptions of what ploughing was really like when the ploughman was coated with mud, of how his mother worked for the farmers in the fields digging potatoes, and of how he picked blackberries to sell in the market are memorable for their unaffected authenticity. Hardly surprisingly, he remarks ruefully that there was "no time for me to go to school to get any education," although he did occasionally attend a dame school for a few weeks "now and then."

In due course Morris married: "After a while I thought that I must do as a great many other young men have done—get married. So I picked out a girl and married her—we were married at the parish church at Ashton under Lyne on the 6th of June 1840. She was an orphan girl, by the name of Jane Higinbotham." She was delivered of a baby girl "about a year after," and died in April 1841, "aged 20 years and 3 months."

This laconic account contrasts with the detail provided for other aspects of his life. Whether it truly represented Morris's view of marriage, or whether for some reason he was reluctant to say more, we do not know. In later life (1863) he entered polygamous marriage, and afterwards he was arrested and tried.

When the writer of an autobiography was a person of superior education or aspired to literary fame, the result was usually less satisfying than

---

[12] E. P. Thompson, *The Making of the English Working Class* (London: Gollancz, 1963), 12.

[13] George Morris (1816–97), Reminiscences, LDS Church Archives.

more humble efforts in the vernacular. George Harris, the son of a Devon-shire cabinetmaker, begins his autobiography thus: "Begoten and born in the usual manner, Gentle reader; I shal not tire U with particulars. Altho it may not be amiss to mention Dec. the 7th 1830 as the time; James and Eliza as the Parents; and the aforementioned lovely Ilfracombe as the location."[14]

He next tells an amusing story that his parents could not agree about his name, with the result that he was christened George Henry, his father always calling him George and his mother, Henry. The affectation of a humorous literary style reaches its extreme in his account of learning to walk: "It would be more difficult than interesting to tel of the number of fals that happened while tutering my pedal extremities to resist the effects of 'Atraction of Gravitation'."

Harris had a strongly Methodist upbringing and was apprenticed aboard a coaster in 1846. He was educated to high school standard and studied navigation. However, his spelling is highly erratic, and one shudders to learn that he actually taught school in Utah for a short time in 1854 before taking up farming. The autobiography is full of amusing anecdotes and short poems, both humorous and sentimental; and the author's self-conscious attempt to write for an audience and to project himself as a very entertaining fellow suggests a fairly sophisticated personality.

Individual personality, indeed, is perhaps the dominant characteristic that emerges from the autobiographies so far cited. Loader, Smout, Free-man, Morris, and Harris all wrote as interesting people in their own right. Yet our purpose in examining these and other testimonies is to see what, if anything, they have in common, to try to discern common assumptions, perceptions, and degrees of consciousness. Virtually all the writers begin by seeking to establish their identity. This they do by reference to time, place, and parentage. By telling the reader the date and sometimes the hour of their birth in a certain town or village, and their father's occupa-tion, they feel that they have located themselves socially. Explanation, apology, or justification follows from this. The location is not usually very extensive. Few autobiographies give details of their grandparents or uncles and aunts unless they were sent to live with them, and siblings appear only as numbers. The family as a center of childhood seems to be taken for granted, of little interest to the reader, or perhaps as irrelevant to the main purpose of the writers, which was to present themselves. Virtually none of the autobiographers spend much time on their childhood. They sometimes mention particular hardships connected with child labor but seldom give much detail or speculate about their childish thoughts at the time.[15] It is as

---

[14] George Henry Abbott Harris (1830–?), Autobiography, BYU Library.
[15] E.g., Thomas Wright Kirby (1831–1908), Autobiography, LDS Church

if the years before the age of puberty were considered of no account, or at most as preparation for earning a living later.

One thing the autobiographers virtually always mention is their schooling, or, more usually, their lack of it. All of them had managed at some stage to become literate, and the writing of their autobiographies reminded them in many cases of the inadequacies that remained after their attendance at Sunday school, dame school, or common day school.[16] Andrew Sproul, a Scottish weaver born in 1816, in a journal that devotes only one paragraph to the whole of his life prior to the arrival of Mormon elders in 1840, nevertheless finds space to comment as follows:

> My father Francis Sprowl and my mother Ann Nicol that being his fathers name were poor but honest and I being set to work at an early age, viz. weaving, I had no oppertunity of getting an education before I was set to work, three months previous to being put to labour and that was between the sixth and seventh years of my age I was put to school and that time was taken up in lerning the alphabet and to read a little this was all the time that was set apart for me in the way of being educated at school.[17]

The children of artisans and tradesmen were usually sent to school to learn at least the three Rs, but it is clear that they regarded schooling primarily as a utilitarian pursuit. It was not education in a broad sense that was expected, but simply the acquisition of a skill, similar to any other craft. The consequent level of attainment was not, by today's standards, high. For example, Robert Hazen, born in 1832 and a molder by trade, says that he "learned to be a good writer, speller, arithmetician, geographer and was naturally quick at learning, perhaps not so quick as others."[18] But a typical entry in his journal runs thus:

> 1853
> Tuesdy 12. long to be remembered. 21 years to day i was ushered into this state of existance. where shall i be 21 years hence. at work this day. went to see my intended. found her ill. administered to her in the name of Jesus. she partook of a good supper after and felt well. the Glory be to God.

For common people, making a living was the central experience of their lives. The lifelong waking hours of all but a small minority of the population were dominated by work of some kind, and this comes through

---

Archives. Kirby describes the working conditions in a Suffolk silk factory to which he was sent at the age of seven.

[16] There is considerable literature on literacy and schooling in the nineteenth century. For the latest study in this area see W. B. Stephens, *Education, Literacy and Society: The Geography of Diversity in Provincial England* (Manchester: Manchester University Press, 1987).

[17] Andrew Sproul (1816–?), Diary, BYU Library.

[18] Robert Hazen (1832–?), Diary, BYU Library.

very clearly in the autobiographies. Two aspects stand out: first, the great variety of types of occupation, from many kinds of laboring to skilled crafts and trades; and second, the many different jobs at which an individual worker tried his hand. Thomas Day, born in 1814 near Wolverhampton, is a good example.[19] First he worked as a blacksmith with his father, who was a machine blacksmith. After his father's death, he left the machine company and worked in a carpet factory at Kidderminster. He records a sixteen-week strike against reduction of wages, accompanied by riots in which, he assures us, he took no part. Nevertheless, he left Kidderminster and went to Worcester, where he worked with his stepfather in a rope yard. Next he got a job in a button factory in Bromsgrove, but gave it up in favor of work in a foundry in Birmingham. Thence he returned to Bromsgrove and the button factory, and his last occupation was in a needle factory in Redditch. Despite, or perhaps because of, his peregrinations around the West Midlands, he apparently made a decent living. He was proud of the respectability he ultimately attained, and it was a sore trial that he forfeited this when he became a Mormon: "My wife and I had been very respectable in society, but we now found that our friends became persecutors for the gospel's sake."

Even when a boy was apprenticed to a skilled trade, he not infrequently ran away before completing his term; and if he finished his apprenticeship he often had to go "on tramp" in search of work. The autobiographies contain many examples of such cases. In fact, the general impression from them is of a good deal of mobility between job and job and from place to place. One senses a certain mood of restlessness, of searching for something that eludes the writer, whether security, respectability, or good health. It implies familiarity with, if not acceptance of, some form of change to an extent not common in traditional, preindustrial society. It is a form of seeking, paralleled by the often-mentioned movement from one religious sect to another before the acceptance of the Mormon message. Joseph Smith's rejection of existing churches and sects because of their competing and contradictory claims is echoed in most of these Mormon autobiographies. This may have been no more than an expected pattern, similar to the conversion experience repeated in countless Methodist autobiographies. But equally it may relate to something more fundamental in the culture of the common people. Some of them were already religious seekers when the Mormon mission arrived in England. Perhaps it was not only their religious quest that made numbers of them receptive to Mormonism, but also the social and cultural context of their worldly experiences.

---

[19] Thomas Day (1814–93), Autobiography, LDS Church Archives.

As with other working-class autobiographies, there is a paucity of emotional and intimate detail. References to marriage and courtship are usually purely factual: "On August the 10, 1842 i began to Pay my address to maryann Case eldes Daughter of Robert and ann Case who was born at Chipenham in the county of wilts in the year of our Lord 1822," wrote George Halliday, a plasterer from Trowbridge, "and we continued to pay our addresses to each other untill the 1 of April 1844 when we was married at the old Church, troubridge."[20] Two weeks later his wife was taken ill with "consumption," and after thirteen months she died. George Spilsbury, a Worcestershire bricklayer, notes baldly, "on Sept 5th I married Fanny Smith of Cradly [Cradley] parish, Herefordshire, England."[21] Only rarely do we find even as much feeling as Thomas Day allowed himself when he described his first wife, Ann Andrus Danks, as "a young widow of quiet, loving and lovable ways." Children too are mentioned only to record the date of their birth and, sometimes, early death.

We would like to learn more about family affairs, the role of women, and the relation between spouses, but our sources are meager indeed. How to force these documents to yield more escapes us at present. The autobiographers are eager to tell us many things about themselves, particularly their religious experiences, but it is their public, not their private, selves that they are anxious to reveal. The historian of the common people perversely is not content with what the text of the autobiography says, but looks for what was never intended to be heard. Sexual mores, for instance, are seldom mentioned directly, but John Freeman's account of his relationship with Hannah Whiting implies much. It is unlikely that prudery was a cause of reticence. Ralph Ramsay, a cabinetmaker born in 1824, described his visits to delinquent and apostate LDS members in the Newcastle upon Tyne area and did not mince his words.[22] In 1854 he visited Elder Joshua Cutts, "who had been charged with having the venereal." Cutts's explanation was that his penis, which had been injured by a fall of stones while he was working in the pit, had become infected by his piles, from which he also suffered. The visiting elders told him that the evidence suggested he was guilty and that he should confess frankly. He protested his innocence and said that "he had not had any connection with any woman but his own wife since he entered the Church, that being about five years — what took place before that no one had any business with." Frankness of this order lets in a little light upon the subject of popular sexuality and suggests that the conventions of middle-class Victorian morality were by no means universal in the 1850s.

---

[20] George Halliday (1823–1900), Journal, BYU Library.

[21] George Spilsbury (1823–?), Autobiography, BYU Library.

[22] Ralph Ramsay (1824–?), Journal, LDS Church Archives.

In contrast to the scarcity of references to sexuality, all the writers have something to say about religion. This, of course, is to be expected, given the nature of the exercise, which was to write what was essentially a spiritual autobiography. In the classic form of this genre, the early events lead up to a crisis out of which is born a new self. The search for personal salvation, the failure to find "rest" in any of the religious modes or institutions tried, and the final conversion experience are familiar from puritan models dating back to the seventeenth century. Methodism revitalized and strengthened this tradition and made it available to thousands of working people in the late eighteenth and early nineteenth centuries. As Malcolm Thorp has shown, Methodism was a very fruitful source of converts to Mormonism in the early Victorian years.[23]

Our Mormon autobiographies conform closely to the classic pattern of conversion narrative, albeit in a somewhat attenuated form (little is said, for instance, about the inner spiritual strivings, more about going from sect to sect). The reasons given for acceptance of Mormonism bear out the conclusions reached by Leonard Arrington and Davis Bitton, Richard Bushman, Jan Shipps, and others.[24] But always the climax of the first part of the autobiography is baptism in the LDS church, usually after hearing a Mormon preacher. George Halliday was finally converted by his brother, John Halliday, who had come from Nauvoo on a mission: "i then heard the docktrine that he taught and i examined it with the Bible and after some examination i found that i had done the Best that i know how in serving the Lord But i found that there ware greater light come into the world and i was then willing to embraice it and on Sunday the tenth of November 1844 i was Baptised."

Looking back over their lives, the Mormon autobiographers were unanimous that their baptism was the most important thing that had happened to them. It was a watershed, the reference point in their lives against which all else was to be assessed. The break with the past, the great discontinuity, was further emphasized by emigration, with its often traumatic journey and the building of a new life in a strange new environment. Time was to be measured as before or after the great event. The effect of this was to introduce a sense of chronology that previously had been absent. Working-class autobiographies tend to be fragmentary, anecdotal, chronologically vague, and reliant on traditional (sometimes generational) concepts of

---

[23] Thorp, "Religious Backgrounds," 60.

[24] See Leonard J. Arrington and Davis Bitton, *The Mormon Experience: A History of the Latter-day Saints* (London: Allen and Unwin, 1979); Richard L. Bushman, *Joseph Smith and the Beginnings of Mormonism* (Urbana and Chicago: University of Illinois Press, 1984); Jan Shipps, *Mormonism: The Story of a New Religious Tradition* (Urbana and Chicago: University of Illinois Press, 1985).

time. Mormonism introduced a greater degree of structure and a more disciplined ordering of events. Dates, notably the exact date of baptism, are more plentifully supplied.

Few of the Mormon autobiographers mentioned external events, although they were living through one of the periods of greatest political, economic, and social change in English history. Instead of relating the episodes in their lives to happenings on the national scene, their reminiscences are, with very few exceptions, essentially local and familial. The things that stuck in the memory were personal and even trivial. George Spilsbury, the Worcestershire bricklayer who dismissed his marriage in one short sentence, described in considerable detail how he caught an infectious disease while on his missionary labors in Herefordshire in the early 1840s:

> Having to sleep in so many different places and sometimes with very undesirable bedfellows, I caught the itch which nearly cost me my life. An Elder that travelled with me on one occasion advised me to get some mercury, dissolve [it] in water and wash wherever I was broken out with this rash, which I did in a cold room which caused it to strike inwardly. O, I was very sick . . . [and he had to travel sixteen or seventeen miles]. The spirit of the Lord suggested to me to get some burdock roots and make some tea and drink it freely, which I did and it killed the effects of the mercury and I recovered.

It may be that this anecdote was included as an example of divine help, but it also reveals an order of priorities and a predilection for herbal remedies common to laboring people at this time. There is, of course, a simple explanation of why the common people did not write about national events: it was because they were not, for the most part, consciously involved in them. Their world was not that of their rulers, and the daily concerns of laboring people, as these autobiographies make clear, lay elsewhere.

A crucial question in assessing the evidence of the autobiographies is the nature of the sample. Davis Bitton lists perhaps 150 entries relating to England in the 1830s and 1840s, and of these I have been able to examine some 35. This is but a tiny fraction of the 17,849 Mormon baptisms and 4,700 emigrants from Britain in the period 1837–46 and makes anything like generalization extremely hazardous. The most that can be said is that the experiences and sentiments recorded in the Mormon autobiographies examined are, by and large, very similar to non-Mormon autobiographies of the same type and period. The sample is biased geographically toward the West Midlands and Lancashire, and also toward religion. But the language of blessings and gifts, the use of greetings such as brother and sister, and the literalness of biblical references are very close to the culture of Methodism and popular evangelical religion generally. Women, as ever, are underrepresented among the autobiographers, and what we hear most clearly are masculine voices.

With these provisos, a few tentative conclusions may nevertheless be drawn from the witness of these autobiographers. First, they were nearly all poor people in the sense that they did not have much of this world's goods, and some of them were at times in want. The pursuit of material well-being and escape from the anxieties and stresses that poverty entails preoccupied most of them for much of their time. A constant theme was the struggle to attain respectability, with its implicit recognition of the division in working-class life between the "roughs" and the "respectables." Second, the common people did not exercise power. They did not, for the most part, make the decisions that affected their lives, but were, in effect, controlled by others. A working man, even a skilled artisan with traditional notions of independence, could do little about external conditions that affected his work. Perhaps the biggest step toward emancipation that he could take was emigration, which seemed to offer a new dimension of freedom.

Despite, or perhaps because of, their poverty and exclusion from power, the common people developed their own consciousness and aspirations that were different from their rulers'. Deeper even than the laboring man's expectation of material sufficiency for himself and his family, there emerges from the autobiographies the elemental desire in all human beings to feel that they are wanted and that their efforts are recognized and rewarded. When this is denied, there is a loss in human dignity and sense of worth. The denial of some of the basic needs of ordinary people, and the constant belittling of their opinions by the educated classes, perpetuated a gulf between "them" and "us." There was a natural retreat into a working-class or popular religious world, where there were other values that recognized men and women for what they were worth, despite the contrary view of the dominant society. The "sons of want" knew that they had only themselves to turn to for help. Experience taught self-help through reliance on the family, the local community, the chapel, the friendly society, or the trade union. It was into this world of the common people that the Mormon missionaries penetrated in 1837 and from which they reaped such a rich harvest.

2

Some Sociological Reflections on the Nineteenth-Century British Mission

ROBERT L. LIVELY, JR.

Historically, millennialist movements which have proclaimed Christ's second advent to be imminent have been transitory. With the disconfirmation of their adventist expectations, such movements have typically evaporated. The distinctiveness of nineteenth-century millennialism was its capacity for persistence. In that century it became increasingly possible, with the expansion of literacy and the development of communications, for religious sects to advance a position on the basis of reasoned argument about the scriptures. The effect was to transform millennialism from being associated with social disruption and ecstatic manifestations as it had been in the past, to millennialism being a quietly assured conviction of the wickedness of the times with the reasonable prospect of a divine intervention of a radical kind to transform society and to justify the righteous. Such attitudes can clearly be seen in the millennial sects in nineteenth-century England, including the Plymouth Brethren, the Christadelphians, the Jehovah's Witnesses, the Seventh-Day Adventists, the Catholic Apostolics, and the Latter-day Saints.

During the period 1837–53, the Latter-day Saints enjoyed a fair amount of success among the working classes in the United Kingdom. They appealed to this particular social group because of their own social background, their approach to missions, and their message. The missionaries themselves were from working-class backgrounds, they frequently missioned to people directly in the streets, and they did not respect the social distinctions often found in the larger, more established denominations — particularly the Church of England. Perhaps the most attractive part of the Mormon message was that a concrete, rational program was offered which had both practical as well as spiritual benefits — to emigrate to Zion and engage in building the Kingdom of God on earth. Whereas most of the adventist groups mentioned above could only ask their members to *wait* for the Second Coming, Mormonism provided a plan whereby their members could *do* something in the here and now. They could improve their life's circumstances (a goal consonant with the Victorian temper), achieve new status in the hierarchy of the church (a commodity not generally available to the British working classes), and at the same time be actively involved in helping to bring about the Second Advent. As a result, Mormonism eventually became one of the most stable and successful of nineteenth-century adventist groups.

THE SUCCESS OF THE BRITISH MISSION
AND THE RELIGIOUS CENSUS OF 1851

By 1851, the British Mission was in its fourteenth year. It had enjoyed success, or the lack thereof, in direct relation to the stability of the church in America and its consequent ability to provide leadership and missionaries for the mission in Great Britain. The mission had been established in 1837 by Heber C. Kimball, Orson Hyde, Willard Richards, and Joseph Fielding. Their biggest gains had been in the Preston region of Lancashire; by April 1838, twenty-four branches were reported with a total membership of approximately 1,500. Another boost came in 1840–41, when twelve U.S. missionaries, including Brigham Young and six other apostles, arrived in England. Within one year membership increased by 400 percent to nearly 7,000; branches and conferences ranged from London to Scotland; a publishing program was established which included the printing of the Book of Mormon, a hymn book, and the periodical *The Latter-day Saints' Millennial Star*; and an emigration program was initiated. The British Mission had become the most active and successful mission in the church.

The period 1844–48, however, was a troubled time for the church—a period which included the death of Joseph Smith, a scandal in the British Mission in which the mission president, Reuben Hedlock, misappropriated mission funds, and the expulsion of the Saints from Nauvoo and their trek to the Great Salt Lake Valley. All three events affected the vitality of the British Mission, and it was not until the Saints were established in the valley that renewed emphasis was placed on foreign missions in general, and on the British Mission in particular. Scores of missionaries were then sent overseas, and during 1849–52, the British Mission experienced its greatest success in the nineteenth century—a success clearly reflected in the results of the Religious Census of 1851.[1]

---

[1] For a detailed discussion of the history of the nineteenth-century British Mission see Robert Lively, "The Catholic Apostolic Church and the Church of Jesus Christ of Latter-Day Saints: A Comparative Study of Two Minority

On Sunday, March 30, 1851, ministers of all denominations through-out Great Britain were asked by the Whig government of Lord John Russell to record the total number of attendances at each of their worship services on that day, as well as to indicate on the form provided the number of buildings available for worship, the total number of sittings therein, and how many of the sittings were free, i.e., were not appropriated or rented. Known as the "Religious Census of 1851," this inquiry was part of the national decennial census, and it is unique in British religious and census history for it remains the only attempt by the British government to quantify the religious activities and institutions of its people.[2] The "Report" of the religious census is also unmatched in the history of British government accounts and papers.[3] Horace Mann, barrister-at-law in Lincoln's Inn and the man responsible for the collection and compilation of the census returns, not only reported the statistical results of the census, but he also included a discussion of the development of religion in England from the time of the Druids down to the mid-nineteenth century, as well as historical summaries on each of the twenty-three religious groups figuring most prominently in the census. More important was his attempt to explain the causes, and to suggest remedies, for the most disturbing fact which he felt the census revealed — that nearly 30 percent of the total national population of 17,927,609, or over 5,288,000 people who theoretically could have attended religious services, stayed away by choice. The vast majority of the nonattenders were from the lower classes or "labouring myriads" who lived primarily in cities and large towns. The churches were not reaching these individuals, Mann claimed, because of a combination of social, economic, and organizational reasons. However, Mann did single out the Church of Jesus Christ of Latter-day Saints as being one of the few churches which was having an effect on this section of the population. Indeed, Mann noted that the Mormons were making "some not inconsiderable progress with the poorer classes of our countrymen," and while the total number of Mormon attendances on Census Sunday represented only a small fraction of the

---

Millenarian Groups in Nineteenth-Century England." (D. Phil. Dissertation, University of Oxford, 1977), 163–232.

[2] The completed census forms can be found at the Public Record Office, Ruskin Avenue, Kew, Richmond, Surrey (Ecclesiastical Returns, 1851, H.O. 129). For a general discussion of the religious census see Owen Chadwick, *The Victorian Church, Part I* (New York: Oxford University Press, 1966), 363–69. Also see Hugh McLeod, "Class, Community and Region: The Religious Geography of Nineteenth-Century England," in Michael Hill, ed., *A Sociological Yearbook of Religion in Britain*, 7 vols. (London: SCM Press, 1968–74)b:29–72.

[3] The "Report" is found in *Census of Great Britain, 1851. Religious Worship England and Wales, Parliamentary Papers, 1852-3, LXXXIX*. The results for Scotland were published in a separate report: *Parliamentary Papers, Scotland, 1854, LIX, Religious Worship*.

total national figure (35,626 out of 10,896,066), Mann was sufficiently impressed with the church's success both in England and the U.S. to observe that the Latter-day Saints were "perhaps the most remarkable religious movement since the days of Mahomet."[4]

The religious census was conducted at the height of the church's influence in nineteenth-century Britain and this would have been a factor in bringing the Latter-day Saints so forcefully to Mann's attention. For present-day researchers this fact is important since the statistics provide a separate body of figures which not only supplement, but which are also an independent point of comparison with, official church records. The "Report" is equally important for in it Mann, while perhaps not fully realizing it, provided valuable insights into why the Mormons were so successful among the working classes in England at midcentury, and why the Latter-day Saint church was in fact the pacesetter among the churches in winning the British working classes during 1837–52.

When reporting the results, Mann divided the various religious bodies into three categories: Protestant Churches; Other Christian Churches; and Jews, with the Latter-day Saints included in the second (along with the Roman Catholics, Greek Church, German Catholics, Italian Reformers, and the Catholic Apostolic Church). For all categories the total estimated attendances for England and Wales on Census Sunday were 10,896,066. The Church of England naturally led with practically one-half of all attendances (5,292,551). The Original Connexion Methodists accounted for the greatest total of Dissenters with 1,544,528, followed by the Independents (Congregationalists) and Particular Baptists with 1,214,059 and 740,752 attendances respectively. Mormon attendances totaled 35,626.[5] There were a total of 34,467 places of worship reported for England and Wales, with combined sittings numbering 10,212,563. Again, the Church of England could claim the greatest proportion, with 14,077 churches having 5,317,915 sittings. Next came the Original Connexion Methodists with 6,579 places of worship and 1,477,580 sittings, the Independents with 3,244 places of worship and 1,067,760 sittings, and the Primitive Methodists with 2,871 places of worship and 414,030 sittings. The Latter-day Saints are shown as having 222 places of worship with 30,783 sittings. Mann also estimated that the overall membership in the LDS church in England was at least 30,000, with an additional 20,000 having already emigrated to the United States.[6]

---

[4] "Report," 106.

[5] Ibid., 182.

[6] Ibid., 181. While the Mormons had far fewer meeting places than the larger religious bodies, Mann noted that the Latter-day Saints' utilization of their places of worship was "much above" the national average: 147 (60 percent) of the Mormon

When the census statistics are compared with Latter-day Saint church records it is found that there is no uniform agreement between the two. Total membership figures agree most closely, with the church showing the total membership for England and Wales to be 28,439 as of June 1, 1851.[7] However, that figure was likely somewhat inflated since there were instances where names were left on membership rolls even after people had left the church.[8] Mann's estimate of 20,000 emigrants is greatly exaggerated. "The British Mission Manuscript History" reflects a total emigration up to and including 1851 for the entire British Mission to be only 7,729, while Taylor's estimate is somewhat higher at approximately 9,000.[9] The biggest discrepancy exists regarding the number of branches in England and Wales. While the census reported 222 places of worship, the church's records show 575 branches.[10] Since conference leaders visited branches regularly, their reports were probably more accurate regarding the number of branches than they were for the number of members. It is doubtful that the census officials could have provided census forms to every branch, for many Latter-day Saint meetings were held in private homes or hired rooms or halls, and Mann acknowledged that many such nonconformist meeting places undoubtedly went unnoticed.[11]

Concerning the geographical distribution of the various religious groups, the census found the Church of England to be strongest in the South and Southeast of England, the Nonconformists in the East, Southwest, and Wales, and neither very successful in the northern counties of Northumberland, Durham, Cumberland, and Westmorland. The largest number of Mormon branches were found in Greater London (London and Middlesex) — 36; followed by Wales — 32; the north Midland counties (primarily

---

meeting places were open in the morning; 187 (84 percent) were open in the afternoon; and 193 (87 percent) were open in the evening. See also, 110, 148.

[7] "Statistical Report of the Church in the British Islands, for the Half-Year Ending June 1st, 1851," *Millennial Star* 13 (July 1, 1851): 207. Total membership throughout the entire British Mission, which also included Scotland, Ireland, the Channel Islands, and the Isle of Man, was 32,226. Ibid., 207.

[8] See Samuel W. Richards to Brigham Young, Liverpool, July 3, 1852, Brigham Young Collection, Archives, Historical Department of the Church of Jesus Christ of Latter-day Saints, Salt Lake City, hereafter cited as LDS Church Archives.

[9] The British Mission Manuscript History, Vol. 12, LDS Church Archives. P. A. M. Taylor, *Expectations Westward: The Mormons and the Emigration of Their British Converts in the Nineteenth Century* (Ithaca: Cornell University Press, 1966), 144–45. "Manuscript History" probably does not include children under the age of eight.

[10] *Millennial Star* 13 (July 1, 1851): 207.

[11] "Report," 143; Horace Mann, "On the Statistical Position of Religious Bodies in England and Wales," *Journal of the Statistical Society of London* 18 (1855): 149.

in Nottinghamshire, Leicestershire, Derbyshire, and Lincolnshire) — 30; the west Midland counties (the majority in Gloucestershire, Warwickshire, and Staffordshire) — 26; and the northern counties of Cheshire and Lancashire — 24.[12] The census geographical distribution is roughly comparable with church records, the implication being that while the census officers may not have canvased every Mormon meeting place, they were fairly successful in obtaining a representative geographical sample.[13]

Social patterns were reflected in the incidence of attendance on Census Sunday. The Church of England had the support of the majority of the upper and upper-middle classes, while the Dissenters' strength was found in the middle and lower-middle classes. In the "Report," Mann observed that the number of attendances among the middle and upper classes was indeed commendable, while in general the attitude of the lower classes toward attending church could be characterized as "negative, inert" indifference. This fact had been noted nearly ten years earlier when Engels observed that "the workers are not religious, and do not attend church," and it was still the situation in 1897 when the *Methodist Times* solicited essays from working men on "Why the Working Classes Do Not Go to Church"; the results of which indicated that "Above all, they are indignant at class distinctions in the House of God."[14]

The relationship between working-class nonattendance and the social differentiations that existed in the churches would not have been news to clergymen in the 1890s, for in Mann's "Report" he had already spelled out those social distinctions which contributed to working-class nonattendance at church and which were symptomatic of a great social chasm that existed between the working classes and the middle and upper classes. In the churches these features included: the pew system and the location of free seats in the place of worship; an alleged indifference of churchmen to the social condition of the poor, especially as regarded disease, poverty, and ignorance; and a widespread belief among the poor that a clergyman's

---

[12] "Report," 184–94.

[13] The church's statistical report for June 1, 1851, showed the greatest number of branches to be in South Wales (83) and London (60), followed by the Sheffield (33), Manchester (30), and Herefordshire (29) conferences. *Millennial Star* 13 (July 1, 1851): 207. It should be noted that the number of branches was not a fully reliable gauge of the concentration of members. The West Midlands, for example, was divided into a number of conferences and it had as great a concentration of actual numbers of members as any, with the Birmingham Conference the largest numerically in Britain and the Birmingham Branch reporting an attendance of 1,200 on Census Sunday.

[14] "Report," 162. F. Engels, *The Condition of the Working Class in England in 1844* (London, 1892), 125; *Methodist Times* (February 3, 1897), 65; quoted in K. S. Inglis, *Churches and the Working Classes in Victorian England* (London: Routledge and Kegan Paul, 1963), 1, 117.

motive for preaching was financial and that he would not minister if he did not get paid for it. Other considerations in regard to nonattendance were the fact that the poverty of the masses held them captive in crowded slums where there were few examples of, and little encouragement for, devout Christian living; and the need for more individuals or "agents" who would aggressively take the Christian message *to* the poor.[15] Most of the churches were guilty of these social distinctions, said Mann, and they accounted for the working class's lack of interest in attending church.

The pew system was the practice whereby worshipers rented or appropriated pews for their exclusive use. For churches with little or no endowments, pew rental was a primary source of revenue and it was not unusual in ill-endowed churches for all of the pews to be rented. In churches that could afford it, free sittings were set aside for the poor along the sides and back of the churches (and frequently behind the pillars), but they were either benches or uncomfortable pews which were smaller than the rented ones; viz. 2 feet 4 inches from front to back for the free pews, versus 3 feet from front to back for the rented ones. The census results indicated that over one-half of the sittings in England and Wales were rented or appropriated (5,407,968 out of 10,212,563), and the greatest majority of these could be found in the Church of England and among the Wesleyan Methodists, the Independents, and the Baptists. The Latter-day Saints were shown as having 264 rented or appropriated seats out of 30,783.[16]

Some observers noted that there was really no opportunity for the working man to achieve much involvement in the Church of England, and since most of its clergymen were upper- and middle-class graduates of Oxford and Cambridge, there was little chance of fruitful communication in either direction. The Quakers and Unitarians showed little inclination to preach among the poor, and some Congregationalists even believed that it was God's will that their outreach should be limited to the middle class. The very success of the Wesleyan Methodists and the Baptists among the poor in the eighteenth and early nineteenth centuries proved in midcentury to be a hindrance in reaching the poor, for with success had come respectability and with respectability had come middle-class values and a middle-class congregation. Perhaps the greatest encumbrance from the past with which the Church of England and the Methodists were burdened was an ecclesiastical organization designed for a rural environment and not for

---

[15]"Report," 158–62.

[16]See Inglis, *Churches and the Working Classes*, 48–57; "Report," 178, 181. Since an appropriated seat did not always have a rental fee attached to it, it is impossible to say how many of these sittings were in fact rented. There is some indication that the few appropriated seats reported by the Mormons were merely seats set aside for those conducting the services and for other church leaders.

large towns and cities. The 1851 Census results showed that for the first time in British history one-half of its population lived in an urban setting and that the large towns were experiencing a great influx of the working classes seeking employment. The Church of England was rooted in the parochial system which in theory placed the care of everyone in the parish in the hands of the curate. As Inglis noted, it worked best in small, socially heterogeneous communities, but it was the wrong system and an impossible task in large towns and cities. The urban Methodists were hampered by Wesley's concepts of itinerancy and the circuit. In a situation which required stability and persistence for effective interaction, the urban Methodist minister found his three-year maximum residence and his role as one of many ministers who circulated among a number of congregations in a district to be largely ineffectual.[17]

The Mormons, however, were different. The key was not necessarily stability, for local leadership was provided by a branch president subject to frequent transfer and by traveling elders, district presidents, and conference presidents, all relatively itinerant. While their watch care varied in effectiveness, their message appealed to many who had not heretofore been won over by organized religion.

> The preachers, it appears, [said Mann] are far from unsuccessful in their efforts to obtain disciples: the surprising confidence and zeal with which they promulgate their creed — the prominence they give to the exciting topics of the speedy coming of the Saviour and his personal millennial reign — and the attractiveness to many minds of the idea of an infallible church, relying for its evidences and its guidance upon revelations made perpetually to its rulers, — these, with other influences, have combined to give the Mormon movement a position and importance with the working classes, which, perhaps, should draw to it much more than it has yet received of the attention of our public teachers.[18]

The Latter-day Saint missionaries unanimously agreed that the British Mission recruited the vast majority of its members from among the poor. During his first mission tour in England, Heber C. Kimball wrote to his wife saying that many of the new converts would frequently share their last loaf of bread with the missionaries, and that there were some who were unable to lodge them overnight for they themselves did not have beds to sleep on. And in 1840, Brigham Young wrote to Joseph Smith that "almost

---

[17] Inglis, *Churches and the Working Classes*, 9, 13, 15, 24–25, 41, 59–60, 85, 89–90. It appears that the only large church which could claim any success among the poor at midcentury was the Roman Catholic Church, which was taxed to its limit with the influx of Irish immigrants driven from Ireland during the depressions and famines of the 1840s.

[18] "Report," 111–12.

without exception it is the poor that receive the Gospel."[19] But just as there were definite distinctions between classes, so, it would appear, were there distinct differences within classes, and it was a particular stratum of the lower class which was attracted to Mormonism. Asa Calkin, British Mission president from 1858 to 1860, observed that the Mormon message was practically without effect among the very lowest levels of people who were "born, reared and live and die steeped in sin, ignorance, degradation and wretchedness altogether beyond the imagination of anyone who has not witnessed it."[20] It was rather the "poor honest working classes" or the "industrious poor," the men and women who wanted to work, but whose social and educational background held them captive to low-paying, dull, and sometimes dangerous jobs, who joined the church. Taylor, in his study on Mormon emigrants, found that approximately 90 percent of them could be classified as working class, while the remaining 10 percent had middle-class backgrounds.[21]

Based on Mann's observations regarding social distinctions in the churches, it is here suggested that part of the appeal of the LDS Church to the lower classes lay in the fact that the church did not make concessions to the status distinctions operative in the wider society. Not only were Mormon missionaries unpaid, and practically all church seats free, but the missionaries, who themselves were from working-class backgrounds (and many of whom were English Mormon emigrants returning to mission in their homeland), were laymen who frequently missioned directly in the streets, not in separate "sacred" places. An appeal of outdoor meetings was that the working person did not have to be concerned about how he or she was dressed; it was a frequent complaint of the poorer classes that they were not well enough dressed to attend church or chapel.

There were other facets of Mormonism that were attractive to the working classes. It has been observed of charismatic movements, and the observation is true of many sects whether strictly charismatic in their leadership, that such movements demand that those who join abandon all previous roles and statuses. Allegiance to the new movement is meant to transcend all other loyalties, and at times to demand their renunciation. The demand to abandon the world, the evil things of the world, is also a demand to abandon the status system of worldly society — a requirement

---

[19] Orson F. Whitney, *Life of Heber C. Kimball*, 5th ed. (Salt Lake City: Bookcraft, 1974), 154. British Mission Manuscript History, Vol. 12, May 7, 1840. LDS Church Archives.

[20] "Journal of Asa Calkin, September 11, 1855 — December 30, 1858," 55, February 27, 1857, LDS Church Archives.

[21] Ibid., 56, February 27, 1857; *Millennial Star* 1 (February 1841): 263; Taylor, *Expectations Westward*, 150.

more easily accepted by the poor than by the well-to-do, of course. Mormonism, like other sectarian movements, demanded the surrender of worldly attachments, and implicitly rejected all worldly status systems. The one status system that mattered was inside the movement, and there all would begin again as equals, and the test of their merit would be spiritual and not material. In Mormonism, in contrast with radical sects which eliminated all formal status (as was the case with the Christadelphians and Plymouth Brethren), all men could win leadership roles in the church, and with faithful, diligent work advance up through the ranks of the priesthood. Thus social mobility, which was largely denied them in the outside world, was available in the context of the Mormon church.

The religious census of 1851 occurred at the height of the Latter-day Saints' success in nineteenth-century Britain, but in spite of the impressive statistics and laudatory comments in the "Report," the *Latter-day Saints' Millennial Star* made no mention of it when it was published. At first glance this is surprising, for one would have thought that it would have had real propaganda value for the British Mission, and indeed it would have had not the situation of the mission changed so drastically between the date of the census and the publication of the "Report" in 1854. On January 1, 1853, the plural marriage revelation was officially printed and promulgated in the *Millennial Star* and soon thereafter the British Mission experienced a rapid decline. Church membership dropped from the nineteenth-century high of nearly 33,000 in 1851, to just over 13,000 in 1859, representing a decrease of 60 percent. Baptisms fell by 88 percent from a peak of 8,620 in 1849, to 1,064 in 1859, while excommunications between 1853 and 1859 account for 50 percent of the total cut off from the church in the nineteenth century (17,649 out of 35,087).[22] By the end of 1856 *Millennial Star* subscriptions dropped from 23,000 to 7,000, and the British Mission was in financial trouble, necessitating a major retrenchment.[23] Emigration jumped over 462 percent between 1852 and 1855 (from 581 to 2,686), and the period from 1852 to 1857 saw the greatest exodus of British Mormons from England in any six-year span in the nineteenth century.[24] The decreases in membership and baptisms and the increases in

---

[22] British Mission Manuscript History, Vol. 12, LDS Church Archives. Another factor which contributed to declining baptisms was the withdrawal of most U.S. missionaries in 1858 in conjunction with the Utah War.

[23] Orson Pratt to Brigham Young, Liverpool, October 31, 1856, Brigham Young Collection, LDS Church Archives. See the essay by Richard Poll in this volume.

[24] The British Mission Manuscript History, Vol. 12, "British Mission," LDS Church Archives. Such an event is perhaps not surprising. Given the unpopularity of the polygamy revelation among non-Mormons, this may have induced the really committed to emigrate to America.

emigration and excommunications naturally affected the number of branches and conferences. Branches decreased from a high of 742 in 1852, to 408 in 1860 (a 45 percent drop); thereafter they experienced a steady decline until in 1900 there were only 73 branches in the British Mission. The number of conferences decreased at a slower rate, but from a high of 52 in both 1853 and 1855, it had dropped to less than 15 by 1871, where it remained for the rest of the century.[25]

It would not be until the mid-twentieth century that the Church of Jesus Christ of Latter-day Saints in Great Britain would equal, and easily surpass, the nineteenth-century success which the religious census of 1851 so clearly brought before the British public, and in a sense helped to explain.

ESCHATOLOGY AND EMIGRATION

The religious movements that arose in the first half of the nineteenth century, radical as they often appeared, represented in their teachings a reworking of a variety of elements that could without too much difficulty be drawn from the plenitude of Christian traditions. Many of the beliefs and practices which the leaders of particular sects assembled were drawn from orthodox teaching and practice, but they were given new emphasis and sometimes new contemporary significance by the sects. Thus the premillennial ideas which were a feature common to early Mormonism, and indeed to a number of other contemporary movements, were by no means unknown within the orthodox churches in both England and the U.S. The application of biblical prophecy to recent and contemporary events was an exercise in which some in the ministry of the churches and denominations were also engaged. What the sects typically did, of course, was to provide these ideas with new urgency and often to provide a single-minded focus on issues that, in the settled order of the churches, were merely particular lines of speculation or doctrine that were embedded among others.

The general feeling in the Mormon British Mission during the 1840s was that the millennial kingdom would be on earth by the beginning of the twentieth century.[26] Regarding the millennium, the *Millennial Star* said "we live somewhere in the latter end of the sixth millennium or thousand years," and in order to prove that the end was near "we shall contrast the present state of the world and the passing events, with the prophecies and

---

[25] Ibid.; see Lively, "The Catholic Apostolic Church," 213–32.

[26] This is clearly stated in the "Preface" to the first issue of the *Millennial Star* (May 1840).

their fulfillment."[27] Thus, a regular feature of the *Millennial Star* was the "Signs of the Times," a column in which fires, floods, earthquakes, plagues, volcanic eruptions, wars, etc., were interpreted as obvious signs that the end was near. The millennium itself, said the *Star*, would be ushered in by the restoration of Israel, the rebuilding of Jerusalem, the Second Advent of Christ, the destruction of the wicked, and the establishment of Christ's universal kingdom.[28]

The early Mormons were powerfully concerned with the imminence of the Second Advent, although this formulative idea was insufficient to provide the determining organization for them. Powerful as was its appeal, it did not ultimately dominate the stage for them. Despite early millennial expectations and the proclamation of the title of the *Millennial Star*, the Mormons over time were unembarrassed by their millennialism. They had not announced dates for the advent of Christ, they found many other religious preoccupations, they oscillated between strictly millennialist and distinctly utopian ideals of a paradisiacal state, and eventually they came to rationalize their expectations by accepting a broadly postmillennial position.

Regardless of the particular type of eschatology current at the time— be it premillennialism, postmillennialism, or realized eschatology—the idea of "the gathering," or that the Saints should go westward to Utah to help build the Kingdom of God on earth, was the most powerful and concrete expression the British Saints could give to their millennialism. Thus another attraction, and one which at midcentury was unique to Mormonism, was that the church had a positive and definite solution to the social condition of the poor; by offering the convert a chance to emigrate, the church was taking him or her out of the crowded city or away from a rural environment of decreasing productivity to a land which held the promise of both spiritual and economic betterment. Through the use of church-chartered vessels at reduced fares, and with the assistance of the Perpetual Emigrating Fund, emigration was a distinct possibility for all but the very poorest of Saints. This religiously inspired alteration of total life circumstances through emigration was a powerful dedication of one's life in an act of faith which was at once symbolic of the higher pursuit of salvation, and in many respects a voluntary step toward it.

This pragmatic element in Mormonism also contributed to its mass appeal. While other religious groups could only tell their members to

---

[27] *Millennial Star* 1 (August 1840): 73.

[28] Ibid., 1 (May 1840): 7. Such columns are also to be found in the periodicals of other adventist groups. There were numerous articles on the Jews in the *Star*. In addition to the one in the first edition, cf. 3 (May 1842): 6–8; 3 (March 1843): 189–90; etc.

anticipate the Second Advent sometime in the future, the Mormons could begin working immediately toward a goal that had both spiritual and temporal benefits. This programmatic element was certainly not alien to the temper of the nineteenth century, even in religion. It was fully consonant with a concern to improve one's everyday living standards by pragmatic action and by the increasing rationalization of activity. There was a powerful alternative appeal to "self help" (in emigration) which was an increasingly significant emphasis in the Victorian weltanschauung, and one to which the working classes were already accustomed from other sources. But that it should be combined as a significant orientation in a movement that also laid stress on the Second Coming is certainly unusual. The practical aspects of Mormonism, the prospect of emigration and the upbuilding of a community in Utah, eventually acquired more significance than the adventist teaching within the movement, and yet this was there as a strong form of premillennialist adventism in the early days. The Mormons succeeded in touching many different notes in the communication of their radical message of hope, and so of appealing to a relatively wide public (even if a public of predominantly working-class origin). Subsequent mass movements were to learn how to direct their appeal to diverse audiences simultaneously, and when democratic party organization eventually evolved in politics, the capacity to offer very diverse (at times possibly contradictory) policies and promises effectively to a large public became a recognized skill in the manipulation of the public. For the Mormons, no such conscious manipulative sophistication need be implied, but even if conscious diversification of appeal is ruled out, it must be conceded that the Mormons managed to provide a many-sided program, in ideology, community relations, practical life skills, and life prospects, in which were the weapons for successful recruiting.

SOCIOLOGICAL ANALYSIS

Millennialism of any direct kind was perhaps too exciting a teaching, at least potentially, to find stable institutional expression as a mass movement in the nineteenth century. The well-to-do could not, in general, be expected to be remotely attracted by such a creed, and the working classes, in general, were incapable of organizing and sustaining commitment. Yet there can be no doubt that millennialism had its attraction for working-class people, as the success of early Mormonism indicates. Mormonism already had a strong leadership, and it had evolved a system of discipline into which converts were inducted. Perhaps most important of all, and this may be the factor which contributed the most telling part of its appeal, it had a realizable millennial goal. It did not rely on biblical exegesis alone.

It indicated practical steps toward the achievement of at least earthly salvation, and to achieve that redemption, obedience to the church authorities, self-discipline, and commitment were all required. The traditional weakness of millennialism — the emotional impact, the urgency, and the inability or at least the unwillingness to engage in systematic planning — were overcome by Mormonism (as they were also later to be overcome by other American millennial movements, including the Seventh-Day Adventists and Jehovah's Witnesses). The practicality of Mormonism lay in its establishment of an ordered pattern of life and in the organization of new agencies to cope with a variety of social and human exigencies. Such a practical pattern was perhaps an essential for new religious movements arising in the American context. There, without the impress of a settled class system through which cultural norms and social organization were already a virtually binding framework of life in a country like Britain, new religious movements could forge, out of the still uncertain and unexplored possibilities of human experience and social response, distinctive patterns of action and life-style for their followers. New religions in America had an impulse to offer practical guidance for a new way of life in circumstances in which traditional solutions were inapplicable and in which "received" status systems and their attendant legitimations had neither relevance nor expression. Without the encumbrance of traditional forms, and without the example, instruction, and restraint exercised by higher social classes in Europe, Americans were free to develop new religious responses and their attendant patterns of moral and social regulation. Clearly, many new religious movements failed, but those which succeeded appear to have had in common a strong measure of practicality, even of pragmatism, of a kind not evident in the traditional orthodox churches. No doubt part of the test of success for an American movement was the measure in which it could blend guidance for a way of life in new conditions with the emotional satisfactions of religious commitment. The exigencies of life in a new world — new socially as well as physically — may have put a premium on such practicality, and it is not an accident that in different ways all the American adventist movements appear to have developed a distinctly rational style in their evangelism and in their provision for the social needs of their members. Mormonism had the advantage of offering to its British converts practical guidance of a kind which it is not easy to conceive as arising in an indigenous millennial mass movement. But undoubtedly, for Mormonism in Britain, the most important part of this pragmatic aspect of the faith was the possibility of taking appropriate steps leading to migration to the United States.

In the process of building up their own society and maintaining their distinctive way of life in the face of considerable external pressure, the

Mormons were obliged to embark on a variety of new strategies. Undoubtedly Mormon religious life underwent change in response to these circumstances, but perhaps most important of all was the fact that the Mormons produced a vibrant social system for which the historical raison d'être was their distinctive religious persuasion: paradoxically, it was the social system which ensured that the distinctive religious system would itself persist.

3

The Religious Milieu of English Mormonism

GRANT UNDERWOOD

In 1837, the first Mormon missionaries set foot on English soil. Within less than a decade one out of every three Latter-day Saints in the world was British, and the vast majority of those were English.[1] What did thousands of English converts see in Mormonism that attracted them to this indigenous American church? With a particular eye for the antecedents of conversion, this chapter surveys the religious landscape in England at the time of the arrival of the first LDS missionaries and explores the appeal of early Mormonism. We shall begin by focusing on the three major divisions of English Protestantism — Anglicanism, Dissent, and Methodism — and then proceed to probe deeper into those aspects of English religion that seem to have been particularly conducive to the establishment of the Church of Jesus Christ of Latter-day Saints in England.

ANGLICANISM

While England and America share a common language and, to a large degree, a common culture, their religious development has been significantly different. The most obvious contrast is that, unlike America, England, since the days of Henry VIII, has had a state religion — Anglicanism.[2] Its

---

[1] Dean L. May, "A Demographic Portrait of the Mormons, 1830–1980," in *After 150 Years: The Latter-day Saints in Sesquicentennial Perpsective*, ed. Thomas G. Alexander and Jessie L. Embry (Provo, Utah: Charles Redd Center for Western Studies, 1983), 39–69. On p. 44, May estimates British membership at 9,882 and the worldwide total at 30,000 as the exodus to Utah commenced. As late as 1870, the U.S. Census shows that a third of the population of Salt Lake County were born in Britain. See Ronald W. Walker, "Cradling Mormonism: The Rise of the Gospel in Early Victorian England," *BYU Studies* 27 (Winter 1987): 34n.

[2] Excellent surveys of religion in England from which the following paragraphs

Civil War, fought more than two hundred years before America's, was in large measure a religious war. At that time Puritanism, which sought to "purify" the Church of England of its "popish" precepts and practices, gained the upper hand, but with the subsequent Restoration of scepter and mitre, non-Anglicans became Dissenters and were sorely persecuted. Even after the Glorious Revolution in 1688–89, toleration for Dissenting religion was limited, and political power continued solely in Anglican hands.

By the nineteenth century, the winds of reform were blowing, stimulated in part by the American and French revolutions and the accompanying advance of democracy, and in part by the international Evangelical movement. An entrenched Anglicanism resisted as long as it could, but the decade before the arrival of the first Mormon missionaries is often regarded as a turning point in English history.[3] A mere five years before Heber C. Kimball and companions set foot on English soil, the monumental Reform Act was passed which gave the vote for the first time to a portion of the upper middle class and redistributed parliamentary seats to provide representation for the industrial cities in the midlands and in the north. Only a few years before that, in 1828, the Test Act, which attempted to limit officeholding to Anglicans, had been repealed. And only the very year before the elders arrived did it first become possible to have marriages solemnized outside the Anglican parish church. Thus, old laws were repealed and new ones enacted that changed the status quo prevalent since the late 1600s.

The missionaries actually arrived midstream, for it still was not possible to bury the deceased in public cemeteries unless performed under

---

are derived include David L. Edwards, *Christian England*, vols. 2 and 3 (Glasgow, 1983, 1984); Ernest Gordon Rupp, *Religion in England, 1688–1791* (Oxford: Clarendon Press, 1986); Ernest E. Best, *Religion and Society in Transition: The Church and Social Change in England, 1560–1850* (New York: E. Mellen, 1982); John R. H. Moorman, *A History of the Church in England* (London: A. and C. Black, [1953]); Alan D. Gilbert, *Religion and Society in Industrial England, 1740–1914* (London and New York: Longmans, 1976); and W. R. Ward, *Religion and Society in England, 1790–1850* (London: Batsford, 1972). See also Owen Chadwick, *The Victorian Church*, 2 vols. (New York: Oxford University Press, 1966).

[3] In addition to the general treatments included in note 1 sources, see G. F. A. Best, "The Constitutional Revolution, 1828–1832, and Its Consequences for the Established Church," *Theology* 62 (1959): 226–34. J. C. D. Clark, *English Society, 1688–1832: Ideology, Social Structure, and Political Practice During the Ancien Regime* (New York: Cambridge University Press, 1985) is a provocative, revisionist work that argues that eighteenth-century England was an ancien régime society, a conservative and confessional "Church-State" bolstered by ideological consensus and popular Anglicanism. Taking the long view, Clark argues that nineteenth-century reform was by no means inevitable and sees the period 1828–32 as a sudden and fundamental discontinuity with the past.

Anglican rites by Anglican clergy, nor would the mandatory tax in support of the established church, called the "rate," become voluntary until the 1850s. Coming from a country where disestablishment had been accomplished several generations earlier and where ministers as such did not wield political power, Mormon missionaries, despite the transformation underway, saw the religious landscape of England as marred by government-sponsored priestcraft.

At the time of their arrival two out of every three English citizens were members of the Church of England. As might be expected of a church numbering in the millions, all was not well in the Anglican household. For centuries there had been complaints and attempts at reform, and the period just before the coming of the Saints was no different. In the 1820s the famous newspaper editor and commentator, William Cobbett, published his *Rural Rides*, which graphically portrayed the malaise of rural Anglicanism and its limited impact upon the people. A few years before his death, the celebrated philosopher, Jeremy Bentham, also heaped scorn on the corrupt and disorganized state of the Anglicans in his book, *Church of Englandism*. While it now appears that much of this was caricature and that the Church of England in the nineteenth century was actually making improvements in pastoral performance, Mormonism profited from this popular image and drew converts from the disenchanted among the large nominal sector of early Victorian Anglicanism.[4]

Nonetheless, by the 1830s there were three major groups seeking to reform the Church of England from within: the "high church" movement — socially conservative Anglicans who emphasized ritual, clergy, and historical continuity; the "low church" movement — essentially the Evangelical wing, with its religion of the heart and call to seriousness in life which resulted in missions and reform societies; and the "broad church" movement — those Anglicans who, as the name implies, ecumenically emphasized ethics over dogma, and were generally learned and liberal, perpetuating the "rational" Christianity of the previous century. Social class distinctions and other circumstances prevented much interaction between humble Latter-day Saints and any of the three groups, yet, in theory at

---

[4] Malcolm Thorp, "The Religious Backgrounds of Mormon Converts in Britain, 1837–1852," *Journal of Mormon History* 4 (1977): 51–65. Edward R. Norman, *Church and Society in England, 1770–1970* (Oxford: Oxford University Press, 1976) challenges the accuracy of the "clerical corruption" stereotype, but, as Thorp notes, nineteenth-century Anglican reforms were "too little and too late to assuage popular images of an indifferent clerical establishment." He also comments that Mormon "reminiscences do not generally reveal a pattern of deep commitment to the [Church of England]" and concludes that Anglicanism, for LDS converts at least, had been a "family tradition" rather than "a source of spiritual satisfaction."

least, Mormonism could have sympathized with aspects of each of these critiques of traditional Anglicanism.

Carrying the "high church" emphasis to a novel extreme were a group of men at Oxford University in the 1830s. Dismayed over the recent breaches in the exclusive privileges of the established church, they began to issue a series of tracts condemning what they called a "national apostasy" and criticizing the weakness of contemporary Anglicanism.[5] These Tractarians, as they were labeled (also known as the Oxford Movement or Puseyites), argued that what made the Anglican Church the legitimate heir of the Apostles was episcopal succession. As a divine institution, therefore, it was sacrilege to have the church compromised by the political expediencies of the day. In their efforts to revive what they considered an effete Church of England, the Oxford Movement looked to the ancient church rather than to the Reformation for precedent and direction. In so doing they rediscovered the richness of the ancient liturgy and architecture. For the Tractarians, the restorationist quest was a return to the Patristic Christianity of the early Catholic Fathers rather than to the Primitive Christianity of the Apostles. Since the ultimate tendency, actually carried out only in a few cases, was to reunite with Rome, the Latter-day Saints could never fellowship the Puseyites. Yet, the Oxford Movement was symptomatic of a broader primitivist or restorationist impulse which, as we shall later see, significantly paved the way for the rise of English Mormonism.

DISSENT

A second major branch of English religion at the time of the Saints' arrival consisted of the Dissenters.[6] Though they often tended to dissent from the procrown politics of the Tories as well, they acquired the name because of their dissent from the established Church of England. They included such

---

[5] The most recent discussion of the Oxford Movement, made especially useful by its up-to-date bibliographical essay, is J. M. Cameron, "John Henry Newman and the Tractarian Movement," in *Nineteenth Century Religious Thought in the West*, ed. Ninian Smart, et al. (Cambridge: Cambridge University Press, 1985), 2:69–109. A good book-length study is Marvin R. O'Connell, *The Oxford Conspirators: A History of the Oxford Movement, 1833–45* (New York: Macmillan, 1969).

[6] The most comprehensive current history of British Dissent is Michael R. Watts's multivolume *The Dissenters* (Oxford: Oxford University Press, 1978–). See also Paul Sangster, *A History of the Free Churches* (London: Routledge, 1983); David M. Thompson, ed., *Nonconformity in the Nineteenth Century* (London, 1972); and Horton Davies, *The English Free Churches*, 2d ed. (London and New York: Oxford University Press, 1963). A recent study of particular value for its treatment of Preston and other early Mormon "beachheads" is Paul T. Phillips, *The Sectarian Spirit: Sectarianism, Society and Politics in Victorian Cotton Towns* (Toronto: University of Toronto Press, 1982).

groups as the Presbyterians, Congregationalists (or Independents, as they had been called in England since the days of the Civil War), Baptists, and Quakers. In a sense, aside from the Methodists, who always considered themselves more loyal to church and state than the Dissenters and therefore in a class by themselves, Dissent was a catchall title for any trinitarian Protestant denomination other than the Established Church. Later, the term "Nonconformists" was also used to describe Dissenters and was a label more congenial to Methodist sensibilities in the nineteenth century. One good reason for distinguishing "Old Dissent" from Methodism is that the former denominations were fundamentally Calvinist in theology, while the latter were usually Arminian. The distinction, however, came to be less important in the nineteenth century as the "New Dissent" rejected the more negative aspects of high Calvinism. Baptists as well as Congregationalists developed a moderate, evangelical Calvinism that elevated human ability in the work of salvation, that perceived Christ's redemption as paying a price sufficient for the salvation of all, and that brought Dissenters into closer harmony with the experiential mood of American evangelicalism. For American readers it is also important to note that in England, Anglicans built churches, Dissenters and Methodists built chapels; the two terms for houses of worship were not used interchangeably as in the United States.

What of the interaction between Mormons and Nonconformists? Though nationally less significant in number, it appears that more Nonconformists joined the LDS Church than did Anglicans.[7] Aside from occasionally shared political perspectives and similar socioeconomic circumstances, religious sympathies were of primary importance. Noncomformists (and, to a lesser extent, Evangelical Anglicans) tended to be responsive to the transatlantic wave of revivalism that swept both England and America during the first half of the nineteenth century. One recent study demonstrates that "the later 1830s and early 1840s" represented the high point of "Nonconformist recruitment" through revivals.[8] This is important since revivalism nurtured Mormonism in the United States. We should not be surprised, therefore, to find that the explosive growth of the first Mormon missions to England coincided chronologically with a surge in evangelical activity.

This connection is typified in an 1838 episode involving Heber C. Kimball and Orson Hyde and a Baptist congregation in Barnoldswicke.

---

[7] Thorp, "Religious Backgrounds," 60. For statistics on denominational affiliation in Britain, see R. Currie, A. Gilbert, and L. Horsley, *Churches and Churchgoers: Patterns of Church Growth in the British Isles Since 1700* (Oxford: Oxford University Press, 1977).

[8] Richard Carwardine, *Trans-atlantic Revivalism: Popular Evangelicalism in Britain and America, 1790–1865* (Westport, Conn.: Greenwood Press, 1978), 59–84.

Hearing of the profound interest in the Mormon message manifest in the nearby north Lancashire villages of Chatburn and Downham, Barnoldswicke Baptists sent for the Mormon elders. According to Joseph Fielding, Kimball and Hyde's traveling companion, "six or seven hundred" crowded into their chapel in eager anticipation. Hyde preached on the millenarian theme of the first resurrection and Kimball followed with a discourse on "the first principles of the gospel." As Kimball told it, "the congregation was overjoyed, tears ran down their cheeks, and the minister could not refrain from frequently clapping his hands together while in the meeting for joy." The service concluded at 10 P.M., but the preacher and some of the people followed the elders to their quarters where discussion continued until four the next morning. So great was the interest that later that morning "a number of influential men suspended operation in their factories to allow their workmen the privilege of hearing us preach."[9]

METHODISM

The single largest contributing group to Mormonism, however, seems to have been the Methodists. According to the only statistical study to date, more Methodists were baptized into the church than either Anglicans or Dissenters. This is significant when it is remembered that at the time of the earliest Mormon missions, there were four Anglicans for every one Methodist in England.[10] For this reason it is important that we take a close look at this branch of English Protestantism.

By 1837, when the first elders arrived, Methodism had been in existence for just about a hundred years.[11] It began as a renewal movement *within* the Anglican Church and remained that way almost until founder

---

[9] Joseph Fielding Diary, 31 March 1838, typescript, 18, Special Collections, Harold B. Lee Library, Brigham Young University, Provo, Utah, hereafter cited as BYU Library; Heber C. Kimball, *Journal of Heber C. Kimball, an Elder of the Church of Jesus Christ of Latter-day Saints* (Nauvoo, 1840), 32–33.

[10] This is based on Thorp's analysis of 298 conversion accounts providing sufficient information to identify prior religious involvements. See Thorp, "Religious Backgrounds," 60, for a statistical table. The Anglican-to-Methodist ratio is documented in Currie, et. al., *Churches and Churchgoers*.

[11] Methodist studies are myriad. Perhaps the most comprehensive and up-to-date is the three-volume *A History of the Methodist Church in Great Britain*, eds., R. E. Davies, A. R. George, and E. G. Rupp, (London: Epworth Press, 1965, 1978, 1983). Recent monographs also useful for what follows include David N. Hempton, *Methodism and Politics in British Society, 1750–1850* (Stanford: Stanford University Press, 1984); John M. Turner, *Conflict and Reconciliation: Studies in Methodism and Ecumenism in England, 1740–1982* (London: Epworth Press, 1985); and Anthony Armstrong, *The Church of England, The Methodists, and Society, 1700–1850* (Totowa, N.J.: Rowman and Littlefield, 1973).

John Wesley's dying day a half century later. Early Methodists attended Anglican services on Sunday and received the sacrament of the Lord's Supper from the hands of Anglican clergy. In this way, therefore, Methodism was to Anglicanism in England what Pietism had been to Lutheranism in Germany. Key characteristics of early Methodism were its basic organizational unit, the "class," which met regularly for prayer and study; its system of unordained, traveling preachers, all carefully orchestrated under the ultimate supervision of Wesley himself; its Arminian, as opposed to Calvinist, theology; and its enthusiastic religion. It is this latter aspect that most concerns us here. In the classical sense of the term, "enthusiasm" meant simply the indwelling of God.[12] Earliest Methodism reveled in the reality of personal spiritual experience. Godly gifts abounded in response to Wesleyan preaching, but all did not perceive this as a shower of divine grace. Belief in such direct interaction and personal communication between God and ordinary men without the aid of intermediaries like clergy or canon had always been a dangerous notion for the religious establishment. It made the individual the ultimate source of religious authority. The philosopher-cleric Joseph Butler, bishop of Durham, told Wesley with a shudder that "pretending to extraordinary revelations and flights of the Holy Spirit is a horrid thing, yes, Sir, it is a very horrid thing."[13]

As time passed, however, Methodism followed the sociological model of movement from sect to denomination. Renewal rigidified into regimentation, and the initial outpouring of the spirit was subordinated to institutional concerns. Even before Wesley's death in the final decade of the 1700s, cries were heard that "primitive" Methodism had been lost. Within only a matter of years, splinter groups began to break away, and by the turn of the century it was no longer possible to talk of Methodism as a single entity. In nineteenth-century England, it is necessary to distinguish Wesleyan Methodism or, more simply, Wesleyanism from Primitive Methodism, Independent Methodism, New Connexion Methodism, and a host of others.[14]

---

[12] Clarke Garrett, *Spirit Possession and Popular Religion: From the Camisards to the Shakers* (Baltimore: Johns Hopkins University Press, 1987); and Ronald Knox, *Enthusiasm: A Chapter in the History of Religion* (Oxford: Oxford Uniersity Press, 1950).

[13] Knox, *Enthusiasm*, 450.

[14] Hempton, *Methodism and Politics*, 216, 230, makes the point that Methodism must not be treated "as a monolith" since there were "many Methodisms in many places at many times." In volume 2 of Davies, et al., *History of the Methodist Church*, separate chapters treat "The Wesleyan Methodists" and "Other Methodist Traditions," 213–329. A recent study quite attuned to such variation is Deborah M. Valenze, *Prophetic Sons and Daughters: Female Preaching and Popular Religion in Industrial England* (Princeton: Princeton University Press, 1985). Also useful for its specific

This is an important distinction generally overlooked in Mormon studies but valuable precisely because it points us to the source of a disproportionate number of early English converts. Perhaps the most obvious example of this was the conversion of the United Brethren. While the story of Wilford Woodruff's marvelous success in bringing hundreds of this group into the fold is well known, what concerns us here is to note that the United Brethren were a break off from the Primitive Methodists who in turn had earlier broken away from the Wesleyans not only for the usual reasons of ecclesiological localism but also on the grounds that the original spirituality had been lost.[15] Clarke Garrett described early Methodism thus: "Like Quakerism in the preceding century, 'methodism' was as much a style of spirituality and an affirmation of the possibility of the immediate experience of divinity as it was an organized religious body. It was the most visible sector of a broad movement of popular piety that affirmed that the age of miracles was not past and that Christianity would regain the purity and vitality of its beginnings."[16]

It appears that in attempting to recapture the early spirit of Methodism in the face of a definite establishmentarian drift in the nineteenth century, non-Wesleyan Methodists were questing for some of the very same values heralded as immediate and available by Mormon missionaries. Interestingly enough, the kinship with early Methodism did not go unnoticed by the Saints. Parley Pratt reprinted one of John Wesley's sermons in the *Millennial Star* with this heading: "JOHN WESLEY A LATTER-DAY SAINT, in Regard to the Spiritual Gifts and the Apostasy of the Church!!"[17]

But of course, the later schismatic or splinter Methodist search for "primitive" Methodism was itself the attempt to restore polity and practice

---

focus on areas frequented by Mormon missionaries is D. A. Gowland, *Methodist Secessions: The Origins of Free Methodism in Three Lancashire Towns: Manchester, Rochdale, and Liverpool* (Manchester: University of Manchester Press, 1979).

[15] The standard work is now Julia S. Werner, *The Primitive Methodist Connexion: Its Background and Early History* (Madison, Wisc.: University of Wisconsin Press, 1984). Also valuable is *From Mow Cop to Peake, 1807–1932: Essays to Commemorate the 175th Anniversary of the Beginnings of Primitive Methodism, May 1982* (Wesley Historical Society, Yorkshire Branch, 1982). In terms of the institutionalization that may have prompted the United Brethren schism, Turner remarks that "Wesleyanism was not the only Methodism that can be shown in development. Primitive Methodism illustrates much more sharply the transition from sect to denomination so beloved of modern sociologists." *Conflict and Reconciliation*, 82.

An important LDS reminiscence of the United Brethren is Job Smith, "The United Brethren," *Improvement Era* 13 (July 1910): 818–23. See also Job Smith Journal, 1–5, Archives and Manuscripts, BYU Library.

[16] Garrett, *Spirit Possession and Popular Religion*, 104.

[17] *Millennial Star* 2:23.

felt to have existed in "primitive" Christianity. What is more, not all Methodists seeking a charismatic religion were separatists. Some, including a number who later converted to Mormonism, could not bring themselves to formally dissociate with Wesleyanism.[18] Therefore, it may be more helpful to look at Methodism from the perspective of a spectrum rather than denominational label. Toward one end of the spectrum would be found those groups, whatever their specific affiliation, who were interested above all else in enjoying a vital, gifted Christianity. Given the tendency of early Mormon missionaries to stress the "signs following belief," it is not surprising that the overwhelming number of Methodists converts, who themselves were the single most statistically significant group, came from that end of the spectrum.[19]

SEEKERS

Beyond Anglicanism, Dissent, and Methodism were the denominational nomads known as "seekers." For them, institutional Christianity was in its darkest day. They had "pondered long over the scriptures, especially the prophecies and promises of the coming of Christ's kingdom." Many of them "had already had some form of inner-light experience, and all were ready to be influenced by visions and dreams. They longed for some authority who would confirm and sanctify these experiences, and who would also cut through the conflicting claims of all the churches. Only the Saviour himself, or at the least his directly appointed messenger, could fulfill such longing."[20]

---

[18] Robert Currie, *Methodism Divided* (London: Faber, 1968) and John C. Bowmer, *Pastor and People* (London, 1975) make clear that the Methodism of the pulpit was not always the Methodism of the pew. Valenze, *Prophetic Sons and Daughters*, and Gowland, *Methodist Secessions*, also illustrate that generalizations are dangerous and that an alternative to formal schism was the private gathering of the pious while retaining nominal affiliation with the parent body. Finally, the rash of regional studies in Methodism, too, is qualifying stereotypes. As just one recent example, David Luker demonstrates how "Cornish Wesleyan Methodism was clearly something very different from orthodox Wesleyanism." See Luker, "Revivalism Theory and Practice: The Case of Cornish Methodism," *Journal of Ecclesiastical History* 37 (1986): 603–19.

Thorp counters P. A. M. Taylor on the proportion of Wesleyan versus splinter-Methodist converts to Mormonism, but the important point seems to be that both types of converts shared a desire for charismatic Christianity regardless of which body held their formal membership or what the attitudes of their denominational leaders were.

[19] This is readily apparent from an examination of English Mormon diaries and from the *Millennial Star*.

[20] J. F. C. Harrison, *The Second Coming: Popular Millenarianism, 1780–1850* (New Brunswick: Rutgers University Press, 1979), 132.

"I was earnestly looking out," wrote one of these individuals, "for some one to be visited by the Spirit, to revive the work, and raise up the cause of God. . . . I went everywhere that I heard of any one being visited by the Spirit of God to prophesy, in hopes of finding the truth." Such seekers often made their way to the site of a Mormon sermon and then made their way into the church. Postulating the dismal and "dead" state of institutional Christianity, their faith was, as another put it, that "something would turn up, either the gospel would be introduced, or afflictions would come upon the nation."[21] Is it any wonder, then, why Mormonism was so successful among this group? It seemed to match seeker hopes and expectations precisely.

MILLENARIANISM

Interest in biblical prophecies was an aspect of the English religious milieu that seemed to penetrate every social class and religious group, and that was particularly helpful in preparing the way for the acceptance of Mormonism. England had had a long history of interest in eschatology.[22] At a popular level along the religious periphery, apocalypticism abounded. From the "Civil War sects" bent on ushering in Christ's millennial kingdom — the literal and terrestrial "fifth monarchy" prophesied in the Book of Daniel — to the French Prophets at the turn of the century to the Shakers and various itinerant millenarian prophets later on, apocalyptic mentalities flourished. Moreover, the educated and the elite also pursued the study of biblical prophecy with vigor.

More than any other era, though, the half century before the Latter-day Saints arrived, beginning with the French Revolution, saw a new wave of eschatological interest sweep through England.[23] As huge armies marched

---

[21] Harrison, *The Second Coming*, 153; Valenze, *Prophetic Sons and Daughters*, 87.

[22] Bryan W. Ball, *A Great Expectation: Eschatological Thought in English Protestantism to 1660* (Leiden: Brill, 1975); Paul Christianson, *Reformers and Babylon: English Apocalyptic Visions from the Reformation to the Eve of the Civil War* (Toronto: University of Toronto Press, 1978); Christopher Hill, *The World Turned Upside Down: Radical Ideas During the English Revolution* (New York: Viking, 1972); Bernard Capp, "The Fifth Monarchists and Popular Millenarianism," in *Radical Religion in the English Revolution*, ed. J. F. McGregor and B. Reay (Oxford: Oxford University Press, 1984), 165–89; Paul J. Korshin, "Queuing and Waiting: The Apocalypse in England, 1660–1750," in *The Apocalypse in English Renaissance Thought and Literature*, ed. C. A. Patrides and Joseph Wittreich (Manchester: Manchester University Press, 1984), 240–65; Hillel Schwartz, *The French Prophets: The History of a Millenarian Group in Eighteenth Century England* (Berkeley: University of California Press, 1980).

[23] Harrison, *The Second Coming*; James K. Hopkins, *A Woman to Deliver Her People: Joanna Southcott and English Millenarianism in an Era of Revolution* (Austin:

across the European continent and regimes toppled, the Revolution excited an atmosphere of millennial prophecy and expectation unparalleled since the Civil War. Serious study of the prophecies reached high tide in England in the late 1820s and 1830s, symbolized by the 1835 publication of Joshua Brooks's massive *Dictionary of Writers on the Prophecies*, and involved a vigorous theological debate between pre- and postmillennialists. The Saints, of course, had much to say on such matters and, as I have pointed out, kept themselves far more abreast of the prophecy literature than has hitherto been assumed. As only one example, in July 1840, Apostle Willard Richards made note in his journal that he had picked up "a new work on the dispersion & history of the Jews, cleansing of the Sanctuary, 2 coming of Christ Reign with his Saints and End of the World by Samuel Kent."[24] He then proceeded to fill several pages of his diary with notes from this book.

When one compares this surge of apocalypticism in the decade preceding the arrival of the Mormons with the Saints' own heavily millennial teaching, one can again sense the relevance of the "message of the Restoration." The flurry of millenarian interest at this time on both sides of the Atlantic was so pronounced that it has caused historian Ernest Sandeen to ask, "Is it only a coincidence that the excitement over the imminent second advent and the dawning millennium broke out in both Britain and America during 1828–32? Is it only a coincidence that a return to apostolic simplicity and power was being sought in both countries just at this time or that speaking in tongues and healing should become local sensations?"[25]

Exactly how millenarianism served as a midwife to Mormonism becomes more clear as we shift from the general to the particular. One apparently significant source of early English converts was the "Christian Society" of Robert Aitken.[26] The group was based in Liverpool and was not yet two years old when the Mormons arrived in 1837. Aitken was a disappointed Anglican who sought ordination in the Wesleyan Connexion, was rebuffed,

---

University of Texas Press, 1982); W. H. Oliver, *Prophets and Millennialists: The Uses of Biblical Prophecy in England from the 1790s to the 1840s* (Oxford: Oxford University Press, 1978).

[24] These matters are discussed at greater length in my "Early Mormon Millenarianism: Another Look," *Church History* 54 (1985): 215–29; and "Apocalyptic Adversaries: Mormonism Meets Millerism," *John Whitmer Historical Association Journal* 7 (1987): 53–61. Willard Richards Journal, Vol. 12, p. 4, typescript, Archives, Historical Department of the Church of Jesus Christ of Latter-day Saints, Salt Lake City.

[25] Ernest R. Sandeen, *The Roots of Fundamentalism: British and American Millenarianism, 1800–1930* (Chicago: University of Chicago Press, 1970), 57–58.

[26] Very little is known about Robert Aitken beyond what is published in the *British Dictionary of National Biography* 1:206. Some information is contained in Gowland, *Methodist Successions*. Malcom Thorp has begun a comprehensive study of the man and his movement.

mingled temporarily with the schismatic Wesleyan Methodist Association, and eventually broke away to create his own society. He had moved steadily toward the evangelical, almost pentecostal, end of the religious spectrum, and had therefore earned the usual caricature of "Ranter." Edward Tullidge likened him to George Whitfield of Great Awakening fame whose evangelism had been so effective it even stirred the thrifty Benjamin Franklin to empty his pockets into the contribution plate.

Furthermore, Aitken became an avid student of the prophecies and a premillennialist. As Tullidge remembered, "his themes on the ancient prophecies and their fulfillment in 'these latter days' were very like" those of "eloquent Sidney Rigdon, before as well as after he became a Mormon" and included "glorious outbursts of inspiration when he dwelt upon the prospect of a latter-day church rising in fulfillment of the prophets."[27] In a published sermon entitled "The Second Coming of Christ," Aitken declared that "the doctrine of our Lord's second advent is a key to the prophetical Scriptures both of the Old and New Testament." To those who chided his interest in prophecy, he remarked, "There is life or death, destruction or salvation, in the taking heed to, or in the despising of unfulfilled prophecy."[28] What it showed him in standard apocalyptic fashion was the overwhelmingly apostate condition of "Gentile Churches." In reasoning that resonated for Mormons, Aitken remarked,

> And now, if we want a standard whereby to judge of the apostasy of the present churches, we must take the church of Christ when the apostatizing spirit was least manifested — that is to say, in the apostolic age. With this pattern in our eye, where, I ask, are the gifts of the spirit — where the miraculous power — where the gift of healing — where the gift of prophecy — where the signs that were appointed to follow — them that believed? What has become of the angel messengers, who so frequently appeared to the primitive Christians? . . . Where is the persecution that all that live godly in Christ Jesus shall endure — and where is the being hated of all men for Christ's name's sake? Alas! alas! my brethren, the gifts of the Spirit are gone, and, I fear, most of the graces have gone with them; and, as to suffering and reproach, to which the Church is called, such things have long been mere matters of history.[29]

By the end of the decade, Aitken's Christian Society had expanded to a number of urban centers, including London where Wilford Woodruff first heard him. Woodruff readily recognized a doctrinal kinship, and wrote that Aitken had "presented some of the most sublime truths that I

---

[27] Orson F. Whitney, *Life of Heber C. Kimball* (Salt Lake City: Stevens and Wallis, 1945), 149–50.

[28] Robert Aitken, *The "Second Coming of Christ," A Sermon* (London: G. & C. Fowler, 1839), 7–8.

[29] Ibid., 11.

had ever herd delivered by a sectarian priest." He was delighted that Aitken had "come out against the sexts" but noted that "he has got as far as he can." Woodruff later reported that "there was some little prospect of the Rev. R. Aitken's A.M. receiving & embracing the work which will open doors to many souls so I felt to rejoice."[30]

Actually, "Aitkenism" had already opened doors, though Aitken himself never joined the LDS Church and eventually returned to Anglicanism. In the published journal of his 1837–38 mission, Heber C. Kimball wrote, "Soon after our arrival in England, great many of the AIKENITES embraced the gospel." The nucleus of the first branch in Liverpool raised up by John Taylor and Joseph Fielding in early 1840 were converts from Aitken's Hope Street Chapel.[31] Prominent English convert and one-time president of the Staffordshire Conference, Alfred Cordon, had previously been an Aitkenite class leader and was responsible for the conversion of other Aitkenites, including an entire congregation in Doncaster, Yorkshire, during his missionary labors. And John Greenhow, president of the large Liverpool Conference, told of his former experience as an elder in the Christian Society, describing how there was a "general consciousness prevailing" among the Aitkenites "that something was wanting."[32] When the Mormon elders arrived, that something was discovered.

Another adventist sect from which British Mormonism may have drawn a small contingent was the "Christian Israelites."[33] John Wroe, an eccentric zealot from Bowling, managed to convince a number of former Southcottians in the 1820s that he should be regarded as prophet and successor to Joanna Southcott. A generation earlier, prophetess Southcott had gathered around herself a significant lower-class movement which was both millenarian and charismatic in character.[34] Wroe added to these elements a Judaizing attempt to revive Old Testament law, liturgy, and priesthood, and called his group the Christian Israelites. Mosaic codes were to be fulfilled to the letter, including circumcision, the eating of kosher food, the wearing of beards, and even the learning of Hebrew. He also accepted the "British-Israel" notion that the English were actually the lost tribes of

---

[30] Scott G. Kenney, ed., *Wilford Woodruff's Journal: 1833–1898 Typescript* 10 Vols. (Midvale, Utah: Signature Press, 1983), 1:498, 512.

[31] Kimball, *Journal*, 48; Fielding Diary, 51–58, 98, 111.

[32] Alfred Cordon, "An Abridgement of His Journal," typescript, BYU Library; *Millennial Star* 2:126; 3:30.

[33] G. R. Balleine, *Past Finding Out: The Tragic Story of Joanna Southcott and Her Successors* (London: S. P. C. K., 1956) has a chapter on this group. Oliver, *Prophets and Millennialists*, and Harrison, *The Second Coming*, deal with Wroe as well.

[34] The most authoritative study is James K. Hopkins, *A Woman to Deliver Her People: Joanna Southcott and English Millenarianism in an Era of Revolution* (Austin: University of Texas Press, 1982).

Israel but did not know it. He promptly assigned converts a lineage, and called these "invisible" as well as the "visible" Jews to gather to the New Jerusalem to be built in Ashton, a little town just outside of Manchester. There they constructed a lavish "Sanctuary" able to hold several thousand. The biblically prescribed walls around the Holy City, however, were never completed since Wroe was run out of town in 1831 for indiscretions with young virgins, given David-like to "cherish" him.

The movement continued for a while, but by 1842 the sanctuary had been sold and, according to William Cooke Taylor on a tour that year of Lancashire manufacturing districts, some Ashton Israelites had been absorbed into Mormonism.[35] The case of James Wood is perhaps typical of the ideological connection. Wood lived in Wroe's new headquarters in Wakefield, Yorkshire, and had been impressed with Wroeite sermons on the "second advent." This in turn heightened his receptiveness to the "Restored Gospel," for when he received from Ashton friends a copy of Parley P. Pratt's apocalyptic *Letter to the Queen*, he wrote to Pratt that Mormonism "if I am not greatly mistaken" is "that Church I have long wished to see established in the earth."[36]

NEW TESTAMENT RESTORATIONISM

Undergirding the charismatic and millenarian aspects of the English religious milieu which we have been examining was the nineteenth-century renaissance on both sides of the Atlantic of what has been called New Testament restorationism or Christian primitivism.[37] Under the maxim "no creed but the Bible," a widespread interest in recasting Christianity along biblical lines spawned groups like Alexander Campbell's Disciples of Christ and Barton Stone's "Christians only" movement in America, or the Plymouth Brethren and the Universal Christian Society in England. Espe-

---

[35] Harrison, *The Second Coming*, 147–48.

[36] *Millennial Star* 2:54. The tract referred to is Parley P. Pratt, *A Letter to the Queen, Touching the Signs of the Times, and the Political Destiny of the World* (Manchester: Parley P. Pratt, 1841).

[37] Donald F. Durnbaugh, *The Believers' Church: The History and Character of Radical Protestantism* (New York: Macmillan, 1968); Richard T. Hughes, ed., *The American Quest for the Primitive Church* (Urbana: University of Illinois Press, 1988); Hughes and C. Leonard Allen, *Illusions of Innocence: Protestant Primitivism in America, 1630–1875* (Chicago: University of Chicago Press, 1988); Hughes, "Christian Primitivism as Perfectionism: From Anabaptists to Pentecostals," in *Reaching Beyond: Chapters in the History of Perfectionism*, ed., Stanley M. Burgess (Peabody, Mass.: Hendrickson, 1986), 213–55; and Nathan Hatch, "The Christian Movement and the Demand for a Theology of the People," *Journal of American History* 67 (1980): 545–67; "Sola Scriptura and Novus Ordo Seclorum," in *The Bible in America*, ed., Nathan Hatch and Mark Noll (New York: Oxford University Press, 1982), 59–78.

cially interesting within this tradition was the English penchant for talking of the "everlasting gospel." The early nineteenth-century poet William Blake illustrated the notion when he declared, "All had originally one language and one religion: this was the religion of Jesus, the Everlasting Gospel."[38] The Saints profited from primitivism by their own admission. In response to the assertion that Campbellism produced Mormonism, English convert and *Millennial Star* editor Thomas Ward replied, "This is an error . . . but if he would say that the principles propogated by Alexander Campbell prepared the way in the minds of many for the reception of the fulness of the gospel, we will accede the point at once."[39] What was true of Campbellism, particularly in the U.S., was also true of English Christian primitivism. Even a superficial reading of the spiritual autobiographies of English converts found in journals, reminiscences, and the *Millennial Star* reveals the presence of primitivist thinking which paved the way for conversion.

So common in society generally was biblical restorationism that one recent student found it necessary to distinguish "between *ecclesiastical primitivism*, wherein the forms and structures of the apostolic church are of paramount concern; *ethical primitivism*, wherein the life-style of the ancient Christians is the chief concern; and *experiential primitivism*, wherein the apostolic gifts of the Spirit are of ultimate concern."[40] Mormonism spanned all three types and precisely because of such comprehensiveness managed to respond successfully and lastingly to Christian primitivism in England.

IRVINGITES

One other group, however, approached Mormonism in the nature and intensity of its ecclesiastical and experiential primitivism—the Catholic Apostolic Church, or more popularly, the Irvingites.[41] Joseph Smith once remarked that the Irvingites "counterfeited the truth perhaps the nearest of any of our modern sectarians," but he might have said, had he had a dif-

---

[38] Harrison, *The Second Coming*, 82.

[39] *Millennial Star* 3:197.

[40] Hughes, "Christian Primitivism," 212.

[41] Still the most important study of the Irvingites is P. E. Shaw, *The Catholic Apostolic Church* (New York: King's Crown Press, 1946). Irving's nephew, G. Carlyle, produced *The Collected Writings of Edward Irving*, 5 vols. (London, 1866). Recent studies intent on emphasizing the experiential primitivism of Irving are Arnold Dallimore, *Forerunner of the Charismatic Movement: The Life of Edward Irving* (Chicago: Moody Press, 1983); Charles Gordon Strachan, *The Pentecostal Theology of Edward Irving* (London: Darton, Longman and Todd, 1973); and Strachan, "Theological and Cultural Origins of the Nineteenth Century Pentecostal Movement," in *Essays on Apostolic Themes* ed. Paul Elbert (Peabody, Mass., 1985), 144–57.

ferent purpose in mind, that they *anticipated* "the truth" closer than any others.[42]

In the 1820s, Edward Irving, a Scot, was ministering to a Scottish Presbyterian congregation in London and had attracted considerable attention with the eloquence of his sermons. His interest in biblical prophecy brought him into contact with Henry Drummond who invited him to a series of prophetic study conferences held annually during the late 1820s at Drummond's palatial estate in Albury. These conferences resulted in the publication of the three-volume *Dialogues on Prophecy* which represents the high point of premillennial discourse in England.[43] The Albury group believed that England had become an "apostate nation." As with the Tractarians, who were almost contemporary in origin, and unlike the Mormons, this was a fundamentally conservative reaction on the part of well-to-do individuals appalled at the unraveling alliance between church and state. It, however, also grew out of an ecclesiastical primitivism which saw the "falling away" as something antedating recent events, as well from their apocalyptic millenarianism which by definition pronounces the present derelict beyond human reform.

In Irving's analysis, much like in Mormon thought, the deaths of the Apostles resulted in the apostasy of the Church, and if ever Christianity were to be restored to its original faith and unity, it would again require a foundation of twelve apostles. "We cried unto to Lord," declared Irving, "for apostles, prophets, evangelists, pastors, and teachers . . . because we saw it written in God's Word that these are the appointed ordinances for the edifying of the body of Jesus."[44] The first apostle was called by prophecy in 1832, and by 1835, the same year the LDS Quorum of the Twelve was reconstituted in Kirtland, the full number of twelve Irvingite apostles had been commissioned. This apostolate and a never fully constituted quorum of "seventies" had the universal oversight for the whole Catholic Apostolic Church. The rest of the Irvingite ministry was essentially episcopal — a supervising bishop, or "angel" as they were called, who presided over a local church or region, a council of elders, and a group of deacons to assist with temporal affairs.

Spiritual gifts were the experiential aspect of biblical Christianity for which the Irvingites felt to pray. When various gifts broke out in Scotland

---

[42] *Times and Seasons* 3:746. A full-length comparison between the two movements in Robert L. Lively, Jr., "The Catholic Apostolic Church and The Church of Jesus Christ of Latter-day Saints: A Comparative Study of two Minority Millenarian Groups in Nineteenth Century England (Ph.D. Diss., University of Oxford, 1977).

[43] So argued in Oliver, *Prophets and Millennialists*, 99–149.

[44] Shaw, *Catholic Apostolic Church*, 34.

in 1830, it caught the attention of Irving and his London congregation. At the final prophetic conference in Albury that year, the chairman made it clear that not only did they have the "responsibility" to "inquire into the state of those gifts said to be now present in the west of Scotland" but that "it is our duty to pray for the revival of the gifts manifested in the primitive Church."[45] Within a year, tongues and prophecy were prominent in Irving's congregation, and healings occurred as well. This prompted the actual break in 1832 with the Presbyterian Church and the formation of the new Catholic Apostolic Church. As it turned out, few Irvingites actually joined the Mormons, although two prominent English-born missionaries from Canada, John Taylor and Joseph Fielding, were influenced prior to their conversion by Irvingite views on the millennium. Irvingites tended to be solidly middle class and more prosperous than most English Mormon converts.

CONCLUSION

What should be obvious by now is that the religious milieu of early Victorian England was highly conducive to the transatlantic establishment of the Church of Jesus Christ of Latter-day Saints. During the Quorum of the Twelve's 1840 mission to England, Brigham Young and Willard Richards wrote to the First Presidency, "We find the people of this land much more ready to receive the gospel than those of America."[46] A major share of the credit, as we have seen, must go to the pronouncedly primitivist, charismatic, and millenarian nature of early Mormonism which capitalized on similar influences in England. One student, recognizing the responsiveness of the English milieu, has remarked that "there was nothing in [Mormonism] that had not been anticipated over the preceding half-century."[47] The appeal of earliest Mormonism was not its foreignness, but its familiar spirit. What it did was to unite into "the fulness of truth" those scattered and isolated insights embedded in the English environment. Unfortunately, some could not see beyond the fragments:

> When we arose to preach unto the people repentance, and baptism for the remission of sins, the cry of "Baptist, Baptist," would be rung in our ears. If we spoke of the Church and body of Christ being composed of Prophets and Apostles, as well as other members, "Irvingites, Irvingites," would immediately dash into the mind. If in the midst of our remarks, we even once suffered the saying to drop from our lips, "The testimony of Jesus is the spirit of

---

[45] Ibid., 32.

[46] Ronald W. Walker, ed., "The Willard Richards and Brigham Young 5 September 1840 Letter From England to Nauvoo," *Brigham Young University Studies* 18 (1978): 472.

[47] Oliver, *Prophets and Millennialists*, 218.

prophecy," "O you belong to Johanna Southcote," would be heard from several places at once. If we spoke of the second coming of Christ, the cry would be, "Aitkenites." If we made mention of the Priesthood, they would call us "Catholics." If we testified of the ministering of angels, the people would reply, "The Irvingites have their angels, and even the Duke of Normandy is ready to swear that he has the administering of angels every night."[48]

And yet, for those thousands who thought they perceived something larger afoot, the religious environment of England was felt to pave the way. "We know," wrote editor Thomas Ward, "that the minds of many of our elders were prepared for the work through the belief and reception of many of the principles propagated by Campbell [and we might add, just as appropriately, the numerous other primitivist, millenarian, and charismatic groups in early nineteenth-century England]; it was our own case, and we shall not cease to be grateful for being permitted to come in contact with them, which as far as we received them, we believe still; and we will even go further and acknowledge that the Lord permitted the propagation of those principles as a forerunner to the fulness of the gospel, though its advocates knew it not." As Orson F. Whitney summed it up, such individuals and movements "shed the lustre of advanced thought over the pathway soon to be brightened by the beams of eternal truth."[49] That the beloved LDS hymn, "The Morning Breaks, the Shadows Flee," was actually an adaptation by Parley P. Pratt of a one-hundred-year-old Charles Wesley hymn by the same title, therefore, is merely symbolic of the numerous ways in which the religious milieu of England was anticipatory of the Restoration.[50] Yet, from a Mormon perspective, whereas Wesley and countless other seekers, prophets, and millenarians wrote in hope and foretaste, Pratt and thousands of English converts actually lived to see the "dawning of a brighter day, majestic rise upon the world," English as well as American.

---

[48] Smith, *History of The Church*, 4:222–23.
[49] *Millennial Star* 3:197; Whitney, *Life of Heber C. Kimball*, 146.
[50] The hymn is cited in Turner, *Conflict and Reconciliation*, 47.

4

Early Mormon Confrontations with Sectarianism, 1837–40

MALCOLM R. THORP

The early growth of the Church of Jesus Christ of Latter-day Saints during the first missionary venture to the British Isles in 1837 can be partly attributed to the conversion of a significant number of former adherents of three nonconformist groups. The first converts were gleaned from Rev. James Fielding's chapel on Vauxhall Road, Preston. Soon after the conversion of the first Saints in Preston, Mormon missionaries John Goodson and Willard Richards made contact with another Christian sect at Bedford, headed by Rev. Timothy Matthews. According to LDS sources, a number of converts were drawn from Matthews's church, and Matthews himself was committed to baptism before he experienced a change of heart.[1] In addition, missionaries in both Preston and Liverpool encountered discontented members of the Christian Society, yet another sect, headed by Rev. Robert Aitken. According to Mormon Apostle Heber C. Kimball's account, as many as fifty Aitkenites in Preston alone at one time defected to Mormonism.[2]

Who were these three sects and their ministers? Aitken was the most important revival preacher of his generation — an English version of Charles G. Finney, claimed one Mormon account. Matthews had gained a local reputation in Bedfordshire as an imposing, but unorthodox figure. When preaching, he wore a black robe with bands and would stand on a stool,

---

[1] James R. Moss, "The Gospel Restored to England," in V. Ben Bloxham, James R. Moss, Larry C. Porter, eds., *Truth Will Prevail; The Rise of the Church of Jesus Christ of Latter-day Saints in the British Isles 1837–1987* (Solihull, England: The Church of Jesus Christ of Latter-day Saints, 1987), 84–86; V. Ben Bloxham, "The Apostolic Foundations," in Bloxham, *Truth Will Prevail*, 123.

[2] British Mission Manuscript History (hereafter cited as BM), vol. 6, 27 August 1837, Archives, Historical Department of the Church of Jesus Christ of Latter-day Saints, Salt Lake City, hereafter cited as LDS Church Archives.

blowing either a copper bugle or a silver trumpet to gain attention. His large physical stature and strong penetrating voice were said to be important to his success as a popular preacher. At least one early LDS missionary account discovered a connection between Aitken and Matthews, suggesting that a ministerial affinity existed between the two men, and that Matthews considered Aitken to be his "son." Furthermore, it was stated that Matthews became the Aitkenite minister of the Hope Street, Liverpool, congregation. Fielding's church, called "the Fieldingites," was an independent church that allegedly broke away from the Methodists.[3] While it is well known that the Reverends James Fielding and Timothy Matthews were brothers-in-law, the ecclesiastical connection between their churches in Preston and Bedford has not been explored.

Historical accounts of the early British mission have not done justice to these three sects and their leaders. Except for several brief references, coupled with errors associated with failure to examine all of the sources closely, historical accounts have been noticeably vague about these groups. Yet, who can doubt their importance to the early history of the British Mission? It is the purpose of this essay to reexamine the relationship between the Saints and these sectarian churches, using new sources that shed interesting light on this problem.

One of the difficulties involved with this essay is that it frankly clashes at some points with the "traditional" Mormon accounts, both past and present.[4] The problem from the outset was that Fielding, Matthews, and Aitken were looked upon as instruments of evil who sought to thwart God's design. Moreover, they were seen as dishonest men who knew the truth but did not act in accordance with the light within them. Thus, the underlying purpose of such histories typically has been the justification of the present by projecting images of a glorified past. Often in such accounts there has been little effort to understand the story from the perspective of the other side — that is, from the point of view of the "gentiles" — even

---

[3] George Albert Smith History, 23 August 1840, LDS Church Archives; Thomas Wright, *Life of T. R. Matthews* (London, 1934), 83; George J. Adams, *A Few Plain Facts, Shewing the Folly, Wickedness, and Imposition of the Rev. Timothy R. Matthews* (Bedford: C. B. Urrny, 1841), 9; Bloxham, "The Apostolic Foundations," 124. Malcolm R. Thorp, "The Setting," in Bloxham, *Truth Will Prevail*, 59. This represents the present author's error!

[4] Traditional Mormon history is written with the avowed purpose of promoting a faithful view of the past and is not necessarily concerned with critical examination of sources. For Mormonism in Britain, an example of this approach is Richard L. Evans, *A Century of "Mormonism" in Great Britain* (Salt Lake City: The Church of Jesus Christ of Latter-day Saints, 1937). This has been superseded by Bloxham, *Truth Will Prevail*. While this latter work is useful, the contributions are uneven in quality.

when sources have been available to make it possible to see both sides of the religious spectrum. This essay attempts to sympathetically understand all of the characters in the opening saga of the LDS Church in the British Isles and to avoid historicist judgments on their ultimate fate.

I

In the early part of the winter of 1836–37, Joseph Fielding, a young English convert to Mormonism living in Upper Canada, expressed a desire to spread the gospel to his numerous relatives still living in England. Somewhat reticent because he feared failure, yet taking courage that "the Lord takes the weak things of the World to confound the strong," Fielding approached John Taylor about his dilemma. As a result of their discussion, letters were sent by both men to family members, including Rev. James Fielding in Preston, and Rev. Timothy Matthews and his wife, Ann, in Bedford. According to Taylor's recollection, this was the first time the restoration of the gospel was announced by authorized servants of God to the inhabitants of England.[5]

Unfortunately, these letters have not survived. However, we do have Ann Fielding Matthews's response to this gospel announcement in a letter she wrote to her brother, Joseph. In addition, we have James Fielding's later statement[6] that he received from America a copy of Orson Hyde's *A Prophetic Warning*, a broadside which intended to pique the interests of millennialists and biblical primitivists who looked forward to a restoration, but which did not spell out the message of Mormonism, including the Book of Mormon.[7] From letters written by members of the Fielding family, it appears that they were also told about the gold plates and the translation of these records by Joseph Smith. But it appears that details of what this implied were purposely kept to a minimum, and none of the letters sent back to America by members of the Fielding family mentioned the story of an ancient Hebrew people in America.[8]

---

[5] Joseph Fielding Diary, 9–10, Special Collections, Harold B. Lee Library, Brigham Young University, Provo, Utah, hereafter cited as BYU Library. Larry C. Porter, "Beginnings of the Restoration: Canada, An 'Effectual Door' to the British Isles," in Bloxham, *Truth Will Prevail*, 33.

[6] James Fielding to Joseph Fielding, 27 August 1837, Bedford, Russell Family Collection, BYU Library.

[7] Orson Hyde, *A Prophetic Warning to All the Churches, of Every Sect and Denomination, and to Every Individual into Whose Hands It May Fall.* This broadside was dated Toronto, August 1836, and was reprinted in *LDS Messenger and Advocate* 2 (July 1836): 342–46. I am indebted to David J. Whittaker, BYU Archives, for the information here, as well as at several other points in this essay.

[8] John Fielding to Joseph Fielding, Gravely, 19 December 1837, LDS Church Archives. See also below.

Thus, on January 18, 1837, the Matthews sent a letter to Joseph Fielding in which they expressed interest in the new movement. Yet, they were also skeptical. Ann wrote:

> At first my mind seemed alternately to rejoice and mourn at one time I have been ready to exclaim then hath God indeed resiled [reconciled] her people and restored to them the lost gifts of her blessed spirit. . . . [Yet] is it possible that my beloved Brother & Sister have fallen into delusion, are they about to defect from the truth of inspiration given to us in Gods Holy word to follow cunningly devised fables which the story of finding the Plates at first glance seem to suggest. Do not I entreat you set me down for an unbeliever. this is far from being the case. No. I am waiting for a revival of primitive Power, the Gifts and the might power of God to be manifested visibly in the eyes of a wicked wo[r]ld.

Rev. Matthews also indicated that he did not want to summarily reject Mormon claims, but that he wanted to "prove all things" before he would agree. What followed was a one-page detailed list of questions they wished answered, including whether Joseph Fielding had actually seen the plates, as well as the Urim and Thummim. Interestingly, there were no questions in this detailed query about the actual contents of the Book of Mormon.[9]

One of the reasons why the Matthews were interested in the new American religion was that they were primitive restorationists who were awaiting the time when their congregation would be baptized by the spirit. In addition, Ann was a visionary who had recently seen God the Father and the Son in two different spiritual manifestations.[10]

At the time that the Fielding-Taylor letters arrived at Bedford, Rev. Matthews was struggling with difficulties that began with his removal as chaplain to the House of Industry at Bedford in 1832.[11] The LDS account of Matthews's removal and subsequent founding of his own religious sect are not entirely accurate. It was said that Matthews's removal occurred as a result of his millenarian views, as well as his belief in spiritual gifts. It is true that Matthews espoused such positions, especially the belief in the imminence of the Second Coming. Ann Matthews wrote in 1833 that the

---

[9] T. R. Matthews and Ann Matthews to Joseph Fielding, Bedford, 18 January 1837, LDS Church Archives.

[10] Ibid.

[11] Joan Varley, "A Bedfordshire Clergyman of the Reform Era and his Bishop," *The Publications of the Bedfordshire Historical Record Society* 57 (1978): 127. It is erroneously asserted in Bloxham, *Truth Will Prevail*, 84, that Matthews was curate of Colnworth and Bolnhurst until he became preacher for the Primitive Episcopal Church, Bedford, in 1821. In actuality, Matthews was replaced as curate for Bolnhurst and Colnworth in 1830, at which time he became chaplain to the House of Industry. It was not until 1832 that he founded the Primitive Episcopal Church. See Varley, "Bedfordshire Clergyman," 114–15.

Rev. Matthews had been approached by a learned Jew who demonstrated to his satisfaction from an old Hebrew Bible that the world was 5,993 years old, and that only seven years remained before Jesus would come down in glory![12]

But, while it might have been unusual to be quite this specific about the Second Advent, these were not necessarily non-Anglican doctrines, and were not the reasons for the loss of his chaplaincy. Rather, the controversy surrounding Matthews's dismissal centered on his accepting ordination from G. A. West as a bishop in the Primitive Episcopal Church, and the fact that Matthews subsequently ordained a man named Nevelle to the Primitive order. West was the English leader of an American sect in Liverpool. The major doctrine taught by this group was that proper ecclesiastical organization consisted of ordained bishops (who were really no more than local ministers) and a lay priesthood of dedicated parishioners. In addition, each congregation within the Primitive Church was autonomous in pursuing truth as dictated by the spirit. These ideas appealed to the impressionable Matthews, who had a deep concern for the welfare of common people, and he saw this lay order as an important means of engaging members of the working class in the Christian effort. In his defense, however, Matthews argued that he had been deceived by West, who had presented to him the seals of twelve bishops supposedly verifying the legality of the ordinations. When pressed by local Anglican authorities, he renounced having fallen for West's scheme as an error of bad judgment caused by deception. Local officials were also perturbed by Matthews's use of his own revised edition of the Book of Common Prayer, a version that excluded the Anglican articles of faith. Matthews insisted that the changes he made were inconsequential, but his reasoning failed to convince the directors of the chapel, and by a narrow margin of one vote he was deprived of his office.[13]

Most of the worshipers of the House of Industry followed Matthews. He also obtained support from a wealthy local benefactress, who financed the construction of a new chapel. Evidently the founding of the new church went extremely well, at least at first. In March 1833, Ann Fielding Matthews wrote two letters to Joseph Fielding in Canada, in which she gave an account of their successes. She reported that about 900 people had joined

---

[12] BM, vol. 6, 15 August 1837; Orson F. Whitney, *Life of Heber C. Kimball* (Salt Lake City: Kimball Family, 1888), 148; Ann Fielding Matthews to Mr. and Mrs. [Joseph] Fielding, Bedford, 18 March 1833, LDS Church Archives.

[13] Varley, "Bedfordshire Clergyman," 127, 134, 135; "Circular to the Clergy," Bedfordshire Record Office, England, MC 136. Yet when Matthews left the Church of England, he appears to have argued authority both through Anglican ordination, and, for the title of "Bishop," through the Primitive Episcopal Church. See Wright, *Life*, 22 and passim.

in Bedford and the surrounding villages, including Barford. In one evening alone, sixteen souls were brought to God. "A Society has of course been formed and more have since been made partakers of the pardoning love of God." Optimism abounded: "We think that the Church will rise to all the power & the glory of the primative Apostolic age before the coming of her Lord." She related that it was now twelve months since Rev. Matthews preached his last sermon at the House of Industry, and that the Lord had vindicated him: "What wonders has God wrought for us in consequence of that apparent conquest of our enemies. We have now a beautiful Church capable of containing nearly twice the number of people. The very thing that was intended to root us out and dismiss us from the town has been the means of establishing & setting us in it & while two of our enimies have been . . . summoned to meet their Judge [Captain Haig and Dr. Thacheray, who had voted in favor of removing Matthews from the House of Industry]."[14]

In spite of Ann's enthusiastic letter, Rev. Matthews soon fell on hard times. Ann became severly ill and was compelled to move to Leamington for treatments. As a result, Rev. Matthews was forced by pecuniary want to press the bishop of Lincoln, his former ecclesiastical superior, for full reinstatement as an Anglican minister. At one point agreement was reached concerning a probationary period of three years, but at this juncture Matthews balked. And, on August 10, 1836, Matthews announced his formal break with the Anglican Church.[15]

At the time of this announcement, Matthews was in Preston, preaching "in aid of a New Church." This "New Church" was none other than the Rev. James Fielding's congregation, the "Fieldingites," the group who eventually were to occupy the Vauxhall chapel. It has not been possible to find, however, any evidence that this group evolved from earlier Methodist connections. To be sure, the Fielding family came from a Methodist background, and it is plausible that James Fielding began his career as a Methodist minister,[16] although the denominational affiliation within Methodism is uncertain, and there is no record of his ordination in the Methodist archives. There does remain a problem, however, because it is not possible to determine when exactly Rev. Fielding first began his ministerial labors in Preston and whether he had a congregation there before founding the Primitive Episcopal group. However, the extant sources all indicate that the "Fieldingite" congregation was founded in collusion with Matthews,

---

[14] Ann Fielding Matthews to Mr. and Mrs. [Joseph] Fielding, Bedford, 18 March 1833, LDS Church Archives.

[15] James Fielding to Joseph Fielding and Sisters, Preston, 23 October 1835, LDS Church Archives; Varley, "Bedfordshire Clergyman," 131, 138.

[16] BM, vol. 6, 15 August 1837, LDS Church Archives.

and that the groups in Bedfordshire and Preston were from the very beginning denominationally connected.

Thus, in March 1833, Ann Matthews reported that Rev. James Fielding was likewise prospering with his new congregation at Preston. She said James had recently reported that over 100 had joined the society, that in one week nine persons had been brought out of darkness into the light of the gospel, and that every week the congregation attracted new members.[17]

In 1835, with Timothy Matthews's momentary departure from the Primitive Church, Fielding was left alone to carry the burden of the ministry: "I assure you it has been a heavy trial to me. I am now left alone — not a single brother minister to communicate with. It seems strange that I should have been almost forced into the work and then disserted." In spite of difficulties he could still claim progress; his congregation had grown to about 150 to 160 regular members, not counting investigators. He also said that there were prospects for a new chapel — that £200 had been collected, and that solicitations among the wealthy in Preston promised enough to soon begin construction.[18]

After Matthews's return, there appears to have been tension between the two brothers-in-law, and in 1837 Joseph Fielding reported that there was some talk of Timothy and James exchanging congregations, but that "bro[ther] J[ames] doesnt trust him long with his people."[19]

In many respects, the Rev. James Fielding appears to have been much more cautious and circumspect about ecclesiastical ideas than the ever rash Matthews. Still, he would countenance change: "Truth never shuns the test of enlightened reason especially when that reason is in professed subjection to the light of revelation."[20] James was, then, a seeker after light and truth, but he was a most conservative one. The sectarian world of the popular marketplace for religious ideas perhaps did not really appeal to him, for he observed that men of his era were like those Paul encountered, who lost the power of reason, but who could not pass the test of faith: "The present signs seem strikingly to answer St Paul's prediction in the 3rd Chap[ter] of 2 Timothy. Yet many run to and fro & knowledge is increased, in fact the form of Godliness abounds, but how little we see of the *power*, and even when a good work *does* break out it is hooted and denounced as

---

[17] Ann Fielding Matthews to Mr. and Mrs. [Joseph] Fielding, Bedford, 18 March 1833, LDS Church Archives.

[18] James Fielding to Joseph Fielding and Sisters, Preston, 23 October 1835, LDS Church Archives. The chapel mentioned here was what became known as the Vauxhall Road Chapel.

[19] Joseph Fielding to Mary and Mercy Fielding, Preston, [1837], LDS Church Archives.

[20] James Fielding to Joseph Fielding, Preston, 15 August 1838, BYU Library.

fanaticism if not insanity."[21] He remarked later that his views on religion were pretty much set. His conservatism made him an unlikely candidate for sudden conversion:

> With regard to my own views of gospel truth &c I rather feel wishful than otherwise to have them sifted to the bottom — and I assure you in the name of the Lord that I am so far from entertaining a high opinion of myself or my attainments, that I really dare not for my very soul shift one inch from the ground on which I have so long stood. I am so deeply impressed with the importance of spiritual matters and the shallowness of my own comprehension that I actually feel a kind of holy dread of trusting myself on new ground.[22]

How accurate was Joseph Fielding when he wrote that "James Fielding had earlier assured his congregation that he could not place more confidence in an angel than he did in the statements of his brother Joseph respecting the Latter-day Saints"? Did he embellish the account when he wrote, "They were thus prepared for the Elders' message"?[23] To what extent did James Fielding know about the doctrines of Mormonism at the time of the arrival of the first missionaries to Preston in July 1837?

In a letter written in 1840, James admitted that he had been initially infatuated with the possibility that a restoration had taken place by the power of God. He recalled that, "I should observ[e] that my prejudice (so to speak) was quite in favour of the new revelation & Notwithstanding my suspicions and fears I felt a strong desire that it might prove true & a kind of excellation [exultation?] at the idea of seeing for myself the miraculous & wonderful works which your letters would reasonably lead me to expect."[24] But he said that his first doubts occurred when the six elders arrived at his doorstep on the night of July 22, for, "No sooner had the Elders come within the door than I was seized with a sudden & strong conviction that they were not men of God."[25]

Nevertheless, James decided to allow the Mormons to preach in his chapel, and on the following afternoon, the first LDS meeting was held. James prefaced this meeting with a warm introduction, including, according to Joseph Fielding, mention of the subject of baptism. On this occasion the Apostle Heber C. Kimball opened the meeting with the first public lecture "on the Fulness of the Everlasting Gospel" in Britain. That evening another meeting was held with equally promising results. However, it is

---

[21] James Fielding to Joseph Fielding and Sisters, Preston, 23 October 1835, LDS Church Archives.

[22] James Fielding to Joseph Fielding, Preston, 15 August 1838, BYU Library.

[23] Fielding Diary, 17.

[24] James Fielding to his Sisters, Preston, 28 May 1840, LDS Church Archives.

[25] Ibid.

clear that Rev. Fielding had deep reservations concerning what had taken place. Brother Joseph fully corroborated his later testimony when he wrote that "he did not seem to receive our testimony himself,"[26] although as a gesture of goodwill he did announce that the elders could use his chapel for a third meeting on Wednesday.

Moreover, James appears to have left the Sunday meetings feeling that he had been duped. From the very beginning, James argued that he had given permission to use the chapel on the provision that no doctrine contrary to those taught in his church be introduced. He claimed that the elders had made that promise, but had broken it during their sermons.[27] He was angered by the influence that the Mormon preachers had on his congregation: "Many of the dear simple souls whom God had made me the means of saving were decoyed away from me & my little church. I could compare the influence the addresses of the Elders had upon the minds of several of the members to nothing but *witchcraft*. I clearly saw that it was according to St Paul a 'seducing spirit.' "[28]

It is clear that between Sunday and Wednesday considerable friction developed between the two Fielding brothers. Rev. Fielding mentioned a confrontation between himself and the elders, a point that is not made in LDS sources. He said that he went to the elders' lodgings "and God gave me power to confound them." He told them that God had never sent them and accused them of employing dishonest means to gain their ends. The elders, he reported, retorted by quoting St. Paul's words, "being crafty I caught them with guile," but Fielding replied that this was not the mean-

---

[26] Joseph Fielding to his Sisters, Preston, 2 October 1837, LDS Church Archives; Fielding Diary, 17, 18.

[27] James Fielding to his Sisters, Preston, 28 May 1840, LDS Church Archives. At dispute was the missionaries' mentioning of baptism by immersion. While we have seen that Joseph argued that James had referred to baptism in his welcoming remarks to the Sunday afternoon meeting, sources suggest that some agreement had been made prior to this occasion. Joseph recalled that, "I had told him that if he should allow us that privilidge we would not run foul upon him at once so that he might judge of it before he repeated that favour and that his people might not be influenced to an undue agree [degree] at first." Joseph Fielding to his Sisters, Preston, 2 October 1837, LDS Church Archives.

In his Diary, Joseph Fielding does not mention the quarrel over baptism. He does state (18) that James had previously read to his congregation the letters from Canada, and that these had created a favorable impression. Later (December 25), however, he wrote of James's sharing these letters with his congregation: "My Brother James had formerly highly recommended to his people, i.e., when he received them, though he kept from them that Part that treated Baptism" (47). This establishes that from the very beginning James was concerned about at least this Mormon doctrine, and it makes it entirely plausible that James was right about a breached agreement.

[28] James Fielding to his Sisters, Preston, 28 May 1840, LDS Church Archives.

ing of this passage. So emotional did this encounter become that one of the missionaries "threw down his book of Mormon on the table with a vengeance."[29]

Joseph later wrote that "the people began to believe more & more, this made Bro James begin to fear." However, his letter suggests, as we have seen above, that James already had doubts, and never really believed in the message of these American missionaries. Joseph continued: "he [James] began to object & he said he had not time to study the subject his mind was so taken upon preaching to the people to repent and belive that he had no time to devote to the study of Mormonism." In addition to baptism, the issue of the Book of Mormon divided the two brothers: "I do not think he ever read the Book of Mormon but to find objections it appeared weak to him and unlike inspiration. he saw no beauty in any thing we advanced." Given James's atttitude toward Mormonism, it is not entirely accurate to assert that he closed his chapel following the Wednesday night meeting because he feared he was losing his congregation.[30] Perhaps a better way of stating the case would be to say that the chapel was closed because James Fielding did not believe the LDS Church to be true and concluded that the missionaries' message was evil.

To be sure, initially nine members of Fielding's congregation, including George Watt, one of its leading members, joined the new sect.[31] Eventually, according to Joseph Fielding, the greater part of James's church joined the Mormons.[32] Not only had James lost part of his congregation,

---

[29] Ibid.

[30] Joseph Fielding to his Sisters, Preston, 2 October 1837, LDS Church Archives; Moss, "The Gospel Restored," 76.

[31] According to LDS sources, James's congregation was so agitated by the doctrine of baptism by immersion that he offered to have them baptized, and he engaged Rev. Giles from the local Baptist church to perform this ordinance. Only one member would come forward. "Mr. Fielding's people also stated that he acted the part of a hypocrite and deceived them when he read the letters to them in public which he had received from America, by keeping back that part which treated on baptism." BM, vol. 6, 1 August 1837. No mention of this occurs in James's letters involving the incident. And Joseph Fielding did not expound on this event. Indeed, Joseph wrote that members of James's congregation were deeply committed to their minister, some even asking if they could continue to attend James's chapel and still be Saints. Joseph Fielding to his Sisters, Preston, 2 October 1837, LDS Church Archives. The real problem appears, however, when Fielding stated that, on September 11, Rev. Matthews was expected in Preston to baptize members of the Primitive Church who desired this ordinance. Fielding Diary, 31. Was this necessary if James Fielding had previously invited Giles to perform this ordinance? Or was the Giles incident (which was based on rumor) really historical?

[32] Of the twenty-eight members who comprised the early Preston Branch, nearly all of these were said to have come from Rev. Fielding's church. See BM, vol. 6, 6 August 1837.

but he could not recover from this reversal. By allowing Mormonism a foothold in Preston, he lost face with the local populace. This probably was what was meant by the comment, "it is said that Bro Jas made religion stink in the minds of the intelligent of the place." He was eventually forced to give up his chapel, which was too large for his now decimated congregation: "We understand the Methodist have proposed to buy his Chapel. the outside is about finished. it is a noble building but it is never likely to be filled."[33]

According to traditional accounts, Fielding became "one of the most bitter opponents the Elders had" in Preston, and not long after these events, James was evidently ritually "cursed" by the Mormon elders. What does this mean? James soon joined forces with Richard Livesey, a local Preston writer, who produced the first tract against the Saints, and the two men appeared together at public meetings where the reputed evils of Mormonism were discussed. To be sure, James was "bitter" about the loss of his congregation because he claimed that the Mormons had defrauded him by breaking their initial bargain not to preach baptism or new doctrines — a contention that was backed by the Fielding family.[34] Yet, in private letters to his brother, he claimed that he was and had been open-minded about the subject of Mormonism, and that it was the Saints who were intolerant. In two letters that James Fielding sent to Joseph in August 1838, he accused his brother of using his family connections to advance the interest of the church at his (James's) expense. It would have been far better to have preached first in Liverpool, "besides had you opened your mission at Liverpool you might have avoided the charge of working with a poor brother's materials." The Book of Mormon issue was also clearly a matter of contention. He accused his brother of going too far in his "assumptions" concerning the book:

> You must recollect that no one has the right to assume the data that is not acknowledged by the other party — you were certainly the aggressor. Your business was not to tell me "in plain terms that the Book of Mormon was the word of God" — this was assuming the thing — I want something to convince my judgment — and I confess I have felt something of what St. Paul felt when at Athens — It was said "his spirit was stirred within" him "when he saw their idolatrous devotions" or according to the original he was in a paroxism of

---

[33] Joseph Fielding to his Sisters, Preston, 2 October 1837, LDS Church Archives.

[34] Moss, "The Gospel Restored," 76; James Fielding to his Sisters, Preston, 28 May 1840, LDS Church Archives; Richard Livesey, *An Exposure of Mormonism* (Preston: J. Livesey, 1838); James Fielding to Joseph Fielding, Preston, 15 August 1838, BYU Library; John Fielding to Joseph Fielding, Gravely, 19 December 1837, LDS Church Archives. See also below.

anger. I felt something of this kind, and no wonder if my feelings carried me a little too far.[35]

James said that he had read the Book of Mormon twice, and had "excercised all the understanding God has given men upon its contents"; yet, he could only question, "How can I embrace as truth such a mass of incoherency and absurdity as appears almost on every page of the book of Mormon[?]" He went on to add that, "The historical part seems to me a complete zigzag—when I had read two or three hundred pages I got so versed in the up-and-down maze that I could and did actually fortell what was coming next, several times running. I could predict when the Nephites would beat and when the Lamanites would beat."[36] James also argued that the Mormons were disingenuous in their public discourses concerning the Book of Mormon: "To give a public challenge at a time when it was impossible for your opponents to furnish themselves with facts and arguments against Mormonism and then refuse to hold an argument when proper information had been obtained upon the subject was quite unreasonable. I am just speaking now according to the standard of common sense and sober reason—I suppose at all event[s] you will not deny me the right to judge according to the principle of common sense and the common meaning of words. In fact, I know of no other method of proceeding in such matters."[37] James wrote out of considerable brotherly affection, and stated his willingness to meet and discuss the issues of Mormonism with Joseph and a small group of Saints, provided all adhered to the rule that only one person should speak at a time.

It was in the midst of this controversy that, in early August, Willard Richards and John Goodson left Preston for Bedford, with the purpose of contacting Rev. Matthews and commencing missionary labors in that town.[38] Matthews was intially receptive, talking to the missionaries for three hours, and then allowing them to preach in his chapel that evening. According to Goodson's account, they were allowed to meet with Matthews's congregation every night that week, and during this time Rev. Matthews "kept growing in the faith." However, on Saturday, August 14, Goodson wrote that Mrs. Matthews returned from the country, "at which time he [Matthews] was almost ready for baptism." Ann Matthews, however, was initially "quite high" against this idea, "but we united in calling upon the Lord that his hand might be upon her, and it fell upon her both in body

---

[35] James Fielding to Joseph Fielding, Preston, 27 August 1838, BYU Library.

[36] James Fielding to Joseph Fielding, Preston, 15 August 1838, BYU Library.

[37] James Fielding to Joseph Fielding, Preston, 27 August 1837, BYU Library.

[38] BM, vol. 6, 2 and 15 August 1837. There appears to be a problem with the dating of this first entry. Elder Goodson, as I will show, said that they were in Preston for a week prior to the episode of 15 August. See below.

and mind, so that she is now partly humble and almost ready."[39] Significantly, however, at the time of writing this account, neither had committed themselves for baptism, and it is highly doubtful that such a commitment was ever given.[40] Later in 1837, Joseph Fielding wrote that it was Ann's influence that kept Rev. Matthews from joining the church.

According to LDS sources, Rev. Matthews committed himself to be baptized the next evening, but left Bedford the following morning instead to visit his congregations in the outlying villages. It is stated that the stumbling block to his conversion was Elder Goodson's sharing with him the vision of Joseph Smith and Sidney Rigdon on the three degrees of glory, which caused him to react negatively to the teachings. There is every reason to believe this part of the story, although Goodson's August 14 letter reveals another clue to Matthews's disaffection. Goodson stated that Matthews received a letter from members of the Primitive Church in Preston concerning troubles in the congregation.[41] While Goodson did not seem to feel that this letter exercised undue influence over Matthews, it seems likely that the disruptions in his church in Preston due to Mormon proselytizing would have an impact on his attitude toward the missionaries, as well as his decision regarding baptism.

At any rate, it is evident that when Matthews returned from his preaching circuit he was openly hostile to the Saints. On August 20, Ann Fielding Matthews sent a letter to Joseph Fielding chastising him bitterly for intruding into James's congregation. The letter stated that both Ann and her husband looked upon Mormonism as a cunning fable and that the Book of Mormon was a fraud. In a later undated letter written by Rev. Matthews to Joseph Fielding, he said, "I saw enough at Bedford to convince me that the Elders who came down there were never lead to the Lord Jesus, nor baptised by the Holy Ghost."[42]

---

[39] John Goodson to Isaac Russell, Bedford, 14 August 1837, Isaac Russell Collection, BYU Library.

[40] Joseph Fielding did relate that 8 P.M. was the time fixed for baptism "but when they should have gone forward they began again to pray. I hardly know why unless it was something like Balaam in Numbers." But, the "praying" could only have occurred the night of August 14. By all accounts, Matthews had gone into the country on the morning of August 15. Thus, while it is possible that the Matthews had committed themselves for baptism, Goodson's letter casts doubt on this point. Goodson stated that they were nearly ready for baptism, but still had not committed themselves at the time he was writing (probably the evening of August 14). In subsequent letters, T. R. and Ann Matthews never mentioned having consented to baptism. Joseph Fielding to his Sisters, Preston, 2 October 1837, LDS Church Archives.

[41] BM, vol. 6, 15 August 1837; John Goodson to Isaac Russell, Bedford, 14 August 1837, BYU Library.

[42] Ann Fielding Matthews to Joseph Fielding, Bedford, 20 August 1837,

According to contemporary LDS accounts, it is argued that Rev. Matthews borrowed the ordinances of baptism and the laying on of hands for the gift of the spirit from the Mormons. It seems entirely plausible that he was influenced by the Mormon elders concerning these doctrines. But this statement must be somewhat qualified. We must remember that Matthews was a primitivist, and that he was already looking forward to a baptism of the Holy Spirit. We should remember, too, that Matthews was already a believer in the the gifts of the spirit. Still, it appears likely that his interest in baptism by immersion was stimulated by his discussion with the elders, although the Mormon account of subsequent events appears to have been embellished. For, it is stated that the day after he failed to appear for his baptismal appointment, "*it was rumored that* Mr. Matthews had baptized himself in the river, and then went to baptizing others."[43] This latter statement must be treated with caution, for the Church Book for Matthews's Primitive Episcopal Church in Bedford has survived, and this record indicates that Charlott Mallows of Haynes was the first person baptized by immersion;[44] this event occurred on November 13, 1837, considerably after the events of the preceding August.

However, Joseph Fielding asserted September 11 that Matthews was expected in Preston, where he was to baptize members of James's church. It was probably on this occasion that Matthews publicly announced that he would never baptize another infant.[45] The obvious meaning here is that Matthews concluded that he would not baptize another child by sprinkling, for Matthews stated in March 1843 that "When I was led about five years ago to adopt the Apostolic mode of Baptism by Immersion, I saw no ground for rejecting the Infants, and I saw that they ought to be baptised in the same manner."[46] Thus, if Matthews was influenced by the LDS missionaries concerning the proper apostolic mode of baptism, he certainly interpreted this in his own way, and not as the Mormon elders had taught.

Joseph Fielding Collection; Rev. T. R. Matthews to Joseph Fielding, Liverpool [undated], BYU Library.

[43] Italics added by the present author. According to the LDS account, it was rumored that Mr. Matthews baptized himself. BM, vol. 6, 15 August 1837. Joseph Fielding said that "*it appears* that Mr. Matthews found some other person the next day to perform the ordinance." See Joseph Fielding to his Sisters, Preston, 2 October 1837, LDS Church Archives.

[44] "Primitive Episcopal Church, Bedford," November 13, 1837, Bedford Record Office, Z 273/1 and typescript.

[45] Fielding Diary, 31; copy of Letters to Mr. Matthews [at] Liverpool, 2 August 1839, BYU Library.

[46] Wright, *Life*, 80.

Rev. Robert Aitken first appeared in LDS accounts following the conversion of a number of members of his Christian Society in Preston. Hearing of these events, Aitken stormed into Preston and vitriolically denounced the Saints as the "Devil's Conjurers," and he pounded a copy of the Book of Mormon against the pulpit and said that it came from hell.[47]

The Christian Society had been founded in January 1836, initially with nine members. But the new sect soon spread throughout the north and the potteries, and by the end of that year, there were 1,500 members, with churches at Liverpool, Manchester, Burslem, Hanley, Congleton, Preston, and Leigh.[48] From the beginning, Aitken looked upon the Society as an alternative to Methodism, for he considered the standard of holiness in Methodist congregations not high. Indeed, all of the churches, he averred, "were living beneath their privileges," adding, "that there is much worldly conformity amongst them; that a secular and temporizing spirit has gained considerable ground throughout the societies; that their standard of holiness is very far beneath the Gospel standard."[49]

The distinctive theological ideas of the Christian Society were its belief in the gifts of the spirit, including the working of miracles, the gift and interpretation of tongues, healings, and miracles. In addition, Aitken was a recent convert to the Old Testament concept of the millennium, claiming that he had been taught this doctrine, not through the intelligence of man, but directly by God. Aitken's millennial views rested firmly upon a conviction that society had been corrupted by vanity and other forms of deceit, and that it stood condemned. As a result, the true Christian must flee from secular Babylon and join a society such as the one he founded.[50]

While there was much talk within the Christian Society of the Second Advent, Aitken's writings on this subject lacked the detailed imagery that one finds in such Bible sources as Daniel, Micah, and Revelation. He really did not have much to say about the events themselves, other than to project a literal fulfillment of all of these scriptures. Thus, he lumped the entire tradition into one cryptic comment: "so every prophecy and promise respecting his second coming—throne—kingdom—reign—judgment—power—with the changes predicted in the world—elements—nature—condition of animals and the like, shall be literally accomplished."[51] But this

---

[47] Fielding Diary, 12.

[48] *Laws, Regulations and General Polity of the Christian Society,. in connection with the Rev. R. Aitken* (1836).

[49] Ibid., 4–5.

[50] *Extracts from the Minutes of the Fourth Annual Convocation of the Christian Society* (Liverpool, 1839), 8; Robert Aitken, *The "Second Coming of Christ," A Sermon* (London: G. & C. Fowler, 1839), 8–10.

[51] *Extracts from . . . Fourth . . . Convocation*, 6.

great day was to be anticipated, for it would only be then that the Holy Spirit would be poured out upon all flesh.

One of the problems with the Christian Society, however, was that it lacked a distinctive theology. It was Methodist in theology and church polity. There was a strong emphasis on teetotalism and refraining from the use of tobacco. The movement also was limited by the social conservatism of its founder. Thus, members of the Christian Society were expected to refrain from radical politics, and not to criticize ministers of the crown or magistrates. And they were forbidden to attend other denominational meetings.[52] The popularity of this movement, in spite of its extreme social conservativism, suggests an undercurrent of disenchantment with the political radicalism normally associated with the working classes of the industrial north.

Aitken's meetings were often scenes of emotional excesses, where individuals would be caught up in the spirit. One commentator mentioned that those seeking salvation were invited to "go down in the cellar to seek for Jesus," where he saw about fifty people in different postures: "some grovelling on their bellies, some kneeling, some standing; some anxious some depressed, and some joyful; but all more or less excited, and the majority uttering a great variety of exclamations."[53] Such emotional exuberance was probably attractive to many working people, and we should not go too far in condemning such scenes. Indeed, LDS meetings also witnessed manifestations of the spirit, especially in connection with speaking in tongues.

Another problem with the Christian Society was the lack of effective leadership. Aitken was successful in attracting adherents, but he could not keep them within the fold. On the one hand, Aitken was authoritarian in his approach to church organization and attempted to mold it into his own image. Yet he did not systematically pursue rigorous supervision of the Society. In early 1837, he even left the north to open up a new chapel in London. His efforts to control the various branches from afar proved disastrous, and major rifts soon developed. In the prestigious Hope Street Chapel, Liverpool, for example, Aitken quarreled with John Bowes, the minister, over Bowes's strict interpretation of teetotalism, as well as Aitken's efforts to interfere in matters of policy that should have been left to the congregation. Bowes also accused Aitken of breaking pledges originally made to him when he assumed the Hope Street Chapel. After protracted conflict, Bowes was eventually forced to leave for Manchester, although many of the local Aitkenites sided with him in this dispute.[54]

---

[52] *Laws, Regulations . . . of the Christian Society*, 8, 27, 38, 40.

[53] Rev. D. Thom, "Liverpool Churches and Chapels," *Historic Society of Lancashire and Cheshire: Proceedings and Papers* 4 (1851–52): 183–84.

[54] John Bowes, *The Autobiography or History of the Life of John Bowes* (Glasgow: G.

Bowes was removed from the Hope Street Chapel in order that Aitken could bring in none other than the Rev. Timothy Matthews as the minister.[55] Indeed, Joseph Fielding wrote on October 2, 1837, that Matthews had left Bedford for London, "I understand in view of another Church, but I have heard lately that he had been in Liverpool with an idea of joining another minister named Aiken of some Methodist order." By the fall of 1837, Matthews had once again fallen on hard times, as his congregation had suffered serious losses, mostly to the Irvingites, but also to the Latter-day Saints. There were legal problems over Matthews's abandoning his chapel in Bedford, however, and he never entirely forsook his ministry in that town. Instead, he went on extended trips to Liverpool, where records indicate that he preached at least eighty-five times at the Aitkenite Hope Street Chapel in 1839 alone.[56]

From Liverpool, Matthews wrote to Joseph Fielding concerning the Book of Mormon. Matthews argued that, "Had I been in America I would have seen the Plates—their being hidden does not look well—Is the way of the Lord to *hide*[?] Does the Lad [Joseph Smith] need *three* or *nine* men to *testify* the *Truth* of the *Bible*. . . . Throughout the whole Book of Mormon a professed Jewish History, [there is] not *one single Reference* . . . made to *Circumcision* which . . . appears a conclusive Argument that the Book was written by Gentiles."[57]

Matthews was not in Liverpool in January 1840 when John Taylor and Joseph Fielding visited the Hope Street Chapel, an occasion which saw the first converts from Liverpool join the LDS Church. But, they were informed by several members of the congregation that Mr. Matthews had examined the Book of Mormon and had concluded that it was "of the devil."[58] Indeed, soon after Matthews's return, a debate was held between the two Mormon elders and Rev. Matthews. In the course of this discussion, an ugly confrontation developed on the question of ecclesiastical authority.

Gallie & Sons, 1872), 176–203.

[55] Ibid., 186–87.

[56] Joseph Fielding to his Sisters, Preston, 2 October 1837, LDS Church Archives; T. R. Matthews and Ann Matthews to Joseph Fielding, Bedford, 18 January 1837, LDS Church Archives; Varley, "Bedfordshire Clergyman," 138; Bowes, *Autobiography*, 186. Entries in Matthews's church book show that sixteen joined in 1837, fifteen in 1838, and twenty-one in 1839. This would indicate a drop from previous years, but still some success in conversions. Bedford Record Office, Z 273/1. Wright, *Life*, 44–45.

[57] Rev. T. R. Matthews to Joseph Fielding, Liverpool [n.d.], BYU Library. This is undoubtedly the letter that Joseph Fielding mentions receiving from Matthews in his diary. The date of receipt was 21 November 1839. See Fielding Diary, 87.

[58] Joseph Fielding to Hannah [Fielding], Liverpool, 26 January 1840, LDS Church Archives.

According to Fielding, "Mr. M[atthews] asked Bro. Taylor where he got his Authority; Ans[wer]: by Prophecy and laying on of hands of those who had Authority, etc. This came by the Ministration of an holy Angel. Bro T[aylor] then asked where he got his. Ans[wer]: from the Bishop of Lincoln, and that was as good as his Angel, 'and you have no more Power than I have if you have, let us see it. . . . I say if you have any Power from Heaven or Hell shew it.' "

Finally, after Matthews repeatedly asked for a sign of their powers, Taylor replied that he would oblige him: "his Body should be afflicted; the Lord should lay his Hand upon him, etc." By this time, the breach between Matthews and the Mormons was complete, and we are told by Fielding that the next day John Taylor pronounced a "curse" on Matthews. Rev. Fielding said of this promise that Taylor prophecied: "God shall smite thee with *sickness*, and *disease*, and *death*."[59] The last mention we have of Matthews's activities involving the Mormons occurred shortly after this incident when he was observed in Northampton circulating hundreds of tracts in which he claimed that the Book of Mormon was written from the Spaulding manuscripts.[60]

II

What happened to these three sectarian leaders? In the case of James Fielding, he eventually found a new church for his diminished congregation in the abandoned Aitkenite chapel at Preston, where he preached and supplemented his income by teaching school. In 1845 he wrote, "Many attacks have been made upon my little flock, but still it exists, and I indulge a confident belief that I shall see the work of God revive and that my latter days will be my best."[61]

As we have seen, defections to the Irvingites and the Latter-day Saints had so impoverished Matthews that he had consented to preaching engagements at the Aitkenite chapel in Liverpool. Even before the collapse of the Christian Society in 1840, Matthews was devoting his primary attention to his emaciated Bedfordshire congregations. His charismatic, if comical, preaching methods soon brought him new followers, and the 1840s wit-

---

[59] Fielding Diary, 116, 117; James Fielding to his Sisters, Preston, 28 May 1840, LDS Church Archives.

[60] Adams, *Plain Facts*, iii–iv, 10–11. Solomon Spaulding had written a romance containing superficial similarities with the Book of Mormon. Anti-Mormon writers argued that Sidney Rigdon, one of Joseph Smith's closest advisors, had provided the Mormon prophet with this text and that it provided the basis for the Book of Mormon. The Spaulding theory has been thoroughly discredited.

[61] James Fielding to Joseph Fielding and Sisters, Preston, 14 January 1845, LDS Church Archives.

nessed his emergence as one of the most successful nonconformist preachers in Bedford. The irrepressible Ann Matthews wrote in 1841 not only of present prosperity but of her future millenarian expectations:

> The Lord is exceedingly gracious to us. He often makes our cup to run over but we are expecting fearful events in which our own Country will according to Prophetic truth have to drink of the cup of trembling. I am also persuaded the time will come when there shall literally be a cry "Flee out of Babylon" and ten men shall take hold of the skirt of him that is a Jew saying we will go up with you for we have heard that God is with you. I think it very likely we shall not end our days in England but if we as a Family emigrate I hope it will be to the Holy land.[62]

Such was not to be, for Timothy Matthews ended his days in Bedford when he died of a heart attack in 1846.

Robert Aitken was never fully at home with nonconformity. As leader of the Christian Society he was plagued with doubts concerning his creating schism by breaking with the Church of England and forming his own sect. In September 1840, he finally concluded that his efforts were wrong and resigned his leadership of the Christian Society. He then reapplied for reinstatement as an Anglican clergyman. After a probationary period in Leeds, Aitken was given the rural Cornwall parish of Pendeen as his living, and he served long and honorably in this capacity until his death in 1870.[63]

On September 7, during dark hours of depression following Aitken's resignation as leader of the Christian Society, Mormon Apostles Heber C. Kimball and George Albert Smith visited him at his home in London. Smith later recalled Aitken's having remarked that, "I am afraid of you, I am afraid of you, you are so near the truth it is impossible to detect you." But, Smith continued, "instead of being honest enough to embrace the truth after making this acknowledgement to us, he right then renounced his religion as an Aitkenite."[64]

Kimball's account of this interview, however, differed considerably from his fellow apostle. On September 11 he wrote: "We made Mr. Aitkin a visit last week. he treated us verry kindly. he told us that he had with

[62] Ann [Matthews] to Joseph Fielding, Bedford, 24 March 1841, LDS Church Archives.

[63] Charlotte E. Woods, *Memoirs and Letters of Canon Hay Aitken* (London: C. W. Daniel Co., 1928), 18–28.

[64] Journal History of the Church, 10 September 1854, p. 8, LDS Church Archives. Wilford Woodruff's report of this meeting was somewhat different than Smith's. He recorded: "He [Aitken] treated them kindly acknowledged their doctrin to be true but was afraid of deception. His mind is in a disturbed state." Scott Kenney, ed., *Wilford Woodruff's Journal Typescript*, 9 vols. (Midvale, Utah: Signature Press, 1983–85), 1: 509.

drown himself from his own society and from all others. he ses [says] all the Sec [sects] are Rong and going the broad way. I never saw a man in such a state before."[65] Thus, while it is entirely possible that Aitken had made a complimentary remark about Mormonism, it is difficult to believe that he had acknowledged his belief in LDS truth claims. Aitken was a Methodist at heart, and doctrinally, both as leader of the Christian Society and afterwards, he represented positions far different than Mormonism. In addition, there is no reason to believe that Aitken ever believed in the Book of Mormon; in fact, the evidence suggests the contrary, and that both before and after the interview with Smith and Kimball he publicly denounced the Book of Mormon. Once again, we have that ever-repeated formulary that he did not join the church because of self-interest! Aitken was basically a man of integrity; such stories reveal more about LDS anticlerical attitudes than they do Aitken's inward beliefs. This episode reminds one of Bryan Wilson's comment that sects tend to deny religious virtue to anyone except their own leaders.[66]

From our discussion here, are there any clues that would help explain the LDS successes among these sects? The issue that appears most important in explaining Mormon conversions of members of the Primitive Episcopal Church, as well as the Aitkenites, was the Saints' more effective claims to sacerdotal authority. Of the three ministers discussed, only Matthews appears to have developed effective counterclaims to the Mormons. As a result, his congregational losses were only minimal. James Fielding never seems to have developed any effective arguments on the issue of authority, and his failure to provide such explanations was probably the reason why half of his congregation abandoned his chapel in spite of their considerable personal attachment to him. Aitken, the most able theologian of the three, rested his claims on the apostolic succession carried through the Church of England. But Aitken was always troubled by fears that he was guilty of creating schism by leaving the bosom of the Anglican Church, and this made it difficult for him to substantiate his claim to authority in a way that would convince doubters within his sect. The Christian Society was always more a voluntary society for promoting Christian values among the working classes than it was a fully developed church. The loose structure and internecine rifts within the society made it difficult to effectively counter the propaganda of the Saints. Aitken's largely negative campaign against the Book of Mormon was not enough; what was

---

[65] Heber C. Kimball to Edward Martin, London, 11 September 1840, LDS Church Archives.

[66] BM, vol. 1, April 1841; Bryan Wilson, *Religion in Sociological Perspective* (Oxford: Oxford University Press, 1982), 91.

needed was a convincing refutation defending the uniqueness of his society against such sectarian attacks as those launched by the Mormons.

One interesting aspect of this study has been the fluidity of the sectarian scene during this period. This is demonstrated not only by LDS missionary successes, but also in the lucrative raids of the Irvingites on Matthews's church. Fielding's troubles, we have seen, were partly from Mormon losses, but also partly from other sectarian intruders. And, we might ask, how many early Mormons abandoned the faith between 1837 and 1840?[67] Perhaps our conception of the sect is not entirely applicable to the fluid structure of popular religion at this time. That is, if we define a sect as a close-knit, highly cohesive structure, with little penetration from outsiders, then this generalization probably has little meaning for the groups that we have studied here.[68] While this definition certainly applied in later years, we might be skeptical about its applicability to this early period.

---

[67] By 1840 there were few more than 1,500 members of the church in England, only a slight increase over the figures when the first missionaries left in 1838. It seems probable that between 1838 and 1840 as many left the church as joined. Apostasy was cited as a major reason. James B. Allen and Thomas Alexander, eds., *Manchester Mormons; The Journal of William Clayton 1840–1842* (Santa Barbara and Salt Lake City: Peregrine Smith, Inc., 1974), 10. See also James B. Allen and Malcolm R. Thorp, "The Mission of the Twelve to England, 1840–41: Mormon Apostles and the Working Classes," *Brigham Young University Studies* 15 (Summer 1975): 501–2.

[68] For a discussion of the characteristics of sects, see Wilson, *Religion*, 90–93 and passim. See also Robert Lively's essay in this collection.

5

The 1840–41 Mission to England and the Development of the Quorum of the Twelve

RONALD K. ESPLIN

Joseph Smith organized the Quorum of the Twelve Apostles in Kirtland, Ohio, in February 1835.[1] Though the apostles often discussed their mandate, as a quorum, to introduce the restored gospel abroad, by 1838 only Elders Kimball and Hyde had preached overseas (in England), and they had returned. Though revelation in March 1835 also declared that the apostles, when united, were "equal in authority and power" to the Presidency of the Church,"[2] during the first three years of their history they seldom demonstrated either unity or power. In the summer of 1838, only one year before finally departing for Great Britain on their long-anticipated mission, the Quorum of the Twelve seemed anything but united, powerful, or impressive. Indeed, in the aftermath of the Kirtland difficulties, the Presidency had removed from office four of the apostles only weeks before.

In Far West, Missouri, July 1838, Joseph Smith reflected on the state of the apostles' quorum. "Show us thy will, O Lord, concerning the Twelve," he prayed. The response, now Section 118 in the Latter-day Saint volume of scripture known as the Doctrine and Covenants, directed that the Quorum of the Twelve be reorganized, and it named men to replace those who had fallen. After promising that if they were humble and faithful "an effec-

---

[1] For a discussion of the calling of the Twelve, see Ronald K. Esplin, "The Emergence of Brigham Young and the Twelve to Mormon Leadership, 1830–1841," (Ph.D. dissertation, Brigham Young University, 1981), 125–32. This paper, a version of which was presented at the Mormon History Association Annual Meeting in Oxford, England, July 1987, is a refinement and expansion of ideas first discussed in the above study. For more detail about the British Mission of the Twelve and its background, see Esplin, "The Emergence of Brigham Young," 392–498.

[2] Doctrine and Covenants 107:23–24, given 28 March 1835, the month following the organization of the Quorum of the Twelve. "The Presidency" was subsequently called the "First Presidency."

tual door shall be opened for them, from henceforth," the revelation then charged the apostles to depart from the Far West Temple site "over the great waters" for England the following April 26.

But this was not the end of hard times for the Twelve. Even before those named in the revelation could be ordained, disaster befell the Missouri Latter-day Saints, as armed neighbors besieged their communities and, eventually, drove them from the state. Within 100 days of the revelation Apostle David Patten died in battle, Apostle Parley Pratt was imprisoned, and Quorum President Thomas B. Marsh apostatized, taking Apostle Orson Hyde with him.[3]

Nonetheless, the July revelation charging the apostles to depart for England contained seeds of renewal for the Twelve and marks the beginning of their eventual ascendancy within the LDS Church. A brief review of the history of the Quorum of the Twelve from 1835 to 1838 helps us understand the essential role the mission to Great Britain played in this transformation.

Two threads ran throughout the initial instructions when the LDS Quorum of Twelve Apostles was organized in 1835:

(1) Though described as equal to the church's Presidency in power and authority, their specific calling was to take the Restored Gospel abroad and "to build up the Church and regulate all the affairs of the same in all nations."[4] Oliver Cowdery counseled the new apostles to prepare for long periods away from home; the Gospel must go to the nations abroad, he told them, and since they held the keys of that ministry, they too must go. It was their duty to unlock the kingdom of heaven to foreign nations, Joseph Smith taught them, "for no man can do that thing but yourselves." Each, he emphasized, had "the same authority in other nations that I have in this nation."[5] Where would they begin?

(2) Emphasis on individual humility and on quorum unity. They must be *one*, "equal in bearing the keys of the Kingdom to all nations," Cowdery stressed in his apostolic charge. Since unity and humility were essential for either authority or success, rather than competing, each must pray for the other. Bonds of fellowship and brotherhood should prevail above all else.[6]

With only a few exceptions, notably in 1836 in connection with Kirtland Temple experiences, the early Twelve seldom fulfilled this commission.

---

[3] See Esplin, "Emergence of Brigham Young," 336–44.

[4] Revelation, 28 March 1835, Doctrine and Covenants 107:33.

[5] Joseph Smith, Jr., *History of the Church of Jesus Christ of Latter-day Saints*, ed. B. H. Roberts, 7 vols., 2d ed. rev. (Salt Lake City: Deseret Book, 1971), 2:193–98; and Record of the Twelve, 27 February 1835, Archives, Historical Department, The Church of Jesus Christ of Latter-day Saints, Salt Lake City, cited hereafter as LDS Church Archives.

[6] *History of the Church*, 2:195–97.

The personality of Quorum President Thomas Marsh was one obstacle. Concerned about his prerogatives as president, Marsh's leadership was often intrusive and officious. His impatience with criticism and tendency to view a difference of opinion, or even initiative by others, as a challenge to his leadership no doubt contributed to the pettiness and self-concern that sometimes plagued the new quorum. Years later, Brigham Young characterized the Twelve in Kirtland as divided by jealousy and "continually sparring at each other." Under Thomas Marsh they met very often, he noted, "and if no one of them needed cleaning, they had to 'clean' some one any how."[7]

In Kirtland the Quorum of the Twelve also lacked the visibility and prestige of the Kirtland High Council, a disturbing reality for Marsh and others.[8] They found it especially unsettling that even the Prophet Joseph Smith often appeared distant and uninvolved with them. Eventually Brigham Young found meaning in the prophet's Kirtland posture toward the Twelve. After Joseph Smith's death, Young's brother asked him why the prophet had often "snubbed" the Seventy — another leading priesthood quorum. In response, Brigham asked rhetorically why Joseph had likewise kept the Twelve "so far from him & snob[bed] them" so much that some exclaimed "We are Apostles[!] it's an insult for us to be treated so." For his part, he now understood: Joseph "snobed us & when we proved ourselves willing to be every bodys servant for Christs sake then we were worthy of power." This was necessary, he concluded, because only "true servants" may receive power, while those who aspire or think themselves great are unfit for leadership.[9]

Disharmony within the Quorum cannot all be laid at Marsh's feet. Others, too, had visions of potential authority and prestige at odds with the actual, creating tensions and leading to anxiety about position and prerogatives. Some of the discord clearly related to the newness of their office and their own relative youth and inexperience. This was a collection of individuals not yet molded into a unit and often without a clear vision of

---

[7] For a discussion of Thomas B. Marsh's personality and role as president of the Twelve, see Ronald K. Esplin, "Thomas B. Marsh as President of the First Quorum of the Twelve, 1835–1838," in *Hearken, O Ye People: Discourses on the Doctrine and Covenants* (Sandy, Utah: Randall Book, 1984), 167–190; Historian's Office Journal, 16 February 1859, LDS Church Archives.

[8] According to Doctrine and Covenants 107:36 "standing high councils, at the stakes of Zion" had authority similar to the Twelve. Because of the nature of their responsibilities, the work of the Kirtland High Council touched the lives of Kirtland Saints more directly than did the Twelve. See Esplin, "Thomas B. Marsh," 101–75, for more information on the Kirtland Twelve.

[9] Minutes, 30 November 1847, Brigham Young Papers, LDS Church Archives; see both versions.

role and purpose. Scriptural models and prophetic instructions could provide guidelines, but their exact role and the precise bounds of their authority could only be the product of shared experiences.

President Thomas Marsh had long expected to lead his quorum to England. For him it was not only a quorum responsibility but, especially after his 1836 blessing in the Kirtland Temple, uniquely his own as president. By 1837, however, his quorum was disunited and scattered. In Ohio several of the apostles spoke of leaving that very summer for England, even as others joined dissidents critical of Joseph Smith. President Marsh, pondering both the proposed mission and the urgency of uniting his divided associates, arrived in Kirtland from Missouri by late spring. Though initially promising, Marsh's efforts at reconciliation failed.[10] Nor would he preside at the opening of work in England. In spite of strife and apostasy in Kirtland—or perhaps because of it—Joseph Smith had felt the mission could not wait. Unaware of Marsh's itinerary, the prophet had dispatched (only days before Marsh's arrival) Apostle Heber Kimball to England. Thus it was that Kimball and fellow apostle Orson Hyde—without President Marsh or other colleagues—landed in Liverpool in July 1837.[11]

In his distress, President Marsh served as catalyst for a revelation that would be significant to his quorum and the later quorum mission to England. Questioning his own status and wondering if the Twelve could ever be acceptable to the Lord, Marsh went to the prophet. In response, Joseph Smith dictated as Marsh wrote "the word of the Lord unto Thomas B. Marsh concerning the twelve Apostles of the Lamb." The writing acknowledged the special responsibility of the president of the Twelve in establishing the work abroad. It also reproved the apostles ("exalt not yourselves; rebel not") even as it reaffirmed that they shared priesthood leadership authority with the Presidency. And it confirmed priorities and assignments: The Twelve were not to trouble themselves "concerning the affairs of my Church in [Kirtland, Ohio]"—that was not their assignment. Instead they should "go . . . into all the world and preach my gospel."[12] Clearly, for the apostles service abroad must proceed any expanded role at home.

Instead of additional apostles following Kimball and Hyde to England under Marsh's direction in 1837, the focus shifted to Missouri where, by the end of 1838, dissent and violence decimated the "first" Quorum of the Twelve. As noted, however, the July 1838 revelation did contain seeds of

---

[10] See Esplin, "Thomas B. Marsh," 178–82.

[11] For Kimball's call to England, see Esplin, "Emergence of Brigham Young," 279–81. For an overview of the Kimball and Hyde mission, see Ronald K. Esplin, "A Great Work Done in That Land," *The Ensign* (July 1987), 20–27.

[12] Revelation of 23 July 1837, Doctrine and Covenants 112:15, 27–28, 30, and heading.

hope and renewal. Despite difficulties ahead, the revelation promised that a faithful and humble quorum would, "henceforth," find "an effectual door" opened for them. By affirming the necessity of the apostles leaving for England the following spring, and by naming John Taylor, John Page, Wilford Woodruff, and Willard Richards to replace "those who have fallen," the revelation pointed to future success.[13]

Only five of the original Twelve remained, and one of them could not be relied upon. However four — Brigham Young, Heber Kimball, Parley Pratt, and Orson Pratt — would prove exceptional in abilities and commitment. Fiercely loyal to Joseph Smith and his vision of a new Zion on earth and bound together by shared perspectives and experiences, they formed a nucleus of extraordinary strength for a renewed Quorum.

When Missouri enemies imprisoned Joseph Smith and his counselors, leadership responsibilities fell upon the remaining apostles. The October 1838 apostasy of Marsh and the death of David Patten left Brigham Young the senior member and acting president of the Twelve. He and Heber Kimball, next senior, superintended removal of the Saints from Missouri and, in the midst of this discouraging season of challenge, began rebuilding the Quorum of the Twelve.

In December, though still mired in Missouri difficulties, Brigham Young ordained two of those named in the July revelation, and a few months later two more. Except for Willard Richards, named by the July revelation but already in England, the cast of apostles who would serve together abroad was now complete.[14] As the new quorum members began working together under Brigham Young, an emphasis on teamwork and unity replaced the concern for status, position, and authority that marked the Marsh years.

Once out of Missouri, preparing for Britain gave purpose and urgency, as powerful shared experiences began to mold a quorum substantially different from the Kirtland Twelve. The bold April return to Missouri, risking their lives to fulfill revelation, marked the beginning of a new era for the apostles.[15] Ordinations at the Far West, Missouri, temple site provided, for the first time in nearly two years, enough apostles for a quorum, while the successful foray into enemy territory launched the new quorum with united confidence. Further, a joyous May reunion with the Prophet Joseph and his brother Hyrum commenced an important season of instruction. In preparation for their mission (and in contrast to the Kirtland

---

[13] Revelation of 8 July 1838, Doctrine and Covenants 118:1–6.

[14] Esplin, "Emergence of Brigham Young," 361–66, 380–83.

[15] See Scott G. Kenny, ed., *Wilford Woodruff's Journal, 1833–1898, Typescript*, 9 vols. (Midvale, Utah: Signature Books, 1983–85), 26 April 1838, 1:325–27; and Esplin, "Emergence of Brigham Young," 380–83.

experience), the prophet now met with and taught the Twelve frequently. In June a penitent and humbled Orson Hyde, among the Missouri casualties, rejoined the Twelve. Parley Pratt, fresh from a Missouri jail, rejoined them in July.[16]

On July 2 the Twelve met in Brigham Young's home for a special meeting before departing for England. There the Prophet Joseph promised that, if faithful, they would reap a bountiful harvest and return safely. Stressing the necessity of humility and unity, he urged them to learn from the mistakes of their predecessors.[17] An epistle issued for publication by six of the Twelve only two days later suggests the degree to which they embraced these priorities. In it the apostles urged elders throughout the church to have patience in the face of oppression, and to "unitedly seek after unity of purpose." If the elders were diligent, faithful, and humble, the epistle promised, "the power of the Priesthood will rest upon you, and you will become mighty in testimony."[18]

Malarial chills and fever, endemic along the river, felled several of the apostles and their families before they could depart. Not until August did the first leave. Young and Kimball, both ill and with families bedridden, remained until September. Even then they had to be lifted into a wagon and hauled the first leg of the journey. For the apostles, leaving their families in the grasp of sickness and poverty was a trial of faith. Though the church had promised to assist, they had no illusions about the resources to do so. Truly they left their families in the hands of God—a difficult trial that was vital to the success of their mission.

These young men—some new in their calling, all new in their associations together in a reorganized quorum under Brigham Young—had yet to develop a full sense of their office and mission.[19] Only experience could

---

[16] Even after the return of Hyde and Pratt, the Twelve still consisted of only ten men: Brigham Young, Heber Kimball, Orson Hyde, Parley Pratt, Orson Pratt, William Smith, John Page, John Taylor, Wilford Woodruff, and George Smith. Willard Richards, already in England, would become the eleventh member. Lyman Sherman, named to the Quorum in the same January 16, 1839, letter that named George A. Smith, died before he could be ordained. Not until 1841 was another called to take his place.

[17] Joseph Smith Diary, 2 July 1839, Joseph Smith Papers, LDS Church Archives; and *Woodruff's Journal*, 2 July 1839, 1:342–44.

[18] See Elden J. Watson, ed., *Manuscript History of Brigham Young*, 1846–1847 (Salt Lake City: Elden Jay Watson, 1968), 43–48. With Parley Pratt still in prison and his brother Orson in Missouri to assist him and with William Smith still apart from the Quorum and Orson Hyde barely returning, only six signed the published epistle.

[19] The average age of the eight apostles who served in Britain was thirty-two. Brigham Young and Heber Kimball, thirty-eight when they arrived in England, were the oldest; George A. Smith, twenty-two, was the youngest.

teach them what it meant to be apostles. For Brigham Young who, as leader, helped set the tone for all, the lengthy journey to New York presented several incidents that quietly confirmed him in his apostolic office. Returning to the Kirtland Temple, where he administered ordinances for John Taylor and other British-bound missionaries who had no opportunity before, touched him deeply. At Fairport, near Kirtland, he and others waited four days for calm sufficient to permit their Lake Erie steamer to dock so they could board. As the ship steamed through the night, winds again assaulted the lake, awakening Young. An uncharacteristically detailed diary entry suggests the significance he saw in what occurred next: "I went up on deck and I felt impres[sed] in spirit to pray to the Father in the name of Jesus for a forgiveness of all my sins and then I fe[l]t to command the winds to sees [cease] and let ous goe safe on our Jorney the winds abated and Glory & [h]ouner & prase be to that God that rules all things."[20]

After arriving in New York, six weeks of preaching and preparation passed before Brigham Young and his colleagues finally had the means to book passage. On March 7, 1840, they sailed aboard the *Patrick Henry* for Liverpool, where they arrived April 6. In a foreign land, Joseph Smith assured Quorum President Brigham Young, "the same spirit [will] rest upon you that now rests upon me to lead, guide and direct."[21] If he were humble and worthy, Brigham believed, it was his right to be taught by that spirit. Full of emotion he let out a shout of hosanna when he touched the shore. "I felt the chains were broken, and the bands that were upon me were burst asunder," he recalled later.[22]

After disembarking, Brigham Young and the four apostles traveling with him held a private meeting to partake of the Lord's supper, give thanks for safe passage, and seek divine assistance for their mission.[23] Two days later, just as Kimball and Hyde had done when they opened the work in England nearly three years before, they traveled to Preston. When Woodruff and Taylor (who had preceded them by two months) joined

---

[20] Brigham Young Diary, 26 November 1839, Brigham Young Papers; and Watson, ed., *Manuscript History of Brigham Young*, 58–59.

[21] Esplin, "Emergence of Brigham Young," 417–18; Minutes, 10 October 1865, General Minutes Collection, LDS Church Archives. Compare this with what Joseph Smith told all the Twelve in 1835: "and you each have the same authority in other nations that I have in this nation." Minutes, 7 February 1835, Record of the Twelve, LDS Church Archives.

[22] Watson, ed., *Manuscript History*, 69; and Brigham Young Discourse, 17 July 1870, *Journal of Discourses*, 26 vols. (London: Latter-day Saints Book Depot, 1854–86), 13:211–12.

[23] Heber Kimball, Parley and Orson Pratt, and George A. Smith traveled with Brigham Young.

them, seven apostles and Willard Richards convened for what Woodruff called "The First Council of the Twelve among the Nations." After ordaining Richards they formalized, for the first time since the apostasy of Thomas Marsh, the presidency of their senior member by setting Brigham Young apart as "the standing President of the Twelve." Eight of the Twelve now stood ready to push forward the vital work in Great Britain.[24]

As witnesses of the remarkably successful mission of Kimball and Hyde in 1837–38, the Saints in Preston had high expectations for the apostles. Less than a year after baptizing their first converts in July 1837, the first apostles to preach in England had presided over nearly 1,500 members and some twenty branches (or congregations).[25] After their departure in April 1838, however, there had been little increase in membership. Hoping for a return of the energy and power of the earlier apostolic mission, the Preston Saints warmly welcomed Woodruff and Taylor—the latter an Englishman returned home—in January 1840. With their American companions, these apostles infused new enthusiasm into the work, and by April optimism and a sense of excitement filled the British Saints.

The arrival of additional apostles, especially the return of Heber Kimball, father of the British work, also had immediate impact. "It was indeed a time of Rejoicing," noted Mission President Joseph Fielding upon seeing them. Although sickness and the rigors of an ocean crossing left them "thin & weather beaten," they seemed to be in good spirits, "and the Spirits of the Saints are greatly revived by their coming." News of the arrivals spread rapidly. By April 12, the Sunday following, more than 500 enthusiastic British converts converged on Preston's Temperance Hall to greet them. That Sunday the apostles testified to the Saints "with power," Kimball reported, "for the Lord was with them." That first week in Preston the Twelve held their organizing council, conducted a general conference (with participants representing more than 1,800 British Saints), and met several times as a quorum.[26]

---

[24] *Woodruff's Journal*, 14 April 1840, 1:435; and Minutes, 14 April 1840, LDS Church Archives. Setting Young apart as "Standing president" formalized the "acting" presidency he had assumed in Missouri following the loss of Marsh and Patten. It also contrasted with the practice in some church councils and conferences of rotating the Presidency so that each presided in turn. Henceforth, when the Twelve met as a quorum, Young was formally and in *each* case the president. Though Orson Hyde passed through briefly on the way to Palestine, only eight apostles served in England. William Smith and John E. Page did not respond to the call. The twelfth, Lyman Wight, was not called until just before the apostles returned from England.

[25] See Esplin, "A Great Work," 27.

[26] Joseph Fielding Diary, 9 April 1840, typescript, LDS Church Archives; and Heber C. Kimball and Joseph Fielding to the Editors of the *Times and Seasons*, 6 May 1840, in *Times and Seasons* 1 (July 1840):138–39. The combination of river

Beginning with these first quorum meetings and conferences in England, Brigham Young consciously strove to operate with harmony and build unity among the apostles and the Saints. Minutes of the Twelve for April 16, 1840, one of the few extant examples with enough detail to illustrate quorum dynamics, show Young providing leadership without being overbearing. As president, Young proposed four of the eleven resolutions, double the number by Kimball and Richards, most active after him, but he did not monopolize. All but two quorum members proposed at least one item, and each of those seconded one or more. After discussion, according to the record, "the above resolutions were unanimously adopted."[27]

President Young later presented this program of proselyting and publication to the assembled Saints for their vote. That he then followed it is evidence that he viewed this voting and discussion as more than formalities.

Public meetings also demonstrated Young's concern for the feelings of others. He deferred to Kimball, for example, to chair the first conference, the beginning of a rotating chair or presidency that saw others of the Twelve, in turn, take the lead at succeeding conferences. Kimball similarly called Mission President Joseph Fielding to the pulpit to conduct, a gesture Fielding recognized as "his desire to support me in my office." Concerned that the British Saints had opportunity to develop confidence in all their leaders, not just in the Twelve, Young did not immediately replace Joseph Fielding's mission presidency. Fielding's emotional diary entry, penned after two weeks with the apostles, preserves his gratitude for this enlightened approach: "my whole Soul rejoiced, yea, I could not express my Joy. . . . I feel that [I] have the good will & Confidence of my Brethren the 12; they have not a Word of Censure. . . . Their desire is to exalt me in the Eyes of the Church."[28]

Expecting a great deal of himself and others, Young could be both firm and demanding. But rather than dictating to his peers or to the Saints, as quorum leader he consciously sought to promote the collegial fellowship that meant so much to him.[29] Several years after the British

---

sickness from the summer before and the rigors of an ocean crossing left Young so thin and worn that his long-time friend Willard Richards at first did not recognize him. *History of the Church*, 8 April 1840, 4:111.

[27] See *Woodruff's Journal*, 16 April 1840, 1:438–39. During the final council meeting one year later, also recorded by Woodruff, Young initiated only one of four proposals.

[28] Quotations are from Joseph Fielding Diary, 12 and 19 April 1840. The meeting on April 12 was only one of several occasions where the Twelve deferred to Joseph Fielding; see, for example, Fielding Diary for 15 April 1840: "I opened the Meeting. Elder Kimball presided."

[29] In 1833 Young copied into his diary an especially meaningful passage from

experience he observed: "When T. B. Marsh was Pres[iden]t of the 12 — he was a[lway]s like a toad's hair comb[ing] up & down," but "since I [h]ave been the Pres[iden]t I am daddy."[30] Not stern father but supportive and affectionate daddy, treating his fellow apostles — and others — more as associates than as subordinates.

If, as president, Young took the lead in emphasizing unity and harmony in quorum relationships, he was not alone. Recognizing the need to conduct themselves with greater unity than before, others, too, made good feelings, mutual support, and cooperation high priorities. One searches in vain for incidents of division or bad feelings; instead one finds concern for one another, communication, fellowship, and commitment to shared responsibilities.[31] Letters and diaries convey a sense that these men viewed one another with mutual respect and genuine affection. After a few months in Great Britain, Heber Kimball, pondering the things most important to him, penned in his diary a prayer reflecting the ethic that had come to prevail among the Twelve. After expressing gratitude for the blessings of the past year, he prayed that the Lord would "myltiply my power" that he might "find favour in Thy sight . . . and be of great use to my brethren, the twelve, that we may all be one in all things both in this world and that which is to come."[32]

By April 17 the Twelve had laid the groundwork for publishing, ordained local member Peter Melling as the first patriarch in England, concluded to quietly encourage emigration without public announcement, decided where each of their number would begin his individual ministry, and agreed to

---

a long Joseph Smith revelation called the "Olive Leaf," a charter for relationships between men involved in Kirtland's religious school and anticipated temple. That he copied this passage into a diary whose pages mostly record contracts and travels underscores his longing for such Christian bonds of fellowship. "Art thou a brother or brethren," reads the passage: "I salute you in the name of the Lord Jesus Christ, in token of the everlasting covenent; in which Covenent I receive you to fellowship in a determination that is fixed, immoveable and unchangeable to be your fri[e]nd and brother through the grace of God, in the bonds of love." Brigham Young Diary, undated entry end of 1833; compare this with Doctrine and Covenants 88:133.

[30] Minutes, 12 February 1849, Brigham Young Papers.

[31] That the records are silent about discord suggests not that they refrained from recording it but that there was little to note. Records for the Kirtland period were not reticent about noting difficulties within the Twelve. There had been severe problems earlier and there would at times be tensions in the future, but the evidence suggests that this was a period when the Twelve were "well united & agree in all things & love one another." *Woodruff's Journal*, 27 April 1841, 2:94.

[32] Stanley B. Kimball, ed., *On the Potter's Wheel, The Diaries of Heber C. Kimball* (Salt Lake City: Signature Books, 1987), 1 January 1841, 31–32. Wilford Woodruff's "Close of the Year" diary entry for 1840, 1:586–87, reflects similar concern for his colleagues.

convene a second conference July 6. Brigham Young then sent Joseph a report of their activities, including a note stressing a theme he would repeat many times during this mission: "If you see any thing in, or about the whole affair, that is not right: I ask . . . that you would make known to us the mind of the Lord, and his will concerning us. I believe that I am as willing to do the will of the Lord, and take counsel of my brethren . . . as ever I was in my life."[33]

When the apostles parted for separate fields of labor, Young and Richards accompanied Woodruff to Herefordshire and its environs to assist in ongoing work there among the United Brethren. Laboring in the region since March, Woodruff had already baptized perhaps 160, including more than three dozen lay preachers. Now, for a month, the three colleagues shared days packed with preaching, teaching, visiting, baptizing, confirming, ordaining, blessing, and counseling. By mid-May nearly 400 had accepted baptism. Working as a team, the apostles formed the main body of United Brethren into Latter-day Saint branches.

In the eyes of the apostles and their new coreligionists, God's hand was evident in Herefordshire. On May 18, traditionally a feast day among the United Brethren, Young, "clothed with the power of God," addressed the gathered Saints as a prelude to sharing a large banquet. It was apparently on this occasion that a "notable miracle was wrought by faith & the power of God." Writing two weeks later Woodruff recorded that the three apostles had blessed Sister Mary Pitt, confined to bed for six years and unable to walk without crutches for eleven, "& her ancle bones received strength & she now walks without the aid of crutch or staff."[34]

It is hard to imagine better circumstances for developing confidence and leadership. Seldom had these young apostles felt more needed, never had the results of their work been more dramatic. Without doubt the experience of transforming the United Brethren into Latter-day Saints helped transform and strengthen them. Though in scale the United Brethren conversions were extraordinary, apostles in other fields experienced similar challenges and successes that had comparable impact on their development as leaders.[35]

The people "beg and plead for the Book of Mormon," Young wrote Joseph Smith from Herefordshire, again seeking permission to publish.

---

[33] Report and Minutes, *Times and Seasons* 1 (June 1840):119–22.

[34] *Woodruff's Journal*, 3 June 1840, 1:455.

[35] This was true both in terms of successful proselyting and in exercising spiritual gifts. George A. Smith, for example, recorded instances of healing in his ministry, adding: "Many have been healed thank the Lord . . . such was there faith in the Ordinance of Laying on hands." Diary of George A. Smith, 13 July 1840; see also 28 August 1840.

The apostles had earlier sought general publishing authority, but no such permission had come.[36] They now knew firsthand the urgency of the need, and when a generous donation from United Brethren converts made immediate publication possible, a decision had to be made. May 20, Young, Woodruff, and Richards ascended to the privacy of the Herefordshire Beacon in the beautiful Malvern Hills where, as Young noted in his diary, "we had Prayrs and a little counsel." Woodruff, as usual, provided more detail: "we united in prayer & held a Council & unitedly felt that it was the will of God that Elder Young should go immediately to Manchester to assist in publishing a collection of Hymns . . . & also to immediately print . . . the Book of Mormon."[37] Later that day, with Young on the way to Manchester, Woodruff and Richards resumed baptizing and confirming among the United Brethren.[38]

So that each of the Twelve could comment on this change in plan, Young followed up the Malvern Hills council with a visit or a letter to each apostle not present. By such personal visits and mail, Young received input from his associates and influenced work throughout the mission. Because he traveled so extensively, he asked his wife to direct mail to John Taylor, Liverpool, and he "will [k]now whare I am for we are constantly wright[ing] to each other."[39]

Communication within the Quorum hardly depended on Young alone, however. Perhaps the fact that they were "in a strange Land among strangers . . . for the Gospel sake," as George A. Smith noted, reinforced the inclination to rely on one another. Genuinely interested in one another's success and well-being, they made the effort to stay in touch. "Wrote a letter to O Pratt in answer to One Received from him," Smith jotted in his journal. The same week he wrote a letter to "Br Young and Recevd One from him."[40] This was typical.

---

[36] Brigham Young to Joseph Smith, 7 May 1840, Joseph Smith Papers. About this same time, Joseph Smith sent word from Nauvoo that they could proceed, but that authorization would not reach Britain until late in the year.

[37] Brigham Young Diary, 20 May 1840; and *Woodruff's Journal*, 20 May 1840, 1:451. That the uneducated Young would oversee publications is ironic; but in this, as in everything, he did what he saw as duty. Not only did he oversee publication (including proofing and indexing) of the Book of Mormon and the hymnal, but while Pratt was away he also took responsibility for the mission periodical. This is another example of how meeting British Mission responsibilities stretched and developed abilities in the Twelve.

[38] *Woodruff's Journal*, 22 June 1840, 1:469. By this time, a month after Young left, Woodruff reflected on the unprecedented blessing of 541 members in the vicinity organized into thirty-three branches; soon the number approached 800.

[39] Brigham Young to Mary Ann Young, 12 June 1840, Philip Blair Family Papers, Special Collections, Marriott Library, University of Utah, Salt Lake City.

[40] George A. Smith Diary, 28 and 31 December 1840 and 1 January 1841.

While keeping his quorum informed of mission developments, Young also wrote letters of personal concern and encouragement. One such letter to Richards illustrates his sense of humor. No doubt this apostle writing to another had in mind debate about the meaning of the Apostle Paul's epistles when he wrote: "Be careful not to lay this letter with the new testment wrightings. if you doe som body will take it for a text after the Malineum [Millennium] a[nd] contend about it." Young's warm, personal touch helped produce among the apostles the result he had longed for. As Heber Kimball expressed to his wife in May: "There never was better feelings among the Twelve than at this time; all things go well."[41]

On June 1, 1840, Young and Kimball organized the first of several Mormon companies to sail for America. This began an enterprise that would become another major success of the Twelve in England, one with lasting impact on British Saints and on their view of the Twelve as men of authority and inspiration. A few individual Saints had sailed previously, but this, a small company of about forty, was the first contracted for by the church with priesthood leaders appointed to preside at sea — a pattern that would endure for decades with the thousands of LDS emigrants to follow.[42]

When the Twelve met with the Saints in July conference, there were represented 842 members more than in April. The apostles used this general mission conference to strengthen, counsel, and further regulate the church. Ordinations, mission calls, interviews, and instruction occupied them for many hours. The Twelve also convened as a Traveling High Council to formally hear cases of alleged misconduct. In general session Young called upon priesthood officers "whose circumstances would permit" to devote themselves full time to the ministry. In a council with officers the following day, the Twelve assigned the volunteers to specific fields of labor.[43] Throughout these proceedings, the Saints witnessed the apostles giving wise counsel, expressing love and concern, and functioning with unity and effectiveness. As a quorum and individually they were gaining an increased sense of authority and ability to perform.

In private council, the apostles accepted Parley Pratt's motion that Brigham Young and Heber Kimball oversee the publications while Pratt returned to New York for his family. Willard Richards soon carried much

---

Such references are sprinkled throughout his diary; see especially August–October 1840. See also similar references in *Woodruff's Journal* for the entire period.

[41] Brigham Young to Willard Richards, 10 June 1840, Brigham Young Papers; and Heber C. Kimball to Vilate Kimball, 27 May 1840, Kimball Family Papers, LDS Church Archives.

[42] *Manuscript History*, 77.

[43] See minutes in *History of the Church*, 4:146–50, and *Woodruff's Journal*, 6–7 April 1840, 1:480–82.

of that load, freeing up the unusually effective missionary Kimball for other fields. From July until October Quorum President Young found himself "much confined to the office . . . conducting and issuing the Millennial Star, Hymn Book and Book of Mormon, giving counsel to the elders throughout the European mission, preaching, baptizing and confirming."[44]

Young longed for association with his brethren in Nauvoo. To Joseph Smith he had written in May that he dreamed of living forever "to enjoy each others society in peace. I long to see the faces of my friends again in that Country once more."[45] He missed not just the friendship, but also the guidance. As he wrestled with each day's challenges, he yearned for the prophet's advice. Although he had several times written for direction, by early September, some five months into the mission, he still had no answers. With a detailed report to the Presidency in September, Young asked again for counsel on a series of pressing questions. He also knew that he could not await a reply: "Our motto is go ahead. Go ahead — & ahead we are determined to go — till we have conquered every foe. So come life or come death we'll go ahead, but tell us if we are going wrong & we will right it.[46]

The October Conference marked the halfway point in the mission of the Twelve. It also marked a shift to a different managerial style. Joseph Smith had instructed them that, when united, they had authority as a quorum to conduct business without constant reference to a sustaining vote.[47] So far, however, they had chosen to present most matters to a conference representing all the British Saints. But as business and numbers multiplied (up 1,115 since the last conference), it became less practical to convene a truly *general* conference, much less to entertain floor motions and discussion on every item of business. The conference accepted Young's suggestion that the number of general conferences be reduced, and that ordinations, the regulation of officers, and other business be conducted by the Twelve as a quorum or Traveling High Council.[48]

---

[44] *Manuscript History*, 79. The *Millennial Star* was a mission periodical founded by the Twelve for the British Saints. For more than a century it was the voice of the church in Great Britain.

[45] Brigham Young to Joseph Smith, 7 May 1840, Joseph Smith Papers.

[46] Brigham Young and Willard Richards to the First Presidency, 5 September 1840, Joseph Smith Papers.

[47] Instructions to Twelve and Seventy, 2 May 1835, *History of the Church*, 2:220; see also Esplin, "Emergence of Brigham Young," 451-52.

[48] See minutes, *History of the Church*, 4:214-18. This conference began by considering individual items of business as had earlier ones. But midcourse, with time running out, it was agreed that the Twelve handle the remainder. Further refining this procedure, the Twelve agreed to do business at the April British general conference "as a quorum," deciding matters in their own councils, then "call upon the church or conference to sanction it." *Woodruff's Journal*, 5 April 1841, 2:80.

Publication and administrative duties did not prevent Young from preaching or insulate him from the pressures and rewards of the front line. In this, too, he attempted to be an example. "Sence we have ben in Manchester," he wrote his wife, "We have don all that we posably could to spread this work we have succeeded in makeing the priest mad, so that they rave like demonds, We keepe Baptiseing every weak which causes much per[se]cution."[49] In late October Young and Kimball took a short mission to Preston then south to the town of Hawarden, Wales.[50] Their preaching in Hawarden elicited a singular response, Young noted in a letter to his wife Mary Ann:

> We have hered from Wales whare Br Kimball and I went, a grate meny of the people was sorry they did not obey the gospel when we ware there the report went out that we had the same power that the old apostles had, it is true we did lay hands on one young man that was quite low with a fevor, we rebuked his fevor and he got well we laid our hands on a woman that had verry bad eyes she emeditly recoverd, they have a gradel [great deal] to say about our preaching. they say that Elder Kimball has such sharp eys that he can look wright through them, and Elder Young Preashes so that every Body that heres him must beleve he preaches so plane and powerful.[51]

Young's experiences illustrate the kinds of emotional and spiritual encounters that helped each of the apostles gain in Britain a greater sense of duty and authority.[52]

In 1849, Young and Kimball instructed four newly called apostles about their office. Their advice distilled their own experiences in England eight years before. According to both, the calling as an apostle should be viewed as a harness that could not be set aside — not a light "carriage harness" either, insisted Kimball, but "an old Penn Wagon harness" suitable for heavy burdens. They would not know the weight of the harness, cautioned Young, until they were in the traces under load. Then, especially, "look out how you walk or you will fall"; be one with the Twelve, for

---

[49] Brigham Young to Mary Ann Young, 16 October 1840, Blair Collection, LDS Church Archives.

[50] Contemporary Mormon sources spell the town as Hardin or Harden. This was most likely Hawarden, a small town of northeast Wales a few miles west of Chester. Thanks to Peter C. Brown for pointing this out.

[51] Brigham Young to Mary Ann Young, 12 November 1840, Blair Family Papers.

[52] Though we do not know that Young and Kimball had any immediate success in Hawarden, an April 1841 report notes 170 members in North Wales centered, it appears, in nearby Overton. *Millennial Star* 1 (April 1841): 302; see also Ronald D. Dennis, "The Welsh and the Gospel," in V. Ben Bloxham, James R. Moss, and Larry C. Porter, eds., *Truth Will Prevail: The Rise of the Church of Jesus Christ of Latter-day Saints in the British Isles, 1837–1987* (Solihull, England: The Church of Jesus Christ of Latter-day Saints, 1987), 237–39.

any variance of feeling "will cut." Young spoke also of the love he had for his brethren of the Twelve, "the love of a tender fat[he]r to his Chil[dren]." And Kimball assured his new associates that if they were humble, faithful, and pulled with "a steady diligent walk the heavens will be opened [and] you will be mighty men."[53]

In Britain Young, Kimball, and their associates learned to wear the harness and pull together. A deep sense of duty reinforced by the enormous expectations of the Saints kept them in the harness and at their task. From leaving America in sickness to laboring in a faraway kingdom renowned for education and religion, this mission intensely challenged these young New Englanders. Reaching beyond what they had done before, sometimes beyond what they thought themselves capable of doing, they increased in confidence and ability.

George A. Smith provides a dramatic example of the results of pulling in the harness. Smith, the youngest of the Twelve, was a large man with poor health and "weak eyes." With limited experience and education, he often felt profoundly inadequate, yet he would not neglect his duty. While laboring in the area of Staffordshire known as the Potteries, for example, he reported to a relative that he seldom got to bed before midnight because of the large number "Who come to hear me talk and Recive instruction from me." To not thus respond would be unthinkable: "I have to be A teacher of good Principles to them that Recieve my testimony." Nonetheless: "You cannot think how foolish it makes me feel to Be Looked up to with So much Earnestness by Persons Who have been Professors of Religion and Preachers. . . . I thank the Lord for the Wisdom he has given me and the Success I have had in teaching these Men . . . they all look to me for instruction as Children to A Father and this Makes me feel vary Small indeed and Causes me to cry unto my father Who is in heaven for Wisdom and Paetence to do my fathers Work."[54] Expected to perform, he did, growing in confidence as the Saints demonstrated confidence in him. The fact that his charges expressed deep appreciation for his efforts reinforced this development. "I cannot describe the Love and gratitude I feel towards you for the great Blessings you have been instrumental in the hands of God of bringing upon our Family and Neibourhood," one wrote. "We can never repay your kindness towards us But God will Bless you for your Labours."[55]

---

[53] Council Minutes, 12 February 1849, LDS Church Archives.

[54] George A. Smith to Lyman Smith, [8?] January 1841, George A. Smith Papers, LDS Church Archives.

[55] George A. Smith understood this process and recommended it to others. One member whom he counseled wrote of the results of doing one's duty despite inadequacies in words that apply equally well to Smith and his peers: "your words

Wherever the American missionaries traveled they found friends. In the words of Brigham Young in December, "I find Fathers & mothers sister & Brothers whare ever I goe."[56] Only the ministers actively opposed them, and even that they saw as confirmation of their calling. The Lord turns all things to good, and they only "drive the people to us," he wrote. As an example he pointed with delight to Manchester sectarians who urged their members to stay away from the Mormons, telling them "they are so intising you cannot keep away if [you] goe once." The Twelve found such admonitions a great boon to their work.[57]

Apparently Joseph Smith's first letter arrived in Britain with Lorenzo Snow in early November; the mission of the Twelve was more than half over before they had the first word of direct instruction since leaving America. Though approving much of what the Twelve had done, the letter also suggested dissatisfaction with some aspect of their publication program. Though mild, the censure carried a sting. Young defended his actions in a letter to his wife. He would have been pleased to consult beforehand on everything "if we could, but it did not seem to be posable, all I have to say about the matter . . . is I have don all that I could to doe good and promote the cause that we are in. I have don the verry best that I knew how."[58] Once they could visit face to face, he was confident Joseph would understand his actions. Communication was so poor that it would be two months before the next letter arrived from the prophet, forcing Young and his brethren to continue to act independently, and mature in the process, even as they longed for additional counsel and instruction.

The last communication from Nauvoo before the Twelve left Britain conveyed Joseph Smith's approbation of their entire course of action.[59] He

---

have been verified for I receive greater blessings and Power every time I get up to Speak even so as to astonish myself." Richard Rushton to George A. Smith, 25 September 1840, George A. Smith Papers.

[56] Brigham Young Diary, 21 December 1840.

[57] Brigham Young to Mary Ann Young, 12 November 1840, Blair Family Papers. See also Brigham Young to Mary Ann Young, 16 October 1840, Blair Collection.

[58] Brigham Young to Mary Ann Young, 12 November 1840, Blair Family Papers. It is unclear why Joseph Smith was dissatisfied. Apparently his letter to Young, not presently available, was ambiguous enough that Young was also uncertain. The problem seemingly had to do with publication, but notations in Smith's papers alongside Young's earlier letter requesting permission indicate that Lorenzo Snow was carrying word from the prophet authorizing publication.

[59] While Joseph Smith did not explain either why he had earlier been concerned about publication or why he now approved, we can assume that by this time he was better informed about the urgent need and had come to accept publication as necessary. Young had kept him informed of what they did, and why, and apparently Smith now agreed.

said he felt their mission was as important as any labor then on earth. Though admitting to some previous anxiety about their ability to accomplish it, he was satisfied that they had acted with diligence and wisdom. He especially commended them for unity and harmony. That the prophet's instructions dovetailed so closely with what Young and his peers had done (or concluded to do) must have boosted their confidence, as did Joseph's decision not to advise on other matters "of much importance, on which you ask council, but which I think you will be perfectly able to decide upon." "I feel much confidence in your united wisdom," the passage concluded. Smith also conveyed an understanding of the probable impact of the British experience on the apostles who, "like the gallant Bark, that has braved the storm unhurt," will henceforth be "more conscious than ever of the strength of her timbers and the experience and capabilities of her Captain, Pilots, and Crew."[60]

With the arrival of the new year, Young finally permitted himself to think of departing. Now that the publishing program was nearly complete and Parley Pratt had returned with his family to oversee the mission when his colleagues left, a return home was possible. After writing his fellow apostles of the decision to leave, Young announced in the February *Millennial Star* an April 6 conference in Manchester so the Twelve, before departing, could meet with the Saints "in general council" for "much business of general interest."[61]

Preparations for departure provide several windows into the relationship between the apostles and their British converts, witnessing to the development of the Twelve as leaders. In March Wilford Woodruff conducted a series of branch conferences as he prepared to leave for America. "I never saw a time I needed more wisdom," he recorded in his diary. Following a meeting in the Gadfield Elm Chapel, members in perplexing circumstances flocked around him "by Scores at a time . . . asking council what to do." After recording dozens of examples of what was asked of him, he wrote: "THESE and a thousand other questions were asked me in the term of an hour or more, & I needed as much wisdom as Solomon to be a councellor in the midst of such a seene." Conferences at other branches

---

[60] Joseph Smith to the Twelve, 15 December 1840, Joseph Smith Papers. Of the many copies of this communication, this is the only dated one. An undated manuscript copy in the Joseph Smith Letterbook, Joseph Smith Papers, is printed both in *Times and Seasons* 2 (1 January 1841): 258–61 and *Millennial Star* 1 (March 1841): 265–69. Because most versions were undated, it was mistakenly inserted in the *History of the Church* with October documents, and it has generally been mistakenly assumed that the Twelve received it in the fall of 1840. See *History of the Church*, 4:226–32.

[61] *Millennial Star* 1 (February 1841): 264.

also involved hours shaking hands, blessing the sick, and giving counsel.[62]

Others experienced similar farewells in branches they had helped raise up. No doubt George A. Smith received special satisfaction from the certificate "To the Saints in America and the World . . . Given by Order of the Assembled Conference," prepared by the Saints where he labored: "This is to certify that Elder G A Smith has faithfully laboured among us in all humility and meekness; and that we feel grateful to the Lord for his goodness in sending him among us. And we hereby recommend him as a Faithful Minister of the Gospel of Jesus Christ and a Shining Ornament to his Profession."[63]

On April 1, 1841, the Twelve assembled in Manchester for their final meetings as a quorum in England. With the addition of Orson Hyde, en route to Israel on a special assignment, nine apostles attended, the most seated together since soon after the organization of the quorum in Kirtland. "Perfect union & harmony prevailed in all the deliberations," Woodruff recorded after several days in council.[64]

The apostles met with the Saints in conference on April 6, 1841, one year after their arrival in England. The accomplishments and changes of the intervening twelve months exceeded all expectations. "It hath truly been a miricle what God hath wrought by our hands . . . since we have been here," wrote Woodruff, "& I am asstonished when I look at it."[65] Reports from churches throughout the kingdom showed an increase of nearly 2,200 since the last conference and well over 4,000 over the course of their mission.[66] The impact of the quorum mission on the lives of thousands of British Saints was profound. The influence on the church as thousands of British emigrants began flowing to Nauvoo likewise was great and would continue. The impact of the mission on Young and his colleagues was similarly enduring.

Before leaving Manchester on April 15 the Twelve performed their last official act as a quorum in England, completing for publication "An

---

[62] *Woodruff's Journal*, 15 March 1841, 2:61–63; 21 March 1841, 2:66, 68–69.

[63] "To the Saints in America and the World," 28 March 1841, George A. Smith Papers.

[64] *Woodruff's Journal*, 5 April 1841, 2:78; see also entries for 2–3 April.

[65] Ibid., 15 April 1841, 2:90. The entry continues: "during our Stay here we have esstablished churches in all the most noted cities & towns in the Kingdom have Baptized more then 5,000 souls Printed 5,000 Books of mormon 3000 Hymn Books 2,500 Volumes of the Millennial Star & about 50,000 tracts, & gatherd to the land of Joseph [America] 1,000 Souls & esstablished a great influence among those that trade in ships at sea & lacked for nothing to eat drink or ware. Truly the Lord hath been good."

[66] With some excommunicated, hundreds emigrating, and some baptized before the first conference, the total converts for the period the apostles were in England was between 5,000 and 6,000. See Esplin, "Emergence of Brigham Young," 475–76.

Epistle of the Twelve" to the Saints throughout Great Britain. In it they expressed thanks for the diligence of the Saints in hearkening "to the council of those whom God has seen fit to send among them, and who hold the keys of this ministry." The result had been union and power. They urged them to remember "that which we have ever taught . . . both by precept and example . . . to beware of an aspiring spirit."[67] The epistle announced the appointments of Levi Richards and Lorenzo Snow as traveling counselors to assist President Parley Pratt, stressed procedures for ordinations, and instructed the Saints in detail about emigration. A few days later they set sail.

A dramatic event during the voyage home illustrates the sense the Twelve now firmly shared that, when united and faithful, the Lord oversaw their lives and labors. At midnight on April 24, contrary winds which had blown since soon after their departure increased to gale strength and blew off the fore-topsail. The next day the seas were "mountains high." All aboard the pitching ship were sick. For days the gale continued until there was fear that the weaker children would die. In spite of the difficulty, Woodruff judged the Twelve "generally well & vary patient well united & agree in all things & love one another." They prayed together and assisted the sick. On the twenty-eighth the storm worsened. Berths collapsed. Baggage broke loose, threatening to crush the emigrants. Facing disaster, the apostles sought the Lord's intervention. The next day Woodruff noted simply: "the Sun Shines plesent & we have a fair wind for the first time since we left Liverpool." Young, the following week, wrote: "when the winds ware contr[ar]y the 12 a gread to humble them selves before the Lord and ask him to calm the seas & give us a fair wind, we did so & the wind emeditly changed and from that time to this it has blone in our favor."[68]

The 1840–41 mission marked the beginning of the Twelve functioning as a united and effective entity. In Britain Brigham Young first presided over a quorum of apostles engaged as one in a common labor. Far removed from Joseph Smith and other leaders, they relied on the Lord and on each other, and together achieved a success unprecedented in the short history of the church. The results reinforced confidence in the authority of their

---

[67] *Millennial Star* 1 (April 1841): 309–12. No doubt thinking of their own experiences in Kirtland and Missouri, they defined such a spirit as one "which introduces rebellion, confusion, misrule, and disunion, and would, if suffered to exist among us, destroy the union, spirit, and power which are associated with the priesthood and can only exist with the humble and meek."

[68] *Woodruff's Journal*, 24–29 April 1841, 2:93–96; and Brigham Young Diary, entries before and after 5 May 1841, Brigham Young Papers. See also Smith's colorful account ("All the Beathren Were sick we Eat Nothing for th[r]ee Days vomiting Was the Principal Employment We had one Gale."), George A. Smith Diary, 29 April 1841, and preceding entry.

office, in the leadership of Young, and in each other. Besides proselyting success, in Britain the Twelve for the first time functioned as an effective agency of ecclesiastical administration. Here, also for the first time, Young had the opportunity to shape the Quorum into a different kind of council than he had experienced under Thomas Marsh. The apostles grew individually, and collectively they nurtured a growing sense of fellowship and collegiality. In Woodruff's words, writing on the high seas: "I never enjoyed my self better with the Twelve. . . . Union prevails among us & we dwell together in love."[69] For the Twelve, this shared mission set a pattern for relationships with one another, set a course for the Quorum, and prepared them to receive new responsibilities soon afterward.

The impact of the Twelve's mission reached beyond Britain. Nauvoo Saints, too, came to look upon the apostles with more respect following their British labors. Extensive news that circulated in Nauvoo of their ministry increased in the minds of the people their stature as leading elders. Without question, in 1841 many more Saints in America looked upon them as effective and trustworthy leaders than would have thought so previously. Nor did it hurt their reputation among Nauvoo Saints to have been preceded by several hundred British converts singing their praises.

The mission to Great Britain — especially leaving families sick and destitute — had been a test of men. Wrote Woodruff, who lost a daughter to sickness while he served: "Never have I been called to make greater Sacrifices or enjoyed greater Blessings."[70] Undertaking the mission at all required greater dedication and faith than had earlier assignments. In spite of poverty, sickness, the torment of leaving families insufficiently fed or sheltered, eight of the Twelve responded to the call and served together in Britain. Orson Hyde, fulfilling a separate assignment, briefly joined his colleagues in Britain. If the thousand-mile march with Zion's Camp was an important preparation for the calling of the original apostles, as they believed, the British experience of unity, success, and power after sacrifice was of crucial importance to the reorganized Twelve.[71] The one helped qualify men to be called as apostles, the other helped prepare them to serve next to the Presidency as apostles in deed.

Young believed that only those willing to sacrifice and serve humbly, as did the Twelve in Britain, were "fit for power."[72] He was probably not

---

[69] *Woodruff's Journal*, 6 May 1841, 2:98. That he should write this after several weeks together in close quarters bespeaks genuine harmony and mutual affection.

[70] Ibid., "Close of the Year" entry for 1840, 1:586.

[71] Joseph Smith in the spring and summer of 1834 led 200 ill-equipped men on foot from Kirtland, Ohio, to Jackson County, Missouri, in a fruitless effort to reinstate Missouri Latter-day Saints on lands from which they had been violently driven.

[72] Minutes, 30 November 1847, Brigham Young Papers.

surprised that the nine apostles who met in Manchester in April 1841 stepped firmly forward as one to lead after Joseph Smith's death, while each of those who failed to serve in Britain soon removed themselves from their quorum and from the church.

In August 1841, the month following the return of the first of the Twelve from their British mission, Joseph Smith informed the apostles that they would now take their place next to the Presidency. In an August 10 council, he charged the Twelve to henceforth supervise "the business of the church in Nauvoo," for the first time giving them responsibility within a fully organized stake of Zion. At a special conference on August 16, Joseph Smith publicly explained that the Twelve would henceforth "assist in managing the affairs of the Kingdom in this place," that is Nauvoo, church headquarters, not as a temporary assignment but as "the duties of their office."[73] Emerging from the shadows after their successful British mission, in Nauvoo the Twelve would serve prominently as Joseph Smith's right hand.

---

[73] Minutes, 16 August 1841, LDS Church Archives; and History of Brigham Young, 2. See also *History of the Church*, 4:402–4, Willard Richards Diary, 16 August 1841, Willard Richards Papers, LDS Church Archives; and the discussion documenting the importance of this transition in Ronald K. Esplin, "Joseph, Brigham and the Twelve: A Succession of Continuity," *Brigham Young University Studies* 21 (Summer 1981): 310–11.

6

The Rise and Decline of the Church in the West Midlands, 1840–77

JOHN B. COTTERILL

The story of the early Latter-day Saint Church in Great Britain is invariably dominated by the great success stories of conversions, focusing on the labors of missionaries such as Heber C. Kimball at Preston, William Clayton at Manchester, and Wilford Woodruff in the remote regions of Herefordshire.[1] Little has been written concerning the slow but perhaps even more significant growth of Mormonism in areas such as the city of Birmingham, as well as the surrounding industrial towns and villages of what is known as the "Black Country." So important was the development of the church in this region that by the mid-1840s it had become the geographical center of Mormonism in the British Isles — not Lancashire, as is popularly imagined. This essay examines the growth of the church in this region, as well as the factors that accounted for the gradual decline in church membership into the 1860s. Indeed, it can be argued that the history of the Birmingham Conference was the history of the British Mission in miniature.

In a letter to William Clayton, dated January 28, 1840, seven days after his arrival in the Staffordshire Potteries, Wilford Woodruff observed, "I feel as though the spirit will soon send one of us to Birmingham."[2] The next day witnessed the departure of Theodore Turley to his native city and his unproductive reunion with his parents. However, as the Staffordshire

---

[1] This essay is part of a chapter from John Cotterill, "Midland Saints: The Mormon Mission in the West Midlands, 1837–77," (Ph.D. thesis, Keele University, 1985). The editors express appreciation to Dr. Cotterill's widow, Jane Cotterill, for permission to publish the essay, which has been edited for publication.

[2] Manuscript History of the British Mission (hereafter MH), entry under "Birmingham Conference," Library-Archives, Historical Department, The Church of Jesus Christ of Latter-day Saints, Salt Lake City, hereafter cited as LDS Church Archives.

Conference to the north was consolidated and the initial converts were made in Herefordshire and Gloucestershire to the south, Mormon attention was redirected upon Birmingham. Grets Green, a community just three miles northwest of the city, was visited by John Cheese, formerly a preacher with the United Brethren in Herefordshire, who on May 17, 1840, performed the first service of baptism in the region, Joseph Evans and Thomas Saunders offering themselves for this ordinance.[3] The church accepted the opportunity afforded by Cheese's labours and commenced directing its missionaries to Birmingham and its neighbouring communities. Within days of the baptisms, Wilford Woodruff and Willard Richards visited and preached at Grets Green; William Clayton and John Needham were appointed to labor in the vicinity of Birmingham; a number of visiting missionaries, including Alfred Cordon and John Bourne, were sent from the Staffordshire Conference; and Lorenzo Snow, an American missionary, was set aside to labor in the city.

Theodore Turley, the founding father of the Birmingham Conference, devoted much of his early labour to Grets Green and West Bromwich. From the former he reported in June 1840:

> All the time I have been here, there have been either preachers or leaders calling upon me, some in the spirit of enquiry, others to try and eat me up. It is hard fighting.
>
> On Saturday I was invited to the house of a gentleman at Hill Top; I had an interview with him. He received me with warmth, received my testimony, said he had tried to preach the gospel for thirty five years, but was convinced that he lacked the power of God, and he had preached the second coming of Christ and the Restoration of the Jews; he had suffered much opposition on account of his going to try for me to preach in their chapel. Sunday — In the afternoon preached in the street and at night I was invited to fill the appointment of a Methodist local preacher. The house was filled and I preached two hours; many believe. Numbers say they must be baptized. The preacher stated publicly that he must be baptized; prayed that God would enable them all to examine the truths they had heard, and obey them. He and his wife have told me they will obey the command. A great fuss was raised. I have no chance to visit the different places around. I pray God to send more labourers in the vineyard. Brother Smith, do come and help me here. There is Birmingham and Wolverhampton and other towns here that are perishing.[4]

From these initial successes in Grets Green and West Bromwich, the impetus took the missionaries into other towns of the Black Country: Needham laboured in Albury, Dudley, Hill Top, and Darlaston, whilst John Bourne addressed meetings at Oldbury and Wednesbury. At Oldbury Bourne attended a service in a Methodist chapel at which the minister

---

[3] MH, entry under "Birmingham Conference."

[4] MH, entry under "Diary of the British Mission," Letter from Theodore Turley to G. A. Smith, 8 June 1840.

invited his congregation to testify to their personal experiences of religion. Bourne was ordered to sit down following his testimony to Mormonism. At Wednesbury he recorded preaching to a large audience, most of whom were Roman Catholic. The Baptist chapel at Wednesbury was made available to Turley on two occasions in June. The second time he had to contend with vociferous opposition, certain of which threatened "to horsewip me and others thretining to put me down a cole pit." At Bilston, Lorenzo Snow delivered a lecture "to a very respectable audience which was made up principally of socialists."[5]

As the missionaries collectively extended their influence from Grets Green and West Bromwich to neighbouring towns, the response to the church in Birmingham remained disappointing throughout 1840. In October, at the general conference in Manchester, Alfred Cordon reported Birmingham to have just four members. During November, Brigham Young and Heber C. Kimball added their weight and influence to the mission, yet growth continued to be associated with the smaller communities rather than with the city itself. By the end of the year, Grets Green claimed forty members, West Bromwich twenty-one, whilst the return for Birmingham was sixteen.

The second most important industrial centre of the Black Country, Wolverhampton, some ten miles to the north of Birmingham, was equally unsupportive of the initial incursions of the missionaries. Lorenzo Snow, who laboured in the town in November 1840, was met with indifference rather than hostility. He was, however, afforded hospitality by one of the curious who attended his meetings, a Mr. Farmer, who "possesses considerable influence among the learned of the town."[6] Farmer's influence extended to his arranging the use of the Baptist chapel for Snow's meetings, the missionary observing of the Baptists that this was "to their horror!" Throughout these difficult months of his mission, Snow retained a sense of perspective and of humour, which must have sustained him and others when faced with apparent failure. Thus he observed that in February 1841, Farmer travelled, at his own request, to Grets Green to be baptized "in a pure running stream, preferring the trouble of this journey to being baptized in a canal."[7] He balanced this, however, with considerable realism, when reflecting upon his task.

---

[5] John Bourne, Reminiscences, LDS Church Archives; Theodore Turley, Reminiscences and Diary, Special Collections, Harold B. Lee Library, Brigham Young University, Provo, Utah, hereafter cited as BYU Library; MH, entry under "Bilston Branch."

[6] MH, entry under "Diary of the British Mission," Letter from Lorenzo Snow to G. A. Smith, 28 November 1840.

[7] Ibid., Report from Lorenzo Snow, 19 January 1841.

I have just returned from Wolverhampton. The work there still moves, but slow and I cannot but believe that a great and mighty work eventually will be performed in that town. But I am quite sensible that much diligence, prayer, faith and perseverance will necessarily require to be exercised. At times the prospects there certainly have presented quite a gloomy aspect; something, however, has always whispered me not to despair, and many times I have trampled through mud and rain to fill appointments at Wolverhampton, when at the same time I might have had much larger congregations nearer home and more easily obtained. It sometimes has been the case that having preached there at night, we were compelled to return to Bilston for a place to lay our heads. In this respect, however, I have been rather more fortunate than those whom I sometimes have sent to fill my appointments.[8]

Birmingham benefited greatly from its proximity to the Staffordshire Conference, for missionaries either laboring in the Potteries or travelling there would often journey to Birmingham. The city thus enjoyed the services of the most eminent missionaries of the day who augmented the labors of those for whom this was the chosen field. The effect upon the enquirer or convert must have been immeasurable when addressed by Brigham Young or Wilford Woodruff, whose labors and feats in America would be familiar to an audience. A West Bromwich convert, Henry Stokes, acknowledged this, recording that he had been comforted and strengthened by visits from travelling missionaries.[9]

The year 1840 had witnessed the Mormon Church attempting to establish itself in the Black Country; by the early months of 1841, however, church leaders and missionaries were far more optimistic when anticipating the prospects for the Saints in the region. Snow commented that "the Church there is moving steadily onward in the increase of knowledge and multiplying of its members. The priests of Baal, however, bark and howl most ferociously." Alfred Cordon was more specific: "The Saints here are in good spirits. Our meetings are quite well attended, considering the circumstances. We had upwards of one hundred attend last Sabbath evening."[10] Both alluded to the opposition the Saints were beginning to meet. In these early stages this antagonism took the form of publishing handbills denouncing the church and disturbing meetings. Paradoxically, opposition to a sect or church is a mark of that organization's success; opposition does not precede or anticipate its adversary's success, it follows it. The opposition the Birmingham Saints were beginning to experience was, therefore, a mark of the conference's development.

The status of conference was bestowed upon Birmingham on February 28, 1841, at which time its three branches—Grets Green, West Bromwich,

---

[8] Ibid.

[9] Henry Stokes, Reminiscences, LDS Church Archives.

[10] MH, entry under "Birmingham Conference," Report from Lorenzo Snow, 19 January 1841; Report from Alfred Cordon, 17 February 1841.

and Birmingham—aggregated 112 members. The newly designated conference developed very slowly from this beginning. Its president, James Riley, recognized the difficulties it was to face during its infancy, particularly the withdrawal of its most famous missionaries, for the conferring of conference status coincided with the majority of the apostles and their fellow missionaries returning to America. Wisely, President Riley concentrated upon instilling discipline and loyalty throughout the conference, consolidating the earlier missionary labor so that any expansion that might occur had a sound base. There was also much energy within the conference, he himself being an indefatigable outdoor preacher. In this he was joined by George J. Adams, a charismatic teacher with a gift for rhetoric:

> There is a great stir about the sect, which is everywhere spoke against. Since our beloved brother, Elder Adams, has been here, the people come out to hear the Word. The able manner in which he explained the Scriptures, the glorious things which he unfolded and brought to light, engaged the attention of the people more than is ordinarily the case, and his persevering and untiring zeal in the prosecution of his mission, causes the Saints to bless him in their hearts, where the memory of him will exist till we meet in Zion to recount our toils and rest from our labours.[11]

The Saints were sustained in their belief but, whilst opposition was voiced, membership grew only marginally. At West Bromwich, fourteen new members were baptized during the first half of the year. Initially this branch met in butcher Joseph Neal's house in Spon Lane, but subsequently the elders hired a large house with a shop front affording a bow window. This shop they had furnished and fitted with seats so that it resembled a chapel and was open to the view of onlookers; a Saint, William Broomhead, resided in the rest of the house. From this preaching house, Thomas Tyler and his wife, Sophie, reported, "We are looking, striving, receiving visions, blessings and gifts."[12] The conference was on the threshold of expansion: its membership was united, its leaders and preachers respected and enthusiastic, its preaching rooms established.

During the winter months of 1841–42 and the following spring, recruitment to the Birmingham Conference accelerated. At its inception the conference numbered just in excess of 100; by May 1842 membership exceeded 300, representing eight branches within a ten-mile radius of the city. The following year, during which 200 new converts were welcomed, Reuben Hedlock, president of the British Mission, on a visit to Birmingham witnessed the good feeling within the conference and observed that there were "some additions every week and many inquiring after the truth."[13] He

---

[11] Ibid., Report from President James Riley, 31 October 1841.
[12] Henry Stokes, *Reminiscences*; MH, entry under "West Bromwich Branch."
[13] MH, entry under "Birmingham Conference," Report from Reuben Hedlock,

appealed for experienced elders to be attached to the conference for "the Saints appear teachable and are willing to do right if they know what to do." Many, he observed, wished to emigrate but were too poor to accomplish it.

At this time the character of the conference underwent a change as its field of operation was expanded to encompass Kidderminster, Leamington, and Stratford-upon-Avon. The pattern of establishing and strengthening the parent branch, developing the conference upon this nucleus, and then radiating outwards, was being repeated in the industrial heart of the Midlands. The Birmingham Conference, however, undertook each stage of this development with impeccable timing, so that expansion did not denude the parent branch or exhaust it of energy or resources. By 1844 membership had passed 700, the original group of branches contributing some 400 members and thus ensuring strength and stability at the centre of the conference. However, the territory covered by the conference now extended into South Wales, Aberdare, Merthyr Tydfil, and Tredegar figuring among these new branches. The extremely influential Welsh Conference, therefore, had its roots in the West Midlands, from whence certain of its founding branches were administered in the middle years of the 1840s. The Birmingham Conference was demonstrating its ability to respond to the pressures associated with a large membership and a vast geographical area.

The Birmingham Conference commemorated the first anniversary of the deaths of Joseph and Hyrum Smith with a service of prayer and fasting which united them with fellow Saints in Britain and America. They shared the occasion with a special guest. Wilford Woodruff had returned to Britain in January 1845 to preside over the European Mission; on June 27 he joined Birmingham Saints in worship and remembrance.

> On the 27th June I kept a day of fasting and prayer in the town of Birmingham with a flourishing branch of the Church of nearly 400 members, under the guidance and teaching of Father Robert Crook. I had an interesting meeting with the Saints on that evening, and while hearing the testimony of various individuals one truth was strongly impressed upon my mind, which was that notwithstanding one year had passed away since the Prophets were martyred at Carthage yet the work which they had established and sealed with their own blood was alive in the hearts of tens of thousands and bringing forth fruit to the honor and glory of God. I attended a council meeting with the officers of the Church in Birmingham and was happy to find that perfect union prevailed among them. I spend an interesting day with them on Sunday 29th June. They held their meeting in a commodious room which they had rented for a year in the High Street. I preached in the morning and afternoon, communed with about 400 Saints, confirmed five, blessed several children, and administered to several that were sick; the remainder of the afternoon was

---

17 December 1843.

occupied by the brethren and sisters in bearing their testimony of the work of God, and truly it was an interesting time. In the evening, the house was crowded to excess and many could not find admission. A large number of strangers were present who had not before attended our meetings. Although I addressed them somewhat lengthy, good order prevailed, and the best of attention was given and I have no doubt but that many will yet be added to the Church in Birmingham. The prospect for the spread of the work in that place was never better than at the present time, and I have the satisfaction of saying that during my stay there, I had no spirit manifest with any member of that branch of the Church but perfect union. Elder Crook is much blessed in his labours and is striving to build up the Kingdom of God, he has the hearts and affections of the Saints.[14]

Throughout the second half of the 1840s and the early years of the following decade, membership of the Birmingham Conference grew at an extraordinary rate, despite the loss of its Welsh branches and those other branches — Stratford and Leamington amongst them — that lay beyond a reasonable travelling distance of the city. At the first quarterly conference of 1848, Cyrus H. Wheelock, president of the conference, announced that membership had exceeded one thousand; during the following twelve months the conference received 434 new members, the Birmingham Branch alone conducting 190 baptisms. The year 1850 witnessed membership passing the 2,000 mark, the last six months of the year recording 360 new members. During the entire period of this unprecedented development, conference spokesmen referred to church meetings being fully subscribed, the confidence of the members, the energy and initiative of the elders, and the prospects of additional future growth. In December 1848, Harrison Burgess informed Orson Pratt that "they have the best chapel here that I have seen among the Saints and are drawing a large congregation. On Sunday evening there were present from twelve to fifteen hundred people of a respectable class."[15]

The chapel to which Burgess referred was the Livery Street Chapel, which the Mormons gained in 1845, a place of worship formerly belonging to the Congregationalists.[16] This was in use at the time of the Religious Census of 1851, which reported an evening attendance of 1,200, which substantiates Burgess's claim and suggests that in Birmingham Mormonism was established as a serious church. Mormon occupation of the Livery Street Chapel illustrates the changing fortunes of religious bodies, the sacred hymns of the Saints replacing the more familiar offerings of English nonconformity. As its own needs changed, the LDS Church was to utilize other former nonconformist chapels: between 1852 and 1858 it occupied

---

[14] MH, entry under "Birmingham Conference."

[15] Ibid., Letter from Harrison Burgess to Orson Pratt, 8 December 1848.

[16] *The Victorian History of the Counties of England: Warwickshire. Vol. 7, Birmingham* (London, 1964), 64.

the Cambridge Street Chapel in the city, whilst in the following decade the Saints succeeded the Methodist New Connexion in worshipping in the Oxford Street Chapel. It is worth reflecting that just ten years prior to their accommodating huge congregations in the Livery Street Chapel, they were using private rooms, such as Joseph Neal's butcher shop in West Bromwich. The individual Saint was still acquainted with poverty, but as a corporate body Mormons had acquired a dignity to accompany their faith.

The Birmingham Conference, which grew to be the largest conference within the British Mission, was also the archetypal conference in terms of its membership, during the 1840s and 1850s the pattern of its growth and subsequent decline mirroring that of the mission as a whole. Yet throughout this period Birmingham knew no peer, for its actual membership exceeded that of other individual conferences; similarities lay in the percentage change of the respective bodies rather than in any comparison of numbers. The Birmingham Conference achieved its peak membership in 1852, a year later than the mission, and then both commenced a parallel decline. In 1856, as Saints in America were posed for the Utah War, both bodies returned membership figures that were 68 percent of their highest recorded memberships; at the end of the decade, identical returns of 42 percent of peak records were recorded. In both instances the difficulties in Utah which affected the missionary program and brought a temporary cessation to church emigration may be seen reflected in membership figures. The Birmingham Conference was an indicator for the entire mission.

Even in decline, however, the Birmingham Conference retained a remarkable numerical strength, the explanation for which lay in the sound organization that had been synonymous with its leadership. Certainly the conference had experienced some occasional difficulties. In 1854 criticism had been expressed at its funding and the necessity to take up collections at every meeting to finance the travelling elders who relied upon the membership to sustain them, and in the same year Saints were asked to consecrate one day's earnings to clear the conference debt. But there is no evidence of widespread dissatisfaction with or within the governing council. In the late 1850s, as the decline in membership became particularly marked, the official reports of the conference depict an enthusiastic and soundly organized body whose activities encompassed both Saints and non-Mormons. The report for 1856 cites a conference strength of 1,516, of whom 146 were elders and 133 priests, the majority of whom were engaged in outdoor preaching and the distribution of tracts.[17] Three thousand copies of *Marriage and Morals in Utah* had been circulated, especially to important civic and religious leaders in the city, obviously in an attempt to counter

---

[17] MH, entry under "Birmingham Conference."

accusations relating to plural marriage. Although an opinion had been expressed that in some parts of the conference the Saints were laboring to little or no avail, the contrary proved to be the case, for within the preceding twelve months 298 persons had been baptized. However, this number was balanced by those emigrating, 178, and those excommunicated for neglecting their duties, specifically those concerning communal worship and the paying of tithes. Within the conference ten Sabbath Schools were maintained, at which, in addition to religious and sectarian instruction, reading and writing were taught to the young attenders. A course of lectures had been undertaken in the ten principal branches of the conference, these apparently being well attended. The impression that is suggested by the report is of an active, well-organized, large, and successful conference, controlled centrally and with understanding and authority; branch records of the period confirm this representation.

Conference reports, however, have a limited value; they deal with the general rather than the particular, with the organization of the conference rather than its individual members. What the report omitted was the struggle against poverty that so many members experienced as they pursued their faith and complied with the regulations and requirements of their church. The decline in the demand for manufactured goods lowered wages in Birmingham in the late 1850s and early 1860s and brought about a scarcity of work, which affected many Saints. During 1861, William G. Mills, writing from Birmingham, twice felt the need to allude to the poverty and unemployment facing members.[18] On the second occasion he related this to their inability to plan their emigration. "The spirit of gathering seemed to burn in every bosom but the times, however, were disabling them from delivering themselves, work was hard to be obtained and wages were lower than ever."

In 1865 the West Bromwich Branch reacted to the realization that certain of its Saints were so impoverished that they could no longer afford to purchase the *Millennial Star*. A fund was instituted to provide the journal for those without the means to purchase it. At approximately the same time the branch announced a day of fasting, requiring of the Saints that they should donate what they would normally have spent on food to provide a Christmas dinner for the poor in their midst. Two years later in the report of the branch's work it formally recorded "that a great deal of poverty existed."[19] This was an important matter, not simply on humanitarian grounds, but because it implied that, many of its more progressive and ambitious members having emigrated, the branch and the conference con-

---

[18] MH, entry under "Birmingham Conference," Letter from William G. Mills to President Cannon, 15 June 1861.
[19] MH, entry under "West Bromwich Branch."

tained a far greater proportion of the poor and, incidentally, the aged, than had been the case during the years of growth and development. In reality, the response to the gathering and the success of the mission's emigration programme, plus external economic factors that resulted in a recession, were having an adverse effect on a church already in decline.

Additionally, the Birmingham Conference was reaping another reward of its earlier success. No stranger to opposition from the early 1840s, it found itself facing an orchestrated attack upon its position within the city that culminated in extreme hostility in 1857, when crowds, having been treated to and incited by the rhetoric of Dr. Brindley, attempted to vandalize church premises and assault individual Saints.[20] It was a paradox that the city noted for its liberalism and tolerance and a press that reflected these values should be the venue for some of the worst anti-Mormon rioting experienced in this country. The extent of their effect upon membership and potential converts is a matter for surmise; that they did have an effect is beyond dispute.

The Birmingham Conference maintained an important and influential presence throughout the 1860s, its membership remaining numerically quite stable although its personnel changed considerably. This resulted from the British Mission's ongoing reorganization of its conferences, for as numbers declined in the smaller conferences and they became more difficult and less efficient to manage, they were closed and their branches annexed to more prosperous neighboring conferences. As the decade progressed, therefore, the territory administered by Birmingham grew, as it assumed responsibility for branches transferred from other conferences. The most significant of these annexations occurred at the end of the decade, following the demise of the Warwickshire Conference, which had enjoyed an independent existence from 1846, when it was founded with seven branches and 168 members, until its closure at the end of 1869. This conference in its early years had been based upon Leamington and had included branches at Stratford, Coventry, and Rugby. It had been fortunate in its presidents. Thomas Smith, formerly a member of the United Brethren and one of their foremost preachers, assumed the presidency upon the founding of the conference; and Alfred Cordon, returning to Britain on a mission in 1848, was confirmed as the second president of the conference. At its most active, it claimed 763 members and twenty-nine branches, an apparently well-established body. Yet in its plethora of branches lay its inevitable problems and ultimate closure since many of these branches must have been very small indeed and, therefore, always vulnerable either to the emigration of their members or neglect of duty, perhaps associated

---

[20] See Cotterill, "Midland Saints," chapter 7, "Opposition and Persecution," 323–29.

with an aging membership. After 1851 numbers declined rapidly, membership halving by 1860, a parallel to the national pattern but a marked contrast to that of the Birmingham Conference; at its close it had just over 200 members.

The Birmingham Conference, therefore, had to confront the situation it had known in the early 1840s, that of having to administer to Saints spread over an excessively large area. Successive presidents in their reports refer to the problems this posed, both the administrative difficulties and those facing Saints who increasingly felt their isolation and the lack of incentive to comply with the expectations of the church. President Andrew P. Shumway, writing in November 1869, recorded his response to the challenge. "I have divided the Conference into two districts, and Brother Eldridge takes one and my brother Charles the other. I take a roving commission to myself, travelling where most needed, and where likely to do the most good. We have twelve meeting rooms in the Conference, where meetings are held on Sundays, as well as evening meetings during the week. The saints are visited once each week at their houses by the visiting officers, except in some cases where the scattered conditions of the saints render it impossible."[21]

Two years later, Joseph Argyle reported in similar manner on the condition of the Saints, many of whom were "very poor and have had to suffer for lack of the necessities of life this winter through the severe frosts." In an extremely pessimistic letter he lamented the lack of converts entering the church, realistically recognizing that when the British Mission commenced "many people were ready to receive their testimony, thousands more baptized, and the power of God made manifest to them to overflowing." Persecution had followed and once that first harvest of Saints had been gathered, it became progressively more difficult to make converts. The non-Mormons, whom he tried to address, "have been dwindling into darkness and it seems as though the whole world are falling into infidelity as fast as time can take them." The following year Charles H. Wilcken, who had only recently taken over as president, reflected in similar vein: "I don't see what more we can do; if people will not listen, we certainly cannot make them, still it makes me feel uncomfortable and uneasy."[22] During his second year in office he defined quite clearly certain of the problems the conference faced.

> You are aware that I have a great many scattered members who are not privileged to assemble themselves with the Saints in meetings; these I have hunted

---

[21] MH, entry under "Birmingham Conference," Letter of President Shumway to Albert Carrington, 17 November 1869.

[22] Ibid., Report of Joseph Argyle, 16 March 1871; *Millennial Star* 34 (19 November 1872): 747.

up, stayed with them, and have cheered and comforted them, and in most instances have administered the sacrament to them. I have found some of them have not partaken of this holy ordinance for years, had also neglected to pay their tithing, nor even saved anything for the emigration, in consequence of which they are "neither cold nor hot." In a few cases the spirit has left them to that extent that they fear lest somebody should find out they are Latter-Day Saints.[23]

The problems with which succeeding presidents grappled were endemic in any large conference in decline, responsible for a large area in which could be found a number of scattered communities, and whose members were aging and therefore less involved in both conference business and church duties. Between 1870 and 1877 membership went into an even more rapid decline: at the commencement of the decade it could claim approximately 900 Saints; at the time of Brigham Young's death, that figure had halved. The conference was still baptizing some fifty converts a year, but waste and natural causes were taking an increasing toll. The pattern for the remainder of the century was determined.

The Birmingham Conference may stand as the example of a large and progressive conference, adapting to respond to the variables of growth and those that accompanied decline; it illustrates the patterns and types of membership throughout this process; it depicts the achievements of and the difficulties that beset both leadership and members. In a church extolled for the efficiency of its organization, the Birmingham Conference demonstrates that successful administration related to flexibility. The management appropriate to a developing conference would be inapplicable to a buoyant membership of 2,300 or a declining body of 500. The organization demanded of a conference, all of whose branches were within ten miles of a central point, differed from that required by a dispersed community whose extremities were 100 or more miles apart. The Birmingham Conference at varying times had to accept all these variables and more, it had to accept radical transformations to its organization and shape so that it might accommodate differing sets of conditions. This is the real achievement of the conference: it could adapt and accommodate. In this it was as successful during its decline as it had been during its development.

---

[23] Ibid., 35 (11 February 1873): 91.

7

A Fertile Field: Scotland in the Days of the Early Missions

BERNARD ASPINWALL

Scotland proved fertile ground for the Mormon missionaries in the early nineteenth century. The first converts to the faith were quickly won, and by the end of the century almost 10,000 Mormons had been converted in Scotland.[1] The reasons for this considerable response were many and varied. Allowing for the zeal and commitment of those early pioneers, Scotland was well-prepared ground: many in their audiences could respond positively to their message.

Scotland was undergoing a massive social, political, and religious transformation in those years. In industrial and entrepreneurial innovation Scotland was perhaps the most advanced in the world; its economists and universities were at the forefront of technical and intellectual thought. The industrial revolution was in full swing. In particular around Glasgow, the University of Adam Smith, the great ironworks were developing, belching forth their romantic flames. The immense chimney stack of the Tennant chemical works reminded at least one observer of the grandeur of Strasbourg Cathedral.[2] Similarly, the great textile mills, including the largest in the world with over 1,000 looms, were booming and winning markets throughout the world. In a mill tenement at Blantyre, the infant David Livingstone

---

[1] Frederick Stewart Buchanan, "The Emigration of Scottish Mormons to Utah, 1849–1900" (Unpublished M.Sc. thesis, University of Utah, 1961). See also his essay, "Imperial Zion: The British Occupation of Utah," in *The Peoples of Utah*, ed. Helen Z. Papanikolas (Salt Lake City: Utah State Historical Society, 1974), 61–114. I am grateful to Dr. Buchanan for his personal help in many ways.

[2] John B. Latrobe, *Hints on Six Months in Europe* (Philadelphia: Lippincott, 1869), 103. On this sense of romantic grandeur and crisis see F. D. Klingender, *Art and the Industrial Revolution* (London: Adams and Dart, 1968); William Fearon, *The Art of John Martin* (Oxford: Oxford University Press, 1975); Morton D. Paley, *The Apocalyptic Sublime* (New Haven: Yale University Press, 1986).

was learning his Latin from a Catholic priest. Throughout the west-central belt of Scotland numerous coal mines were opening. The new railways were revolutionizing attitudes and expanding horizons. Scots had a belief in progress, "a metaphysic, a scientific credo, a value judgement, a philosophy of history."[3] The old order had irrevocably changed.

The fortunate, wealthy Scots who benefited from these developments could face the future with the certainty that Progress and Providence were on their side. The less fortunate had to find consolation elsewhere. In the hard times following the end of the Napoleonic Wars in 1815, the displaced handloom weavers were often reduced to starvation and despair; their position consistently deteriorated through to the 1840s. Those in employment worked long hours in unhealthy conditions in mills and mines. Endemic fever raged in the overcrowded cities of Glasgow, Edinburgh, and Dundee.[4] Even amid such miserable conditions optimistic political or religious convictions flourished; the promised future strength compensated for the depressing present weakness.

The new industrial proprietors and merchants were vigorous, uncompromising men. They sought recognition for their wealth, talents, and political interests in the unreformed parliament. Men like Kirkman Finlay and Henry Monteith, liberal and conservative alike, were part of a social revolution.[5] With the reform of parliament in 1832, the new order seemed well ensconced at least in the hearts of the "respectable" if not the excluded, unrepresented, and resentful masses. Their hopes had been dashed. Previously, Scotland had effectively been in the control of a machine, a small group of political professionals around the Melville family.[6] The disintegration of that controlling interest, which had well represented and protected traditional aristocratic privilege, was symptomatic of larger social and political changes. Now the new larger but restricted electorate seemed preoccupied with containment rather than innovative change; it gave political power to the new entrepreneurs. To the unenfranchised, as E. P.

---

[3] Gladys Bryson, *Man and Society: The Scottish Inquiry of the Eighteenth Century* (Princeton: Princeton University Press, 1945), 43.

[4] See Edwin Chadwick, *Report on the Sanitary Condition of the Labouring Population of Great Britain* (1842), ed. M. W. Flinn (Edinburgh: Edinburgh University Press, 1965), for evidence; Thomas Ferguson, *The Dawn of Scottish Welfare* (London: Nelson, 1948), 111–65; James E. Handley, *The Irish in Scotland, 1788–1845* (Cork: Cork University Press, 1943) and his *The Irish in Modern Scotland* (Cork: Cork University Press, 1947); Alexander Wilson, *The Chartist Movement in Scotland* (Manchester: Manchester University Press, 1970), among the considerable literature.

[5] I. G. C. Hutchison, *A Political History of Scotland, 1832–1924: Parties, Elections, Issues* (Edinburgh: John Donald, 1986), esp. 1–5.

[6] See Holden Furber, *Henry Dundas, Viscount Melville* (London: Oxford University Press, 1931), and Cyril Mathison, *Life of Henry Dundas* (London: Constable, 1933).

Thompson has suggested, it was often an alien world.[7] In this atmosphere the old British sense of social justice within a moral economic order had been undermined in the interests of the factory and mine owner. The alien developing capitalist economy was fast eroding the right of the worker to the fruits of his labor.[8]

Against this background popular demands for political, social, and economic reform grew markedly. Scottish workingmen inspired by the French and American revolutions demanded real representation.[9] From the Friends of the People in the 1790s to the Chartists of the 1830s and 1840s, various Scottish political movements demanded greater popular participation in the political process, in controlling the rapid social and economic changes. That desperation produced a small revolutionary rising in 1820 which was crushed with ruthless severity. Even the reformed parliament failed to meet the demands for greater popular participation and for greater protection from exploitation under the developing capitalism, or to sustain a humane sense of community.[10] The restoration of old values was necessary.

Hitherto lands had been increasingly concentrated in the hands of few wealthy families. Farms had become increasingly large-scale operations providing few opportunities to new younger, small-scale tenant farmers. Population pressures on the small holdings available increased. So too did rent. Many were forced to migrate to the new industrial towns like Glasgow, to England, or increasingly further afield to America.[11] The landed dom-

---

[7] See E. P. Thompson, "The Moral Economy of England in the Eighteenth Century," *Past and Present* 50 (1971): 76–136. A comprehensive account is E. P. Thompson, *The Making of the English Working Class* (New York: Pantheon, 1964). Also see Robert Q. Gray, *The Labour Aristocracy in Victorian Edinburgh* (Oxford: Oxford University Press, 1976), and H. Hont and M. Ignatieff, *Wealth and Virtue: The Shaping of Political Economy in the Scottish Enlightenment* (Cambridge: Cambridge University Press, 1983).

[8] Thompson, *The Making*, 803, quoting the Chartist Bronterre O' Brien.

[9] G. S. Veitch, *The Genesis of Parliamentary Reform* (London: Constable, 1913), and W. H. Meikle, *Scotland and the French Revolution* (Glasgow: Maclehose, 1912) remain classic accounts.

[10] See for example Henry Weisser, *British Working Class Movements and Europe, 1815–1848* (Manchester: Manchester University Press, 1975), and Peter Beresford Ellis and S. Mac A'Goahain, *The Scottish Insurrection of 1820* (London: Gollancz, 1970). In addition to Thompson and Wilson, *Scottish Chartism*, see for example, "Patrick Brewster and Scottish Chartism," in Stewart Mechie, *The Church and Scottish Social Development, 1780–1870* (Oxford: Oxford University Press, 1960), 100–18.

[11] See J. M. Bumsted, *The People's Clearances: Highland Emigration to British North America, 1770–1815* (Edinburgh: Edinburgh University Press, 1982); Bernard Bailyn, *The Peopling of North America* (Madison: University of Wisconsin Press, 1985), and his *Voyagers to the West: A Passage in the Peopling of America on the Eve of the Revolution* (New York: Knopf, 1986); Malcolm Gray, "Scottish Emigration: The Social Impact

inance in the political life of the nation came under attack. From the days of American independence popular movements had been restive at these developments. As early as 1771 Rev. William Thom of Govan had attacked the destruction of the sturdy yeoman Scot through the concentration of land in few hands.[12] More radical criticisms were heard by 1850. Patrick E. Dove bitterly attacked the reduction of many Scottish farmers to savagery through the high rents of rapacious landlords.[13] Many had emigrated. The old village and community were being destroyed, and seeking a new world overseas became a normal fact of Scottish life.

A strong tradition of transatlantic trade, emigration, and religious sentiments bound Glasgow into a transatlantic moral world; America was merely Scotland renewed and regenerated and the Atlantic but a Scottish loch.[14] Whatever the distance in miles, the ethnic, intellectual, and spiritual link was close. Emigrant Scots could rediscover and reestablish their identity within this new moral world economy. Some 40,000 Scots had already emigrated to America in the late eighteenth century; by 1890 almost a quarter of a million Scots had emigrated there.[15] Greater economic opportunities in developing textile mills and ironworks, asylum in a freer political and religious atmosphere, made the early nineteenth-century prospect even more attractive.[16] Emigration, either temporary or perma-

---

of Agrarian Change in the Rural Lowlands, 1775–1875," *Perspectives in American History* 7 (1973): 95–174.

[12] William Thom, *A Candid Enquiry into the Causes of the Late and Intended Migrations from Scotland in a Letter to J. R. Esq. . . . Lanarkshire* (Glasgow, 1771), 14, 19, 28–29, 40–41.

[13] Patrick E. Dove, *The Theory of Human Progression and the Natural Probability of a Reign of Justice* (London: Johnstone and Hunter, 1850), esp. 41, 44. Dove edited the Glasgow *Witness*, visited America, and was a forerunner of Henry George and his ideas. J. Morrison Davidson, *Concerning the Four Precursors of Henry George and the Single Tax* (Port Washington, N.Y.: Kennikat Press, 1971), 57–71.

[14] See Howard Miller, *The Revolutionary College: American Presbyterian Higher Education, 1707–1837* (New York: New York University Press, 1976); Douglas Sloan, *The Scottish Enlightenment and the American College* (New York: Columbia University Press, 1971). My book, *Portable Utopia: Glasgow and the United States, 1820–1920* (Aberdeen: Aberdeen University Press, 1984), covers the later background. Also see my essay, "Scottish Religious Identity in the Atlantic World, 1880–1914," in *Studies in Church History* 10 (1982): 505–18.

[15] See my *Portable Utopia*, passim; Ben J. Wattenberg, ed., *Statistical History of the United States from Colonial Times to the Present* (New York: Basic Books, 1976), 116–17, and Rowland T. Berthoff, *British Immigrants in Industrial America* (Cambridge, Mass.: Harvard University Press, 1953), 5, 7.

[16] See for example David J. Jeremy, "British Textile Technology Transmission to the United States: The Philadelphia Region Experience, 1770–1820," *Business History Review* 47 (1973): 24–52, and his *Transatlantic Industrial Revolution: The Diffusion of Textile Technologies between Britain and America, 1790–1830* (Cambridge, Mass.: M.I.T. Press, 1981); Tamara K. Hareven, *Family Time and Industrial Time: The*

nent, became normal in most families; it was a well-established Scottish tradition. In 1830, for example, 90 percent of American carpet weavers were from Ayr and Kilmarnock; many were concentrated in the Scottish town of Thompsonville, Connecticut.[17] A decade earlier Scots had banded together to form Caledonia, LeRoy, and Scottsville in western New York. As John Duncan, a Glasgow visitor, noted on his return, "a kind of America mania has possessed many of my countrymen."[18] Group migration and settlement, therefore, was not unusual.

Not all Scots who emigrated became thoroughgoing democrats by any means; not a few radicals returned home disenchanted. Scottish Tories were confirmed in their prejudices against extending democracy. Even some Scots who succeeded in making vast American fortunes merely welcomed the greater opportunities and questioned universal suffrage. A few railed at "the idea of social equality entertained by the most worthless members of society."[19] Egalitarian notions and merit were threatening to birth and connection: "No man of high principles can enter American political life."[20] Optimistic ideas of man's inherent goodness jarred against traditional Calvinist notions.

Relationship Between the Family and Work in a New England Industrial Community (Cambridge, Mass.: Harvard University Press, 1982), 16–21; Constance McL. Green, *Holyoke, Massachusetts: A Case History of the Industrial Revolution in America* (New Haven, Conn.: Yale University Press, 1939), 48–49, 76; Caroline F. Ware, *The Early New England Cotton Manufacture: A Study in Industrial Beginnings* (Boston: Houghton Mifflin, 1931); R. Ginger, "Labour in a Massachusetts Cotton Mill, 1853–1860," *Business History Review* 28 (1954): 57–91.

[17] R. T. Berthoff, *British Immigrants*, 39. See also Clifton K. Yearley, Jr., *Britons in American Labor* (Baltimore: Johns Hopkins University Press, 1957), passim.

[18] John M. Duncan, *Travels Through Part of the United States and Canada in 1818 and 1819* (London: Glasgow University Press, 1823), 338. Also see among other contemporary works Peter Neilson, *Recollections of a Six Years' Residence in the United States* (Glasgow: D. Robertson, 1830); Thomas Hamilton, *Men and Manners in America* (Edinburgh, 1843); A. Prentice, *A Tour in the United States of America with Two Lectures on Emigration* (London: John Johnstone, 1849). Government-assisted group emigration to Canada had been well established in the 1820s. Robert Lamond, *A Narrative of the Rise and Progress of Emigration from the Counties of Lanark and Renfrew* (Glasgow: Chalmers and Collins, 1821); Helen I. Cowan, *British Emigration to British North America* (Toronto: University of Toronto Press, 1961), 47–64; Norman MacDonald, *Canada: Immigration and Colonisation: 1841–1903* (Aberdeen: Aberdeen University Press, 1966), 1–68. Significantly, a number of early Scottish Mormon converts like Samuel Mulliner had originally emigrated via Canada.

[19] J. Dawson Burn, *Three Years Residence Among the Working Classes of America During the Recent Civil War* (London: Smith, Elder, 1865), 168. Also G. Lewis, *Impressions of America and American Churches* (Edinburgh: W. P. Kennedy, 1845), 34, noting a Scot with $30,000 and a loathing of democracy.

[20] Hamilton, *Men and Manners*, xxii.

their frequent visits to Glasgow drew considerable audiences.[38] They radiated optimism, confidence, and love of God and man. Their revivalistic techniques, well established in previous generations, enjoyed a great resurgence. From the 1820s onwards they constantly heightened religious sensitivity and renewed evangelical enthusiasm in Glasgow. Temperance, education, Bible, missionary, and tract societies followed in their wake; their thrust was to uplift the laboring masses. Their message gave a very personal experience of salvation, a sense of identity within a community of like-minded folk. They were quietly challenging the prevailing social, economic, and religious ethos. In effect, they were founding their own parallel community. They had direct access to God outside of the existing ecclesiastical structures; direct access to love and justice outside of the unjust, exploitive social order; and they confidently awaited the Lord.

The millennial preaching of Rev. Edward Irving encouraged exuberant expectations of the imminent Second Coming.[39] He was part of an established west of Scotland tradition; popular millenarianism was not uncommon. It was a constant theme of numerous preachers and women visionaries. The eighteenth century had seen the millenarian Buchanite enthusiasts whose disappointment later led them to America.[40] The idealism of Robert Owen and his social experiments at New Lanark, Lanarkshire, and New Harmony, Indiana, tapped a similar vein of popular consciousness.[41] Likewise, Scottish social theorists like the preacher "Shepherd" Smith,

---

[38] *United Presbyterian Magazine* (October 1870), 540. See my *Portable Utopia*, and R. Carwardine, *Transatlantic Revivalism: Popular Evangelicalism in Britain and America, 1790–1865* (Westport, Conn.: Greenwood Press, 1978).

[39] See Margaret O. W. Oliphant, *The Life of Edward Irving*, 2 vols. (London: Hurst and Blackett, 1864), and Gordon C. Strachan, *The Pentecostal Theology of Edward Irving* (London: Darton Longman Todd, 1973). On the background, W. H. G. Armytage, *Heavens Below: Utopian Experiments in England, 1560–1960* (London: Routledge, 1961), 77–286; W. H. Oliver, *Prophets and Millenialists: The Uses of Biblical Prophecy in England from the 1790s to the 1840s* (Auckland, New Zealand: University of Auckland Press, 1978); Clarke Garrett, *Respectable Folly: Millenarians and the French Revolution in France and England* (Baltimore: Johns Hopkins University Press, 1975).

[40] See Hugh White, *The Divine Dictionary* (Edinburgh: A. Brown, 1785), and *Eight Letters between The People called Buchanites and a Teacher near Edinburgh* (Edinburgh: Elliot, 1785); J. F. C. Harrison, *The Second Coming: Popular Millenarianism, 1780–1850* (New Brunswick: Rutgers University Press, 1979), 32–38, and John Finlayson, *An Admonition to the People of All Countries That Our Saviour's Second Coming Is At Hand* (Edinburgh: Author, 1797), and *The Last Trumpet and The Flying Angel* (London, 1849).

[41] J. F. C. Harrison, *Robert Owen and the Owenites in Britain and America: The Quest for the New Moral World* (London: Routledge, 1969), and R. G. Garnett, *Cooperation and the Owenite Socialist Communities in Britain, 1825–1845* (Manchester: Manchester University Press, 1972).

the translator of Saint-Simon and Lamennais, endorsed these notions, which found a ready audience among Scottish Chartists. Some of them were to follow John Alexander of Ayrshire to found a short-lived model community in Texas.[42] These and several others contributed to an ethos which anticipated such developments.

Scottish society, then, was a state of flux when the first Mormon missionaries arrived. Their optimistic, confident message met several local Scottish concerns: the necessity for a right relationship with God; the vision of a moral, cohesive community; the promise of well-being here on earth and in the hereafter. Above all, they came from America, a land with a very positive image of freedom, self-determination, and opportunities for greater prosperity. The opportunity to begin a new life in a new world in a new moral dimension proved irresistible to a goodly number of Scots. The message was all the more convincing in that Scots were among the first Mormon missionaries in Scotland.

The first missionaries arrived in 1839. Alexander Wright, a Banffshire man, had become a Mormon following his emigration to America.[43] He returned to begin a very successful mission in 1839–41. With Samuel Mulliner, a Haddington emigrant, he worked around Paisley and Glasgow, winning large audiences and some 100 emigrants within a few months. Shortly afterwards the apostle Orson Pratt arrived to share in the labors. Solid growth followed.[44]

Converts in the west-central areas of Scotland were mainly from the working classes: miners; iron mill and textile workers; the literate, politically aware craftsmen; and a few farmers. Interestingly enough, these converts included some Chartists and at least one Methodist minister.[45] They

---

[42] William Anderson Smith, *"Shepherd" Smith, The Universalist: The Story of A Mind* (London: Low Marston, 1893), and W. G. Roe, *Lamennais and England* (Oxford: Oxford University Press, 1966), 164, 203–5. Ray Boston, *British Chartists in America, 1839–1900* (Manchester: Manchester University Press, 1971), 43. Also Wilbur S. Shepperson, *Emigration and Disenchantment: Portraits of Englishmen Repatriated from the United States* (Norman: University of Oklahoma Press, 1965), 71–77.

[43] Missionaries of the Church of Jesus Christ of the Latter-day Saints, 1839–1848, Archives, Historical Department of the Church of Jesus Christ of Latter-day Saints, Salt Lake City, hereafter cited as LDS Church Archives.

[44] Manuscript History of the British Mission, 8 April 1840, LDS Church Archives. See also Buchanan, "The Emigration of Scottish Mormons" and "Imperial Zion," cited above.

[45] Together with six of his congregation, January 1838. Manuscript History of the British Mission, LDS Church Archives, which also notes that on 6 April and 15 June 1840 Irvingites were converted.

were largely found in the small, tightly knit industrial communities, mainly in the west of Scotland. Compared to Glasgow, Kilmarnock, Gourock, Paisley, and their like provided a disproportionately high number of converts to their population.[46] These features show marked similarity to those areas of Methodist success, described by E. P. Thompson, in northern England, but not repeated in the poorer Scottish towns; small Scottish congregations found the financial burdens far too great.[47] Significantly, in his research sample, Fred Buchanan has shown that almost two-thirds of those Scottish Mormon converts emigrating to Zion needed aid from the Perpetual Emigrating Fund.[48] In a real sense, the oppressed and deprived were the backbone of the movement. By sharing the hardships and poverty of their people, Mormon missionary leaders won their loyal support. In that respect their rapport was similar to the Irish clergy with their Scottish flock.[49] Not surprisingly, in the most densely populated artisan area of Britain, Parley P. Pratt's *Voice of Warning* proved influential, as did his subsequent claim: "Here, too, we are all rich — there is no real poverty, where all men have access to the soil, the pasture, the timber, the water power, and all the elements of wealth without money or price."[50]

An analysis of membership of the church in the west of Scotland in 1844 shows its strength in the major towns, particularly the coal and textile areas of Lanarkshire and Ayrshire.[51] Some 568 were found in Glasgow; 104 in Airdrie; 93 in Paisley; 86 in Kilmarnock; 85 in Holytown; 83 in Tollcross; 82 in Kilbirnie; 77 in Greenock. Others were scattered in smaller groups throughout the area. Seven years later the Religious Census of 1851

---

[46] See Glasgow Conference, Emigration Deposits, 1869–93, LDS Church Archives, especially entries for 5 February and 31 December 1841. See Buchanan, "The Emigration of Scottish Mormons," 18–20, 55–58.

[47] Thompson, *The Making of the Working Class*, 379, and A. J. Hayes and D. A. Gowland, eds., *Scottish Methodism in the Early Victorian Period: The Scottish Correspondence of Rev. Jabez Bunting, 1800–1857* (Edinburgh: Edinburgh University Press, 1981); Callum G. Brown, *The Social History of Religion in Scotland since 1730* (London: Methuen, 1987), 72.

[48] Buchanan, "The Emigration of Scottish Mormons," 17, 71.

[49] See for example Bernard Canning, *Irish-Born Secular Priests in Scotland, 1829–1979* (Greenock: Author, 1979).

[50] Quoted by P. A. M. Taylor, *Expectations Westward: The Mormons and the Emigration of their British Converts in the Nineteenth Century* (Edinburgh: Oliver and Boyd, 1965), 27. Similar backgrounds appear in James B. Allen and Thomas G. Alexander, eds., *Manchester Mormons: The Journal of William Clayton, 1840–42* (Santa Barbara, Calif.: Peregrine Smith, 1974).

[51] Glasgow Conference Records, LDS Church Archives. Also see British Mission: Scotland, Manuscript History, LDS Church Archives.

Table 1.
Meeting Places and Attendance, 1851, in Various Burghs of Scotland

Burghs	Meeting Places	Attendance
Airdrie	1	95
Dundee	1	109
Dunfermline	1	50
Dysart	1	84
Glasgow	1	400–450
Greenock	1	50–60
Paisley	1	25–33
Rutherglen	1	30

Table 2.
Meeting Places and Attendance, 1851, in Various Counties of Scotland

Counties	Meeting Places	Attendance
Ayrshire	2	30–158
Dumbartonshire	1	21–28
Fife	3	39–173
Haddingtonshire	1	44
Lanarkshire	6	524–659
Linlithgowshire	1	13–35
Renfrewshire	4	75–118
Perthshire	1	12–25[52]

revealed much the same picture.[53] In spite of emigration to Zion, expulsions, and missionary endeavor, the heartland of Scottish Mormonism remained the west-central belt.

The skilled artisans amid the social, economic, and religious dislocation were willing converts to this new, attractive faith. Present hardship was a prelude to future joy. Amid the collapse of their old world, their old rhythm of work, community, and place, they were more receptive to a new gospel. The prospect of salvation here below and in the hereafter, material improvement, and spiritual fulfilment proved irresistible. In tapping the Scottish religious sensitivity to the millenarian tradition, appealing to poorer

---

[52] Ibid., 18, 23–33. On later developments see M. Hamlin Cannon's classic accounts, "Migration of English Mormons to America," *American Historical Review* 52 (1947): 436–55, and "The English Mormons in America," Ibid. 57 (1952): 893–908.

[53] *Census of Great Britain, 1851: Religious Worship and Education: Report and Tables.*

people, echoing the ideal of a moral economy, and through their association with the democratic American image, Mormons were able to win a hearing and many Scottish converts among the less fortunate. The missionary endeavor was arduous, but the ground was well prepared. It seemed providential to all concerned; a new phase of Scottish life had begun.

8

From a *Seion* of Lands to the Land of Zion: The Life of David Bevan Jones

D. L. DAVIES

The early nineteenth century witnessed a revolutionary religious transformation of Wales.[1] It has been estimated that whereas circa 1811 Nonconformists accounted for between 15 and 20 percent of the Welsh people, by 1851 the proportions of Nonconformists to Anglicans had been almost exactly reversed.[2] In some districts—particularly the iron and coal communities of Glamorgan and Monmouthshire—the preponderance was far greater. In the Merthyr Tydfil district (then inclusive of the booming Aberdare Valley), the religious census taken Sunday, March 30, 1851, showed that of the 30,168 who attended Protestant services that evening only 6 percent adhered to the state church while an amazing 94 percent dissented from it in one form or another. Of these dissenters, an imposing 39 percent adhered to chapels of the Baptist persuasion. The impression exists that some Baptists came to see the Merthyr-Aberdare nexus as rather a fiefdom of theirs. Such an outlook was probably a factor in shap-

---

[1] The phrase "A *Seion* of Lands" appearing in the title of this essay alludes to the poem *Caru Cymru* (Loving Wales) by the Rev. Crwys Williams (1875–1968). After praising the beauty, language, and humble people of his homeland, Crwys lauds it for its two-thousand-year-old Christian heritage: "The home of the Gospel, a *Seion* of lands is she." The poem and most of the sources for this paper are set in the Welsh language. This is an ancient Celtic tongue, the last of its type in Europe to command widespread modern usage; it was the indigenous language of Britain before the Anglo-Saxon invasions introduced English. All translations from Welsh are my own. *Seion* (Zion) is pronounced "Sigh-on," with penultimate stress, as in most Welsh words. The pronunciation of the Welsh terms most widely used in this paper are: *Udgorn Seion* (It-gorrn Sigh-on); *Dewi Elfed* (Deh-wee El-ved); and *Gwawr* (Goo-ah-oor: this is monosyllabic). *Udgorn Seion* (The Trumpet of Zion) was the major periodical of the early Mormon Mission to Wales and appeared from 1849 until 1862.

[2] G. A. Williams, *When Was Wales?* (London, 1985), 158–59.

ing the attitude of Baptist leaders like William Robert Davies[3] (minister of Caersalem Chapel, Dowlais) and Thomas Price[4] (minister of Carmel Chapel, Aberdare) toward what must have seemed a novel and intrusive faith being preached in their midst by Latter-day Saints. By 1851 nonconformity had become almost a national religion of Wales, and the Nonconformist chapel was the center of life for most Welsh people. Professor Gwyn A. Williams has written that "Everything outside [the chapels] came to seem only half-Welsh, [the Nonconformists] were the *real* Welsh . . . they came to feel that they, as a Nonconformist people, *were* the Welsh nation."[5]

Early Latter-day Saint missionaries to Wales sought to challenge the supremacy of those denominations that had come to represent not just popular religion but also a powerful political Liberalism and even the nation itself. In the wider Merthyr district, Mormon proselytizing begun by William Henshaw in 1843 and by Captain Dan Jones in 1845 was successful enough that on Census Sunday in 1851 Mormon attendance at afternoon meetings was 1,190 — only 647 fewer than the maximum attendance claimed by the state church on the evening of the same Sunday. A key factor in the growth of Mormonism at Aberdare was the conversion on November 2, 1847, of William Howells, who had been a lay preacher attached to the Baptist congregation of Thomas Price at Carmel Chapel, Aberdare.[6] Through the labor of Howells and others, Aberdare came to

---

[3] I. G. Jones and D. Williams, eds., *The Religious Census of 1851: A Calendar of the Returns Relating to Wales* (Cardiff, 1976), 1: 682; "Captain Dan Jones vs. the Revd. W. R. Davies," unpublished essay by Ronald D. Dennis, Brigham Young University (Provo, Utah, 1986).

[4] The role of Thomas Price (1820–88) in expanding the Baptist denomination at Aberdare is briefly mentioned in the text below. It has been said his "leadership in a well-organized cohesive denomination . . . provided the basis for an equal authority within the body of Nonconformity as a whole in Aberdare, and, to a lesser extent, in the constituency [of Merthyr] in general." I. G. Jones, *Communities: Essays in the Social History of Victorian Wales* (Llandysul, 1987), 270–72. Apart from being a dominant clerical figure, Price was active on the district board of health; school board; as a guardian of the poor; in the temperance movement; as a patron of workers' Friendly Societies; as a local newspaper editor; as a Liberal politician; and as a powerful arbitrator in industrial disputes. Benjamin Evans, *Cofiant Dr Price, Aberdar* (Aberdare, 1891), 61–64; Jones, *Communities*, 263–321; see also *Y Bedyddiwr* (October 1848), 388; (February 1849), 64–65; (May 1850), 129, 159.

Price and W. R. Davies, both archenemies of Mormonism, were in close touch with each other until the latter's death in 1849. Evans, *Cofiant Dr Price*, 31–36.

[5] Williams, *When Was Wales?*, 205–6.

[6] T. H. Lewis, *Y Mormoniaid Yng Nghymru* (Cardiff, 1956), 10–21; see also R. D. Dennis, "The Welsh and the Gospel," in V. Ben Bloxham, James R. Moss, and Larry T. Porter, eds., *Truth Will Prevail* (Solihull, England: The Church of Jesus Christ of Latter-day Saints, 1987), 236–67; I. G. Jones and D. Williams, eds., *The Religious Census of 1851*, 1: 163–90, 682; R. D. Dennis, "William Howells: First

rival Llanelli as the Mormons' second centre in Wales, after Merthyr Tydfil itself.

In 1851 Aberdare was the scene of perhaps the most dramatic of many confrontations between Mormonism and nonconformity in nineteenth-century Wales. The antagonists were Thomas Price, Baptist minister of Carmel Chapel, and David Bevan Jones, ex-Baptist minister of Gwawr Chapel, in nearby Aberaman.

David Bevan Jones, or "Dewi Elfed" according to the poetic nom de plume he adopted and by which he came to be widely known, was born in 1807 in the parish of Llandysul, Cardiganshire. He was christened on June 30, 1807, by the vicar of Llandysul, the Rev. H. Bowen, in the local parish church.[7] His christening into the state church in 1807 suggests that his parents, like most Welsh people until that time, retained at least a token allegiance to that church. Yet, as with the majority of the Welsh nation, it is likely they felt increasingly drawn toward one or another of the Nonconformist denominations. The period 1800 to 1830 was one of considerable growth in the following these churches commanded; and their expansion was further fueled by the final secession from the Church of England in 1811 of the powerful Methodist tendency in Wales. Yet at the time of his birth Dewi Elfed's family appear to have remained nominally Anglican. It would seem that this did not long remain the case, for Dewi himself indicated in a statement made years later that he entered the Baptist faith at the age of fifteen or so, in about 1822.[8]

Dewi Elfed was baptized into the congregation of Pen-y-bont, established in 1774–76. In 1833 a division occurred within the congregation which led to the establishment of a separate cause at Ebeneser. From the evidence of a Pen-y-bont register book which the minister and dissentients took with them to their new home it appears that Dewi Elfed's family were among those who made the move to Ebeneser.[9] Dewi Elfed had married

Missionary to France," in Donald Q. Cannon and David J. Whittaker, eds., *Supporting Saints: Life Stories of 19th Century Mormons* (Provo, Utah: Brigham Young University, 1985), 43–81; Thomas Price, *Jubili Eglwys Calfaria, Aberdar . . . Hyd Y Flwyddyn 1862* (Aberdare, 1863), 16.

[7] The year of his birth is suggested by details in the 1851 Census at Aberdare (H.O. 107.2460) and is confirmed by an entry in the bishop's transcripts of christenings in Llandysul parish for the period Easter 1807 to Easter 1808 (National Library of Wales, Church in Wales Records, SD/BT). See also W. J. Davies, *Hanes Plwyf Llandysul* (Llandysul, 1896), 67.

[8] Gareth Elwyn Jones, *Modern Wales* (Cambridge, 1984), 273, 276–77; *Udgorn Seion* (29 October 1853), 286.

[9] *Llawlyfr* (Handbook) of the Baptist Union of Wales for 1917, p. 83, and 1987, p. 34; also correspondence between Mr. J. Tyssul Jones, secretary of Penybont Chapel, and the writer, 22 July 1983; and Davies, *Hanes Plwyf Llandysul*, 66–67; National Library of Wales (NLW) Minor Deposit 1099A.

by 1833, and at the time of the 1851 census he and his wife, Anna, lived in the Abergwawr neighbourhood of Aberdare with five children.[10]

Dewi Elfed was active in a literary direction as an aspiring lyricist and as a competent litterateur serving denominational ends in the Baptist journal *Seren Gomer* from 1841 on. In the bibliography of his home county for the years 1600–1964, three early "secular" writings by Dewi Elfed are mentioned: (1) *Eos Dyssul* (Rhan 1), a twenty-four-page booklet containing "a little of the poetical work of David Jones, Llandysul, (Dewi Elfed)," printed by William Jones at Newcastle Emlyn in 1838; (2) *Can Newydd yn dangos Niweidiau Meddwdod ynghyd a'r budd a'r Lles sydd o lwyrymwrthod a hwynt*, a song in favour of teetotalism and against the evils of alcohol, printed by W. Jones at Newcastle Emlyn; and (3) *Serch Gerdd a gyfansoddwyd ar daer Ddmuniad y sawl y perthynai iddynt ac yn neillduawl y Claf o gariad*, a lengthy ballad to a lovelorn girl.[11] I have been able to locate a copy only of this last item on the list—the song to a lovelorn girl.[12]

At the time Dewi Elfed's son Aneurin was born in 1837 the family resided in Llandysul. It is not known by what means Dewi made a living at this stage in his life, but by June 1841 he had become an ordained Baptist minister. There is no evidence that he took formal ministerial training at a denominational college. The more likely course by which he entered the full-time ministry was by serving an apprenticeship as an accredited lay preacher for some years. This would mean his being sponsored by his home congregation and journeying around the Baptist chapels of the district on as wide a basis as possible in order to make his mark. Having achieved this he might receive a *galwad* (a call) from a particular congregation to minister to them; but recognition of his propriety so to serve would also be required of the relevant district authority within the denomination. This was usually the county association.

There is every indication that this is what occurred in Dewi Elfed's case, for it is said directly that he was "reared to be a preacher" by the congregation meeting at Ebeneser, Llandysul.[13] His first pastoral charge

---

[10] 1851 Census, parish of Aberdare, Glamorgan, enumeration dist. 2(i), no. 113.

[11] See *Seren Gomer*, December 1847, April 1848, and January 1849 for examples; also Lewis, *Y Mormoniaid*, 104–5; Glyn Lewis Jones, *Llyfryddiaeth Ceredigion, 1600–1964* (Aberystwyth, 1967), 2: 548. At this point the bibliography is based upon an essay by John Davies (1860–1939), entitled *Llenorion a Llenyddiaeth Ceredigion*, being NLW MS.8705.

[12] There is an original copy in the pamphlet collection of St. David's University College Library, Lampeter, and a 1905 reprint in the Goodwin Collection of 19th Century Welsh verse at the Library of the University College of North Wales, Bangor.

[13] Davies, *Hanes Plwyf Llandysul*, 67; also Edward Thomas, *Canmlwyddiant Eglwys*

was at Seion Baptist Church, Cwrtnewydd, in the parish of Llanwenog, Cardiganshire. This chapel stood only seven or eight miles from Llandysul and had been constituted in 1829. Unfortunately, the records of the chapel do not commence until 1869, so no detailed account of his period there survives today. Yet it is known he was inducted as minister at Cwrtnewydd on June 17–18, 1841.[14]

Even at this early stage Dewi Elfed was prone to attract a controversial response as the following passage, written in reply to one of his articles, illustrated: "What is this constant backbiting and throwing of vitriol when no-one was doing anything at all to provoke him. . . . To tell the truth, we see Dewi as rather too small (not only of body but also of spirit) to bother to engage him in battle. The truth is that he has nurtured some immeasurable ideas about himself."[15]

Since no representation of Dewi is likely to have survived it is interesting to note the implication here that he was short of stature. It must be admitted that, whilst religious acrimony was frequently directed by Nonconformists and Anglicans at each other, and by both at Roman Catholicism, it is very unusual for one Baptist writer to publicly refer to another of his denomination — and he an ordained minister — in terms such as the above.

Dewi remained at Cwrtnewydd until the autumn of 1846, when the Baptist journal *Seren Gomer* for November records the transference of "the Revd D. B. Jones (Dewi Elfed)" to take charge of the Baptist church "gathered at Jerusalem (chapel), Rumni."[16] This new pastorate was in the northwest corner of industrial Monmouthshire, in one of the iron and coal towns of south Wales, close to Merthyr Tydfil, and a very different environment to rural south Cardiganshire. His stay at Rhymney was short-lived and not without trial. It is only fair to note that none of the relevant commentaries suggest Dewi Elfed was in any way reponsible for the difficulties which he and the congregation soon faced.

During 1847 the local economy was in a depressed state, "on account of which many were in low circumstances and the church was unable not only to pay any of the debt, but even to pay any of the interest." Toward the end of 1847 the mortgager of the chapel premises, who was owed nearly £1,000, became restive. Dewi Elfed as minister advised the congre-

---

Gwawr, Aberaman (Aberdare, 1948), who says: "He was raised to preach at Ebeneser, Llandysul, *in 1835* [my emphasis]," 9.

[14] D. Cledlyn Davies, *Hanes Plwyf Llanwenog* (Aberystwyth, 1939), 46 (see also p. 54 for mention of Mormonism locally); and correspondence between the church secretary, Mr. Walter Harries, and the writer, July 1983; *Seren Gomer* (August 1841).

[15] *Seren Gomer* (January 1842), 44.

[16] Ibid. (November 1846), 360.

gation there was no choice but to surrender the chapel to the mortgager, who would seek to recoup his money by an auction of the premises. Events dragged on until November 1848 when a special conference of ministers in the Monmouthshire Baptist Association reluctantly agreed to surrender the building. Dewi apparently resigned his pastorate voluntarily and left Rhymney sometime around the fall of 1848. He arrived at his next pastoral charge at Gwawr, Aberaman, near Aberdare, in late 1848 or early 1849, and was formally recognized as the minister of that cause in June 1849. Yet there were already suggestions of his holding unorthodox views in the direction of Unitarianism.[17]

The Welsh word *Gwawr* means "dawn," and Gwawr Chapel was one of sixteen churches renewed or founded in the Aberdare district between 1845 and 1865 in direct or indirect association with Thomas Price.[18] In the case of Gwawr the association was direct. Since 1846 Baptists at Aberaman had held services in private homes and at the King William Inn. In 1848, Price and his colleagues began negotiations to lease land and build a new chapel at Aberaman with a view to work starting in early 1849. Almost at once, however, the Aberaman Baptists requested that the new church at Gwawr be constituted separately and independently of the mother church at Carmel, Aberdare, whereas the usual practice was to sustain a close and formal relationship between two congregations for some years after one had been established out of the other. The request was acceded to, and the church at Gwawr was formally incorporated on June 14, 1848, with 121 members comprising an independent congregation. Dewi Elfed arrived somewhat later, between early autumn 1848 and the spring of 1849, and was acknowledged as minister of Gwawr in June 1849. At a later date, Thomas Price claimed this separation occurred in 1849 and, by inference, that Dewi Elfed was behind it. This view is incompatible with sources which record Price's participation in the separation service of 1848.[19]

Once Dewi Elfed was settled at Aberaman, the task of completing the construction of Gwawr Chapel was taken out of the hands of the church at Carmel. To ensure this, the names of Thomas Price and John Davies were

---

[17] J. S. Jones, *Hanes Rhymni a Phontlottyn* (Denbigh, 1904), 78–79, 132–33; also "A History of Monmouthshire Baptists," being NLW.1218B, Box 12 (part of the Monmouthshire Baptist Association deposit); *Llythyr* (Letter) of the Glamorgan Baptist Association, June 1849; Abel Edmunds, *Crybwyllion am Ddechreuad y Bedyddwyr ym Mlaen Cwm Rumni* (Aberdare, 1862), 27; also "A History of the Monmouthshire Baptists."

[18] See note 4 above.

[19] Thomas, *Canmlwyddiant Eglwys Gwawr*, 8–9; *Seren Gomer* (August 1848); *Y Bedyddiwr* (The Baptist) (July 1848), 263–65; also Glamorgan Baptist Association *Llythyr*, June 1848, June 1849; Thomas Price, *Jubili Eglwys Calfaria . . . Hyd 1862* (Aberdare, 1863), 28; and *Y Bedyddiwr* (July 1848), 265.

removed from the lease and those of Dewi Elfed and one David Richards were inserted in their place. Price and other Baptist writers have always maintained this step was one of willful deceit.[20] Yet there are grounds for other views, including a presumption on the part of Dewi Elfed that as minister of Gwawr direct amendment of its deeds was within his compass; and also that the ground landlord was publicly reported as having raised no objection to similar amendments when these were openly put to him.[21]

Trouble began brewing between Dewi and his Baptist ministerial colleagues by the beginning of 1850. Dewi said that some of them had tried to obstruct the completion of Gwawr Chapel despite his efforts at raising sufficient money for the job. He claimed to have raised the then considerable sum of £340 toward offsetting construction costs in less than eight months by preaching throughout Glamorgan and Monmouthshire. Yet, acccording to Dewi, such endeavours counted for little with "the reverends" because they objected to his doctrine.[22] The most contentious issue in the disagreement seems to have been that of "The Laying On of Hands." Essentially, the issue turned on whether the rite whereby an ordained priest or minister blessed those of lower rank by the laying of hands did so in order to symbolically invest the recipient or whether the act was spiritually significant in itself. The laying on of hands was very widely practiced in the Baptist churches of Wales in the early nineteenth century. However, while some Baptists saw the practice as a symbolic but valid action confirming the views of the gathered church, others increasingly saw it as subversive of sound Protestant church polity. A major cause of the disrepute into which the practice fell—especially in Glamorgan—is said to have been its espousal by the Mormons.[23]

Dewi Elfed contended that the Baptist clergy of his district were outraged not just at his teaching—particularly concerning the laying on of hands—but by the demand for it among their own congregations as well as his. Matters came to a head on November 5, 1850, when Dewi was invited by the quarterly conference of the Glamorgan Baptist Association to attend a meeting at Aberdare the following night to discuss the orthodoxy of his doctrine and practice at Gwawr Chapel and elsewhere.[24] In his written response Dewi denied that there was anything out of order in the affairs of his congregation at Gwawr and implied that the conference had no right to

---

[20] Price, *Jubili Eglwys Calfaria*, 28–29; Benjamin Evans, *Cofiant Dr Price*, 109, and Thomas, *Canmlwyddiant Eglwys Gwawr*, 9.

[21] *Millennial Star* 13 (1 April 1851): 110.

[22] *Udgorn Seion* (29 October 1853), 286.

[23] Professor John Griffiths, sometime principal of the Cardiff Baptist College, in *Cyfrol Goffa Cymanfa Bedyddwyr Neilltuol Morgannwg* (Carmarthen, 1933), 25–28; Rev. W. R. Jones, ibid., 70–71.

[24] *Udgorn Seion* (29 October 1853), 277–87.

involve itself in those affairs unless invited by him. A final dig was some unsolicited advice to the other ministers that they improve their current condition by casting out their old leaven "that you may be as new dough."

At the conference numerous charges of unorthodox conduct were levelled at Dewi. He later listed these from memory.[25] They were that he had

1. Denied the Bible

2. Contravened the five principles laid down in the Letter issued by the Association to member churches, and said that the Letter should be burned[26]

3. Baptized for the forgiveness of sins

4. Stressed the importance of the laying on of hands

5. Preached that the Holy Spirit cannot be received without baptism

6. Declared that by baptism one is reborn in water

7. Preached on topics of too great a complexity, and instructed others in them during secret sessions

8. Taught millenarianism and the restoration of all things to their primitive form

9. Preached the personal rule of Christ on earth

10. Called himself an apostle

11. Judged wrongfully the sermons of other ministers

12. Tended in his own sermons toward an espousal of Mormon doctrine and encouraged Baptist churches in that direction

13. Denied that three Persons in the Godhead can ever be one Person

14. Taught that the Holy Spirit is received by the laying on of hands

15. Preached that where God's Spirit is present miracles can be performed by those upon whom it has descended

16. Asserted that the New Testament alone is insufficient to redeem a man to eternal life

17. Maintained that God extends blessings and revelations of a divine nature at the present time as in previous days

---

[25] Ibid., 283.

[26] Neither the five principles nor the association letter concerned is identified in the original.

18. Preached that profiteering for self-gain was the object of ministers, and that they were utterly devoid of God's Spirit and power.[27]

Dewi said that the presentation of charges was followed by acrimonious outbursts aimed at him and those officers of his church who had accompanied him to the hearing.[28] They were denied an opportunity to speak in defense of the charges levelled. He recounted how "the Reverend from Aberdare," Thomas Price, had told him he would rather be under the Devil's nails than under Dewi's. Yet Dewi Elfed was not amiss himself to throwing a few verbal bombs among the assembled ministers. He told them they were "pot-bellied and pompous Reverends," which was hardly calculated to have a calming effect. It must be remembered this is Dewi's account alone, and he was obviously bitter at the affair although writing of it three years on in October 1853.

No account survives to document the accuracy of the charges against Dewi Elfed, but the accusation of leanings toward Mormonism, and of attempting to influence other Baptist congregations in the direction of Mormonism, foreshadowed later developments. It is not known precisely how Dewi Elfed first came into contact with Latter-day Saint teachings, nor can it be ascertained whether Mormonism led to changes in Dewi Elfed's Baptist ministry or simply corresponded with and confirmed beliefs he already held. At any rate, in March 1851, after the expulsion of Dewi

---

[27] Baptists in the Welsh county associations have never adopted a creed more detailed than direct personal avowal of Jesus Christ as their redeemer uniquely revealed in the New Testament. While there is scope for individual emphasis in such a situation, it has been taken further in at least two specific regards: a trinitarian theology and a requirement of the symbolic baptism of confessing adult believers. Doctrinal conformity in these basic tenets would be essential for full membership of all but a tiny minority of Welsh Baptist churches and certainly of those with which Dewi Elfed had hitherto been associated in Glamorgan.

The question of ultimate church authority is open to some interpretation. The origin of the earliest Baptist churches in Wales was "congregational" in that they established themselves as communities of like-minded believers; but from the start they were sustained, ordered, and disciplined by each other in associations which later developed into the county associations of which the Glamorgan body of 1850 was one. Historically, therefore, the authority of the county association in disciplinary matters was paramount; but it was customary for congregations to exercise considerable local autonomy in practice. An important elucidation (in Welsh) by M. J. Williams may be found in the *Trafodion* (Transactions) of the Welsh Baptist History Society, 1986, p. 24.

[28] These are named as David Richards (whom Price said was Dewi's accomplice in altering the lease to Gwawr Chapel), Josuah Evans, and John Johns. Also named as a sympathizer in Dewi's account was the David Rees alongside whom Dewi was subsequently baptized into the Mormon faith. In all, five were baptized on that occasion, and it is possible the three not named were the officers of Gwawr who accompanied Dewi to this hearing.

Elfed and his congregation from the Glamorgan Baptist Association four months previously,[29] he took the initiative to contact William Phillips, then president of the Mormons' mission in Wales. Phillips's report of their meeting, published soon afterwards in the *Millennial Star*, indicated that Jones was about to defect to the Latter-day Saints, that he appeared to have about fifty or sixty members of the congregation with him in that intent, and that the landlord was seemingly compliant toward a change of use in the Mormon interest concerning the lease by which the chapel was held.[30]

Despite this development, when the Religious Census of 1851 was taken, on March 30, Dewi Elfed defined the Gwawr Chapel as one serving the Baptist cause.[31] The return indicates a substantial drop in attendance that Sunday morning as compared to Dewi's estimate of average attendance during the previous twelve months, from 250 attendees and 40 scholars to 100 attendees and 30 scholars. There is also a less marked drop in the number of "scholars" in afternoon attendance, from 80 to 60. At evening services there appears to have been no diminution at all, although the constant figure of 450 is suspiciously "round"—as are so many other statistics in this census. It may be that in general terms such a throng continued to frequent Gwawr during this tense interim period in its history and that of its pastor. As to their motives, let alone their sympathies, that is another question.

During this period there was preliminary skirmishing between Dewi Elfed and Thomas Price. Dewi locked the doors of Gwawr on Sunday, April 20. Thomas Price accused him in an intemperate letter to the newspaper *Yr Amserau* (The Times) of having done this surreptitiously against Dewi's allegedly few remaining followers; Dewi retorted that the step was necessary only because Price and a ministerial colleague, John Daniel Williams of Cwmbach, "in conjunction with their brothers," had earlier broken the lock of the chapel door without authority to do so.[32] Dewi intimated in the same response that he had already denounced Price and his colleagues either generally or by name from the pulpit of Gwawr as caring "more for the wool than for the life of the flock."

The following Wednesday evening Dewi reopened the chapel for a Latter-day Saint meeting conducted by William Phillips. During this meeting Dewi and David Rees, probably a recognized lay preacher within the congregation at Gwawr, and a few others announced their intention to be baptized on the following Sunday.[33]

[29] *Y Bedyddiwr* (December 1850), 373.
[30] *Millennial Star* 13 (1 April 1851): 110.
[31] Jones and Williams, eds., *Religious Census*, 187.
[32] *Yr Amserau* (28 May 1851); *Udgorn Seion* (14 June 1851), 186.
[33] *Udgorn Seion* (14 June 1851), 184; *Millennial Star* 13 (1 June 1851): 172.

On Sunday, April 27, 1851, in a crossing of the theological Rubicon, Dewi Elfed finally broke with the Baptist cause. At age forty-three, within sight of Gwawr Chapel and where he had previously baptized others into the Baptist faith, David Bevan Jones underwent baptism as a Latter-day Saint. It was a step that was to change his world quite literally.

William Phillips reported that a crowd of about 2,000 were present at the baptism, of whom "there were a great many ready to raise a riot, but most of them were on my side." In a brief service at the riverside, Rees, Jones, and Phillips all preached. In addition to Rees and Jones, three other members of Jones's congregation were baptized. At two o'clock that afternoon the Latter-day Saints held a service at Gwawr Chapel at which Phillips took the minister's chair and confirmed the five newly baptized converts. Dewi Elfed and David Rees were then ordained priests in the Church of Jesus Christ of Latter-day Saints, after which Phillips addressed them on the duties and responsibilities of that priesthood. According to a Latter-day Saint report, the chapel was packed for the occasion. Phillips addressed the meeting in Welsh and the Mormon printer John Davis in English.[34]

Another service followed that evening. Phillips was pleased that the chapel was again "very full of people" and that "a great many believed." He confided to Franklin Richards that "I expect many will be baptized in that neighbourhood this week." It was a triumphant occasion for the Mormons. Yet it may be thought surprising that only five were baptized that day whereas Phillips had first foreseen "about 50 or 60" entering the Mormon faith at the same time as Dewi Elfed.

The *Amserau* newspaper, based at Denbigh in north Wales, carried a short report of the baptisms in which it referred to "the minister and congregation" of a Baptist chapel at Aberdare regrettably going over to the Saints, and to "the baptism of them all in the river Cynon." A propaganda war followed, in which Thomas Price attacked Dewi Elfed and his followers and sought to kill any impression of a mass defection.[35] On the other side, Dewi probably overstated his support. Price gave a more balanced account twelve years later, when he wrote that Dewi Elfed

> was supported by some Baptists, and in being abetted by a few mistaken families, he was able to . . . plant poisonous weeds that have left their effect upon Aberaman to the present day . . . he deceived some of the members into accompanying him. So, the church at Aberaman was entirely destroyed, and none were rescued from this badness except a few who returned to us. . . . [Dewi Elfed was] a wolf in sheep's clothing, being helped by a few Baptist families, some of these being old members, old enough to know better . . . we

---

[34] *Millennial Star* 13 (1 June 1851): 172–73, and *Udgorn Seion* (3 May 1851), 141–43.

[35] *Yr Amserau* (14 May 1851), (28 May 1851).

had every obstruction from the few Baptists who had a hand in the matter . . . indeed the effects have not entirely passed even today.[36]

Dewi would have regarded this as an unintended compliment. Especially interesting is Price's contradiction in 1863 of his statement in 1851 that most Gwawr members had returned to other Baptist churches rather than associate with Dewi Elfed. Price's allusions to a continued Mormon influence at Aberaman are most intriguing; but without baptismal or other records from the Aberaman and Aberdare branches of the Mormon Church one must discern what one can of this influence via the columns of *Udgorn Seion* and occasionally elsewhere. Evidence for it chiefly concerns reports in the *Udgorn* of disseminating mission literature in the district; religious verse by local members in the journal; occasional reports of religious works (as when the leg of a young boy named William Phillips was miraculously healed once annointed with oil); and references to Dewi Elfed and David Rees in particular travelling through Glamorgan and Monmouthshire on preaching tours to promulgate their new faith.[37]

For a brief period Thomas Price and Dewi Elfed exchanged acrimonious charges and countercharges, Price in *Yr Amserau* and Dewi in *Udgorn Seion*. Finally, Price probably realized he had more to lose, and Dewi more to gain, by feeding the issue between them with publicity. Despite repeated challenges from Dewi, Price did not respond in the public press after the end of May 1851, although he continued to denounce Dewi long afterwards in Baptist sources.[38]

The Latter-day Saints busily used Dewi Elfed's ability with words and his standing as a converted Nonconformist minister in furtherance of their mission.[39] Within a fortnight of the publication in *Udgorn Seion* of the

---

[36] Price, *Jubili Eglwys Calfaria*, 29–30.

[37] See *Udgorn Seion* (14 June 1851), 195; (27 December 1851), 416; (29 January 1853), 81; (5 February 1853), 100; (2 April 1853), 228; for an account of the healing of the young boy see *Udgorn Seion* (31 May 1851), 169–70. For details of Mormon meeting places in the area in 1857 see Orson Pratt, *Angenrheidrwydd Am Wyrthiau* (The Necessity of Miracles), translated by Dewi Elfed and published at Swansea that year.

[38] *Udgorn Seion* (14 June 1851), 184–86 and *Yr Amserau* (18 June 1851). E.g., in his retrospective *Jubili* of 1863; in *Seren Cymru* (Star of Wales), (4 January 1867); and in remarks to his biographer, Benjamin Evans, printed in the latter's *Cofiant* of 1891.

[39] Although Latter-day Saint membership in Wales reached a declared peak of 5,244 in December 1851, only two ordained Nonconformist ministers seem ever to have been among the converts. Dewi Elfed was one. The other, also at first a Baptist minister, was John Parry (1789–1868), initial conductor of what became the Mormon Tabernacle Choir. Converts from amongst accredited lay preachers (such as William Howells at Aberdare and David Rees at Aberaman) were more usual. Converts came from all the Nonconformist denominations in Wales, but especially

report on his baptism the first of Dewi's many hymns and prose translations to figure in that journal appeared there. It was a song about escaping Babylon in pursuit of the Saints' Zion.[40] Indications of Dewi's contribution to the missionary effort by way of itinerant preaching engagements also rapidly appeared in the *Udgorn*. Among these are comments in an imaginary dialogue of exhortive intent that he, as a Mormon protagonist, spent much of his time and energy preaching "hither and thither across the countryside, in persecution and disrespect from place to place; frequently in suffering and in need."[41]

A particular example of field missionary work by Dewi Elfed and David Rees (previously colleagues at Gwawr) relates to neighbouring Monmouthshire. A local correspondent, Thomas Giles wrote to *Udgorn Seion* from Tredegar June 6, 1851, of the Saints' success in that area in opening new places of worship. Three halls had recently been opened, one of them at the Belle Vue Inn between Victoria and Ebbw Vale. Here, Dewi Elfed and David Rees bore witness to hundreds of people. The hall was so full in the morning that many could not gain entry. In the afternoon the crowd was so large it was decided to preach from the window to satisfy a tumult both inside and outside which Giles claimed numbered between 1,000 and 1,500 people. In the evening the crowd was said to be even bigger; and Giles recounted how the testimony of Dewi Elfed and his companion "caused an agitation among the people."[42]

Giles anticipated the opening of another three premises in the near future, and expressed on behalf of the Saints and (it is said) "several Baptists" the hope that Dewi Elfed in particular would be present to address them at one of these occasions on June 15. There must have been many other such visits of which no record survives, for it can be assumed that every effort would have been made to maximize the impact of converting to Mormonism a minister of the denomination most fiercely opposed to the Saints.

Although Dewi Elfed had been baptized in April 1851, the battle for final possession of Gwawr was not yet resolved. The issue of legal title to the chapel was to be settled in court. Regrettably, none of the case papers and no newspaper reports of the proceedings seem to have survived. This is surprising since the wrangle over Gwawr had already attracted public

---

from among the Baptists. This would appear to have caused a special acrimony between the two faiths. One likely cause of the Baptists' particular vulnerability and ire was Mormon espousal of what they saw as their own hallmark: the adult baptism of confessing believers.

[40] *Udgorn Seion* (17 May 1851), 162–63.
[41] Ibid. (2 July 1853), 17.
[42] Ibid. (14 June 1851), 195.

attention; and the eventual triumph of the Baptist interest was to be recounted proudly for the next 100 years in Baptist circles as the justified comeuppance of the Mormons. Edward Thomas in his centennial history of Gwawr[43] gives the most detailed information about the proceedings at the Glamorgan summer assizes which convened at Cardiff on July 12, 1851.[44] The court gave judgement for repossession of Gwawr Chapel to the Baptists, and the property was conveyed by the court from the custody of the sheriff of Glamorgan to the care of Llewelyn Howells, farmer, who had attended court on behalf of the Baptist remnant at Gwawr.[45] Shortly thereafter, Howells issued an assignment of the chapel to Thomas Price and a group of sixteen trustees handpicked by the Baptists to secure future title to the premises against repetition of past events. According to Benjamin Evans, biographer of Thomas Price, Dewi Elfed's lawyer tried unsuccessfully to have Price pay his own costs despite an award that Dewi should meet them.

It remained for Thomas Price and the Baptists to take physical repossession of Gwawr Chapel, which did not occur until November 4. According to Price and his biographer, a crowd of about 2,000 set out behind Price, accompanied by the sheriff of the county of Glamorgan. When the marchers reached the site they found that Dewi Elfed and an unnamed supporter had entered the building, bolted the door, and fastened down all windows so that access was impossible without breaking an entrance. The sheriff gave Price to understand that he had no authority to break an entry into a place of worship. For a moment no one knew what to do next. The crowd began to get restive and voices were raised at those inside the chapel. At this, Price strode forward, "wild in appearance, walking quickly and looking purposefully, with his every gesture declaring that Gwawr was shortly to be a chapel for the Baptists and not the Saints." After trying the bolted door to no effect, he obtained the assistance of David Grier, a mason who had with him the tools of his trade, and Philip John, one of Price's deacons at Carmel. A window was forced open and Price was helped in by the mason and the deacon, both of whom followed him into the building. It is said that Price chased Dewi Elfed and his companion about the chapel, finally coming to grips with them in the chapel lobby.

---

[43] Baptist Union of Wales Assembly *Llawlyfrau* for 1915, 1947, and 1964; Thomas, *Canmlwyddiant Eglwys Gwawr*, 10.

[44] *Cardiff & Merthyr Guardian*, 5 July 1851, announces the forthcoming assizes; the issues of 19 July and 26 July report on the court's deliberations, but nowhere is there mention of the Gwawr case. Likewise *Seren Cymru*, 13 August, and *The Cambrian*, 18 July, make no reference to the Gwawr case in their retrospective reports.

[45] *Trafodion* of the Welsh Baptist History Society, 1983, pp. 25–29; his obituary appears in *Y Bedyddiwr* (April 1857), 120.

There, single-handed, Price is said to have grasped the two "with the grip of a giant," and, after the main door was opened, "literally booted both rascals one after the other out of the chapel until they descended distantly amidst the congratulations of the large crowd." Price proclaimed the incident "a pretty good example of the casting out of devils in the 19th century." Later that day the chapel was placed securely in trust for the Baptists once more. The next Sunday, November 9, Gwawr was reopened to the Baptists in a service under the auspices of the churches at Aberdare and Cwmbach. Thereafter, the meeting was placed under the guidance of Price's most trusted lieutenant, J. D. Williams of Cwmbach. By then the county Baptist association had decided that the Baptists at Aberaman were to become members of the Cwmbach church while having the facility to meet for worship in their own locality.[46]

Dewi's parting shot at his Baptist adversaries was to have published in *Udgorn Seion* a lengthy poem lampooning his favorite target — the Nonconformist "reverends." He worked this song into an assertion of Mormon truth, and sent it to the editor of the *Udgorn* signed, "Dewi Elfed, Capel Gwawr, Aberaman."[47]

In the same issue of the journal he also had printed a single *englyn* (stanza) which contains an oblique reference to events on the November 4. This verse had one purpose: to reassure Dewi's audience among the Saints, who cannot but have heard of how things had gone for him at Gwawr, that despite the triumph of his opponents he and his colleague had escaped in good spirits. The verse read:

> Despite a coup by evil — through coarse war
>   in a cursed quarrel;
> In freedom flies each angel,
> They're of good cheer — "All is Well."

It was a spirited gesture of defiance, the more so for invoking William Clayton's classic Mormon pioneer hymn; but by the time it had appeared in print Dewi Elfed had literally been turned out onto the road.

Dewi himself remained at Aberaman only until January 1853, fourteen months after his ejection from Gwawr. In the meantime, he wrote fifty-seven of the 575 hymns — all in Welsh — that appeared in a Latter-day Saint hymnal published by John Davis in November 1852.[48] Collectively, these hymns display Dewi's zeal and energy in propagating his new faith,

---

[46] Price, *Jubili Eglwys*, 30, and Evans, *Cofiant Dr Price*, 110–12. *Seren Cymru* (22 January 1852), also formally notes the resolution of the case. *Y Bedyddiwr* (December 1851), 369–79.

[47] *Udgorn Seion* (15 November 1851), 369–72.

[48] *Casgliad o Hymnau, Caniadau ac Odlau Ysbrydol at Wasanaeth Saint y Dyddiau Diweddaf yn Nghymru* (Merthyr Tydfil, 1852).

though it must be noted their themes and images are not so different from what one would expect of any Nonconformist hymnist of the day in Wales. A half dozen specifically Mormon espousals were exceptions to this. One of the hymns (no. 462) was a paean for his conversion.

Until the autumn of 1852 Dewi does not seem to have held any specific post of responsibility among the Saints, although he was certainly busy as an itinerant missionary. Then in October 1852 the Welsh Mission held a representative conference at Merthyr at which it was resolved to publish the fortnightly *Udgorn* as a weekly with effect from January 1853. Also agreed was that Dewi Elfed should acquire a knowledge of accountancy, maintain the financial records of the mission, and make them available to its component parts.[49]

Following this, Dewi seems to have moved rapidly to a wider role. At a meeting of the general council of the Welsh Mission at Merthyr on January 3, 1853, it was decided that Dewi Elfed be appointed the new president of the Llanelli Conference, succeeding Abednego Jones, who would be emigrating to Zion. Dewi's son, Aneurin L. Jones, was appointed conference secretary. Upon taking up this post Dewi established an address in the town of Llanelli, care of Mr. John Lewis, Saddler, Thomas Street.[50]

A British Mission membership report for December 31, 1852 indicated that the Welsh Mission had 4,872 baptized adherents, distributed between fourteen area conferences. The Llanelli Conference had 398, making it the fourth largest in Wales. Six months later the effect of continuous emigration and of a gradual slackening in the pace of conversions throughout Britain begins to be discernible. Wales reported 4,397 members and Llanelli 346.[51]

A significant moment in Dewi Elfed's life came in December 1853 when William Phillips, president of the church in Wales who had baptized him into the faith, and John Davis, the Mormon printer who had preached at his ordination, prepared to emigrate to Zion. Dewi Elfed composed a fourteen-verse *Annerchiad* (address) on the occasion of their departure from Liverpool to New Orleans on January 27, 1854.[52]

---

[49] *Udgorn Seion* (16 October 1852), 336–38, and (30 October 1852), 344–47; Lewis, *Y Mormoniaid*, 46, 96.

[50] *Udgorn Seion* (8 January 1853), 33–34; (16 October 1852), 325–26; (29 May 1852), 180; and (12 February 1853), 132.

[51] Ibid. (29 January 1853), 82–83, (30 July 1853), 82–83. For a discussion of growth and decline in Latter-day Saint numbers in Britain as a whole during this period, see Cowan in chapter 7 of Bloxham, et al., *Truth Will Prevail*, esp. 213–17, 442.

[52] *Udgorn Seion* (31 December 1853), 421–22. This was the last issue of the *Udgorn* that Davis edited, and he entitled his final address "*Udganiad Olaf yr Udganwr Cyntaf*" ("The Final Blast of the First Trumpeter"). Other than Dan Jones, it is

In June 1854 Dewi wrote to Dan Jones, editor of *Udgorn Seion*, reporting difficulties faced by the mission in his Llanelli area. He related the
attitude of some local authorities in the following terms: "We are occasionally welcomed by some policemen. . . . Our names are taken by them. . . .
At such times they are tools in the hands of the Reverends, stewards, societies and the Lords of the Sects."[53] He also noted a Latter-day Saint
preaching meeting held in the "chief hostelry" at Porth-y-Rhyd, near
Llanwrda in the parish of Llanddarog, Carmarthenshire, where the *Sectau*
(Nonconformist denominations) assembled legions of Sunday School scholars, drew them up in regimental order, and then, when the Saints began
their service, drowned the Mormons with "the noise of catechismic guns
firing traditional bullets against the Saints."[54]

On August 2, 1854, Dewi and his family transferred their membership to Swansea, centre of the West Glamorgan Conference, where Dewi
had recently been appointed president. The move coincided with Dan
Jones's decision to transfer the headquarters of the Welsh Mission from
Merthyr to Swansea in September 1854.[55] From that time on, *Udgorn Seion*
and the office of the church in Wales were both based in Swansea. This
proximity of Dan Jones and Dewi Elfed was not a happy one for Dewi in
the long run.

Soon after settling at Swansea Dewi organized an *eisteddfod*, or competitive literary festival, within the church in accordance with a practice rapidly gaining in popularity at the time. This was a unique departure in
which all topics were focused on the endeavours of the Saints in West
Glamorgan.[56]

Dewi's presidency came to a most unhappy end by July 1855, when he
was publicly denounced and excommunicated for financial misdemeanors.
It seems there had been financial impropriety and also animus between
Dewi and Dan Jones since the beginning of 1855. Matters became public
in July with a denunciation of Dewi Elfed in *Udgorn Seion* by Daniel Daniels,
a Latter-day Saint "pastor" supervising three area conferences in west
Wales, who was to follow Dan Jones as editor of the *Udgorn* and president

likely no one made a greater contribution than Davis to the success of the early
Mormon mission to Wales. Ronald D. Dennis, *Welsh Mormon Writings from 1844 to
1862: A Historical Bibliography* (Provo, Utah: Brigham Young University, 1988),
169–171; see also Lewis, *Y Mormoniaid*, 52–53.

[53] *Udgorn Seion* (24 June 1854), 385–87.

[54] Ibid. (22 July 1854), 447–50.

[55] Llanelli Branch Record of Members, film 104169, membership nos. 353–59,
Family History Library, The Church of Jesus Christ of Latter-day Saints, Salt
Lake City, hereafter cited as LDS Family History Library. *Udgorn Seion* (November
1854), 543.

[56] Lewis, *Y Mormoniaid*, 56.

of the Welsh Mission. Daniels and Jones had been close colleagues ever since they had returned to Wales in each other's company in 1853 to undertake missionary work in their homeland. Daniels's denunciation was endorsed by Dewi's own counsellors and upheld by Franklin Richards, recently reappointed British Mission president.[57]

Dewi allegedly complained to mission officials that his excommunication was unjust, being based on Jones's supposed ill will toward him, and that money discrepancies were in reality of only a few pounds. In response, charges against him involving about fifty pounds were published in the *Udgorn*. Every bit as damaging as assertions about money were those which focused upon Dewi's supposed ill will toward the then Welsh president, Dan Jones. He was a revered figure, widely regarded as father of the faith in Wales.[58]

This affair marks the nadir of Dewi Elfed's personal standing. Dewi withheld from any public confession of wrongdoing for almost a year. During this time — in what must have been a very lonely period — he maintained profession of the Mormon faith.

On April 19, 1856, Dan Jones emigrated to America for the third time aboard the *Samuel Curling* from Liverpool with 707 converts. Prior to his departure, peace was made between him and Dewi Elfed. This was witnessed by Jones's successor as Welsh president, Daniels, and by Thomas Harries, Dewi's successor as conference president in West Glamorgan.[59] In a fulsome published statement Dewi repented of offenses to Jones and other leaders, acknowledged the justice of his excommunication, and expressed his intention to be thoroughly obedient to church leadership. He made no overt reference to money.

Dewi concluded his recantation with an eight-verse poem entitled *Emyn y Profiad* ("Hymn of Tribulation"), in which he sought to "sing away a little of my burden." It is an accomplished and finely tuned piece; and there are striking images and allusions in it as when Dewi wrote of the effect upon him of being excluded from the communion of the Latter-day Saints:

> Doors shut fast on all life's pathways!
> Darkly dammed were sunny rays!

---

[57] *Udgorn Seion* (21 July 1855), 235–38.

[58] *Bywgraffiadur Cymreig* (Dictionary of Welsh Biography) (London, 1953), 422; also Ronald D. Dennis, "Dan Jones, Welshman: Taking the Gospel Home," *Ensign* 17 (April 1987): 50–56.

[59] *Udgorn Seion* (3 May 1856), 136; (10 May 1856), 156–60. Jones had led an earlier company of 326 Welsh Saints to America in February and March 1849, aboard the ships *Buena Vista* and *Hartley*. R. D. Dennis has used the emigrants' own words to retell the story of this previous crossing in *The Call of Zion: the Story of the First Welsh Mormon Emigration* (Provo, Utah: Brigham Young University, 1987).

> A freezing shower on burning love!
> Grief where once I uttered praise!

Or again when he stated the constancy of his Mormon faith even whilst outside the church:

> Through the trials of my turmoil
>   My strong witness had its birth,
> Speaking truly of the tenets
>   In that gospel of great worth . . .

Dewi was examined by the president of the church in Europe, Franklin D. Richards, as well as by the president in Wales, Daniel Daniels, and was warmly received into fellowship again. Church leaders in Wales publicly acknowledged Dewi's humility and repentance and indicated that he had concurred readily in what had been asked of him. This may be code to signify that whatever the penitent said or did not say in his letter, Dewi had made sufficient recompense to the church to permit his restoration to the faith in accordance with Franklin Richards's observations on the matter. Daniels wrote that Dewi had "continued to maintain and defend with vigour the principles of this religion the whole time he was on the outside." He recommended Dewi to the faithful of the church and asked that the previous problems be buried. Welsh leaders charged Dewi Elfed to go forth into the world with "redoubled industry" to spread the Mormon gospel among those who dwelt "in Babylon." In this, they were surely crediting him with a particular gift for reaching hearts and minds as a preacher. It would also seem to be a vote of confidence in his orthodoxy which made him a suitable standard-bearer at a time when mass breakthroughs were increasingly difficult to achieve.

Between 1856 and 1860 Dewi Elfed was employed as a rallier of the baptized and as a frontline soldier in an attempt to take the Mormon faith forward. It is likely he was sustained in his labor by seeing it as a redemptive period in his life. Not long after his reinstatement Dewi Elfed was out and about in south Wales preaching the gospel and visiting branches of the church in order to strengthen them in faith. In September 1856 he declared his spirits to be high, and those members of the church upon whom he had called to be for the most part of good cheer and determined faith. Open-air meetings were held twice or three times each Sunday, and Dewi reported, "hundreds coming to listen, yes, thousands sometimes; and an excellent reception everywhere. It appears hosts of people are ready to be baptized. There is some new stirring amongst the people as if they were in a state of constant excitement — restless in their feelings . . . enquiring quietly of Jesus' servants."[60]

---

[60] *Udgorn Seion* (27 September 1856), 315–17.

He remarked that during his own open-air meetings he had experienced virtually no obstruction to his work, although he had met several people full of wrath, bitterness, jealousy, and enmity toward the Saints. Such types were usually under the influence of the Nonconformist churches, he declaimed. As in the days of his clashes with Thomas Price, Dewi reserved a special vitriol for the "reverends" who headed these denominations, and was in bold form when he wrote: "Ha, ha, the sects are in a giddy spin — the talent of preaching has become something of a boring whistle — the days of the beast having swallowed them alive — and the time of their downfall nearing in the hour when Mighty Babylon will fall and collapse, she being the mother of prostitution and earthly accursedness." Having said he had experienced little opposition whilst preaching, it is a bit inconsistent to refer to "bitter" and "jealous" opposition emanating from the dissenting churches, and to refer to that furor in Wales as elsewhere concerning plural marriage among Mormons in America. Dewi loyally defended it as a proper aspect of the patriarchal order that bestowed blessings. Yet he had to concede that "Hardly anything is heard anywhere . . . except a barking against the plural marriage of the Mormons."

Disdain of Mormonism often focused upon plural marriage and can hardly have made for an easy reception in most places. Having defended the practice in his report, Dewi produced in translation a detailed defense of the custom delivered by Parley Pratt to the Utah legislature on December 31, 1855. This pamphlet, printed and published at Swansea by Daniel Daniels in September 1856, bore the title *Priodas A Moesau Yn Utah* ("Marriage and Morals in Utah").[61] It was an appendage to eight other pamphlets prepared by Dewi Elfed in 1856-57, all meant to convey to the Welsh observations by Orson Pratt upon the Mormon faith. Published as well at Swansea, they represent a further substantial contribution by Dewi Elfed to the mission work of the Latter-day Saints in Wales.[62]

---

[61] Lewis, *Y Mormoniaid*, 73-78; also Alan Conway, ed., *The Welsh in America: Letters from the Immigrants* (Minneapolis: University of Minnesota Press, 1961), 311, 315, 318; *Priodas a Moesau yn Utah*, translated from the *Deseret News* by Dewi Elfed, Swansea, 1856. It had first appeared in *Udgorn Seion* (7 June 1856), 177-83; (21 June 1856), 193-201.

[62] The main series of eight titles was comprised of: (1) *Y Wir Ffydd* (The True Faith), 1856; (2) *Gwir Edifeirwch* (True Repentance), 1856; (3) *Bedydd Dwfr* (Water Baptism), 1857; (4) *Yr Ysbryd Glan* (The Holy Spirit), 1857; (5) *Doniau Ysbrydol* (Spiritual Gifts), 1857; (6) *Angenrheidrwydd Am Wyrthian* (The Necessity of Miracles), 1857; (7) *Gwrthgiliad Cyffredinol* (Universal Apostasy), 1857; and (8) *Brenhiniaeth y Dyddiau Diweddaf* (The Latter-day Kingdom), 1857. See Dennis, *Welsh Mormon Writings*, 207-19. Dennis estimates the print run of each to have been 3,800.

After 1857 details of Dewi's activities on behalf of the church are scantily documented. In a report published in *Udgorn Seion* of April 1857 he indicated that in addition to proselytizing he was seeking a revival of faith among the Saints themselves in conjunction with what became known as the Mormon Reformation. He identified several groups in need of reinvigoration: the lethargic; the meddlesome; those who disregarded dietary rules; those who held back from full commitment to the faith; those who begrudged tithing; and those who moved frequently from place to place, thereby loosening their roots in the church until overpowered by the spirit of "the world." This latter group, he maintained, was especially noticeable at Merthyr Tydfil and Aberdare. The thoroughness of his labours are indicated by this statement: "[I] try to do my best to preach to the world, to visit the Saints, to teach and train them, and to build up the Church in every way I can. I am determined to preach and bear witness in every town, village, valley and corner I have already spoken in, and also where I have not yet been if I come to know of them somewhere in the domain of my labour."[63]

Reckless and rash he may have been, but this is the voice and endeavor of a devoted servant of that faith he had embraced in a maelstrom of antagonisms at Aberaman six years before. These lines are a testimony to Dewi Elfed's convictions as he continued to propound the faith of the Latter-day Saints in south and east Wales in the years after 1856, labouring faithfully in the vineyard but not, as yet, called forth to Zion.

The last discernible reference to Dewi's missionary labors occurs in the *Millennial Star* in 1859, indicating that he was still a travelling elder in January of that year.[64] One reason for the lack of further information is undoubtedly the defective survival of *Udgorn Seion* from these years. Possibly the slow contraction into which the Welsh Mission slipped during the late 1850s and the increasing emphasis of the church in Britain on using the English language may have had a bearing in reducing the perceived role of Welsh-language missionaires such as Dewi Elfed.[65]

Ultimately, permission was given for Dewi and those members of his family still sharing his life to emigrate to Zion. He had waited long for the

---

[63] *Udgorn Seion* (25 April 1857), 129–32.

[64] *Millennial Star* 21 (22 January 1859): 62.

[65] *Udgorn Seion* (March 1856), 86; Lewis, *Y Mormoniaid*, 65; Journal of William Ajax, last editor of the *Udgorn*, 15 March and 9 April 1862. A typescript of Ajax's journal exists in the archives of the Harold B. Lee Library, Brigham Young University, Provo, Utah. I am indebted to R. D. Dennis for references from it and from all other unpublished transatlantic sources assembled by The Church of Jesus Christ of Latter-day Saints at its repositories in Utah and which have been used in the preparation of this paper.

moment. His swan song to Wales may be heard in the concluding verse of his *Annerchiad* to William Phillips and John Davis:

> If I am for some passing time
>   To boldly strive in Babylon,
> There'll come a day when I'll be free
>   And its oppression will have gone;
> To distant Zion your road leads,
>   Oh, joyful hour there to dwell;
> I too look forward to that day—
>   Dear brothers now, farewell! farewell!

Dewi Elfed, his wife, and their two youngest children, Daniel and Eleanor, sailed from Liverpool aboard the *William Tapscott* on May 11, 1860, part of an emigrating company of 731 Saints under the leadership of Asa Calkin. Their voyage across the Atlantic took a month and five days, arriving at New York on June 16, 1860. They apparently stayed in New York for two years, then with several other New York Saints joined a large company of emigrants recently arrived from Liverpool for the long trek west to Salt Lake City. They arrived in the Great Salt Lake Valley on October 17, 1862, as part of one Captain Henry W. Miller's ox train.[66] They had reached their destination in slightly under four months. For Dewi Elfed, however, there was not to be much time during which the reward of Zion might be savoured. He settled at Logan, about a hundred miles to the north of Salt Lake City, where he died of tuberculosis less than a year later, on May (or June) 18, 1863.

A terse report of Dewi's death appeared in the Welsh-American newspaper *Y Drych* (The Mirror) and was picked up shortly afterwards in Wales by the Baptist publication *Seren Cymru*[67] The latter was certainly seen by Dewi's old adversary, Thomas Price. While the summer of 1863 represented the end of Dewi's earthly days in distant America, it represented a peak in Price's career at home. He was elected chairman that year of the Glamorgan Baptist Association, from which Dewi had been expelled thirteen years before, and was awarded the degrees of M.A. and Ph.D. by Leipzig University.[68]

---

[66] British Emigration Records, 13 May 1860, film 25691; and New York Passenger Lists, 16 June 1860, film 175557, ship no. 473, both in LDS Family History Library; Ajax Journal, 27 June 1862. *Deseret News* (17 October 1862), 92. Thanks to Bert J. Rawlins of Midvale, Utah, for additional help in securing this last reference.

[67] *Y Drych* (8 August 1863), 244, reported Dewi's death date was May 18; *Seren Cymru* (28 August 1863), 261 reported June 18. My thanks to Huw Walters of the National Library of Wales for bringing the latter reference to my attention.

[68] *Seren Cymru* (26 June 1863), and Evans, *Cofiant Dr Price*, 131.

Such considerations bring the story of David Bevan Jones, alias Dewi Elfed, to a humble end, far removed from that comparative security and esteem upon which he could have reclined in Wales had he not "crossed the floor" from the Baptist church to the Latter-day Saints. He did not shy away from boldly confronting Thomas Price in the latter's own sphere of influence, and his memory and motives were to suffer a century and more of vilification for having done so. He was a minor poet of competence and, occasionally, of real ability. He was skilled in the art of popular polemics. His letters and essays, although sometimes self-righteous and repetitive, frequently smack of a talented turn for vivid phrases and cutting humour. There is a quicksilverlike edge to his writing, well suited to the battle in which Saints were locked with Nonconformist denominations in the Wales of the day. This may be one reason why Price and a host of ministerial colleagues so despised him: he was one of their number who had not only abandoned the faith of youth for another, but set about projecting that new faith with such verve and energy.

His contribution to the Saints' Welsh Mission as a hymnist, essayist, debater, itinerant preacher, and propagandist must be considered substantial, especially in the context of the age in which he lived. He was clearly highly thought of for his ability as a preacher from the beginning of his association with the Saints until its very end. Yet was there not in this quicksilver a mercurial indiscipline? Dewi seems to have had rather an awkward ability to get on the wrong side of too many too easily. In relation to sometimes bitter theological opponents this was probably par for the course: he gave Price and others no more and no less than he received. His propensity to fall out with his colleagues, however, was a most regrettable trait. Likewise, his tendency to act rashly in response to short-term difficulty, born no doubt of a vibrant but intemperate nature. His quarrels with Dan Jones, Daniel Daniels, Thomas Harries, and others did his standing among Latter-day Saints in Wales no good at all; and the financial ill repute in which he landed himself must be seen as a sorry example of someone with immense potential undermining his own achievements.

The real plus factor that remained with him during his entire alignment with the Saints was the constancy with which he continued to espouse the Mormon creed even in adversity. This much was most readily conceded by those who had previously reviled him publicly in forceful terms. No matter what personal shortcomings he was accused or found guilty of (and they are not the same), there was never an inference that he disavowed the essential tenets of the creed he had affirmed when baptized in the river Cynon by William Phillips in April 1851.

It is a pity that *Udgorn Seion* ceased publication in April 1862, about a year before Dewi Elfed's death. Otherwise, there would almost certainly have been a retrospective assessment there of his life. The last contemporary opinion published about Dewi Elfed was a poem of three memorial *englynion* (stanzas) written by William Lewis, a member of that first party of Welsh Saints which had sailed to America on board the *Buena Vista* under the guidance of Dan Jones in 1849.[69] Lewis used a nom de plume "Gwilym Ddu," and, like Dewi, shared a degree of accomplishment in traditional Welsh metrics. These verses appeared in *Y Drych* in August 1863. Because of the pattern of assonance and rhyme demanded by the rules of *cynghanedd*, in which these verses are set, it is virtually impossible to reproduce in English that fusion of sentiment and technique found in the original Welsh. A free translation would be:

Unrivalled Dewi Elfed — fleet of song,
 Fluent and inspired;
Oh, sad news, his muse is dead,
His art by earth is fettered.

Impressive as a preacher — an agile,
 Engaging adviser
A witty, bold orator,
Choice singer this chosen hour.

Though laid in earth is Dewi, the gifted
 There given to tarry,
With hosts of saints most worthy
From that bond he'll be set free.

For a Latter-day Saint such as Dewi Elfed, who, like other protagonists of the early Welsh Mission, went through so much in furtherance of faith, there can hardly be a more fitting conclusion to this account of his journey "from a *Seion* of lands to the land of Zion."

---

[69] Dennis, *The Call of Zion*, 60–61, 114, 211; a photograph of Lewis appears on 99. Prior to his conversion, Lewis had also been a Baptist; see *Y Bedyddiwr* (August 1847), 309.

9

The Essex Conference, 1850–70*

ANDREW PHILLIPS

One of the most promising new approaches to the study of The Church of Jesus Christ of Latter-day Saints in the British Isles has been the study of LDS congregations from a regional perspective. Indeed, the diversity of local circumstances makes it possible to distinguish trends and conditions that do not necessarily correspond to national patterns. In this essay we will analyze significant social trends within the Essex Conference during the period 1850 to 1870.

Essex is one of the larger English counties, often termed, from its proximity to London, one of the "Home Counties." In 1850 Essex was predominantly agricultural, the nation's best wheat-growing area. It boasted several old market towns and one fairly large one, Colchester, in the north of the county. There was no significant industrialization. The key to its communications was the historic road running diagonally across it from London via Colchester and Ipswich (in Suffolk) to Norwich (in Norfolk). By 1850 this had been effectively supplemented (even displaced) by the Great Eastern Railway, following the same route. With agricultural wages desperately low and its old market towns economically stagnant, Victorian

*This essay is largely based on Records of Members for Latter-day Saint branches and the original returns for the British censuses of 1851 and 1861. Branch Records of Members, on microfilm, are located at the Family History Library, The Church of Jesus Christ of Latter-day Saints, Salt Lake City, hereafter cited as LDS Family History Library, and can be viewed at branch family history libraries throughout the world on loan from the central library. Enumerators' Returns for the British Censuses of 1851 and 1861 are held by the Public Record Office, Chancery Lane, London, hereafter cited as PRO.

An earlier draft of this essay, written for an Essex readership, appears in *Essex Journal* 18, no. 3 (Winter 1983–84).

Essex exported people, mostly by railway, mostly to London.[1]

Because of close proximity to London, it is not suprising that the Essex Conference was formed in 1851 as an offshoot of the rapidly expanding London Conference. For purposes of this study we will concentrate on three branches that varied in size and social composition, yet might also be construed as typical of communities within the Essex Conference. Colchester was the county's largest town; Maldon, one of the more successful branches, was a medium-sized town; and Boxford, technically in the county of Suffolk, was chosen for its rural location. Since all three branches were established and reached their peak membership within a year or so of 1851 and since this was also a census year, by comparing LDS records with the enumerators' returns a brief analysis of Mormon converts can be made.

It is hardly surprising that the Saints established a branch in Colchester. Membership, however, was never large, and in 1854 it was disbanded, its remaining five members being transferred to Boxford. It revived briefly in 1857, but soon faltered again and was closed in 1859. During the initial period fifty-eight people were accepted into membership, mostly by conversion and baptism, but a few, usually the itinerant leadership, by transfer from other branches. Peak membership was about thirty-two, falling to five in less than two years. Despite this poor record the church's visibility should not be underestimated. In the Religious Census of 1851 the branch claimed an average attendance of 100 at their Sunday evening services over the previous nine months.

Colchester was certainly a fertile ground for "religion" during these years. The Religious Census of 1851 records sixteen dissenting congregations, with a minimum attendance on Census Sunday of 5,098.[2] That was over a quarter of the town's population. One Roman Catholic and fifteen Anglican congregations (one of which on grounds of principle sent no return) mustered a minimum attendance of 3,975. It can be estimated that perhaps as much as 75 percent of Colchester's adult population attended church on a regular basis. According to one calculation this was the high-

---

[1] See D. Friedlander and R. Roshier, "Internal Migration in England and Wales," *Population Studies* 19 (1965–66): 239–79. At the 1851 census London had over 57,000 inhabitants who had been born in Essex.

[2] Census of Religious Denominations, 1851. The census lists total attendance at each service at each place of worship on Census Sunday. It is, however, impossible to know how many people attended two or three services — or more than one church — on the same day. Our minimum figure is obtained by adding the highest single attendance at each place of worship. It does not therefore include the unknown number who only attended the less numerously attended service that day. For problems associated with interpreting the Religious Census of 1851 see W. S. F. Pickering, "The 1851 Religious Census — A Useless Experiment?" *The British Journal of Sociology* (December 1967): 57–65.

Stockwell Chapel, Colchester. This chapel housed one of several flourishing Nonconformist congregations, active opponents of the Mormon message, in mid-nineteenth-century Colchester. Courtesy of Colchester and Essex Museum.

est level of churchgoing of all large towns and cities in the country.[3] Several Nonconformist congregations were very large and led by pastors who were both experienced evangelists and powerful personalities. The Rev. Joseph Herrick at Stockwell Chapel, whose entry for the 1851 census he turned characteristically into a small sermon, records a total attendance of over 2,000 at three services on Census Sunday. Sectarianism flourished. There were four shades of Baptists, two of Methodists, plus Independents, Quakers, and a Church of New Jerusalem. Doctrinal disputes proliferated, while the same passions produced a devotional intensity that can only be fully appreciated by reading the private reflections of Charles Haddon Spurgeon, who from his conversion in Colchester in 1849 rose to become the best known preacher of Victorian England, and one of Colchester's most famous sons.[4]

Perhaps in this competitive field the Mormon preachers provided less evangelical impact. It is well established that the Saints recruited most successfully in large cities, notably London and urban Lancashire, where a smaller percentage attended church than elsewhere in the country. Perhaps in a citadel of nonconformity like Colchester pastors watched lest any of their flock should be attracted by the new teaching, while godly employers exercised like vigilance over their employees.[5] Social pressure from one's peers was also potent. Given such sanctions, active persecution of the Mormons, for which there is no evidence in Colchester, might not be necessary. In February 1858 a young Colchester woman, called upon to answer for her church inactivity, responded candidly that "she could not bear to be laughed at as she went to the factory, she had so much to put up with she thought she would give it up for the present."[6] She and her brother were formally excommunicated a month later at their own request.

Why, then, did the LDS Church fail in Colchester? Certainly one could argue that of 100 attending the LDS Sunday evening services in March 1851 a high percentage might be "sermon tasters," while those who joined the new faith may have been more impressionable than resolute. Indeed, most of the fifty-eight baptized Mormon converts in Colchester had left the membership in less than two years. A majority of these Saints were "cut off" — expelled from membership because of desertion, failure to

---

[3] K. S. Inglis, "Patterns of Religious Worship in 1851," *Journal of Ecclesiastical History* 11, no. 1 (1960).

[4] S. Spurgeon and J. Harrald, *C. H. Spurgeon, An Autobiography*, vol. 1, *The Early Years*, Banner of Truth Edition (London, 1962), ch. 10.

[5] J. A. Tabor, a leading contemporary Colchester Nonconformist, left among his papers a pamphlet providing arguments against Mormon teaching. Colchester and Essex Museum, Accession number 5210-1926.

[6] Colchester Branch Council Minutes, in Colchester Branch Record of Members, 28 February and 24 March 1858, LDS Family History Library.

accept church teachings, or falling into sin. It is doubtless also significant that from early 1853 few new converts were added to the branch. This coincides exactly with the public announcement of the church's adoption of plural marriage, a doctrine strikingly at variance with the ethics of mid-Victorian England.

There is a parallel to Colchester in Ipswich, also a Nonconformist stronghold and a known centre of Mormon persecution, where, despite its early evangelization by the Mormons (1839–40), its branch numbers dwindled, and in December 1857 the surviving seven members were, like those of Colchester, transferred to Boxford. They did not apparently make the twelve-mile journey, and in 1858 were "cut off," casualties perhaps of the high demands made of members during the Mormon Reformation of this period. During the 1850s and 1860s a number of anti-Mormon pamphlets and broadsides, published in Ipswich, may well have influenced opinion in Colchester and vicinity.[7]

Though well inside the Suffolk border, Boxford was doubtless placed within the Essex Conference because of its close links with the Colchester Branch. This is clear from the only reference during these years to LDS activity in the local press. It records the failure of "the Mormonites of Colchester and Boxford" to make any converts in nearby Nayland despite visits to the village, and distribution of tracts to all the houses.[8]

With two exceptions, Boxford was the only rural branch in the original Essex Conference, all others being based in medium-sized towns. This rural aspect is the more striking when it is appreciated that its centre was not Boxford itself (population 986), but the hamlet of Stone Street (population 224) one-half mile to the south. Here a private dwelling was converted into the LDS chapel and was recorded as such in the 1861 census. Indeed it is still identifiable today. Given that the British Mission was most successful in urban areas, Boxford deserves examination. Nothing is more contrary to the picture of Mormonism as a mainly urban phenomenon than the absorption of the faltering branches at Colchester and Ipswich by the humble brethren of Stone Street, a hamlet whose thatched roofs and country gardens seem, even in 1989, the epitome of rural seclusion. Not suprisingly, the majority of Boxford converts were agricultural laborers and their families. In addition the branch attracted several rural craftsmen

---

[7] W. W. Woodhouse, *Mormonism an Imposture* (Ipswich: N. Pannifer, 1853). G. Harris Hancock, *Beware of the Mormons!* (Ipswich, [1850s]). Charles Henry Wainwright, *Mormonism Tried by the Bible and Condemned* (Ipswich, 1855). J. Benjamin Franklin, *A Cheap Trip to the Great Salt Lake City*, 3rd and 4th eds. (Ipswich: J. Scoggins, 1864).

[8] *Essex Standard* (4 March 1853).

"Old Chapel House," Stone Street, Boxford, Sussex, ca. 1978. Boxford Branch Latter-day Saints met in the house at left in the 1860s. Courtesy of Andrew B. Phillips.

(a shoemaker and a carpenter), and three female workers at Boxford's silk "factory."[9]

The Boxford Branch was organized in October 1849 by two British converts, Ebenezer and Esther Gilles, and rose to twenty-seven members in nine months. From then until 1858 there were seventy-nine baptisms. By then the branch had started to decline. Peak membership—in 1855— was never more than thirty-five. The branch's existence was thus sustained by continuous conversion offsetting an equal loss of faith. The distinction between the initial and later membership is very marked. Of seventy-five second-phase members, ten were arriving and departing church officials, thirty-three were "cut off," eighteen "removed" (in a few cases to named LDS branches), three died, and one emigrated. This left ten still active— one elder and nine single females. By contrast, of the initial twenty-seven members, only four were "cut off," six removed on church business, and one died. The rest—sixteen—were still active eight years later. In this nucleus were five married couples. All five men were agricultural laborers;

---

[9] 1851 Census Enumerators' Returns, PRO. Forty-five Boxford members were identified from the census: seventeen males and twenty-eight females. Thirteen males were agricultural laborers, and sixteen females were wives or daughters of agricultural laborers.

three lived at Stone Street and four held church offices. Here surely is the real leadership of the Boxford Branch, and an explanation of its sturdy survival when the urban branches at Ipswich and Colchester faltered. No such resident nucleus existed at Colchester, which was dependent for leadership on the comings and goings of outsiders. The Boxford Branch stayed active during the lean 1860s, with a membership of twenty-five in 1862, twenty-one in 1865. Only in 1868, twenty years after its formation, did it shrink to five and was thereafter disbanded.

It is not surprising that with LDS membership declining nationally, the Boxford Branch should falter, too. Its catchment area was small compared with an urban branch. Although efforts were made to evangelize adjacent villages, these, as we have seen with Nayland, were often fruitless. Given Mormonism's increasingly negative public image, social pressure effectively precluded acceptance of the Mormon message. After proselytizing Sudbury, Bures, Monks Eleigh, and Kersey — all near Boxford — in late 1853, a local Essex Mormon missionary summarized: "Generally speaking the people manifested a calm, determined opposition to the truth."[10] It took a resilient convert to make the regular journey, doubtless on foot and in all weather, to the small chapel at Stone Street. In view of patterns seen in other village settings, the social pressure brought to bear against these rural Saints was probably at least as great as that to which the Colchester converts were subjected, and only the most dedicated of adherents could have resisted such communal animosity.[11]

Maldon was the only branch of the three studied that survived from its founding, in 1851, until the contracted Essex Conference was merged back into the London Conference in 1869. The Maldon Branch had twenty-nine baptisms in its first eight months and a further eighty-six by the end of 1856. These figures were not very different from Boxford. At Maldon, however, only eighteen members were "cut off" compared to forty-three at Boxford during the same period. On the other hand, Maldon lost fifty-six members (over half the converts) by removal. Two groups of nine apparently represent block transfers to other branches, for Maldon increasingly drew its members from outside Maldon. Alternatively some of those removed may have been on the first stage of a journey that ended with migration to Utah.

No easy explanation can be found for the survival of the Maldon Branch when those at Colchester and Boxford were closed. In terms of

---

[10] District Council Minutes, Maldon, Essex Conference, 13 December 1853, Archives, Historical Department, The Church of Jesus Christ of Latter-day Saints, Salt Lake City.

[11] Malcolm R. Thorp, "Sectarian Violence in Early Victorian Britain: The Mormon Experience 1837–60," forthcoming in *Bulletin of the John Rylands Library*.

Maldon, Essex, ca. 1840. A small, self-contained, ancient town, standing on a river close to the sea (note the lobster pots in the cart). Courtesy of Essex Society for Archaeology and History.

population Maldon with 4,558 was closer to Boxford's 986 than Colchester's 19,443. Nor was it a spiritual desert. According to the 1851 census at least 1,220 adults attended the town's three dissenting congregations. Even allowing for visitors from outlying villages, this probably represents over 40 percent of its adult population. Unfortunately, Anglican and Quaker figures are not available to make a full comparison with Colchester.

One possible key to Maldon, as at Boxford, is the calibre of its early members. In this it owed much to the charismatic leadership of its founder and first elder, Charles W. Penrose. Between April and December 1851, starting from nothing, Penrose baptized thirty-one converts, who formed the core of the later church: sixteen women, fifteen men, nine of whom were in their forties. Three families provided eleven converts, one of whom became Penrose's wife. As with Boxford this initial group provided stability over time, demonstrating greater staying power. Thus ten of the first thirty converts ultimately migrated to Utah, compared with nine of the subsequent eighty baptized members. Most of these nine were related to the initial ten, and four surnames cover sixteen of these nineteen emigrants.

It is well known that evangelizing sects—and this was often said of the Saints—appealed mostly to the young and to women. Such was not the case at Maldon. By occupation Maldon's "mature" men reflect the artisan class which both contemporaries and recent commentators have found prominent in Mormon membership. There was a cabinetmaker, a carpenter, a blacksmith, a wheelwright, a gardener, a fisherman, and a "vermine destroyer." Only one, John Holland, described as a "Master Tailor employing 3 men," might merit marginal middle-class status.[12]

This leads us to an examination of Mormon leadership and organization. The first Essex branches seem to have been founded as a result of a missionary initiative between 1849 and 1851.[13] When organized, each branch was led by an elder, a position usually achieved after rising through several junior ranks. All the elders of the Essex Conference appear to have been British converts, and a very large proportion were relatively young men. One is struck, too, by evidence of their spiritual durability. Despite the high desertion rate in these three Essex branches, of eighteen elders, priests, teachers and deacons appointed within them, only two, one from the collapsing Colchester Branch and one the brother of a very successful elder, were cut off from membership. It could perhaps be argued that priesthood promotion tended to encourage loyalty and conviction. Leadership responsibilities were soon thrust upon promising converts. For example, Charles Penrose was baptized at Kennington, London, in May 1850. A year later he was sent as an elder to a town he had never seen to found the Maldon Branch. Other examples abound. David Paxman, 22, also baptized at Kennington in 1850, was at North Minns by 1852, and an elder within a year. David Pudney, baptized in 1853 at age 18, was an elder the following year. Pudney and Paxman were both Essex men who had moved to London. Ebenezer Gilles, 31, the first Boxford elder, was a Scot, his wife from Durham. John Spriggs, 32, the first Colchester elder, was Welsh, but lived previously in Ipswich as elder there.[14]

To undertake these missionary responsibilities extraordinary sacrifice was called for. The experience of Charles Penrose, recorded in his diary, may not be untypical.[15] Living by faith, early missionaries were enjoined to proselytize "without purse or scrip."[16] Faithful to this injunction, the

---

[12] Maldon Branch Records of Members, LDS Family History Library. 1851 and 1861 censuses, Enumerators' Returns, PRO.

[13] *Millennial Star* 13 (1 November 1851): 333.

[14] Maldon, Colchester, Boxford, and Ipswich Branch Records of Members, and Computer File Index, LDS Family History Library; 1851 and 1861 censuses, Enumerators' Returns, PRO.

[15] For biographical detail, see Kenneth W. Godfrey, "Charles W. Penrose, One of Britain's Most Influential Converts: His Life and Thoughts," paper delivered at Mormon History Association 22nd Annual Conference, Oxford, July 1987, copy in my possession.

[16] See Richard L. Jensen, "Without Purse or Scrip? Financing Latter-day

nineteen-year-old Penrose, accompanied by another young elder, set out, penniless but for the clothes he wore, and walked the sixty-odd miles from London to Maldon, sleeping rough at night for the first time in his life. The two youths arrived in Maldon knowing no one. Their first night they spent in a haystack, not having eaten the entire day. The following morning Penrose's companion gave up and returned to London. Begging a drink of water later that day, Penrose broke down and cried. From this stark beginning he went on to found a branch, filling his limited free time by studying Latin, French, and Algebra, playing the flute, and writing articles for the *Millennial Star*.

These young British Mormons were also highly mobile, transferred from branch to branch as a matter of church policy, often at regular six- or twelve-month intervals. Thus, Penrose spent only about one year (April 1851–April 1852) at Maldon before he was tranferred to Colchester where he served for eight months (May 1852–January 1853). He then served at Boxford for six months (January–July 1853). The same is true of Paxman, who served briefly in both Colchester (June–November 1853) and Maldon (November 1853–January 1854) before spending approximately twenty-one months in Boxford (January 1854–September 1855).[17]

We might reasonably speculate that the decline of the Essex Conference after 1853 was related in part to a lack of a permanent and stable leadership. Having come and founded branches, the leaders were transferred. Leadership is crucial to any organization, particularly one like the Saints where central direction was so important. Without any intention to do so, a two-tier system of membership might result: on the one hand the active leadership, moving about the conference, psychologically based in London and in close contact with the American missionaries; on the other hand the small congregations at the end of the line. Despite the services of the Great Eastern Railway, considerable problems prevented the Saints of Maldon and Boxford from attending one of those large and heartening rallies so readily accessible in the London Conference. Apart from anything else, the return rail fare cost a week's wages.

The Mormons were always a small sect and a peculiar people. Persecution and ridicule were frequent occurrences. The capacity of the smaller community, compared with the anonymous city, to target such ridicule in a telling way may have been a factor in the durability of LDS branches, particularly when the leadership of those branches had—they would not have seen it as such—a sense that "here we have no abiding city." Extraor-

---

Saint Missionary Work in Europe in the Nineteenth Century," *Journal of Mormon History* 12 (1985): 3-14.

[17] Colchester, Maldon, and Boxford Branch Records of Members, and Computer File Index, LDS Family History Library.

dinary commitment was called for from a "local" Saint, and extraordinary fortitude was often exhibited — but by what percentage of those baptized? Indeed, excommunication may have been as big a factor in the decline of the British Mission as migration, for the LDS Church could never become "respectable," recognized, or patronized by a general public for whom churchgoing was a norm of middle-class and even artisan behavior. Such respectable church-going was undoubtedly a factor in both Anglican and Nonconformist expansion. We may be struck by the large number of Mormon converts "cut off" from membership, but this was largely a reflection of high standards and a rejection of nominal church membership. Eld Lane Baptist Chapel in Colchester, a centre of old Nonconformity, might on Census Sunday have over 600 in its congregation, but they had far fewer baptisms and lapsed members in the ensuing five years than the small LDS branch.[18]

P. A. M. Taylor, in his authoritative account of the migration of British Saints to Salt Lake City, argues that this exodus was the major factor in the sect's declining British numbers.[19] During the first twenty years of the British Mission 76,218 converts were baptized into membership. During the same period 17,618 Saints were gathered to Utah. This represents nearly 25 percent of the total baptized membership, and only includes those who travelled in official Mormon parties. If we confine our totals to the period of peak membership, 1849–57, migrants represent 30 percent of total baptisms. Yet during these same years there was a high level of excommunication, too. If even half those excommunicated were members for less than eighteen months (as was the case in the three Essex branches) it is not difficult to show that well over half the enduring national membership left for Utah. On the other hand, the sources show that the three branches studied here provided only seven emigrants to Zion (five from Maldon and one each from Colchester and Boxford) for the peak period 1849–57! In the Essex Conference, membership decline was clearly not a phenomenon associated with the building of the kingdom in America. Rather, the figures for the three branches suggest that problems of ecclesiastical discipline and internal migration to other branches were the major ingredients in decline.

---

[18] Records of Eld Lane Baptist Church, Colchester, Essex Record Office, Accession No. 5667.

[19] P. A. M. Taylor, *Expectations Westward: The Mormons and the Emigration of their British Converts in the Nineteenth Century* (Edinburgh and London: Oliver & Boyd, 1965), ch. 7.

	Cut Off	Removed	Died
Colchester	29	38	0
Boxford	43	36	3
Maldon	18	56	0

If there was a national emigration rate of over 25 percent, why did these branches contribute so few? One explanation may lie in the large number of members "removed" — a term presumed to mean they left the branch because of leaving the district. This can be deduced from the few cases where the individuals who removed, usually elders, promptly reappear at another Essex branch. Is it possible that some of those removed had gone to London or Liverpool on the first stage of their journey to Utah? If so, how were they different from the seven known emigrants in the three branches where their entry states unequivocally: "emigrated"? Taylor himself seems to have found no evidence of two-stage emigration. The problem is not resolved by examining the records of another Essex branch, that of Orsett. Here, too, there was a large turnover in membership. For the period 1851–56 the figures are:

Members	Cut Off	Removed	Emigrated
113	24	57	13

Of those removed, thirty-three left together on the same date, presumably to join — or found — another branch. For a block of ten, who also left together, the branch record clearly states that they emigrated — and, interestingly, the entry notes that four of these were from London and four from the neighboring branch of Grays. On this basis Orsett, like Maldon, had but five emigrants during these years.

Emigration did not, of course, cease in 1857. Between 1859 and 1861 a further fourteen Maldon emigrants — all from the core group of families — left for Utah. This must have left a serious gap in the ranks, though it is clear that the branch was still actively proselytizing and encountering local hostility in 1868.[20] A search through church records also shows that a number of Colchester and Boxford members who "removed" eventually did leave for Utah.[21] Partly these were the transient branch leadership, who cannot count as local converts. However, there were at least five Colchester Saints and either ten or eleven Boxford members who were listed as removed, but who eventually found their way to Utah. This rep-

---

[20] *Colchester Mercury* (27 July 1868).

[21] Boxford and Colchester Branch Records of Members, European Mission Emigration Passenger Lists, Index to LDS Passengers, and Family Group Sheets, LDS Family History Library; Frank Esshom, *Pioneers and Prominent Men of Utah* (Salt Lake City: Utah Pioneers Book Publishing Company, 1913), 836. I am indebted to Richard L. Jensen for his assistance with this research.

resents over one-third the total of those who were listed above as removed. In addition, these sixteen converts took with them to Utah eighteen dependent minors, all too young to count as Essex converts. It is perhaps significant that in all known cases they migrated from the London Conference. We cannot, of course, be sure that this is a complete list; nor were those who removed from Maldon similarly researched.

Nevertheless, when all reservations have been made, the record still suggests that these three Essex branches contributed such low numbers to the LDS gathering that this was not the main cause of their demise. This was more due to desertions outpacing conversions. The same may be true of the larger Essex Conference. Taylor found only sixty-nine Essex emigrants — compared to 1,301 from London — for the period 1850–62.[22]

Finally, what was the age, sex, and occupational mix of our Essex Saints? As we have already suggested, there was not the preponderance of impressionable young people and single women that their critics suggested. Over the three branches 42 percent of baptized converts were men, 58 percent were women. These figures include a few — mostly female — who were under eighteen years old. It seems likely that if we could restrict ourselves to those over twenty-one the percentage of men would be higher. In short, the Essex Saints probably had a greater percentage of men to women than many contemporary Nonconformist congregations. Colchester's leading Nonconformist church, Lion Walk, at a slightly later date, had 27 percent men to 73 percent women, in a membership of 236.[23] The three Mormon congregations also contained several examples of whole families and a balanced cross section of all age groups. This general picture matches Taylor's analysis of Mormon emigrants. The same is true of social background. Nineteenth-century observations that Mormon membership drew heavily from the sober artisan is true of the three branches. At Colchester and Maldon of twenty-four initial male members identified from the 1851 census, only three were unskilled laborers and only one was himself an employer. The rest pursued named occupations involving traditional skills. With those women whose families can be identified, the same pattern emerges. Only one, the daughter of a Maldon well borer, had a parent likely to be an employer. Of those wives not married to Mormon converts all but one had artisan husbands. The social background of the Boxford Branch we have already discussed.

All this differs from Taylor's analysis of Mormon emigrants in one important respect. He found that for the decade 1850–59, 12.9 percent were "middle class."[24] In the Maldon, Boxford, and Colchester branches

---

[22] Taylor, *Expectations Westward*, 248.

[23] *Essex Standard* (26 June 1874).

[24] Taylor, *Expectations Westward*, 150.

this stratum of society is all but totally absent. Here may be one clue to their small contribution to emigration: Taylor points out that the more affluent Saints were more able to afford the cost of this, even though the church tried to reduce the initial outlay via the Perpetual Emigrating Fund.

In conclusion then, the Essex Conference confirms the established pattern that the Saints recruited heavily among respectable artisans, and that converts cut across the whole age range, with entire families at the heart of their greatest stability. We have noted the high caliber of the native Mormon leadership, mostly young, unstinting and unfailing in their devotion. Yet, we must question whether the constant transfer of such leaders was wise and whether this contributed to the failure of the British Mission to sustain its growth rate after 1851. The Essex Conference also highlights the high desertion rate among those baptized and points to the need to study this phenomenon. Certainly on the evidence the growing unpopularity of the LDS Church and the ability of local communities to direct nonviolent sanctions against converts were important contributing factors.

10

Artisans, Millhands, and Laborers:
The Mormons of Leeds and
Their Nonconformist Neighbors

SUSAN L. FALES

A stranger traveling to Leeds in Yorkshire's West Riding in the early 1850s might question whether the city was dominated by the factory chimney or by the spires of its churches and chapels. Dickens declared of Coketown: "Who belonged to the eighteen denominations? Because, whoever did, the labouring people did not."[1] The same question could be asked regarding Leeds.

Although Owen Chadwick in 1966 wrote that "Victorian England was religious," contemporaries would have agreed with Dickens.[2] Horace Mann, the compiler of the first and only religious census, taken on Sunday, March 30, 1851, bemoaned what he termed the "alarming number of . . . non-attendants."[3] It was not nonattendance in general which worried contemporary observers, but nonattendance in the "large manufacturing districts" of the Midlands and the North.

Leeds was such a large manufacturing district in 1851 with a population of over 172,000, making it the fifth largest city in England, with only London, Liverpool, Manchester, and Birmingham larger. The borough was comprised of the township of Leeds with 101,343 inhabitants and ten out-townships. Although the majority of the borough population was concentrated in Leeds township it comprised only 2,672 acres out of the total

---

[1] Charles Dickens, *Hard Times: For These Times* (New York: New American Library, 1961), 32. Coketown was a fictitious northern industrial city in Dickens's novel *Hard Times*, based on the city of Preston, which Dickens visited during a severe and lengthy strike in the 1860s.

[2] Owen Chadwick, *The Victorian Church*, 2 vols. (New York: Oxford University Press, 1966), 1:1.

[3] *1851 Religious Census of Great Britain: Report and Tables on Religious Worship: England and Wales* (London: Edward Eyre for HMSO, 1853; reprint ed. Shannon, Ireland: Irish University Press), clviii.

Townships and Wards of the Borough of Leeds.

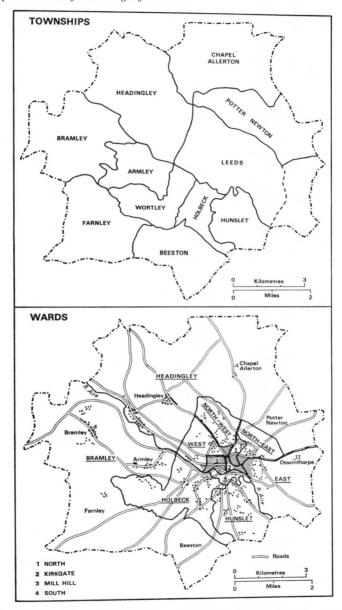

Source: Derek Fraser, "Areas of Urban Politics: Leeds, 1830–80," in H. J. Dyos and Michael Wolff, eds., The Victorian City: Images and Realities, 2 vols. (London: Routledge and Kegan Paul, 1973), 2:767. Reprinted by permission of the publisher.

borough acreage of 21,450.[4] The remainder of the borough was made up of the working-class out-townships of Holbeck and Hunslet; the pastoral townships of Farnley, Chapel Allerton, and Potternewton; Beeston, most noted for coal mining; Headingley-cum-Burley, advantageously located to the north and above Leeds township; the townships of Wortley and Bramley, textile centers, with Bramley especially strong as a handloom weaving center; and finally, Armley, along with Wortley, an increasingly important center for engineering associated with railways.

By 1851 Leeds was noted as a transport center with a strong turnpike network, and water transport, which took advantage of the River Aire. Vessels of 100 tons were able to reach Leeds on the waterways of the West Riding by the 1830s. In the 1840s and 1850s Leeds became linked with major cities, such as York, Manchester, and London, and small towns throughout Yorkshire and beyond by an intricate network of railways. In fact, the Borough of Leeds became a leader in industries associated with the railroads, especially locomotive building in the township of Hunslet.[5]

Leeds was also known as an important market town and commercial center. In fact contemporaries suggested that Leeds was the greatest provisions market in the north of England, with the possible exception of Halifax.[6] The hilly landscape of Leeds was dotted with markets and especially cloth halls for the sale of Leeds's most important commodities — woollen and flax cloth. The availability of water and rail transport, the proximity of the River Aire to fuel the factory steam engines, and sheep to provide the wool, created the dominant industry of Leeds up to the middle of the nineteenth century — the manufacturing and finishing of woollen cloth. It was expansion in the woollen and flax industries that attracted an expanding work force, not necessarily to work directly in these industries, but to provide all of the necessary trades to keep a city functioning. E. J. Connell and M. Ward estimate that an increase of 1,000 textile workers actually drew up to 3,000 new inhabitants to the borough.[7]

---

[4] Robert Baker, "On the State and Condition of the Town of Leeds in the West Riding of the County of York," in *The Chadwick Report on the Sanitary Condition of the Labouring Population with the Local Reports of England and Wales and other Related Papers, 1837-42*, vol. 2 (London: W. Clowes and Sons for HMSO, 1842; reprint ed. Shannon, Ireland: Irish University Press, 1971), 992.

[5] R. W. Unwin, "Leeds Becomes a Transport Centre," in Derek Fraser, ed., *A History of Modern Leeds* (Manchester: Manchester University Press, 1980), 128–29, 136.

[6] Kevin Grady, "Commercial, Marketing and Retailing Amenities, 1700-1914," in Fraser, *Modern Leeds*, 179.

[7] E. J. Connell and M. Ward, "Industrial Development, 1780-1914," in Fraser, *Modern Leeds*, 145.

Was the city dominated by the factory chimney of its woollen and flax mills rather than the spires of its churches and chapels? At first glance the religious fears of contemporaries would seem to be justified. For the entire borough population there were only 137 churches and chapels, with sittings to accommodate 44 percent of the inhabitants. But Leeds was in a relatively good position when compared to Liverpool, Manchester, or Sheffield where there were only enough sittings to accommodate 32.55 percent, 31.56 percent, and 32.66 percent of their inhabitants at religious worship respectively. Leeds was also somewhat different from most of the northern industrialized cities of Great Britain in terms of percentage of its population that attended religious worship.

The Religious Census of 1851 showed that all places of worship in England and Wales experienced attendance of 61 percent, with rural and small towns at 71.4 percent and larger towns of 10,000 or more, 49.7 percent. Even this figure is misleading, however, as most of the largest towns were well below that average. Leeds revealed an index of attendance of 47.4, which was considerably higher than many of the larger towns. Of the four cities larger than Leeds all experienced a lower index of attendance with London at 45.4, Liverpool at 45.2, Birmingham at 36.1, and Manchester at 34.7.[8]

Leeds was also heavily Nonconformist, prompting the new vicar of Leeds, Walter Farquhar Hook, in 1837, to write that the city's "*de facto* established religion is Methodism."[9] John F. C. Harrison has commented that despite Hook's great efforts in Leeds, the religious milieu of Yorkshire's West Riding continued to be one of Dissent. In fact, in 1851, out of the 983,423 attendees on Census Sunday in Yorkshire, 61 percent were at dissenting chapels and 72 percent of the Dissenters were at Methodist meetings.[10]

---

[8] Kenneth S. Inglis, "Patterns of Religious Worship in 1851," *Journal of Ecclesiastical History* 11 (1960): 81–82. At first glance there seems to be a discrepancy between the 44 percent of the population accommodated by sittings in the Borough of Leeds and the 47.4 percent attendance indicated by Inglis. This occurs because Nonconformists were more inclined than Roman Catholic and Church of England adherents to attend two or sometimes three services on a Sunday. When Inglis developed his index of attendance he used the total attendances at all specified places of worship within a given area, expressed as a percentage of the population, but because of heavy nonconformity in Leeds this probably slightly inflated the actual percentage of attendees. Of course the same inflation factor would be evident in all of the index of attendance figures for every city.

[9] W. R. W. Stephens, *Life and Letters of Walter Farquhar Hook* (1878), quoted in Fraser, *Modern Leeds*, 250.

[10] J. F. C. Harrison, *The Birth and Growth of Industrial England, 1714–1867* (New York: Harcourt Brace Jovanovich, 1973), 120.

Leeds certainly fit the West Riding pattern with 59.4 percent of its worshippers at Nonconformist meetings, and 7.1 percent at Roman Catholic worship, leaving only 33.5 percent attending Church of England services. Liverpool and Manchester represent a different picture with Nonconformist worship at 26.8 and 42.3 percent, Roman Catholic worship at 32.5 and 23.3 percent, and Church of England worship at 40.7 and 34.4 percent respectively.[11]

The Mormons of Leeds were a small part of the borough's religious population in 1851, representing one chapel out of 137, located in the Leather Market of the South Market complex.[12] Of the total sittings of over 76,000, 240 were available to the Mormons for formal worship. The growth of Mormonism in Leeds was slow as well as small. The first recorded Leeds baptism was on 24 June 1841, when John Barnes, Sr., a shoemaker, was baptized by Lorenzo Barnes, a missionary from Nauvoo.[13] No more baptisms were recorded in 1841, and in 1842 only five baptisms were conducted, including John Barnes's wife, Elizabeth, and son, John, Jr.

When Lorenzo Barnes returned to Leeds on June 8, 1842, he found twenty-six Latter-day Saint members that he described as generally poor but "kind and glad that I have come and appear willing to even sacrifice their own comfort to make us comfortable."[14] Membership, however, fluctuated drastically from year to year. By December 1847 Leeds Branch contained seventy-six members of whom only three were elders. It was an excellent year for baptisms with fourteen; however, eleven people left the branch to go to other towns. The branch's apex was in March 1851 when there were 303 members. Thirty had been baptized the year before, and significant emigration to the Salt Lake Valley had not yet begun. A steady decline in numbers ensued from this year, so that by December 1859 only ninety-four members remained on the Leeds Branch records.[15]

---

[11] Inglis, "Patterns of Religious Worship," 82–83.

[12] The manuscript returns of the Religious Census of 1851 give the Leather Market as the Mormon place of worship. It is not known whether the Mormons occupied all or part of this complex.

[13] However, Mormonism was not unheard of in Leeds prior to John Barnes's baptism, as in 1840 a *Leeds Times* article entitled "A New Sect," succinctly and unflatteringly outlined its fanaticisms and its introduction in Britain. Although some of Mormonism's teachings were inaccurately described, its belief in baptism by immersion was accurately reported. *Millennial Star* 1 (October 1840): 205–6. There is no known relationship between John Barnes and Lorenzo Barnes.

[14] Lorenzo D. Barnes Letters, Archives, Historical Department of The Church of Jesus Christ of Latter-day Saints, Salt Lake City, hereafter cited as LDS Church Archives.

[15] Leeds Branch Records of Members, 1841–1948 and 1844–1928, Family History Library, The Church of Jesus Christ of Latter-day Saints, Salt Lake City.

The Leather Market in the Leeds South Market. The Latter-day Saints conducted their meetings at this site, according to the Religious Census of 1851. Photographed ca. 1900. Courtesy of Leeds City Libraries.

The Mormons never represented large numbers of worshippers in any area of England, but it was in the larger towns of the manufacturing districts of England that considerable missionary successes occurred. Despite this fact, we have had almost no studies of the early Mormon converts within one of their more common settings—the city.[16] In studying the Mormons of early Victorian Leeds this essay concentrates on the social composition of the urban Mormons in comparison with other Nonconformist denominations. Three areas are specifically examined: occupational structure, migration, and residential patterns. This comparison identifies factors that may help explain why some Leeds residents were more receptive to the message of Mormonism than others. Leeds, because of its strong religious pluralism, is an obvious city in which to study these questions.[17]

---

[16] Susan L. Fales, "The Nonconformists of Leeds in the Early Victorian Era: A Study in Social Composition (M.A. thesis, Brigham Young University, 1984); Jan Harris, "Mormons in Victorian England" (M.A. thesis, Brigham Young University, 1987).

[17] In this study a statistical population of 2,385 people was gathered by listing all the entries from the 1830–37 birth and baptismal registers for twenty-three Nonconformist chapels in Leeds. The denominations were the Unitarians, Independents, Baptists, Friends, Wesleyan Methodists, Methodist New Connexion, and Primitive Methodists. The Leeds Branch Mormon membership lists of the

Because class structure in Victorian England was determined to a great extent by types of employment, the occupations of the early Mormon converts of Leeds were examined first to gain insight into their experiences.[18] In Coketown, according to Dickens, the laboring population did not belong to the city's eighteen denominations. But in Leeds that generalization did not hold true for at least one religious movement. There, for example, James Bywater, a former flax worker, did belong to a chapel — the Mormon. James was baptized on February 4, 1852, in the Leeds and Liverpool Canal by Joseph Horton, a Birmingham native who had been baptized less than three years earlier in Leeds and was now serving as president of the Leeds Branch. James was confirmed the following Sunday by Elder Robert Dransfield, a missionary in the Bradford Conference.[19]

Interestingly, Bywater did not grow up in a particularly religious household. In fact, he states that his father was actually an "unbeliever in [any] sectarian version of religion," and that he had in his possession some "infidel" works which James read. Although a Sunday school attender, James apparently never formally joined a church because he rejected the "Idea and tenant [tenet] that faith alone would save a person. . . . I grew up with a firm conviction that a religion which taught such a doctrine was false, and I believed firmly that man would be judged according to his works."[20]

Bywater was a member of the laboring classes of Leeds. At age nine he started work at Marshall's Flax Mill, where his father and grandfather before him had labored. He was only a half-timer for five years, going to school in the morning and working in the afternoon. He also, with his father's encouragement, attended an evening school in Wortley, taught by

---

1840s and early 1850s were used to gather people for the twenty-fourth chapel. The subsequent checking of these individuals against the 1851 Census of Population brought together families. Male heads of household were utilized for comparability; and the numbers for each denomination (after the census check) included Unitarians, 20; Independents, 91; Baptists, 76; Friends, 22; Wesleyan Methodists, 183; Methodist New Connexion, 21; Primitive Methodists, 31; Mormons, 33.

[18] Occupation has been central to two major national studies of early British Mormons: Malcolm Thorp, "Social and Religious Origins of Early English Mormons," *World Conference on Records: Preserving Our Heritage, August 12–15, 1980,* 13 vols. (Salt Lake City: The Church of Jesus Christ of Latter-day Saints, 1980), vol. 6, Series 444; and P. A. M. Taylor, *Expectations Westward: The Mormons and the Emigration of Their British Converts in the Nineteenth Century* (Edinburgh and London: Oliver & Boyd, 1965). In addition another recent local study of Manchester has also utilized occupational structure as an important sociological element. Harris, "Mormons in Victorian England."

[19] James Bywater Journal, 221–22, LDS Church Archives.

[20] Ibid., 205.

Mr. Joseph Smith, where he paid three pence per week for the opportunity.

By the age of nineteen he had been working in Marshall's Flax Mill for ten long years, and as he says: "I had become heartily tired of it and there had been springing in my heart a longing desire for employment in the open air. I desired very much to till the ground raise the crops of the field and the fruits of the orchard . . . and my dislike for that factory work [became] more pronounced . . . and I became resolved I would not raise a family in England to suffer the hateful labor of a factory life."[21] Apparently Bywater saw little hope of realizing his dream of working the land as an independent man if he stayed in England, where the land was held by a small and exclusive landed gentry.

Bywater worked in the garret on the seventh floor of the mill, sorting the dressed flax, and he consequently bore the hallmark of all laboring men — he worked with his hands. No matter what the wages or the skill, a man's social status in Victorian England was determined by the type of work performed. An ill-paid schoolteacher or lowly clerk would always consider himself the social superior of a more highly paid skilled artisan, simply because that artisan used his hands to perform his work. Additional hallmarks of the laboring man were the insecurity of the job and the wide divergence of skill and pay within the working classes. A skilled artisan could earn 35 to 40 shillings a week, whereas a laborer might only earn 10 shillings a week on an uncertain basis. Yet both men were part of the laboring population of England.[22]

The middle classes also showed a wide range of pay and skill, but more importantly, physical labor was not performed by this class. The upper end of the middle-class scale was represented by men who could mingle easily with the gentry. In Leeds the upper middle class, in fact, formed a city oligarchy. Edward Baines, an Independent, a Liberal M.P. from Leeds, and the proprietor of the *Leeds Mercury*, represented the professional category of the middle classes, as did Richard Constantine Hay, an Independent and member of the Royal College of Surgeons. Newman Cash, a Quaker and prominent woollen merchant, was typical of the powerful merchants of Leeds. On the other hand, the lower middle classes were closer to the laboring classes in pay and were mostly noted for the "taint of trade" or the performance of a paid service. They were the £10 householders (eligible to vote in parliamentary elections) who included a shopkeeper, coal merchant, innkeeper, commerical traveler, schoolteacher, and clerk. The Wesleyan Methodist John Anderson (a tea dealer and gro-

---

[21] Ibid., 207.

[22] John F. C. Harrison, *The Early Victorians, 1832–1851* (London: Weidenfeld and Nicolson, 1971), 22–23.

cer on 20 Park Lane), the Quaker William Broadhead (who maintained a Coffee House on Meadow Lane Road), the Independent Thomas Buckton (a grocer and druggist in Wortley), or the Mormon Robert Warne Reeve (a manufacturing chemist), were all men who fit easily the lower middle-class mold.

Although £300 a year was often mentioned as a minimum for middle-class living, teachers and clerks earned as little as £60 a year, which was much less than a skilled artisan. Nevertheless, these people were considered middle class because of their educational attainments, and because there was no taint of manual labor associated with their jobs. These qualities provided the middle classes with the social status that James Bywater and John Barnes, Sr. (the first recorded Latter-day Saint convert in Leeds), could not and did not enjoy.[23]

John Barnes, Sr., grew up during the rise of the great manufacturing cities of England, at the height of the Industrial Revolution. What of Barnes, whose coarse red hands indicated he did something with them for a living? Was he, a shoemaker, typical of Mormons in Leeds? (See Table 3.) Based upon occupation, 91 percent of the Mormon families were working class, with only 9 percent middle class. As noted above, however, there was a wide divergence within the laboring classes, and in such a breakdown of the Mormon social composition it was found that artisans predominated among the Mormons. Over 48 percent engaged in occupations such as shoemaker, tailor, carpenter, tobacco pipe maker, hatter, and blacksmith. As artisans were generally considered the elite of the working classes and often made more money than clerks and schoolteachers, it is interesting to note the high percentage who were artisans in all of the denominations.

Because the samples for all the denominations were based on male heads of household found on the 1851 Census of Population, this may have eliminated some of the adult, unmarried males who were impossible to identify on the census. However, Alan Gilbert, in his seminal sociological study of church and chapel adherents in early industrial England, provides ample proof that nonconformity was attractive to artisans. He found that 59.4 percent of adult male members of Nonconformist churches were artisans—a concentration between two and three times as high as that of artisans in the general population of England (23.5 percent). Interestingly, the proportion of artisans Gilbert found among Primitive Methodists—47.7 percent—is almost identical to that of artisans among the Mormons in Leeds—48 percent.[24]

---

[23] Ibid., 103–4.

[24] Alan D. Gilbert, *Religion and Society in Industrial England: Church, Chapel and Social Change, 1740–1914* (London: Longman, 1976), 63, 66–67.

Table 3. Occupations of Male Heads of Household, 1851, in Leeds Arranged by Denominations

Occupations	1 Professional		2 Clerks/ Bookkeepers		3 Manufact		4 Salesman		5 Shopkeeper		6 Artisan		7 Factory/ Supervisor		8 Factory/ Skilled		9 Factory/ Unskilled		10 Laborer		11 Farming		Totals
Denominations	No.	%	No.	%	No.	%	No.	%	No.	%	No.	%	No.	%	No.	%	No.	%	No.	%	No.	%	
Unitarians	1	5.0	1	5.0	1	5.0	4	20.0	2	10.0	9	45.0	0	0.0	0	0.0	1	5.0	1	5.0	0	0.0	20
Independents	10	11.0	4	4.4	3	3.3	9	9.9	10	11.0	29	31.9	1	1.1	7	7.7	12	13.2	6	6.6	0	0.0	91*
Baptists	1	1.3	0	0.0	4	5.3	1	1.3	5	6.6	39	51.3	1	1.3	4	5.3	5	6.6	10	13.2	6	7.9	76**
Friends	1	4.5	0	0.0	4	18.2	4	18.2	5	22.7	7	31.8	0	0.0	0	0.0	0	0.0	1	4.5	0	0.0	22
Wesleyan Methodists	5	2.7	3	1.6	11	6.0	12	6.6	20	10.9	73	39.9	8	4.4	12	6.6	16	8.7	19	10.4	4	2.2	183***
Methodist New Connexion	0	0.0	0	0.0	1	4.8	0	0.0	3	14.3	11	52.4	1	4.8	0	0.0	4	19.0	1	4.8	0	0.0	21
Primitive Methodist	0	0.0	1	3.2	0	0.0	3	9.7	0	0.0	10	32.3	0	0.0	0	0.0	7	22.6	7	22.6	3	9.7	31
Mormon	1	3.0	0	0.0	1	3.0	0	0.0	1	3.0	16	48.5	1	3.0	4	12.1	2	6.1	7	21.2	0	0.0	33
Totals	19	4.0	9	1.9	25	5.2	33	6.9	46	9.6	194	40.7	12	2.5	27	5.7	47	9.9	52	10.9	13	2.7	477

Middle-Class Occupations (Columns 1–5) = 132/477 = 27.67%
Working-Class Occupations (Columns 6–11) = 345/477 = 72.33%

* One Chelsea pensioner, one not occupied
** One not occupied
*** Two parish relief, one not occupied

Source: Great Britain, 1851 Census Enumerator's Schedules. Townships of Leeds and Great Britain. 1851 Census, Enumerator's Schedules, Borough of Leeds.

The proportion of Mormons who were middle class—9 percent—was lower in Leeds than in populations analyzed for two earlier studies, using much larger samples, which showed 11.49 and 12.68 percent Mormon middle class respectively.[25] To determine whether the small size of the sample (33 adult male heads of household) might be affecting the final figures, occupational information from the 1841 census and Mormon emigration lists was added to the information from the 1851 census.[26] These sources combined showed a Mormon population of 49 adult males in Leeds (not necessarily heads of household). Of these, 12.24 percent were middle class and 87.75 percent working class.[27] Thus sample size may indeed have had an effect on the final outcome of the figures. Although the proportions of middle and working classes altered somewhat with the larger sample size, there were no substantial changes within the categories previously established. Artisans still represented the largest single group of Mormons, with 46.94 percent.

Artisans were undoubtedly the working-class elite financially; but according to E. P. Thompson, artisans were also at the forefront of new political—indeed radical—movements within society. He makes special note of the role artisans played in the London Corresponding Society at the turn of the nineteenth century, and shoemakers are cited as especially prominent in radical movements.[28] Whether political or religious radicalism played a part in the personality of the early Mormon converts, certainly a high proportion of the Leeds members were artisans and in fact four (17.4 percent) of the artisans were shoemakers.

---

[25] Thorp, "Social and Religious Origins," 2; Taylor, *Expectations Westward*, 149–51.

[26] The small size of the sample may also be responsible for some skewing between middle and working classes for the Independents, Society of Friends, Methodist New Connexion, and the Primitive Methodists. Mormon occupational categories with new sample size of 49: Artisan, 23, 46.94%; Mill Workers, 9, 18.37%; Laborers, 11, 22.45%; Farmer, 2, 4.1%; Manufacturer, 2, 4.1%; Shopkeeper, 1, 2.04%; Professional, 1, 2.04%; Working Class, 43, 87.75%; and Middle Class, 6, 12.24%.

[27] For the Mormons, the category of farmer, considered as working class in Table 3, has been categorized as middle class for this sample, because the two men were listed as farmers rather than agricultural laborers or farmer's men. This is consistent with the categories used by Taylor, *Expectations Westward*, and Thorp, "Social and Religious Origins." The original occupational profile in Table 3 has not been altered to move agriculture from middle class because in only two instances out of thirteen were the occupations listed as farmer and the remainder were farm laborers.

[28] E. P. Thompson, *The Making of the English Working Class* (New York: Vintage Books, 1963), 155–57.

Among all the denominations the working classes predominated with 72.33 percent (Table 3).[29] This makes the smaller percentage of the working-class members found among the Friends, the Unitarians, and the Independents more intriguing when one considers how large the Leeds working-class population was; Leeds has variously been described as three-quarters to four-fifths working class during this period.[30]

In his lifetime we know that John Barnes, Sr., the early Mormon convert, moved several times. Church membership records tell us that he was born in 1801 in Bolton Percy, about seventeen miles northeast of Leeds; but by 1841 he and his wife, Elizabeth, and their five children were residents of Leeds. In a pattern not unfamiliar in the nineteenth century, John and his wife apparently moved short distances more than once, as their third and fourth children, John, Jr., and Eliza, were both born in Huddersfield, only twenty miles southwest of Leeds, and their youngest child, Thomas, was born in Leeds.

Leeds township was sustained by the in-migration of people like John Barnes before 1851. But by 1851 the pattern had changed and Leeds Borough had 69 percent of its population born in the borough and only 31 percent in-migration. In-migration was low for the borough when compared with Bradford and Preston, for example, which had migrant populations of 55 and 53 percent respectively.[31]

Assuming that uprooting caused by migration creates some disruption in an individual's life, an examination of the birthplaces of Leeds's Nonconformists might indicate different patterns of migration suggesting experiences of social dislocation. Alan Gilbert observed and tested the idea that anomie, a social disorganization brought about by the breakdown of long-established social and cultural systems, played a significant role in the late eighteenth- and early nineteenth-century growth of nonconformity in England. By the Victorian era he claims that the change from the agrarian to the industrial system was complete and hence the declining Nonconformist numbers of the 1840s and 1850s. Anomie then brings about an increased need for new "associational and communal" ties to replace those which have been lost.[32]

---

[29] This discussion represents a return to the original sample of 33 Mormon male heads of household as found on the 1851 census and portrayed in Table 3.

[30] David Ward, "Environs and Neighbours in the 'Two Nations' Residential Differentiation in Mid-nineteenth-century Leeds," *Journal of Historical Geography* 6 (April 1980): 146; R. J. Morris, "Middle-class Culture, 1700–1914," in Fraser, *Modern Leeds*, 200.

[31] C. J. Morgan, "Demographic Change, 1771–1911," in Fraser, *Modern Leeds*, 61.

[32] Gilbert, *Religion and Society*, 89, 145–46.

In studying the migration patterns of Leeds's dissenting families, the birthplace of only male heads of household was used. Because the sample population was gathered primarily from Leeds Borough baptismal records of 1830–37 (other than among the Mormons), the use of the families' children as part of the migration patterns would have skewed the sample toward a heavy native population pattern.[33] (See Table 4.)

Interestingly, all the dissenting religions reveal a higher borough in-migration pattern than the 31 percent noted above, with the exception of the Unitarians who had 30 percent in-migration. The Mormons and the Friends show a significantly higher borough in-migration pattern, with 75.8 percent and 63.6 percent, respectively. In Jan Harris's study of Manchester Mormons, an in-migration pattern of 66 percent was found, almost 10 percent less than the Mormons of Leeds.[34]

Short-distance migration (which included the rest of Yorkshire and the contiguous counties of Nottinghamshire, Derbyshire, and Lancashire) was common among most of the denominations. Among the Mormons, however, 30.2 percent of the males were born outside of areas relatively close to Leeds, presenting a picture different from other Dissenters. To further test this phenomenon, all 197 members from the branch were examined and it was found that 28.64 percent were born within Leeds Borough. This figure, only about 4 percent higher than the study done solely with the male heads of household, suggests that the Mormons were relatively recent arrivals in Leeds as few of their children had been born in the city.

Forty-nine percent of the Mormons were born in the rest of Yorkshire and the three counties of Derbyshire, Lancashire, and Nottinghamshire. Twenty-two percent were born elsewhere in England or Scotland. Mormon in-migration was high in comparison with the other denominations, but similar to a study of Manchester Mormons in which 66 percent were in-migrants. In addition, in Manchester, 18.8 percent of the Mormons traveled long distances to settle in that city. Short-distance migration was slightly more important to the growth of the church in Manchester than it was in Leeds.[35]

As many people were not daunted by a walk of twenty miles or more to see friends and family, the possibility of some contact with their birthplaces was possible for many of the Mormon converts, but for many others

---

[33] Because the major source for the present study was the 1851 census for the Borough of Leeds, it was impossible to identify changes in a family's place of residence within the city. Using city directories over a ten-year period to find the heads of household revealed little in the way of migration patterns. Too few of the male heads of household were listed in these directories, and often only the place of business was given.

[34] Harris, "Mormons in Victorian England," 112.

[35] Ibid., 111, 112.

Table 4. Birthplace of Male Heads of Household in Leeds by Denomination

Denomination	Borough of Leeds	Rest of Yorkshire	Counties Contiguous to West Yorkshire	Rest of England	Scotland	Ireland	Other	Total
Unitarians	70.0%	25.0%	5.0%	0.0%	0.0%	0.0%	0.0%	4.1%
Independents	49.5	35.6	3.2	5.4	1.1	2.2	2.2	19.3
Baptists	66.2	32.5	0.0	1.3	0.0	0.0	0.0	15.9
Friends	36.4	50.0	0.0	13.6	0.0	0.0	0.0	4.6
Wesleyan Methodists	53.2	39.2	1.1	5.9	0.5	0.0	0.0	39.5
Methodist New Connexion	61.9	33.3	4.8	0.0	0.0	0.0	0.0	4.3
Primitive Methodist	45.2	51.6	3.2	0.0	0.0	0.0	0.0	6.4
Mormon	24.2	39.4	6.1	24.2	6.1	0.0	0.0	6.8
Totals	52.4%	38.1%	2.1%	5.8%	0.8%	0.4%	0.4%	100.0%

Source: Great Britain, 1851 Census Enumerator's Schedules. Townships of Leeds and Great Britain. 1851 Census, Enumerator's Schedules, Borough of Leeds.

their long-distance migration prevented this intermittent contact. Distance and isolation from friends and family was a factor which could create social dislocation. These potential feelings of social dislocation might be tempered somewhat if the migrants' type of birth community was similar in size and composition to Leeds. For example, it could be argued that the Mormon migrant might not have had as difficult a time adjusting to life in a new city if his past living situation was similar to life in Leeds.[36] By 1851 this adjustment process could also be eased by the neighborhood working-class network already established in the cities. Such institutions as the pubs, the Friendly Societies, and self-help groups could all have made the transition easier from one town to another.

A careful examination of the types of communities indicates that the majority of Mormon migrants came to Leeds from at least marginally similar towns. For example, 21.3 percent of all migrants came from cities with 50,000 or more population and an additional 26.2 percent came from sizeable towns of 5,000 to 50,000 population (47.5 percent thus migrating from large towns).[37] Almost 22 percent more of the Mormon migrants came from industrial villages — many of them noted for woollen and cotton manufacture. (See Table 5.)[38]

A comparison with the Mormon migrants to Manchester (using only the Lancashire-born migrants) during this same time period shows some similarities between the Mormons of Leeds and Manchester. The migration from large towns is comparable for Leeds and Manchester, exhibiting 47.5 percent and 55.5 percent respectively. Unfortunately it was impossible to tell what role the largest of cities played in Manchester migration as Harris did not separate cities of 50,000 and over from the smaller towns. However, industrial villages were much more important to Leeds migration (21.3 percent) than to Manchester (11 percent). And agricultural villages were considerably more important to Leeds (15.6 percent) than to Manchester migrants (1.1 percent).[39]

As people were lured to the large cities seeking new opportunities, the city's population mushroomed and the residential patterns became more

---

[36] Michael Anderson, *Family Structure in Nineteenth Century Lancashire* (Cambridge: Cambridge University Press, 1971), 37.

[37] In fact most of the largest cities had populations of over 100,000, such as Chesterfield, Birmingham, Bradford, and Sheffield (these cities contributed a total of eight Mormon migrants); and London (which contributed nine Mormon migrants) had a population of almost 2 million at this time.

[38] Unfortunately, without extensive research using the manuscript census, it is impossible to determine whether the Mormons were truly unique in their migration patterns in relation to the entire population of Leeds. The statistical reports listed birthplace only by county at this time.

[39] Harris, "Mormons in Victorian England," 120.

Table 5. Mormon Migrants of Leeds by Type of Community

Community	Short-Distance Migration		Long-Distance Migration		Total Migration	
	No.	%	No.	%	No.	%
Large Towns	10	10.2	20	46.5	30	21.3
Towns	27	27.6	10	23.3	37	26.2
Industrial Villages	30	30.6	0	0.0	30	21.3
Mixed Villages	4	4.1	1	2.3	5	3.5
Agricultural Villages	13	13.3	9	20.9	22	15.6
Undefined	14	14.3	3	7.0	17	12.1
	98	100.0	43	100.0	141	100.0

Large Towns: Places with population over 50,000 in 1841.

Towns: Places with population 5,000 to 50,000 in 1841.

Industrial Villages: All villages with less than 5,000 inhabitants that were described as manufacture being the principle business of the village.

Mixed Villages: Places where both agriculture and industry were mentioned as principle occupations of the inhabitants.

Agricultural Villages: Locations where only agriculture was noted as the occupation of the villagers.

Undefined: All places which did not fit into the categories above.

Source: The definitions of community type were adopted from Michael Anderson, *Family Structure in Nineteenth Century Lancashire*, (Cambridge: Cambridge University Press, 1971), 38. The nature of the communities was identified in Samuel Lewis, *A Topographical Dictionary of England*, 4 vols. (London: S. Lewis and Co., 1844), and Samuel Lewis, *A Topographical Dictionary of Scotland*, 2 vols. (London: S. Lewis and Co., 1846).

differentiated. Members of the working classes, the James Bywaters and John Barneses of the large towns, were tied closely to both work and home, because their hours of work were long, public transport was limited, and casual labor was frequent.[40] In addition, those who were better educated and wealthier removed themselves from the disagreeableness of the inner city. Unlike the working man, the well-to-do tradesman or industrialist did not have to live near his work, and it was this fact which exacerbated the isolation of class from class. Consequently, the most important social effect of urbanization was segregation by class.[41]

[40] Morgan, "Demographic Change," 54.

[41] James Hole, *The Homes of the Working Classes with Suggestions for their Improvement* (London: Longmans, Green & Co., 1866), 4; Harold Perkin, *The Origins of Modern English Society 1780–1880* (London: Routledge & Kegan Paul, 1969), 118.

Perkin paints a picture of town functions localized into concentric rings which presents an exaggerated picture of social segregation: "shops and offices in the centre, factories and poorest working-class housing hard by, artisans' and poor clerks' houses somewhat further out, middle-class homes in the inner suburbs, merchants', industrialists' and higher professional men's villas in the outer ring, or when the railways came, in detached satellite suburbs strung along the railway lines."[42]

Leeds was no exception to this general pattern, although opinions vary as to the extent of the differentiation. According to J. F. C. Harrison the working classes lived in well-defined areas of the North, North-east, and Kirkgate wards in the Leeds township, along with the out-townships of Holbeck and Hunslet, and the middle classes were more pleasantly located in the Mill Hill, West, and North-west wards. He sees this social segregation far advanced during the early Victorian era, with the differences of dress and speech further accentuated by physical isolation.[43]

David Ward agrees with Harrison that residential segregation was a commonplace of mid-nineteenth-century Leeds, but he sees the segregation as more weakly differentiated. He arrives at this conclusion after studying the extent of the middle class evident in what contemporaries and other historians have traditionally designated as working-class areas.[44]

The most important contemporary account of social segregation was that of Robert Baker, a Leeds physician, surgeon to the Poor Law Commission, and later factory inspector. In 1833 Baker prepared an initial report of Leeds's cholera cases for the Leeds Board of Health. This report contained a map which portrayed, perhaps for the first time, a concept of social geography.[45] Baker concluded that the greatest instance of cholera was in the working-class areas of the eastern portions of the city, whereas the West and the North-west were relatively immune.[46]

Baker also devised an intriguing scheme to determine the number of working-class population in each of the wards in the township of Leeds (see Table 6). Using a census ratio of 4.5 people to a house combined with the number of houses under £10 annual rent, he found that the working classes were indeed heavily concentrated in the city's east and south wards. The housing valuation was conducted in the town between 1838 and 1839.

---

[42] Perkin, *Origins*, 118.

[43] Harrison, *The Birth and Growth of Industrial England*, 92.

[44] Ward, "Environs and Neighbours," 133–62.

[45] Robert Baker, "Report of the Leeds Board of Health" (Leeds, 1833) in Ward, "Environs and Neighbours," 140. He later elaborated on this theme in his Leeds local report, which became a part of Edwin Chadwick's *Report on the Sanitary Condition of the Labouring Population*.

[46] Baker, "On the State and Condition of the Town of Leeds," 992–1053.

Although this was thirteen years earlier than the period in question, the increase in population was no doubt distributed in similar proportions.[47]

It was expected that the Mormons' residential patterns would be similar to the occupational and class profile already described.[48] Within the bounds of Leeds Township this did hold true, with 51.5 percent of the Mormons living within the predominantly working-class wards, and only 8.8 percent living within the more middle-class wards of Mill Hill, West, and North-west. As anticipated, the Primitive Methodists also had few of their members living within these middle-class wards, with only 9.7 percent residence.

To emphasize the class segregation of Leeds Mormons, an examination of the consequences of living in certain wards was undertaken. The Mormons lived predominantly in the North-east Wards where a death rate of 43.5 per thousand occurred, and the East and South Ward, with a death rate of 33.3 per thousand in 1839.[49] The death rate of 43.5 per thousand was approximately twice the national average (21.6 per thousand in 1841). Interestingly enough, all of the areas in Leeds experienced a higher death rate than the national average.[50]

Moving to the ten out-townships of Leeds Borough, the working-class districts of Hunslet and Holbeck contained 36.4 percent of the Mormons. A total of 87.9 percent of the Mormons lived within predominantly working-class areas, which is consistent with the working-class composition of the Mormons.

These statistics represent a general and crude touchstone for the measurement of social status by residence. A more refined measurement is an examination of the type of housing found by ward and township within the Leeds Borough.

Using the 1850 Ordnance Survey five-foot plans for Leeds, Hunslet, and Holbeck, it was discovered that the Mormons continued to fall into the pattern of the working classes with 52.94 percent, representing nine families, living in the infamous back-to-backs.[51] These were the "one up, one downs" with no ventilation, because the cottage was surrounded on three

---

[47] Ibid., 993.

[48] Only the 33 male heads of household and their place of residence as found on the 1851 census were used in this study of residential patterns.

[49] Baker, "On the State and Condition of the Town of Leeds," 1011.

[50] B. R. Mitchell and Phyllis Deane, *Abstract of British Historical Statistics* (Cambridge: Cambridge University Press, 1962), 36.

[51] Not all of the 33 addresses of the Mormon families found on the 1851 census were identifiable on the 1850 Ordnance Survey five-foot plans. There are no indexes to these maps, and some of the streets or courts were impossible to locate, thereby making it impossible to identify the type of housing. The percentages used are based upon the fifteen families and their addresses located on these maps.

Table 6. Proportion of Working Class, Leeds, by Ward

Wards	Population of the Ward	Dwellings under £10 Annual Rent	Population of the Working Classes at 4½ to a House	Working Class Percentage of Population Estimating 4½ to a House
North	12,506	2,100	9,450	75.6%
North-east	16,269	3,422	15,399	94.7%
East	14,271	2,947	13,251	92.9%
South	5,630	943	4,243	75.4%
Kirkgate	3,138	348	1,233	39.3%
Mill Hill	5,167	274	1,566	30.3%
West	15,483	2,104	9,468	61.2%
North-west	9,656	1,465	6,592	68.3%
Totals	82,120	13,603	61,212	74.5%

Source: Robert Baker, "On the State and Condition of the Town of Leeds in the West Riding of the County of York: in *The Chadwick Report, on the Sanitary Condition of the Labouring Population with the Local Reports of England and Wales and Other Related Papers, 1837–42,* 2 vols. (London: W. Clowes and Sons for HMSO, 1842; reprint ed. Shannon: Irish University Press, 1971), 2: 993.

sides by other cottages and shared walls. Each house was no larger than five yards by five yards. The first such cottages were constructed as early as the 1750s, when the old yards and courts of Briggate, Kirkgate, and the Headrow were lined with these five-yard cottages. The only difference between these early back-to-backs and the newer variety of the 1800s was the irregular and haphazard appearance of the former, contrasting with the symmetrical and monotonously straight lines of the latter.[52]

With characteristic and understandable concern for the morals of the inhabitants of Leeds in the 1850s, Edward Hall, a Unitarian domestic missionary in Holbeck, emphasized what daily life was like:

> They are built back to back, with no possibility of good ventilation, and contain a cellar for coals and food, the coal department being frequently tenanted with fowls, pigeons, or rabbits, and in some cases with two or all three of these—a room from 9 to 14 feet by from 10 to 12 or 14 feet, to do all the cooking, washing, and the necessary work of a family, and another of the same size for all to sleep in. Think for a moment what must be the inconvenience, the danger both in a moral and physical sense, when parents and children, young men and women, married and single, are crowded together in this way, with three beds in a room, and barely a couple of yards in the middle for the whole family to undress and dress in.[53]

---

[52] Maurice W. Beresford, "The Back-To-Back House in Leeds, 1787–1937," in Stanley D. Chapman, ed., *The History of Working-Class Housing: A Symposium* (Newton Abbot: David & Charles, 1971), 97–98.

[53] Quoted in Harrison, *The Birth and Growth of Industrial England,* 92–93.

Table 7. Denomination by Type of Housing, Leeds

Denominations	Back-to-Back (1)	Terraced No Gardens (2)	Terraced with Gardens (3)	Separate Dwelling Surrounded by Gardens (4)	Estate (5)	Undefined (6)	Totals
Unitarians	46.15%	30.77%	15.38%	0.00%	0.00%	7.69%	6.30%
Independents	35.29	23.53	21.57	0.00	1.96	17.65	24.52
Baptists	60.00	10.00	10.00	0.00	0.00	20.00	4.81
Friends	15.38	30.77	38.46	7.69	7.69	0.00	6.35
Wesleyan Methodists	48.28	17.24	11.49	0.00	0.00	22.99	41.83
Methodist New Connexion	45.45	9.09	0.00	0.00	0.00	45.45	5.29
Primitive Methodist	66.67	0.00	16.67	0.00	0.00	16.67	28.85
Mormon	52.94	29.41	5.88	0.00	0.00	11.76	8.17
Total %	44.23	20.19	14.90	0.48	0.96	19.23	100.00
Total Numbers	(92)	(42)	(31)	(1)	(2)	(40)	(208)

Source: Great Britain, *Ordnance Survey of Leeds* (5 feet to a mile, 25 sheets) (Southhampton, 1850).

Among the Mormons living in back-to-back housing were William Eddison, a brickmaker, at 24 Lion Street; Thomas Green, a mariner, at 14 Little Line Street; and Francis Fishburn, a tobacco pipe maker at 6 Hezmalhach's Yard, all in the North-east Ward.

The next step up in housing was the terraced or row house without a garden. The Mormons had 29.41 percent of their members (five families) living in this type of housing. Families such as William Shires, wool dyer, 24 Little Lemon St., North-east Ward; Henry John Harvis, a hatter, at 22 Briggate, Mill Hill Ward; and William Emsley, pipe maker, 10 St. Peters Court., North-east Ward.

The terraced house with a garden represents a third level of housing quality. It generally appeared on the maps with a front yard, sometimes small, but often long and narrow. The yard served to insulate the house and its inhabitants from the street. Only one Mormon (5.88 percent) was found in this housing category; Thomas Young, an inland revenue officer, lived with his wife, Harriet, and five children at 10 Byron Street, North Ward. His terraced house was not as grand as that of John Peele Clapham, the treasurer of the county court, an Independent, because Thomas Young's house had the garden in the back of the house with what appeared to be a privy. In contrast to the 5.88 percent of Mormons living in terraced housing with a garden, over 16 percent of the Primitive Methodists lived in this more desirable housing. Perhaps this suggests the more recent arrival of the Mormons into Leeds.

No Mormons lived in the most desirable type of housing, separate dwellings surrounded by gardens or estates. However, it should be recognized that the area of Leeds under examination was not large. Leeds Township contained almost 2,700 acres, Hunslet, 1,100 acres, and Holbeck only 760 acres. Although men such as Newman Cash, a Friend, and Edward Baines, an Independent and Member of Parliament, could somewhat insulate themselves in their homes in the West Ward at Springfield Lodge and Hanover Square respectively, the vast majority of the population lived in back-to-back or terraced housing.

Were these urban Latter-day Saints different in social composition from the other Nonconformists in the city of Leeds? The answer must be yes. They were the most likely to be working class in composition, the most likely to live in the predominantly working-class areas, the most likely to be housed in the least desirable housing—the back-to-backs and the terraced or row houses with no gardens, and the most likely to have emigrated to the borough of Leeds, especially from long distances.

Did these experiences of potential social dislocation play a role in making the early Mormons of Leeds religious seekers? With the evidence gathered in this study, that is a more difficult question to answer. The inclination is to conclude that this group of early Mormons must have been

Little Lemon Street, Leeds, the street where William Shires lived in 1851, with his wife and son and daughter. Photographed 1908. Courtesy of Leeds City Libraries.

Portion of Briggate, Mill Hill Ward, Leeds, believed to be the section of the street where Henry John Jarvis conducted business as a hatter and lived with his family. Photographed ca. 1903. Courtesy of Leeds City Libraries.

St. Peter's Court, North-east Ward, Leeds, on wash day. William Emsley, pipe maker, lived in this courtyard in 1851, with his wife, a son, two daughters, and a lodger. Photographed ca. 1899–1901. Courtesy of Leeds City Libraries.

more open to the need for new "associational and communal ties" brought about by their recent moves and their inferior social status in the community of Leeds.[54] But perhaps Leeds itself—a city with a strong Nonconformist tradition, within a region with the same strong tradition—might make a religious commitment to Mormonism easier than it would be in a more traditional Church of England community. There is perhaps then a uniqueness in the experiences of Leeds's Mormons which might not be evident in other urban areas.

Like Dickens's Coketown, which has become a caricature of itself, it is tempting to make the Leeds's Latter-day Saints a prototype of all the early Mormons in England and thereby attribute to this study more significance than it deserves. To date the emigrant has received most of the attention from historians. Without more comparative studies conducted at the sites of the early Mormon conversions in England, there will be little possibility of understanding the social composition of those converts who stayed in England as well as those who left.

---

[54]Gilbert, *Religion and Society*, 89.

11

Church Councils and Governance

RICHARD L. JENSEN

With good reason, the Church of Jesus Christ of Latter-day Saints has become known for the effectiveness of its centralized leadership. Still, insights into the nature and vitality of the movement are to be found at the congregational level.[1] For Mormonism in the British Isles and Europe a helpful perspective comes from local church councils, where many of the decisions were made that affected the daily life and worship of church members in the nineteenth century. This preliminary study seeks to explore some of what can be learned about those councils, and what they reveal about the church in the last century.

In the British Isles, as in America, much of the business of the LDS Church during its early years was conducted in conferences, following the principle of common consent. As the church grew, smaller deliberative bodies than conferences became necessary and councils were established.[2] In early years the terms conference and council seemed almost interchangeable; however, their roles were gradually separated. The role of deliberating, initiating action, and coordinating church discipline was increasingly

---

[1] See, for example, Ronald W. Walker, " 'Going to Meeting' in Salt Lake City's Thirteenth Ward, 1849–1881: A Microanalysis," in Davis Bitton and Maureen Ursenbach Beecher, eds., *New Views of Mormon History: Essays in Honor of Leonard J. Arrington* (Salt Lake City: University of Utah Press, 1987), 138–61.

[2] See Doctrine and Covenants 26:2, 28:13, 72:7, and 20:65–67; and Donald Q. Cannon and Lyndon W. Cook, eds., *Far West Record: Minutes of The Church of Jesus Christ of Latter-day Saints, 1830–1844* (Salt Lake City: Deseret Book, 1983), 1–74. Verses 66 and 67 of Section 20, which correspond to Section 17:16–17 of the Doctrine and Covenants of the Reorganized Church of Jesus Christ of Latter Day Saints (hereafter cited as RLDS), were added after initial publication of the revelation, probably not before July 1833. See RLDS Doctrine and Covenants, introduction to Section 17.

concentrated in the council. High councils, established initially at Kirtland, Ohio, and Clay County, Missouri, in 1834, became presiding quorums at church headquarters. Later, however, high councils proliferated and were given responsibility only for specific geographical areas, eventually for stakes.[3] No high councils were organized in the British Isles during the nineteenth century. However, on the congregational level much of the day-to-day business requiring both deliberation and a degree of common consent was conducted in branch councils.

Branch councils were to make available to the branch president the "combined wisdom of his council on various subjects, and it is his duty to come to a decision as he shall be led by the Spirit of God."[4] The branch president's decision was binding, but if council felt it was unrighteous they could appeal to higher authority — generally the conference president. From available accounts it appears that decisions were reached with remarkable unanimity, and were generally passed after discussion by a vote of the council, rather than being the function of the branch president after hearing advice from the council. There was thus seldom any necessity for an appeal.

The local council meeting was the business meeting for priesthood bearers of the branch, and this was the main priesthood meeting they attended. By involving even relatively inexperienced male Latter-day Saints in administration and decision making at the congregational level, branch councils gave added emphasis to the significance of a lay priesthood.

Other church members, including women, were frequently present. Sometimes nonmembers of the church also attended. Without further study it would be difficult to determine whether in actual practice council meetings limited to the priesthood were the general rule or the exception. In theory, it should have been the general rule.[5]

Local councils met weekly, fortnightly, monthly, or as needed. They adopted fairly uniform procedures. Decisions were finalized by the presentation of a motion, which was seconded and then voted upon. Minutes were kept, varying in the amount of detail recorded, and usually number-

---

[3] Doctrine and Covenants 102; Lyndon W. Cook, *The Revelations of the Prophet Joseph Smith: A Historical and Biographical Commentary of the Doctrine and Covenants* (Provo, Utah: Seventy's Mission Bookstore, 1981), 206-7.

[4] *Millennial Star* 7 (March 1, 1846): 90.

[5] In discussing the Manchester Branch Council of 1840 James B. Allen concludes that the inclusion of women "was probably an aberration even at that time," in that it contradicted the pattern already established in Doctrine and Covenants 102. James B. Allen, *Trials of Discipleship: The Story of William Clayton, a Mormon* (Urbana and Chicago: University of Illinois Press, 1987), 26. However, as I point out hereafter, Section 102 was apparently not considered applicable to branch councils.

ing each item of business transacted. Generally the president and the clerk signed the minutes of each meeting after they were approved by the council.

Many of the concerns of councils were mundane necessities like arranging for rent, light, heat, and cleaning of the meeting place. In councils many details of religious observance were settled. Early councils determined when the sacrament would be offered to church members. Councils established fast days on an ongoing basis and for special occasions. In 1852 the Nottingham Council voted "that we fast and pray every Seventh Sunday for more of the gifts and Blessings and that the work of the Lord may Revive amongst us."[6] The Christiania (later Oslo) Branch council in Norway voted to celebrate Christmas Day 1856 by fasting to separate themselves from the "gluttony and drunkenness" that they felt too frequently dominated the world around them on that day. The Nottingham Council decided in 1851 to use water for the sacrament rather than "raisin water" that had been used in the branch earlier.[7]

Councils and their presidents directed the establishment of Sunday schools, of prayer meetings and fellowship meetings, and of meetings in which priesthood bearers could practice preaching as missionaries would do before an audience of fellow church members. Recreation was also a focus of the councils. They regularly directed planning of branch tea parties or soirées. The Nottingham Branch established a tradition of a branch tea party each Easter Monday, with additional parties throughout the year.[8]

Local initiative was evident in other measures the councils adopted. Officers of the Rutherglen Branch in Scotland decided in 1849, before the establishment of the Perpetual Emigrating Fund, that they would save the money they otherwise might have spent on "smoking, chewing, snuffing, drinking whiskey, porter, ale, tea, coffee, etc.," and with the collective savings send people to New Orleans, who would then send their earnings from America to help other branch members emigrate.[9] In 1875 the Dundee

---

[6] Nottingham Council Minutes, 17 June 1852, Library-Archives, Historical Department, The Church of Jesus Christ of Latter-day Saints, Salt Lake City, hereafter cited as LDS Church Archives. All council minutes cited hereafter are located at the LDS Church Archives. Most are found among Records of Members of the respective branches. Access to other council minutes is presently restricted.

[7] Carl Christian Anton Christensen Diary, 18 December 1856, translation by Orson B. West, typescript, LDS Church Archives. Nottingham Council Minutes, 15 July 1851.

[8] See, for example, Nottingham Council Minutes, 8 April 1851.

[9] Eli Kelsey to Orson Pratt, May 3, 1849, in *Millennial Star* 11 (July 1, 1849): 200–202. The editor of the *Star* approved of the general idea, but suggested that individual savings should be the focus.

Branch agreed to establish a revolving emigration loan fund for branch members with money willed to the branch by a deceased member.[10]

The Christiania Branch Council agreed in 1856 that the branch would pay for missionary C. C. A. Christensen to receive instructions in the English language from an Englishman, with the agreement that Christensen would then teach branch members in evening classes.[11]

Local councils were responsible for the well-being of branch members. Each branch generally had a fund for the poor and appointed a person to be responsible for disbursing its limited means to those in most urgent need. District teachers reported to the council on the health and financial condition of those they visited, as well as their relationship to the church. As a rule, these teachers were a limited number of mature men assigned two by two to sizeable geographical areas in the branch. In some branches, confidentiality was considered essential to the branch leadership's ability to respond effectively to individual needs. The Nottingham Council agreed in 1851 that anyone who passed information beyond the council would be disfellowshipped for three months.[12] Some other branches allowed more widespread access to council proceedings.

Teachers were also collectors of various funds for their districts. They each kept a book in which donations were listed. Some local councils made a practice of reading the list of contributors, either in the council meeting or in a worship service.

Councils helped supervise the gathering of funds to provide clothing for missionaries. This was usually done without incident, but occasionally tensions arose when the misuse of scarce resources was suspected. In the Nottingham Council in 1855 half a dozen men pointed to the apparent injustice in filling the request of a missionary for additional clothing. After all, they had provided him only four months earlier with a suit worth five pounds sterling. If his present request were to be granted, they contended, it would require special donations from "Brethren and sisters some who where [were] prevented attending to the means of Grace [sacrament meeting] — thro the want of clothing and where [were] actually wanting bread." Nearly a month later the missionary clarified his request, and with good feelings they donated funds for a strong pair of winter trousers and appointed a committee of women to collect funds for undergarments.[13]

---

[10] Dundee Branch Council Minutes, 25 July 1875. In the minutes, the agreement was signed not only by ten members of the council, with a designation of the position each held, but also by twenty-four branch members, including a mark for each of four illiterate members.

[11] Christensen Diary, 12 June 1856.

[12] Nottingham Council Minutes, 30 December 1851.

[13] Ibid., 23 January 1855; 19 February 1855.

The teachers bore initial responsibility for helping settle disputes between members and for encouraging them to be faithful in all their church obligations. Problems that could not be settled in the course of their personal contact were brought to the council. In some branches a teachers' council, sometimes called the petty council, dealt with relatively minor and routine problems, reserving matters of a more serious nature for the general branch council.[14] The number of individual problems handled by councils suggests that teachers, as a rule, were relatively vigilant. The president of the Nottingham Conference told an offender in a council meeting in 1855, "You cannot do wrong long in this Church without being found out[;] all hidden things must be brought to light."[15] The councils' involvement in dealing with wrongdoing occupied a major part of their effort.

The summons to appear before a church council was not to be taken lightly. Those who refused the invitation risked church discipline for "contempt of council," which in many cases resulted in excommunication. Those who showed sincerity and appropriate humility in expressing a desire to do right usually fared much better before the council than those who did not.

In matters of church discipline, local councils in the British Isles and on the Continent did not adhere to the specific procedures for high council action prescribed in Doctrine and Covenants 102 (RLDS 99). There was no assigned division of council members to represent the different sides of any case. The formal requirements for high council discipline were presumably considered not binding on other councils.

Being called before the council to answer for one's conduct was at least a pointed reminder of duties as a Latter-day Saint. In many instances the Nottingham Council heard a church member's response to concerns that had been raised, then dismissed the case, directing that the individual be "left in the watch care of the Teacher of his District." A similar approach was evident when they heard a member express his desires to continue in the church as a faithful member and voted, "We bid him god speed."[16]

Other cases, however, resulted in disfellowshipment or excommunication. The 1850s were volatile years for church membership in the British Isles, which saw a rapid increase beginning in 1848 and reached its peak in 1851. Excommunications during the 1850s far exceeded any other period. Examination of this phenomenon on a local level may begin to suggest helpful areas of inquiry into the dynamics of church life in that significant period.

---

[14] See, for example, ibid., 1 July 1851; 31 October 1854; 28 November 1854; 23 January 1855; 29 April 1855.

[15] Ibid., 14 June 1855.

[16] Ibid., 6 May 1851; 26 June 1852.

Nottingham Council minutes show a total of 284 cases of excommunication in the years 1851–57. Ten individuals were excommunicated more than once; thus, the actual number of persons excommunicated was 274. Because of brief gaps in the record, there may have been a few more excommunications. Nottingham averaged 41 excommunications per year during this seven-year period. The years 1851 and 1856 saw the fewest excommunications, with 30 and 23 respectively; 1852 was highest, with 61. 1853, 1854, 1855, and 1857 were close to average, with 43, 41, 41, and 45 respectively.

A striking characteristic is that for 38 percent of the excommunications recorded, neglect of duty was named as a reason. This was by far the most frequent reason mentioned. Apostasy was mentioned for 24 percent. Eighteen percent had requested excommunication — a notation that by itself gives little hint of the motivation for the action, but for several of these additional reasons were listed. Fourteen percent were cited for contempt of the council, which tells little about any underlying cause but may indicate that relationships had deteriorated. Only 15 percent of the reasons given were what might be classed as sins of commission (bad conduct, adultery, lying, drunkenness). In some cases more than one reason was given for an excommunication.

Apostasy was mentioned in 30 percent of Nottingham's excommunications in 1851 (9 cases); 23 percent in 1852 (14 cases); 37 percent in 1854 (14 cases); and 42 percent in 1857 (19 cases). Because district teachers were generally assigned to investigate the situation of those called before the council, it is likely that council records reflected fairly accurately the number of excommunicants who were willing to make their disagreement with church teachings known.

It comes as little surprise that apostasy was a major factor in the excommunications that took place during 1854, shortly after the introduction of controversial teachings about plural marriage and about Adam as God.[17] Discussion of the year 1857 below will give some idea of the reasons apostasy might have become evident that year. Further study is needed before any conclusions can be drawn about relatively high rates of apostasy in Nottingham in 1851 and particularly in 1852. Rumors of plural marriage in Utah prior to the official announcement in Europe in January

---

[17] The official announcement of plural marriage to the British Mission is found in *Millennial Star* 15 (1 January 1853): 9–11. The teaching of Adam as God was presented in *Millennial Star* 15 (26 November 1853): 769–70; (10 December 1853): 801–4; (1853 Supplement): 13–18. For a discussion of Brigham Young's teachings about Adam, see David J. Buerger, "The Adam-God Doctrine," *Dialogue* 15 (Spring 1982): 14–58. Although taught by Young, the Adam-God doctrine remains only partially defined and is not today official Latter-day Saint doctrine.

1853 may well have been a factor. However, documentation of apostasy in the British Isles stemming from opposition to polygamy remains circumstantial and relatively infrequent. While missionary diaries report considerable dismay among church members over the teaching, especially soon after its official announcement,[18] they give little direct evidence of excommunications that may have resulted from it. The limited council minutes available provide few details and seldom specify the basis for charges of apostasy. Nottingham records suggest that even in 1853–54 apostasy — probably including opposition to plural marriage — was only one of a variety of reasons why individuals left the Latter-day Saint Church, and apostasy never accounted for a majority of excommunications in any given year. On the other hand, disenchantment with doctrine was undoubtedly involved in some of the defections connected with neglect of duty.

Council proceedings occasionally gave glimpses into the process of coming to terms with new teachings. After the systematic payment of tithing was introduced in 1856 a Nottingham teacher remained optimistic that the wife of one reluctant man would eventually convince him to comply, just as she had earlier overcome his opposition to the teaching of plural marriage: "She had Tongue Banged him into Plurelity [plurality] and she would have to Tongue Bange him into Tything." Indeed, at her insistence they were already paying a tithe. A district president reported that his greatest difficulty in teaching tithing was at home, where his wife was "always ready to find fault," while otherwise tithing met with general acceptance throughout his district.[19] Domestic interaction did not always result in accommodation to new teachings. In May 1854 the Nottingham Council forgave a man for alleged failure to perform his duties after he expressed a desire to do right and explained that his wife's opposition to the teaching of plural marriage was creating discord between them. A council member advised that if the man would get the spirit of God the conflict would end. Three years later the man and his wife were both excommunicated for apostasy.[20]

The unusually rapid gains in British Mission membership in 1848–51 apparently included thousands who were never effectively assimilated into the faith. This is illustrated by the Kilmarnock Branch in Scotland. The twenty-two who had been members of the Kilmarnock Branch and who were excommunicated in the years 1849–51 had an average tenure in the church of only one year and five months. The thirty-one excommunicated between 1852 and 1856 averaged three years and four months' tenure; the

---

[18] See, for example, William A. Empey Diary, 5 and 7 January 1853, typescript, BYU Library.

[19] Nottingham Council Minutes, 19 August 1856.

[20] Ibid., 16 May 1854; 23 June 1857.

nine excommunicated in 1857–58 averaged nine years and two months.[21] Of those excommunicated in the decade 1849–58, thirty-five (56 percent) had been baptized within three years, 1848–50.

British Mission conversions to the Latter-day Saint Church declined significantly in the years 1852 and 1853, but then held at a relatively stable rate for five years, 1853–57 (see Figures 1 and 2). Baptisms for each of those years averaged 4,240, which was an average annual increase of 15.1 percent over the number of members at the beginning of each year. If reported deaths had been the only loss of members, the mission would have experienced a respectable 13.6 percent average annual growth rate for 1853–57. Thus, while the impact of plural marriage on Mormon conversions may have been significant, by itself it was not decisive at this time. However, the combination of excommunication, emigration, and unexplained disappearance of members from church records resulted in a net loss of membership every year from 1852 through 1859. The most rapid declines were in 1855, with a net loss of 11.7 percent; 1856, with 13.5 percent; and 1857, with 32.4 percent. For the decade, the excommunication of 31,820 members nearly doubled the loss of 15,678 due to emigration.[22]

Local church councils played a leading role in carrying out the churchwide Reformation that reached its high point in 1857. This saw an intensification of the sifting process and of the calls for rededication that had been major functions of the councils since their inception. The spirit of the Reformation caught on quickly, and local leaders sometimes had the process underway before instructions were published from Liverpool. Coming on the heels of the systematic introduction of the Law of Tithing, the renewal movement focused heavily on compliance with that law and with

---

[21] Kilmarnock Branch, Scotland, Records of Members, LDS Church Archives. Excommunications of one-time Kilmarnock members were also documented in records of members for Glasgow, Irvine, and Stewarton branches. In addition to the sixty-two excommunicants reported here, eleven more were excommunicated during the period 1849–59, but these were omitted from consideration because of incomplete information in the records.

[22] European Mission Statistical Reports, in *Millennial Star* 12: 15, 207; 13: 15, 207; 14: 15, 318; 15: 78, 510; 16: 78, 478; 17: 75. European Mission Statistics, 1855–76, LDS Church Archives. Reports submitted from the various conferences did not cover identical periods until 1850. Beginning that year semiannual reports gave figures for 1 June and 1 December; beginning in December 1852 the dates were changed to 30 June and 31 December. Baptism figures make no distinction between converts and children of members. Emigration totals do not include children under the age of eight. I have used the statistics reported, although some reports were admittedly less than accurate. Figure 2, "increase not accounted for" and "decrease not accounted for" suggest the extent of accounting problems in the reports.

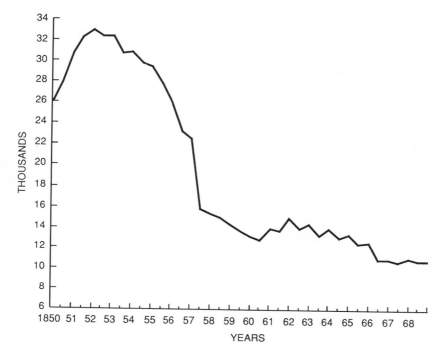

Figure 1. Total Mission Membership, 1850–68, from semiannual reports

the Word of Wisdom, but went well beyond that. Nottingham's branch president rejoiced that the time had come for a "complete Eradicating reform."[23] Church members were to put their homes in order, pray regularly with their families, control their passions, and eradicate anything that would stand in the way of building the Kingdom of God. Rebaptism was to signify a renewed determination to live according to gospel precepts.

Council members, in confessing their own shortcomings and expressing determination to overcome personal obstacles, reinforced one another's enthusiasm and became the core of the Reformation's fire. Many faced significant challenges. A Nottingham priest reported that he and his family were observing the Word of Wisdom and were paying tithing despite the fact that they were "much clammed for the want of Bread" and most of them were barefooted.[24]

Summonses to the council were delivered in batches in 1857, requiring even more than before that those whose devotion was marginal or

---

[23] Nottingham Council Minutes, 17 February 1857.
[24] Ibid., 3 March 1857.

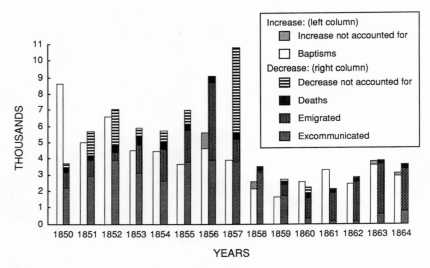

Figure 2. Changes in Mission Membership, 1850–64

doubtful gave an accounting and discussed their intentions. As a result, the ranks continued to be thinned by excommunication—but at no higher a rate than in most of the preceding seven years. Councils also played a significant role in the affirmative side of the Reformation, obtaining a recommitment by those who remained in the church. In Nottingham those who declined to appear before the council were charged with contempt of the council, in addition to other charges pending, and were generally cut off. As a rule, those who appeared before the council confessed their short-comings, expressed willingness to do better, and received encouragement and even a degree of leniency. A seventy-eight-year-old teacher "said his chief support was a little coffee, he used a little tobacco but he wished to do right." The branch president counseled that he might continue with the coffee, but that he must stop using tobacco. An elderly woman whose income was only one shilling per week was counseled to pay her tithing, but allowed to continue to drink tea.[25]

Council meetings during the Reformation became more introspective than before, with officers being repeatedly asked to express their feelings about their standing as church members. Sobering as the Reformation must have been, however, there are occasional signs that humor survived. By March 1858 the Nottingham branch president advised his council that he did not want to hurt feelings, but that he must point out that in their

---

[25] Ibid., 1 and 3 March 1857.

meetings there was "too much laughter and trifling," and that they needed to get the spirit and proceed expeditiously with the business at hand.[26]

Excommunication figures for Nottingham suggest that the Latter-day Saint Church in this area was undergoing a relatively intensive process of sifting and self-renewal for the entire period 1851–57. Emphasis on the urgency of moving the Kingdom of God forward was intimately connected with church discipline. With sins of omission serving as the most frequent reason for strong discipline, the Nottingham Branch was striving for qualitative growth. Branch officers labored with those who were not vigorous and valiant in doing their duty, and with those who did not believe, and cut off what seemed to be dead wood when the response was not promising.

Further study is needed to see to how the patterns evident at Nottingham for 1857 may have compared with other areas in the British Isles and in the European Mission as a whole. Excommunication totals for the British Mission (see Figure 2) indicate vigorous sifting of its membership throughout the 1850s and are compatible with the suggestion that the so-called Reformation years were not very different in this regard from the rest of the decade. Yet with a precipitous drop in mission membership in the first half of 1857 — the peak months of the Reformation — clearly something unusual was happening. During the Reformation new membership records were created for church branches, listing only those who were rebaptized. More than 5,000 who were not formally excommunicated simply disappeared from the records. It appears that the remaining membership by the end of 1857 consisted only of those who had made a renewed commitment which included the payment of tithing.[27] Whether formally excommunicated, those unwilling to actively support the Latter-day Saint Church now found themselves outside the fold.

By contrast, two decades later, 1877–79, twenty-eight members of the Aalborg Branch in Denmark were excommunicated in a twenty-five-month period. None were excommunicated for sins of omission, for apostasy, or for contempt of the council; eighteen were disciplined for sins of commission, eight at their own request, and no reasons were listed for two. A different kind of sifting was taking place. This was no pruning of dead

---

[26] Ibid., 16 March 1858.

[27] Branch Records of Members for the British Mission are far from complete for the period 1856–67, but the present author's sampling of those still extant showed new records beginning in 1857 in most instances. As Richard Poll suggests elsewhere in this volume, those who disappeared from membership records at this time probably included many whose affiliation was marginal and whose location was by now unknown.

branches, but a severance of those whose active conduct seemed to dictate the separation.[28]

Priorities varied between Nottingham of the 1850s and Aalborg of the 1870s, although behavior probably varied as well. The 1850s featured an interesting combination of enthusiasm and restraint. The counsel of Nottingham's branch president in 1854 is instructive: "Hold out the hand of mercy—where there is life cherish the tree[;] if there is no life they are dead branches."[29] Later the same year the Nottingham Council was advised to "carefully and cautiously consulte and deliberate together in the things pertaining to life and salvation and not to be hasty in rising to move or second a motion." In 1855 the council "felt inclined to hide [a brother's] weaknesses beneath the mantle of charity."[30] Yet clearly council members felt impelled to prune where it seemed necessary to keep the church vigorous.

Excommunication did not preclude later readmission into the church. Twenty-four of the excommunicants at Nottingham were eventually rebaptized. In 1858, at the end of the period for which records have been located, fifteen of these were still church members.

Branch councils demonstrated a striking degree of internal unanimity in their decisions. One of the few exceptions was a case in the Bergen Branch, Norway, where in 1884 half of those attending opposed the verdict of excommunication for a man accused of disobedience to the priesthood. The branch president consulted afterwards with his conference president, who directed that the man should be excommunicated immediately.[31]

The local council bore major responsibility for coordination of proselytizing. Shortly after the creation of the Vale House Branch, east of Manchester, members of its council approved a motion "that wee the Vale house saints take for hour [our] District to warn.[:] Glossop Dale as far as the town hall and Hadfield and Padfield Watherside Tintwistle Arnfield and Woodhead." They also agreed on a proposed division of the mother branch's inventory of tracts.[32]

The local council generally assigned local priesthood bearers and others who volunteered to distribute tracts and other church literature. Women

---

[28] Aalborg Branch, Denmark, Historical Record, 1877–79, LDS Church Archives.

[29] Nottingham Council Minutes, 25 July 1854.

[30] Ibid., 19 September 1854; 6 December 1855.

[31] Record of council action in Bergen Branch Record of Members, Entry for 16 March 1884, LDS Church Archives.

[32] Vale House Council Minutes, 6 September 1849, found in Cowdenbeath, Scotland, Branch Record of Members, 1867–1873, LDS Church Archives. The mother branch was Mottram in Logdendale.

frequently volunteered. In April 1857 the Aalborg, Denmark, Branch Council received reports of the priesthood brethren's missionary labors, after which several sisters reported selling many pamphlets and talking with several good people in and out of town." The men had apparently sold less literature and held fewer discussions. The conference president commended both brethren and sisters, although each male's name was duly recorded, while the sisters remained anonymous in the minutes.[33]

Councils directed the establishment and operation of tract societies in the branches, which encouraged the purchase and distribution of tracts. The Falkirk Branch, in Scotland, apparently published tracts of their own by 1852, and branch members personally bought additional tracts from Liverpool in order to distribute them along with those produced locally.[34]

Councils assigned priesthood bearers to hold meetings in outlying areas and report back. Sometimes a deacon and a teacher would be appointed to this assignment.[35] Councils sometimes called priests and elders to missionary assignments further afield. The experience of C. C. A. Christensen is instructive in this regard. At a council meeting in Copenhagen in January 1853 Christensen was ordained a priest and called on a full-time mission to Western Sjaelland, where he helped establish a branch of the church some eighty kilometers southwest of Copenhagen. Later, as a traveling elder, Christensen's proselytizing assignments to various areas in Norway were made in council meetings.[36]

Traveling elders whose full time was spent in proselytizing and related church work were under the jurisdiction of their conference presidents, not of branch councils. However, conference presidents seem to have utilized local council meetings as if they were conferences in the sense of Doctrine and Covenants 73:2, "And then, behold, it shall be made known unto them, by the voice of the conference, their several missions." In the terminology of the day, each separate assignment to labor in a particular location, whether for part of a day or for months, was referred to as a mission. Thus officers of branches had the opportunity to approve changes in missionary assignments. Although minutes and diaries provide little detail on the matter, mutually beneficial discussion — either formal or informal — probably accompanied the transaction of this business. Such an approach helped integrate the efforts of full-time missionaries with those of local church members. There seems to have been a feeling of shared responsibility for proselytizing.

---

[33] Aalborg Branch Council Minutes, 6 April 1857.

[34] Falkirk Branch, Scotland, Council Minutes, 1852–1880, entry for 7 March 1852, LDS Church Archives.

[35] See, for example, Nottingham Council Minutes, 20 May 1851.

[36] Christensen Diary, 24 January 1853; 21 October 1853; 14 January 1855.

Changes in conference presidencies were sometimes approved by local councils. When church authorities wished to proceed with the change before a conference could be called, the council's approval immediately preceded the change.[37] This bespoke not only a flexibility in matters of jurisdiction but also a continued observance of the principle of common consent. So smoothly could jurisdictional matters be juggled that some minute books contain minutes of branch and conference councils side by side in chronological order, sometimes with nothing to distinguish between the one and the other, along with "special councils" bearing no notation whether their jurisdiction was the branch or the conference.[38] Diaries frequently mention council meetings without specifying what jurisdiction was involved. Conference presidents frequently attended branch council meetings; in some instances they requested changes in meeting times so they could attend consistently. It appears from the minutes that actual conference council meetings — sometimes called conferences of delegates — were relatively infrequent, as they would generally require representation from each branch. They were most easily held in conjunction with each conference's "conference" meetings. In the interim, conference business was conducted in the branch council meetings the conference president attended.[39]

Council meetings became merely an occasional formalized extension of weekly worship services in at least one branch in Norway near the turn of the century. When cases arose that required church judicial action, the branch president announced after the commencement of the regular service that prior to partaking of the sacrament the branch was convening a council meeting. In the presence of all the worshipers the case was tried, and afterwards the regular service resumed.[40] Further study will be required to ascertain how widespread this practice became.

Local church councils of the 1850s reveal the dynamics of church life at the grass roots. They show a beehive of activity, a pattern of concerns and endeavors that were the focus of Latter-day Saints' daily lives. Records of relatively few councils are presently available for later years. They indicate that patterns of church discipline changed dramatically, and they sug-

---

[37] Ibid., 14 January 1855; 24 May 1868.

[38] A good example is the Nottingham Council Minutes, 1851–58.

[39] In the 1850s and 1860s councils were held occasionally at the mission level for the British Mission, the European Mission, the Swiss and Italian Mission, and the Scandinavian Mission. Reports of some of these yield important historical insights, but most of them varied little in function from conferences and bore little similarity to branch councils. See, for example, *Millennial Star* 14:243ff; 16:465ff and 705; 18:547ff; 21:69ff; 24:33ff; 27:291–93; 28:49ff. Particularly insightful is the information reported from the council of June 26–28, 1854, in volume 16.

[40] Bergen Branch, Norway, Historical Record, 1880–1906, LDS Church Archives.

gest erosion in the functioning of the once-vital church councils by the turn of the century. The effectiveness of local councils was heavily dependent on relatively intensive efforts by dedicated district teachers. In many branches, that level of effort must have been difficult to maintain over an extended period of time.

After 1870, with many local members of the lay priesthood having emigrated or defected from the faith, it became largely impracticable to base local church operations on the deliberations of councils. Increasingly, decisions were made unilaterally by missionaries from America, or by local individuals serving as branch presidents. This development ran parallel to the centralization of leadership in the American church in ward bishoprics, after priesthood councils, and particularly teacher's quorums, had played a major role in church governance for many years.

A key to the vitality of the Latter-day Saint Church in the British Isles and Europe in the early years of the missions appears to have been broadly based local participation in many facets of church activity, particularly church councils. Further study of this phenomenon and of the demise of the council approach could provide significant insights into the achievements and the decline of the LDS Church's missions in Britain and elsewhere.[41]

---

[41] One aspect deserving scrutiny is suggested by Andrew Phillips's observations elsewhere in this volume about the relative success of branches in Essex. The dynamics of local involvement in councils and proselytizing, and the concomitant commitment of individuals and families to the Latter-day Saint cause, would be a fruitful area for comparative study.

12

LDS Pastors and Pastorates, 1852–55

WILLIAM G. HARTLEY

When Apostle Franklin D. Richards returned in 1854, after a two-year absence, to serve again as British Mission president, he felt pride in one change he had implemented during his previous term. "It was during that period," he told coworkers, "that the first appointment of Pastors took place, and I find it has been a good arrangement."[1]

Starting in 1852 and continuing into the 1860s, pastors filled a leadership layer between mission presidency and conference presidents in the British Mission. Local initiative gave rise to several Latter-day Saint auxiliary organizations in the nineteenth century, but this creation of an ecclesiastical position, limited to Europe, was unusual for a church with strong centralized authority at its headquarters. Here I define, explain, and illustrate the office and calling of a pastor in Britain during a four-year period, 1852–55. I focus on these years because they were the formative period when the office of pastor was introduced, implemented, and refined, and because there is an unusually rich pool of information about pastors who served then.[2]

By mid-1852, church membership in the British Mission was nearly double that of 1848, although it had declined slightly from an all-time high in 1851. The mission was experiencing rapid turnover in its membership. President Franklin D. Richards and his one and sometimes two counse-

---

[1] *Millennial Star* 16 (August 19, 1854): 513. In its sixth "Article of Faith," The Church of Jesus Christ of Latter-day Saints states belief in biblical church officers, including pastors.

[2] Not explored here is pastoral work in Britain after 1855 nor in Denmark, where pastors also served. See Andrew Jenson, *History of the Scandinavian Mission* (Salt Lake City: Deseret News Press, 1927), 124, 129, 153, 170.

lors[3] struggled to manage member and missionary work in 700 branches grouped in 50 conferences containing 32,000 Saints in England, Wales, Scotland, Ireland, and nearby islands.[4] In addition, Richards as European Mission president was faced with the task of overseeing church operations on the Continent.

Many of the mission's conference presidents, branch presidents, and missionaries were British Mormons who were likely to emigrate to Utah in view of newly offered assistance from the Perpetual Emigrating Fund and an increased emphasis on the gathering to Utah. To replace them and to train and supervise their successors would pose a formidable challenge for a mission presidency already straining to maintain the gains of past years. In 1850, when rapid growth had increased the need for local supervision, mission leaders had assigned missionaries to serve as district presidents to help strengthen branches. Now Franklin Richards needed supervisory help for the conferences.[5] Thus, at a special mission conference in April 1852 Richards called five experienced elders to supervise from two to five conferences and dubbed them "district presidents" at first, then "pastors."[6] Two pastors and pastorates were added during the remainder of 1852.[7]

---

[3] Daniel Spencer and John Van Cott were mission counselors as of May 14, 1853. Van Cott departed to preside over Scandinavia in August 1854, leaving Samuel Richards and Spencer as the Presidency. In mid-1854 Franklin D. Richards became president and kept Spencer as his sole counselor. Cyrus Wheelock is listed as second counselor on September 8, 1855. British Mission Manuscript History, Archives, Historical Department of The Church of Jesus Christ of Latter-day Saints, Salt Lake City, hereafter cited as LDS Church Archives.

[4] British Mission Manuscript History, December 30, 1853. Each conference contained from four to forty branches. Manchester, the largest conference, had 3,048 members in 33 branches; Carlyle, the smallest, had 142 members in 6 branches.

[5] *Millennial Star* 12 (January 15, 1850): 26; (February 14, 1850): 58; 14 (June 19, 1852): 257–60. Levi Richards had provided similar assistance in 1850, when mission president Orson Pratt sent him to Wales.

[6] Ibid., 14 (May 8, 1852): 171; (May 15, 1852): 177. As listed by the *Star*, the initial pastors were:

Pastor	Conferences in His Pastorate
Jacob Gates	London, Reading, Kent, Essex
Cyrus H. Wheelock	Manchester, Liverpool, Preston
Robert Campbell	Glasgow, Edinburgh, Dundee
Appleton Harmon	Newcastle-on-Tyne, Carlisle, Hull
Moses Clawson	Lincolnshire, Bradford, Derbyshire Warwickshire

[7] Isaac C. Haight and Dorr P. Curtis. *Millennial Star* 14 (July 10, 1852): 319; (December 11, 1852): 666.

New Mission President Samuel W. Richards, learning that a small battalion of perhaps eighty elders was arriving from Utah in 1853, picked twelve to be pastors—five to replace departees and seven to fill newly created pastorates.[8] For the next several years, the British Mission operated between twelve and sixteen pastorates at a time.

To effectively represent the mission presidency in supervising the work of local church leaders and missionaries, pastors needed to be men of experience. It was apparently felt that a period of residence in Utah provided the advantage of more thorough initiation into church doctrine and practices. A composite profile of the thirty-four pastors who served between 1852 and 1855 shows that thirty-three were elders from Utah, and only John Parry, Jr., of Wales had never emigrated.[9] British-born elders from Utah included James G. Willie, William Clayton, Edward Martin, and Charles Smith (England); William C. Dunbar, James P. Park, and Robert Campbell (Scotland); Thomas Jeremy and Daniel Daniels (Wales); and probably John McDonald of Ireland. Most of the thirty-three pastors were married men. Of twenty-nine for whom we have located birthdates, the average age was forty, two were beyond age fifty, and only three were in their twenties.[10]

The mission president picked pastors either from the ranks of newly arriving elders from Utah or from among conference presidents. Pastors normally did not have counselors, and they served in an average of two pastorates. Calls and releases came at year's end. After calls were made, the *Millennial Star* announced them. New pastors, armed with a letter of appointment, introduced themselves to conference presidents over whom they would preside. At the next quarterly conference of the conferences involved, pastors were presented for sustaining votes.[11]

---

[8] *Millennial Star* 14 (November 27, 1852): 634. Departees were Wheelock, Gates, Clawson, Haight, and Harmon. Utah elders picked as pastors were John S. Fullmer, John Van Cott, James G. Willie, William Clayton, Chauncey Webb, Richard Cook, Charles Smith, Sylvester Earl, Thomas Jeremy, Daniel Daniels, Benjamin Brown, and John McDonald. See *Millennial Star* 15 (July 30, 1853): 511, and Missionary Record Book A, LDS Church Archives.

[9] The thirty-four pastors were Millen Atwood, Israel Barlow, John Barker, Benjamin Brown, Edward Bunker, Robert Campbell, James Carrigan, Moses Clawson, Richard Cook, Dorr P. Curtis, Charles A. Dana, Daniel Daniels, David C. Dille, William C. Dunbar, Sylvester Earl, Edmund Ellsworth, John S. Fullmer, James Ferguson, Jacob Gates, William S. Glover, George D. Grant, Isaac Haight, Appleton Harmon, Thomas Jeremy, Wm. H. Kimball, Edward Martin, John McDonald, John Parry, Jr., Charles Smith, Daniel Tyler, John Van Cott, Chauncey G. Webb, Cyrus Wheelock, and James G. Willie.

[10] Andrew Jenson, *Latter-day Saint Biographical Encyclopedia*, 4 vols. (1901; reprint ed., Salt Lake City: Western Epics, 1971); and Missionary Record Book A.

[11] John Van Cott Journal, January 2, 1853, Special Collections, Harold B. Lee

Latter-day Saint elders, Liverpool, 1855. Courtesy LDS Church Historical Department. Front row (l-r): James Bond, Spicer Crandall, William C. Dunbar*, James Ross, Daniel D. McArthur. Middle: Edward Bunker*, Chauncey Webb*, Franklin D. Richards (mission president), Daniel Spencer (mission counselor), Dan Jones, Edward Martin*. Back: Edmund Ellsworth*, Joseph A. Young, William H. Kimball*, George D. Grant*, James Ferguson*, James A. Little, Philemon Merrill. *Pastors, 1852–55.

Pastors filed reports, not regularly but frequently, with the Liverpool presidency. Fullmer's diary notes his sending pastoral reports by mail or submitting them in person. Records indicate that pastors occasionally visited headquarters, and that presidency members visited and worked in the pastorates. Counselor Daniel Spencer traveled constantly in the pastorates from 1853 to 1855. The most important contact between pastor and mission presidency came during a special London council of elders, May 26–28, 1854, which conference presidents also attended. Here, the presidency clarified mission policies regarding emigration and the calling of local men to be missionaries; discussed doctrinal topics including plural marriage and Adam-God teachings; and directed that branch Sunday schools

Library, Brigham Young University Library, Provo, Utah, hereafter cited as BYU Library.

be started and that branch debts be retired, even if special fast days would be required to do so.[12]

A pastor's primary work was training, assisting, and supervising conference presidents and, through them, the branches. Conference presidents were appointed by the mission president, frequently after nomination by a pastor. Conference presidents were experienced local men or missionaries from America. They depended on church members for their support and sometimes lived in "conference houses" rented with funds contributed locally. Some conference presidents had their families with them, who also required local support. Except in very large conferences, presidents served without counselors.[13] Each conference had a clerk who handled money, accounts, and reports.

Conference presidents were required to train and oversee branch presidents, among whom there was high turnover; to see that conference and branch records were kept; and to be sure the conference book agent did his job properly. Conference presidents called quarterly conferences, and they visited the branches where they helped the leaders, spoke in meetings, and ate and lodged with members.[14]

Branches varied in size from ten to several hundred members. Some owned meeting halls or chapels, others rented. Branch presidents, usually local men who earned their own livings, served without counselors.[15] They were assisted by a clerk, a book agent, a council of priesthood holders, and priesthood visiting teachers assigned districts within the branch. On Sundays, branch presidents conducted morning, afternoon, and evening services. They held weekly priesthood council meetings and a midweek preaching or prayer meeting. Some conference presidents grouped branches into districts, supervised by district presidents, who were missionaries pulled partially and sometimes fully from proselyting.[16]

Conferences supported from one to ten traveling elders, who were Utah elders or local men serving full time. Traveling elders, when not assigned as district presidents, proselyted by traveling, usually alone, from

---

[12] Pastors were responsible to see that conferences submitted reports; see *Millennial Star* 17 (January 13, 1855): 24–27; (August 11, 1855): 505. For pastor-presidency contacts see John S. Fullmer Diary, April 8 and July 12, 1853; James G. Willie Diary, April, August, and September 1854, photocopy of holograph, Special Collections, BYU Library; and Daniel Spencer Diary, 1854–55, LDS Church Archives. The London Conference proceedings were published in *Millennial Star* 16 (July 29, August 5, 12, 19, 26, and September 2, 1854). On Adam-God teachings, see note 34.

[13] *Millennial Star* 18 (May 24, 1856): 321–24.

[14] Ibid., 12 (August 15, 1850): 246–51; 14 (June 19, 1852): 257.

[15] Ibid., 18 (May 24, 1856): 321–24.

[16] Ibid., 12 (February 14, 1850): 55.

town to town distributing tracts and trying to hold public preaching meetings. Conference presidents chose specific areas for the traveling elders and notified the mission president of these assignments. A few traveling elders were assigned to cover entire pastorates. One was Elder John McAllister, in Pastor Dorr P. Curtis's pastorate, who described one of his circuits: "[May 20, 1854] I now commenced my travels through the conferences, visiting all the branches of the Church, opening new places, also attending to the several conferences held in the Pastorate."[17]

Typically, pastors followed a circuit, visiting one conference after another and then repeating the process. Pastor John S. Fullmer, for example, started his ministry in late January 1853 by staying with Liverpool Conference President Alexander F. MacDonald for a week while they visited branches. Two weeks later he moved to the Manchester Conference and lodged at its conference house where President Perrigrine Sessions lived. He and Sessions spent a week touring branches. Then Fullmer went to Preston, and with Conference President Robert Menzies he preached to full houses in various branches. He spent several days among Saints in Preston "teaching privately." After visiting nearby branches, he returned to Liverpool for a quarterly conference there. Fullmer then repeated his circuit of the three conferences.[18] Such grass-roots contacts let pastors strengthen and improve local operations and commitment.

Starting in May 1853, Pastor Bunker spent twenty months supervising the Bradford, Sheffield, and Lincolnshire conferences. He lived with Sheffield Branch President John Memmott but traveled constantly. If he had visited a different branch each week, he could not have visited in one year each of the sixty branches in his three conferences. By mid-1853, his pastorate included:

Conference	President	Clerk	Branches	Members
Sheffield	Wm. Glover	J. C. Sanderson	19	888
Bradford	Jn. Albiston	H. J. Jarvis	22	846
Lincolnshire	Chas. Derry	None	19	465[19]

Critical to the pastor's work was his attending each conference's quarterly conference, where he presided. This gathering let him meet with and instruct local priesthood officers, preach to the Saints, review finances, monitor special projects the mission was stressing, hear appeals from local members, mingle with the Saints, and visit them in their homes. Typi-

---

[17] Ibid., 14 (June 5, 1852): 227. Richards acknowledged that it was impossible for him to fix the particular fields of labor for traveling elders. John D. T. McAllister Diary, May 20, 1854, Special Collections, BYU Library.

[18] Fullmer Diary, January through March 1853.

[19] *Millennial Star* 15 (July 30, 1853): 511.

cally, conferences within the same pastorate held quarterly gatherings a week or two apart, to allow pastors to attend.

Pastor Willie penned a good description of a quarterly conference he attended in late March 1854. On Sunday, "the Saints began to flock to Bridport from all the country branches at an early hour," and "many walked 24 miles" to be there. The meetings began with singing at 10:30 A.M. Willie gave the opening prayer. This being a business meeting, leaders reviewed branch reports and finances, "after which the Presidents of branches, expressed their views, and desires in spreading the Principles of the Gospel in their immediate neighborhoods." At the 2 P.M. meeting, Willie talked about sales of books and the *Millennial Star*, emigration and conference funds, and "gave general instruction." At 6:30 P.M. Willie spoke to a large gathering of Saints and nonmembers about the resurrection, and a "good spirit was manifested by all present."[20]

Among pastors' major responsibilities was the supervision of proselyting work within their pastorates. Although many of them were effective preachers, they carried strict orders to have others proselyte, not themselves. Some conferences, such as Wales, Preston, Liverpool, South, Derbyshire, and Nottinghamshire, had become pockets of resistance to missionary work, believing that enough preaching had been done already or that their areas were dead to missionary work. By mid-1854 pastors claimed they had reversed these negative feelings.[21]

The mission employed five methods of proselyting. First, traveling elders, when not burdened by responsibilities for congregations, went from house to house and town to town, leaving and retrieving tracts and holding special preaching meetings. Pastors and conference presidents assigned these elders to specific areas to proselyte.

Second, nonmembers were invited to specially called camp meetings, debates, lectures, and discourses. Missionaries publicized the meetings by going door-to-door, distributing flyers, or hiring the town crier to cry it out. Despite strict orders to let other elders do the proselyting, pastors, being good preachers, sometimes contributed their services. For example, on August 14, 1853, Pastor Charles Smith and about fifty Saints and the Leicester Branch choir boarded conveyances to go to a camp meeting they sponsored at Dunton. Smith spoke in the afternoon and Conference Pres-

---

[20] Willie Diary, March 26, 1854.

[21] *Millennial Star* 16 (July 29, 1854): 465–68; (August 12, 1854): 501. Negative views about proselyting were based on (a) millennialistic feelings that the preaching had been done once and that was enough, (b) long-term lack of converts in an area, and (c) a reputed cursing or shaking the dust off the feet by a high church authority.

ident Edward Frost at night. "The meetings were well attended," Smith noted.[22]

Not all outdoor meetings went well. In September 1855 Pastor Dana and Traveling Elder Wolcott sent the town crier through Luton to announce their outdoor preaching. A crowd came, and, when riled up by a minister, started shoving Dana and Wolcott out of town. A nearby townsman shamed the mob until the crisis passed. Being opportunists, the elders called a meeting for the next night, where they and opponents each lectured for one hour. Some 900 people paid to witness the event.[23]

Third, branch elders and priests did open-air preaching on Sundays and sometimes on weeknights. In mid-1854, for example, the Glasgow Conference had "open preaching in fifty places." Because of shortages of traveling elders, pastors encouraged local men to do Sunday public preaching.[24]

Fourth, individually and through "tract societies" which some branches organized, local members obtained LDS tracts and loaned them out to nonmembers personally or in letters. Pastors encouraged this sharing of tracts.[25]

Fifth, nonmembers came to branch meetings by invitation or from curiosity. In Manchester, members "placarded the towns, and now many strangers come to hear us."[26] When strangers appeared, leaders usually turned the meeting into a preach-to-proselyte session, especially when pastors were the speakers.

The mission president assigned Utah men who became traveling elders to a pastor's jurisdiction, and the pastor assigned them to one of his conferences. A conference president then assigned the elder to a particular district or region to proselyte or to be a district president. However, a pastor could transfer a traveling elder from one conference to another in his pastorate without the mission president's permission. Likewise, the mission president could transfer that elder from one pastorate to another without a pastor's concurrence. A local man called to be a traveling elder by his conference president could be transferred by pastor or mission president. This explains one pastor's complaint that he had had several travel-

---

[22] Charles Smith Diary, August 14, 1853, LDS Church Archives.

[23] Charles R. Dana Journal and Reminiscences, September 29, 1855, LDS Church Archives.

[24] *Millennial Star* 16 (July 29, 1854): 466.

[25] British Mission Manuscript History, October 29, 1853. Bristol Branch, Manuscript History, LDS Church Archives, April 3, 1854, mentions a "circulating Tract Society" in the branch. Also see Dundee Conference report in *Millennial Star* 16 (July 29, 1854): 467.

[26] David B. Dille correspondence, *Millennial Star* 16 (July 29, 1854): 467.

ing elders but "they were called to travel in other conferences or retired to their shoemaking, etc."[27]

Traveling Elder William Budge illustrates the jurisdictional realities. Mission Counselor Daniel Spencer assigned him to the Norwich Conference in Pastor Dana's pastorate. Dana told Budge to report to Norwich Conference President Charles Harper. Harper assigned Budge to the Yarmouth District and its six branches. Budge there became part of the "traveling priesthood" consisting of Conference President Harper and six traveling elders, including himself. Later, to Harper's surprise, Pastor Dana transferred Budge away to the Cambridgeshire Conference. A month later, the mission president surprised Dana by moving Budge to the Swiss-Italian Mission.[28]

Baptisms for 1853, 1854, and 1855 averaged close to 4,260 per year — about 85 per conference or 6 per branch.[29] Mission leaders indicated that baptisms would have increased greatly if more proselyting elders were called. In June 1854, when at least sixty-three traveling elders were at work, some conferences called for more; several poor conferences asked for more elders, but only if the men would work "without purse or scrip."[30]

Three causes were cited for the British Mission's shortage of traveling elders in the period 1852–55: First, Utah could not supply enough. Second, branches could not support British elders if these men had families who had to be supported, too. Pastor Dana admitted he did not call local men to be missionaries. He hesitated because "there was so much opposition by some of the brethren and the Saints generally on account of their poverty, as they said." Later, he called and ordained five "and sent them forth to labor in the pastorate, shifting them as it was deemed wisdom." Third, there was a "practice universally adopted by persons who have sons of suitable age, to send them to the Valley, as pioneers, or to procure means to emigrate the balance of the family."[31]

Some branches relied too heavily on the district presidents for local leadership. Sensing this, Pastor Dana and Conference President Harper in mid-1854 "concluded to cut loose the traveling elders" and "set them to preach among the Gentiles and make Presidents of Branches responsible for the Saints in their charge."[32] Late in 1855, Pastor Fullmer eliminated

---

[27] Dana Journal, mentioned between his July 22 and October 14, 1854, entries.

[28] William Budge Diary, LDS Church Archives, entries for March, April, July 25, and August 28, 1854.

[29] See Table 8 in text.

[30] *Millennial Star* 16 (July 29, 1854): 467; (August 5, 1854): 482; (August 12, 1854): 501–2.

[31] Dana Journal, commentary after January 1 and July 22, 1854 entries. *Millennial Star* 17 (May 26, 1855): 324.

[32] Dana Journal, July 14, 1854.

district presidents from his conferences, and, for the first time apparently, held a conference-wide meeting of all branch presidents: "This was thought advisable because the Districts had been disorganized at the last conference, so these [branch presidents] were called up to receive instruction direct from the President and Pastor and that they might be made to feel the direct responsibility that rested upon them and in short that they might realize there was now no more a middle wall between them and him who presided over the whole conference."[33]

Pastors were spokesmen for church teachings and policies. Utah elders who arrived for early 1853 missionary duty brought with them the church's first public announcement of plural marriage and were called upon to explain it. During Fullmer's first visits to branches, he preached the new revelation to "full and crowded" meetings. In Liverpool he thought that "the Saints feel first rate about the late revelation," but five months later at Upholland he found the Saints "begin to cavil about the Revelation." At the elders council at London in mid-1854, one conference president observed that "polygamy has got over pretty well, that cloud has vanished away." More troubling, he said, was the last "cat that was let out of the bag"—the teaching "about Adam being our Father and God," a controversial concept then circulating in Utah.[34]

Whether these teachings caused widespread apostasy or severely reduced conversions is yet to be determined, but sources consulted for this study do not indicate dramatic initial impacts. The president of Land's End Conference reported, "Relative to the principles recently revealed, we have not the least difficulty." A late-1854 memorial honoring President Samuel Richards's retirement stated that the shock that leaders expected the two teachings to cause had "to a great extent been prevented."[35] However, long-term effects were yet to be seen.

Pastors explained baptism for the dead, consecration, and proper ways to perform ordinances. Pastor Fullmer corrected one branch for lengthy prayers and for prayers asking for the spirits of Joseph and Hyrum Smith to be with them. He explained that their spirits, unlike the Holy Ghost, were in one place and could not be jumping around the universe. At Oldham Branch, Fullmer ruffled feathers by announcing that men need not advance through each office of the Aaronic Priesthood, as most believed,

---

[33] Fullmer Diary, January 13, 1855.

[34] *Millennial Star* 16 (August 5, 1854):482. Regarding the Adam-God teaching, see Leonard J. Arrington, *Brigham Young: American Moses* (New York: Alfred A. Knopf, 1985), 205.

[35] Land's End President Joseph Hall, in *Millennial Star* 16 (August 5, 1854): 482–83, and Richards in *Millennial Star* 16 (October 7, 1854): 629.

and then he ordained a man a priest who had not been a deacon or teacher first.[36]

Pastors were responsible for the promotion of all mission and church programs. A major emphasis during this period was emigration, and pastors exhorted church members to prepare to emigrate and to donate to the Perpetual Emigrating Fund. Pastors supervised each winter's emigration process. During 1853, 1854, and 1855, about 2,000 Saints departed annually. All missionaries were expected to help with emigration from January to April, along with devoting themselves to their normal labors. In January 1854, Pastor Bunker met with Sheffield Conference President Matthew Rowan and together they chose six local people to fill that conference's Perpetual Emigrating Fund quota for that season. A year later, in Bradford Branch, Bunker and President Millen Atwood "told old Saints in our Branch to emigrate before the year is out," and then released Branch President Joseph Bean and counseled him to emigrate.[37]

On December 13, 1854, President Franklin D. Richards discovered unfilled space on a ship he had chartered for Danish emigrants. Desperate to fill berths, he asked Pastor Smith to recruit additional emigrants on short notice. Smith contacted Brother West of Barrowash, who agreed to take his family of nine.[38]

Financial concerns claimed much of the attention of mission personnel. Pastors spearheaded a campaign to retire branch debts for church books and the *Millennial Star*. Saints had been able to maintain subscriptions to the *Star* until they were asked to subscribe to two new church periodicals, *The Seer* and the *Journal of Discourses*, when English prices were rising and unemployment spreading. As a result, branches fell into debt for the publications sent them.[39]

When Millen Atwood became Bradford Conference president in January 1854, Pastor Bunker told him that the conference owed a formidable debt for mission publications. Bunker and Atwood "laboured diligently" to raise money to retire the debt but had little success. Following the June 1854 elders council in London, however, "new life was given to the [Bradford] Conference" and most branches paid their debts. Atwood was pleased, and

---

[36] Fullmer Diary, April 29 and May 1, 1853. After Fullmer ordained Albert Oaks a priest, Oaks related a vision he had had four weeks earlier in which Brigham Young told him he had a great work to do but must await ordination by Fullmer. Oaks had seen Fullmer in the vision and immediately recognized him when he first saw him.

[37] Matthew Rowan Diary, January 23, 1854; Joseph Beecroft Diary, January 7, 1855, LDS Church Archives.

[38] Smith Diary, December 13 and 14, 1854, LDS Church Archives.

[39] *Millennial Star* 16 (August 19, 1854): 514.

credited God, the "wise counsels of Pastor Bunker," and priesthood unity for the success.[40]

Pastors encouraged tithe paying, which, Fullmer learned upon arriving in England, "has hitherto been considered more as a free will offering or donation than a tithing, and is an annual thing, and not limited as to amount." Not until 1856 was tithing more fully explained and expected. Pastors also promoted the Salt Lake Temple fund by preaching and reviewing donation reports. Bunker, for example, talked at a Bradford Conference "particularly about Temple building, and their use, and the great sacrifices that people ought to make to rear these places."[41] Pastors also solicited funds for foreign missions.

Vigilant for signs of backsliding, contention, and iniquity, pastors generally dealt firmly with problems that came to their attention. In late 1853, Pastor Fullmer attended a Manchester quarterly meeting conducted by Conference President Perrigrine Sessions. When an officer "in a bad spirit" criticized a former district president, other members caught his spirit. Sessions failed to calm the situation, and "the Devil was about to take the conference." Fullmer took charge and spoke bluntly, and, said he, "My battle axe, and the manner I used it had a most happy effect."[42]

Pastor Fullmer visited the Hyde Branch in April 1853 and found a problem. At the Saturday branch social, Saints used tea instead of other drinks, and on Sunday, few came to meeting and most who did come, slept. To counter the dull spirit, the branch president asked Fullmer to speak. He spent five minutes rebuking the president and members for preferring tea, socials, and sleep to worship. Fullmer told the congregation they were "cold and indifferent, stupid or asleep," depriving the branch of the Lord's Spirit.[43]

In the branches and conferences, whenever pastors found disputing, disagreements, and faultfinding, they tried to straighten matters out. Pastor Fullmer once found Bury Branch rife with contention. He cited branch leaders to a hearing and told them "they very well knew that they had quarreled with every President and Pastor that had been appointed in the conference for years," something he would not tolerate. Pastor Charles Smith learned of a couple who became parents six months after they were married and instructed the Derbyshire Conference president "to deal with them"—i.e., excommunicate the couple. As part of their disciplinary respon-

---

[40] Ibid., 18 (March 29, 1856): 203.

[41] Fullmer Diary, February 23, 1853; Joseph A. Young's mission report in *Millennial Star* 18 (August 2, 1856); Beecroft Diary, July 3, 1853.

[42] Fullmer Diary, September 24, 1853.

[43] Ibid., April 23 and 24, 1853.

sibilities, pastors also participated in excommunication proceedings for missionaries.[44]

Once, when Pastor Dana visited Hemel Hempstead Branch, he discerned darkness and iniquity. The branch president said Dana's feelings were wrong. It took two days but Dana ferreted out two priesthood holders who had taken liberties with female church members. Before Dana left, the two men were excommunicated and the branch president reproved.[45]

Pastors discovered that excommunicated Saints could become festering sores. For that reason, Pastor Fullmer, for one, taught branch presidents not to be too quick to cut off members, sometimes for trivial transgressions. He urged presidents to "not bury the Saints before they are dead."[46]

Pastor Charles Smith and Nottinghamshire Conference President Henry Savage witnessed an explosion at an Ashfield Branch council meeting. A faction insisted that a couple be excommunicated. When Savage refused, several said they could not sustain him and asked for their own excommunication, which the council granted. Two men threatened Savage, and "many of them went on with disgusting and filthy language, showing they were of the Devil." Pastor Smith interviewed the two people that the dissenters wanted cut off, and was satisfied with President Savage's decision.[47]

More than once pastors had to settle differences between a district president and branch president. For example, Pastor Willie once settled a feud that erupted when District President Ward removed the Southampton Branch president from office for wife beating. Branch members felt aggrieved, claiming Ward lacked authority over their branch. Willie heard their case, then determined that Ward had transcended his calling by assuming the duties of branch president. Willie reinstated the branch president, who declined to serve. So Willie appointed Ward, whom the members now agreed to accept![48]

But most pastoral visits to branches were positive. For example, Fullmer once attended a Wednesday night meeting in the Liverpool Branch where "we had a fine time. Speaking in tongues and interpretations."[49]

At quarterly conferences, pastors watched for practices, attitudes, or ideas that needed correcting. At Preston, Fullmer heard one branch president admit he had not visited all his flock for years, and another say that he deferred to older, more knowledgeable men. Fullmer countered that "a

---

[44] Ibid., May 26, 1853 and January 7, 1855; Smith Diary, September 7, 1853; Willie Diary, May 4, 1854.

[45] Dana Journal, October 29, 1854.

[46] Fullmer Diary, July 5, 1853.

[47] Smith Diary, October 1, 1854.

[48] Willie Diary, November 8, 1854.

[49] Fullmer Diary, August 3, 1853.

shepherd should look after his flock," and that a branch president, no matter how young, would be upheld by God and given wisdom to govern the branch.[50]

Pastors had occasional differences with conference presidents. As one example, Sheffield President Rowan once disagreed with Pastor Bunker about how to report "scattered" and "lost" members on the half-year report.[51]

Overall, however, pastors and presidents seemed to function smoothly together. President Robert Holt reported in late 1855 a "union of feeling that exists between myself and Pastor [George] Grant, for I can truly say, there has never been the least unkind feeling towards each other. The Saints have seen and felt this." Elder Holt felt pride in carrying out "every measure" that Pastor Grant devised to benefit the work. At the 1854 mission-wide council of elders, Pastor Tyler boasted that he "had the united operations of the four Presidents in supporting me in all things." Pastor Dana said that "the Presidents and I have seen eye to eye all the time." Pastor Willie was pleased that he and Conference President George Bramwell "were one in all things."[52]

Church members were expected to provide pastors and conference presidents with lodging, clothes, and other necessities. To enable Pastor Bunker to attend a special London leadership conference in late June 1854, the Sheffield Conference voted to give him £1.10.[53] At a Feast of Oysters held by the Bosham Branch, Pastor Willie noted that "The Saints assisted me with some little means to defray my expenses." Willie kept track of everyone who donated to help him, and when he received an inheritance during his mission, he repaid the donors.[54] In December 1855, the Bristol Branch held a fast day to raise money to buy clothes for Pastor Millen Atwood. Pastor Dana said of his two years: "I have not had to make calls upon any of the Saints, for the small presents I have had have met my demands."[55]

After three years the office of pastor needed refinements. In 1855–56 President Franklin D. Richards made four changes. Henceforth, he said, mission presidency approval was required before pastors could publish any book or pamphlet, transfer missionaries, hold pastorate-wide conferences,

---

[50] Ibid., July 1 and 2, 1853.

[51] Rowan Diary, June 24, 1854.

[52] *Millennial Star* 18 (February 9, 1856): 92; 16 (August 12, 1854): 500, 504.

[53] Rowan Diary, June 24, 1854.

[54] Willie Diary, May 29, 1854, in Marilyn Austin Smith, ed., *Faithful Stewards: The Life of James Gray Willie and Elizabeth Ann Pettit* (Logan, Utah: Author, 1987). Donors are listed on the last page of volume 1.

[55] Bristol Branch Manuscript History, LDS Church Archives; Dana's report is in *Millennial Star* 16 (August 12, 1854): 504.

or attend conferences outside their jurisdictions. Also, in 1855, church members were urged to recognize the pastors' authority and to "pay the most strict attention to their counsels and instructions."[56]

The individual contributions of pastors to the mission varied. Fullmer's journals indicate that he was a veteran churchman, knowledgeable about doctrine and practices, and an authoritarian leader who spoke his mind and tackled problems head on. Dana's journal reveals him to be an extremely hard worker. "I lost no time when I was traveling either on foot, in the carrs, or omnibuses," he said, to preach "if an opportunity afforded."[57] Willie, an Englishman, spent much time visiting outside his pastorate and seemed less forceful as an administrator. Bunker was a kindly man and a good public speaker.

Although records show no attempts to have a pastor removed or reprimanded, pastors occasionally provoked the ire of at least some with whom they had contact. The local priesthood disliked Fullmer's "sharp reproof" of the Bury Branch. Pastors caused some confusion when they explained practices and procedures differently than their predecessors had done. Some pastors disliked aspects of British society or customs, and expressed it. Fullmer, for example, rebuked the Hyde Branch for tea drinking, and walked out of a Royton Branch social, disliking the people's low tastes in amusement and judging the town to be "a dirty stinking place. No Saint ought to live in it."[58] Pastors, like other officers, probably upset people by soliciting new donations and payments on old branch debts from poor Saints.

By the time the last of the 1852–53 elders who had served as the first pastors sailed home in 1856, they had given vital leadership to church operations in the British Isles. Certainly a dozen pastors laboring at a given time eased the mission presidency's burden and provided conferences and branches with closer supervision than the presidency could have given. Pastors had supported, reformed, and enhanced more than four dozen conferences, about 100 conference presidents, and scores of traveling elders. Several felt they had livened up many units which were dead when they arrived. Pastors helped many conferences reduce their debt loads, tighten up their record systems, and overcome bitternesses caused by elders who had mishandled or misappropriated conference funds.[59]

---

[56] *Millennial Star* 17 (July 21, 1855): 457; 18 (March 22, 1856): 185–87; Spencer Diary, November 20 and 25, 1855, LDS Church Archives.

[57] Dana Journal, narration before his May 11, 1854, entry.

[58] Fullmer Diary, April 24 and 27, 1853; January 1, 1855.

[59] See pastor reports at the London council in *Millennial Star* 16 (August 12, 1854): 497–505; (August 19, 1854): 513–20.

Despite these contributions, any assessment of the effectiveness of pastors must take into account the fact that their addition failed to reverse the mission's decline in membership, a fact that haunted mission leadership at the time. Seeking an explanation for lack of progress, in mid-1854 Daniel Spencer, counselor in the mission presidency, gave pastors and other leaders partial blame for low missionary and member zeal in some places. He said he did not think "there is such energy as might be manifested on their part. We are dull and stupid in comparison with those who have gone before us." Leaders, he added, did not "realize our positions sufficiently, or we could create means for building up of the Kingdom." Specifically criticized were those pastors and presidents who harbored beliefs that increased preaching was fruitless, more traveling elders need not be called, finance agents did not need close supervision, elders could not labor without purse or scrip, and members' poverty excused them from church financial obligations. Yet the overall assessment of Spencer and of conference and branch leaders who worked with the pastors seems to have been positive.[60]

As shown in Table 8, the British Mission's membership declined during the 1853–55 period by 6,338, a number almost equal to the emigration total. Baptisms exceeded excommunications; had it not been for emigration there would have been no net loss. Branches declined by 65, although the number of pastorates held steady. Close scrutiny of the figures reveals a loss of nearly 1,500 members unaccounted for by deaths, excommunications, and emigration; why these disappeared from the records is unclear. The lack of mission growth during the pastors' period of service deserves further study; it was probably due largely to factors beyond their control.[61]

Released pastors continued to give leadership to the church when called. Of those discussed above, many left for home early in 1856. During the journey, several presided over shiploads of Latter-day Saint emigrants and four became captains of four of the five handcart companies that year — Ellsworth, Bunker, Willie, and Martin.

The British Mission utilized the office of pastor beyond the 1852–55 period studied here. Pastors continued to serve in a similar fashion until Apostles Amasa Lyman, Charles C. Rich, and George Q. Cannon became the new mission presidency in 1860. They ordered pastors to vacate the conference houses (where they were spending too much time in residence), to do more visiting of officers and branches, and to preach more. The trio changed the name of pastor to "district president" and decreed that con-

---

[60] Ibid. (August 5, 1854): 490–92. See, for example, Spencer's report of his mission-wide tour in *Millennial Star* 17 (May 26, 1855): 323–26.

[61] Essays by Phillips, Jensen, Peterson, and Poll in the present volume discuss the numerical decline in the British Mission, which accelerated further after the period considered here.

Table 8. British Mission Semiannual Statistics, 1852–55[62]

Period	Conferences	Branches	Members	Baptized	Excom.	Emigrated
1852(B)	51	742	32,339			
1853(A)	53	737	30,690	2,601	1,776	1,722
1853(B)	49	726	30,827	1,976	1,413	58
1854(A)	50	698	29,797	2,213	1,330	1,380
1854(B)	51	702	29,441	2,317	1,396	629
1855(A)	48	703	27,771	1,876	1,491	1,589
1855(B)	51	677	26,001	1,835	2,345	482
		−65	−6,338	12,818	9,751	5,860

ferences henceforth send reports and monies direct to mission headquarters, not through the pastors.[63]

A steady and serious decline in church membership made the pastor layer of leadership unnecessary. Membership, which stood at 30,747 in 1850, slid to 13,853 in 1860 and down to 8,804 in 1870. Conferences decreased from 53 in 1853 to 14 in 1870, or one-fourth the number that existed when the office of pastor was first introduced.[64] The pastoral office of district president was phased out by 1869.[65]

Nearly a century later, in response to renewed membership growth, leaders created the position of regional representative to help supervise church units throughout the world. Similar in many ways to the office of pastor in the 1850s and 1860s, which was limited to Europe, it became a new level of supervision and communication between general authorities and stake or mission presidencies.[66]

---

[62] Statistics were reported twice yearly in the *Millennial Star* for 1853 and 1854. The 1855 figures are in the British Mission Statistical Reports, LDS European Church Archives. Statistics for the half year ending December 31, 1852, from *Millennial Star* 15 (January 29, 1853): 78, are also cited here to show changes over three full years.

[63] Leonard J. Arrington, *Charles C. Rich* (Provo, Utah: BYU Press, 1974), 231; *Millennial Star* 23 (January 12, 1861): 24–25.

[64] Richard O. Cowan, "Church Growth in England, 1841–1914," in V. Ben Bloxham, et. al, eds., *Truth Will Prevail* (Solihull, England: The Church of Jesus Christ of Latter-day Saints, 1987), 216.

[65] I have found mention of a district president with jurisdiction over several conferences as late as October 18, 1868. *Millennial Star* 30 (November 14, 1868): 733.

[66] Briefly, regional representatives supervised stakes and mission representatives supervised missions. Since the mid-1970s regional representatives have served throughout the church.

13

The 1857 Reformation in Britain

PAUL H. PETERSON

"With the help of God I am on hand to kick the scales from the eyes of the people," declared the Mormon apostle. "[We need] to arouse, stir, shake them, and if necessary, kick and thump, hammer and pound them, until we are satisfied with the result."[1] For students of Mormon history such railing conjures up images of Jedediah Grant preaching repentance and pelting the Saints with strident rhetoric during the Mormon Reformation of 1856–57. The image is only partially correct. While the statement is rooted in a reformation context, it was Ezra Taft Benson, not Jedediah Grant, who was advocating reform, and it was given in Liverpool, not Salt Lake City. But if the preacher and the place were different, the purpose and the cause were the same. The Mormon Reformation had crossed the Atlantic and was being visited upon Saints in Great Britain. It lasted only about six months but its impact was considerable. The purpose of this essay is to chart the course of reform in Great Britain and tell something of its significance.

The basic context and outline of the Mormon Reformation in Utah Territory are familiar to most students of LDS Church history.[2] The roots of the Reformation can be traced to the millennial attitudes of Latter-day Saints in that era, the relative isolation of the Mormons in Utah Territory in 1856–57, and the personal charisma of Jedediah Morgan Grant.

---

[1] *Millennial Star* 19 (February 28, 1857): 129–34; 19 (March 12, 1857): 290.

[2] Standard treatments of the Reformation include Gustive O. Larson, "The Mormon Reformation," *Utah Historical Quarterly* 26 (January 1958): 45–63; Paul H. Peterson, "The Mormon Reformation" (PhD dissertation, Brigham Young University, 1981); Howard Claire Searle, "The Mormon Reformation of 1856–57" (Master's thesis, Brigham Young University, 1956).

A subdued but ever-present millennial notion was an integral part of Latter-day Saint theology in the 1850s. To most church members the millennium was not immediately around the corner, but a few blocks down the road. Certainly most church members believed the Parousia would occur in their lifetimes. They were also convinced their destiny was to usher in that blessed day by establishing the Kingdom of God on earth. Unity was considered paramount in such an undertaking. Early attempts to establish the kingdom on a permanent basis in Ohio, Missouri, and Illinois failed. The failure was due to the Saints' inability to solve internal disorders and to live harmoniously with non-Mormon neighbors. With the move to Utah Territory the threat of Gentile interference was removed, nurturing hopes that God's kingdom on earth could be established. With such lofty expectations it could be expected that any deviation from the norm, any contention or unity-breaking distraction would be viewed ominously. Thus it was not surprising that reform impulses were observed shortly after the Saints arrived in the valley.

But it was not until 1856 that a systematic program of reform was carried out. In September 1856, Brigham Young's outspoken and zealous second counselor, Jedediah Grant, led a contingent of home missionaries to Kaysville, Davis County, to conduct a conference and preach reform. Seemingly, while there Grant was moved upon to ask all Saints to recommit to gospel principles and indicate their willingness to do so by being rebaptized.[3] Grant's success eventually culminated in a reform movement that affected every level of the church. Although the crusade obviously had Young's enthusiastic approval, Grant was both its architect and prime mover. All Saints located in Salt Lake City and nearby environs were required to measure their worthiness by submitting to a catechism consisting of twenty-seven questions, exhibit increased dutifulness in adhering to gospel principles, and manifest their commitment to become more pliable and obedient by being rebaptized. In encouraging Saints to improve themselves, church leaders oftentimes punctuated their discourses with denunciations and even threats. The Saints were given to understand that the Lord would no longer countenance slothfulness — that lackluster and lukewarm church members would no longer be dallied around with. It was sometimes an intense and nearly always a soul-searching time for Latterday Saints. And, at least for a brief period, the Reformation met the tandem objectives of church leaders of encouraging lethargic but wellintentioned church members to rectify their deficiencies and/or prodding (or sometimes harrassing) intractable ones to improve the spiritual climate of Zion by going elsewhere.

---

[3] *Deseret News*, September 24, 1856.

The course of Reformation in Great Britain was less ardent but just as consequential. It had its origins in Liverpool, the major embarkation center in the mid-1850s for thousands of emigrants, and the hub of missionary/migratory activities for European Saints. On January 26, 1857, Orson Pratt, mission president and apostle, received a directive from Brigham Young instructing him to initiate a reformation immediately. Young's letter, dated October 30, 1856, stressed the need for an awakening and gave general advice on how the crusade should be conducted. Pratt was told that a reformation was needed in England, Scotland, and Wales. "The Saints are dead," Young wrote, "and do not drink at the living fountain; the fire of the Almighty is not in them, and we make the same observation in regard to the elders who are sent to preach." Pratt and his assistant, Ezra Taft Benson, were told to rejuvenate themselves spiritually, then go throughout the entire mission and arouse the people. They were instructed to "trim off the dead branches, so that the tree may thrive, grow, and expand." Benson, a tenacious, fiery apostle, was given the specific charge to "kick the scales" from the eyes of the Saints.[4] Young concluded his correspondence with a series of predictions, some of which were not fulfilled, at least in an immediate sense: "If you, brother Benson, and the other brethren, go forth with the spirit of reformation through England and the British Conferences, as we have suggested you will find a large increase of members, and means donated to the benefit of the work; you will find your hands untied, and be out of debt, and able to help us all that we shall require, and also be able to operate efficiently and successfully, in regard to emigration."[5]

What did Brigham Young know of actual conditions in Great Britain? Had he been informed by mission leaders that spiritual lethargy and backsliding had reached alarming proportions in the British Isles? The evidence is contrary. Correspondence between Young and mission leaders in preceding months gives no indication of a spiritual crisis in that land.[6] In all likelihood, the Reformation was a logical outgrowth of a successful reform in Utah Territory. There the results of the reform were obvious. Meeting attendance improved dramatically, tithing and freewill donations increased, and a preoccupation with things spiritual came to characterize the community. Why not, Young must have reasoned, should Saints else-

---

[4] Brigham Young to Orson Pratt, October 30, 1856, Brigham Young Letterbooks, Archives, Historical Department of The Church of Jesus Christ of Latter-day Saints, Salt Lake City, cited hereafter as Letterbooks and LDS Church Archives.

[5] Ibid.

[6] I have reached this conclusion after examining Young's Letterbooks, Incoming Correspondence, and Outgoing Correspondence in the 1850s.

Orson Pratt, 1856, courtesy of Utah State Historical Society. As president of the British and European missions, Pratt oversaw the introduction of the Mormon Reformation throughout his jurisdiction.

where not participate in spiritual renewal and enjoy the resulting salient benefits. An examination of Young's correspondence also reveals that the letter to Pratt was but one of several letters he sent at the same time to

Ezra T. Benson (1811–69), courtesy of LDS Church Historical Department. Benson, a member of the Quorum of the Twelve, was assigned major responsibilities for the Mormon Reformation in the British Isles.

mission leaders in diverse locales urging them to commence reform.[7]

Pratt acted on Young's advice with dispatch. Waiting a few days until Benson returned from an assignment, he organized a meeting for all per-

---

[7] See, for example, letters from Brigham Young to John Taylor in New York, October 30, 1856, and Erastus Snow in St. Louis, October 31, 1856, Letterbooks.

sonnel in the Liverpool mission office. On February 4, 1857, Pratt confessed to the assembled brethren that when he read of the daily spiritual ministrations of Nephi, Elijah, and Elisha, he realized his own spiritual barrenness. He observed that while truly remarkable external manifestations of the Most High would not transpire until the times of the Gentiles had been fulfilled, the Saints still should be exhibiting more of God's power than was presently the case.[8]

Other elders in attendance were given an opportunity to express their feelings concerning the projected reform. All declared their intention to participate fully. Benson was especially vibrant, responding that he was ready "to cut myself loose." "This letter [Brigham's]," said Benson, "has put fire on the fire, and with the help of God, I am on hand to kick the scales from the eyes of the people."

It was at this meeting that Pratt charted the course the Reformation was to take in the British Isles. Mission leaders and presidents of the various pastorates, districts, conferences, and branches were to reform first, then lay members. Those willing to recovenant to keep the commandments more diligently were eligible for rebaptism. Members reluctant to enter into this pledge were not. An especially key question had to do with tithing. The principle had been but recently introduced in England and prior to this time Saints had not been cut off for noncompliance. Pratt instructed the elders that Church members unwilling to covenant to pay tithing were not to be grafted in.

Orson Pratt was confident that the principle of rebaptism would act as a needed sifter. Those that refused the ordinance (and thereby indicated their refusal to pay tithing and comply with other commandments), were dead branches that needed to be removed that the tree might remain healthy. "If one-third would be cut off, and the rest remain united," Pratt wrote, "it will be one of the greatest works that was ever accomplished in this land."[9]

The following day, February 5, Pratt, Benson, and other Liverpool elders met acccording to appointment at a local bathhouse to be rebaptized. It was typical Reformation procedure for file leaders to demonstrate the importance of rebaptism by being the first to submit to the ordinance. Pratt and Benson baptized each other and then baptized the rest of the brethren.[10] Charles Dana, president of the Manchester Conference, recorded that he had never had a more enjoyable evening in his life. "I almost envied the Elders the blessing of laboring in those lands now," observed Dana, "for in the last three years, if an Elder should reach out or strike

---

[8] *Millennial Star* 19 (February 28, 1857): 129–34.
[9] Ibid.
[10] Ibid.

ahead, there was someone to pull him back by the coattail, or in some other way."[11]

Following the baptismal, Pratt speculated on how the upcoming reform movement fit into the eternal scheme of things. He reasoned that something of great magnitude was near at hand. "It may be," Pratt suggested, "that the Lord intends this purification to prepare the Saints for entering into the Temple, in which we expect such manifestations and blessings to be given as the Church has never had." Whatever the specific purpose, Pratt concluded that the Lord was preparing the Saints to be nearer his presence.[12]

Indications are that the reform was carried out according to Pratt's instructions. Expectedly, proselyting elders quickly recovenanted to keep the commandments and were rebaptized. Once they had completed the procedure, efforts were concentrated on urging members in local branches to follow suit. It would appear that other missionary activities were temporarily curtailed until this process was carried out. This effort commenced in late February 1857 and continued until early fall, but the bulk of it was completed before the end of June.

The reform effort extended throughout Great Britain and eventually throughout other Europeon nations. Ezra T. Benson introduced the Reformation in Wales on March 12, 1857, and apparently James Ure instigated the movement in Scotland about this time.[13] In Scandinavia, Hector Haight called his presiding elders together in Copenhagen in late February 1857 to "lay before them the council [counsel] and instructions given by President Pratt that the Elders and saints renew their covenants by baptism."[14]

Ezra Taft Benson, the passionate counselor to Orson Pratt, became the prime articulator of reformation principles in the European Mission. In an effort to reform those worth reforming, to "cleanse the British mission from every kind of rubbish," Benson traveled to as many branches as possible, holding both elders conferences and general meetings.[15] English convert Elijah Larkin noted that Benson was successful "in kicking the scales from off the eyes of the old Saints and the young."[16] Matthias Cowley, a missionary from Utah, recorded that Benson went about "like a

---

[11] Charles Root Dana Journal, February 4, 1857, LDS Church Archives.

[12] *Millennial Star* 19 (February 28, 1857): 129–34.

[13] Ibid. (May 9, 1857) 289–96; James Ure Diary, February 9 and 15, 1857, LDS Church Archives.

[14] Hector Haight Diary, February 20, 1857, LDS Church Archives.

[15] Ezra Taft Benson to John Taylor, January 29, 1857, *The Mormon*, February 21, 1857.

[16] Elijah Larkin Diary, April 11, 1857, Special Collections, Harold B. Lee Library, Brigham Young University, Provo, Utah.

two-edged sword, cutting on all sides everything that is impure." "He is in this country," said Cowley, "as Jedediah was in that, in bringing about the Reformation."[17]

While Benson provided enthusiasm and incentive in his addresses, local elders bore the responsibility of carrying the Reformation to individual branches. They methodically called on individual branch members, patiently urging them to confess their sins, renew their covenants, and agree to rebaptism. Some members, buoyed up by the zeal of Benson and local leaders and encouraged by reading reports of reform success among Utah-based Saints in the *Millennial Star,* enthusiastically recommitted and were rebaptized. But a surprising number did not. Missionary John Freckleton noted that some Scots were not keen about a reformation. Freckleton became president of the Dysart Branch when his predecessor refused to be rebaptized.[18] William Jefferies in Sherbourne, England, like Freckleton, soon learned that many Saints saw little need of reform. On May 8, 1857, Jefferies visited for a second time with Brother Rawlings and his family, "trying to induce them to renew their covenants."[19] Shortly afterwards he labored with the Ware family — unsuccessfully as it turned out.[20] In June Jefferies visited a sister and "found her with but little of gospel life." "I preached reformation to her," recorded Jefferies, "and endeavored to create faith enough in her to cause her to renew her covenant." Still later, Jefferies visited William Davis. "I labored hard to induce him to pay his tithing," he noted, "but could not get him even to promise to do so." Davis was later suspended from fellowship.[21]

Exactly what criteria British members had to meet before they were either suspended or rebaptized is not completely clear. A catechism was never sent overseas, leaving local leaders some latitude in formulating guidelines. Clearly, the vast majority of church members were not guilty of grievous sins, and in many cases, the importunings of visiting elders amounted to little more than urging British saints to become more Christian by overcoming transgressions that almost all people are prone to commit. "They are by far, the best people in England," wrote a *Millennial Star* editorialist, "and they have repented of many sins, such as have been made manifest to them from time to time, but they are not yet perfect neither will they be while surrounded by the corrupt influences of Babylonish

---

[17] Matthias Cowley to James McKnight, April 4, 1857, Manuscript History of the British Mission, LDS Church Archives, vol. 17, citing *Deseret News,* 7:26.

[18] John Orr Freckleton Journal, 5, LDS Church Archives.

[19] William Jefferies Journal, May 8, 1857, LDS Church Archives.

[20] Ibid., May 13, 1857.

[21] Ibid., June 14, 1857.

christianity." The editorialist then singled out two sins that the Saints frequently indulged in—slander and light-mindedness.[22]

Expectedly, in a time when Saints were asked to measure themselves against the strict law of God, various sins and deficiencies surfaced. Orson Pratt was concerned with too much cooking and feasting on the Sabbath and too little attendance at meetings and it is likely that these items were emphasized. Surprisingly, Word of Wisdom observance, never stressed by church leaders during this era in Utah, was emphasized a good deal, especially by Benson. Saints in Great Britain were also criticized for their casual approach toward emigration and a general lack of concern with their temporal salvation. Certainly the law of tithing was the major concern. In most cases those unwilling to commit to at least try to observe this practice were suspended from church membership.

Cutting off disenchanted Saints was, of course, one objective of the Reformation, both in Zion and abroad. Young had instructed Pratt to cut off dead branches, and Pratt had mentioned at the outset of the Reformation in England that the church would benefit by lopping off about one-third of its membership.[23] Asa Calkin, Pratt's successor as mission president, shared his mentor's optimism that a pruning of lukewarm members would strengthen the church. Calkin, in fact, viewed the Reformation in watershed terms, believing it to be the beginning of a new era in the history of the church in England. He noted that real Saints took hold of reform but that bogus ones shunned it, claiming that "Mormonism isn't what it used to be." That was fine, according to Calkin, for it was better for them to "apostatize here than after they go to the valley."[24] Matthias Cowley noted that "basswood Mormons are obliged to kick out and none but the hickory Saints stand."[25]

It soon became disconcertingly apparent, however, that there would be an alarmingly high number of "bogus" or "basswood" Saints. Indeed, when Pratt realized how many Saints refused to renew their covenants, he must have wondered if his missionaries had been too efficient in carrying out the sifting process. Missionary Jesse Hobson of Worcester Conference lamented that in one branch only six or seven members out of a membership of sixty had chosen to be rebaptized.[26] By May 1857 enough had severed relationships with the church that Pratt predicted in a letter to

---

[22] *Millennial Star* 19 (May 2, 1857): 281–84.

[23] Brigham Young to Orson Pratt, October 30, 1856, Letterbooks.

[24] Asa Calkin Diary, April 27, 1857, LDS Church Archives. There were other leaders who viewed the Reformation as a new beginning. Benson observed on one occasion that "a new Church was being made." See Manuscript History of the London Conference, April 5, 1857, LDS Church Archives.

[25] Cowley to McKnight, April 4, 1857.

[26] Jesse Hobson Diary, October 6, 1857, LDS Church Archives.

Brigham Young that "when the branches are all trimmed and set in order, the Saints in these lands will not number more than about one half as many as . . . in 1850."[27] Four weeks later Pratt reported to Young that "many of those claiming to be Latter-day Saints, and of long standing, do not drink deep into the Spirit of the Reformation. They cannot receive the law of Tithing," wrote Pratt, "and Mormonism as it was in the days of Joseph is good enough for them." Pratt further speculated that the Saints in the British Isles numbered no more than 20,000.[28]

But as the Reformation progressed, Pratt soon realized that even this estimate had been too optimistic. At the end of July 1857, he noted that "in some Conferences not more than half of the Old Members have been rebaptized," and that the total number of Saints in the British Isles was less than 17,000.[29] A month later Pratt, now somewhat sombered by the reduction in membership, summarized the effect of the Reformation: "The reformation has greatly reduced the numbers of Saints; still those that are left are faithful, but poor and can do but little after paying their Tithing. They are anxious to emigrate but can do but little towards it. Almost universally those persons who have any means other than their Daily wages, have neglected to renew their covenants or pay Tithing."[30]

The rather severe reduction in church membership in the British Isles is puzzling. Why did thousands of church members eschew Mormonism? Were British Saints unaccustomed to receiving dictates or impositions, especially financial ones, from file leaders? It would seem not. For some years church members had been asked to donate monies to a variety of enterprises. Besides tithing, there were the Perpetual Emigrating Fund, temple offerings, funds for distribution of pamphlets, funds for local operating expenses, and collections for missionaries. Even the word "reform" would have caused little consternation. Latter-day Saints were always being told to reform. Indeed, reform was being preached in the British Mission with some regularity before the Reformation was instigated. It is instructive that Benson wrote Young that "I thought I was preaching reformation through this mission but when I read your letter [calling for a Reformation] I found there was great room for improvement."[31]

In addition, it is clear the Reformation was not a radical or even a novel departure in doctrine or practice. Rebaptism was not an uncommon

---

[27] Orson Pratt to Brigham Young, May 1, 1857, Brigham Young Incoming Correspondence, LDS Church Archives.

[28] Pratt to Young, May 29, 1857.

[29] Pratt to Young, July 28, 1857.

[30] Pratt and Ezra Taft Benson to Brigham Young, August 27, 1857.

[31] Ezra Taft Benson to Brigham Young, March 20, 1857, Incoming Correspondence.

practice during the nineteenth century, and it would appear that it was engaged in with some frequency in the British Mission in 1856, the year preceding the Reformation in that country.[32] The payment of tithes had been emphasized from mid-1856 on. In early July 1856, during the mission presidency of Franklin D. Richards, it was noted in the *Millennial Star* that in previous months mission leaders had permitted some elders to introduce tithing in their branches on a trial basis. Apparently the response was so favorable that leaders were now "constrained by the Holy Spirit to recommend to all the conferences to adopt this law practically."[33] Two weeks later the *Star* provided a rationale for this new emphasis by indicating the "Lord has made it manifest that the law of tithing should be introduced, that it may serve to separate the chaff from the wheat, and that the Saints may have an opportunity of proving, to a greater extent than they have yet done, whether they are worthy of being gathered home to Zion."[34]

Apparently, even though mission leaders had decided to introduce tithing on a uniform basis in the British Mission in 1856, it was not made an absolute test of fellowship. This decision represented an important difference between this period and the Reformation. Perhaps this call for an actual response or action rather than the acceptance of a mere verbal promise represented a commitment many Saints were unwilling to make.

Undoubtedly, the most significant factor in reducing church membership during the Reformation era was the determination of church leaders to conduct a general housecleaning. They were convinced that unwieldy and stubborn members had become a drag and a detriment to church vitality and growth. Clearly, Young had been concerned for some time with converts who embraced the gospel for "no other motive than to have the privilege of being removed from their oppressed condition."[35] In 1855 he expressed his desire to Orson Pratt to stop the flow of unconverted emigrants.[36] As indicated previously, Young's initial letter to Pratt directing him to instigate reform contained explicit directions to remove the recalcitrant. "Trim off the dead branches," Pratt was told, "so that the tree may thrive, grow and expand; so that it may furnish the living waters, where the Saints can come and drink of the fountain."[37] That mission leaders understood this to be a prime reformation objective is made clear in Benson's response to Young. "According to your instructions we forth-

---

[32] James Carrigan to Franklin D. Richards, *Millennial Star* 18 (February 16, 1856): 108.

[33] Ibid. (July 12, 1856): 442–43.

[34] Ibid. (July 26, 1856): 475.

[35] Brigham Young sermon, April 6, 1855, *Journal of Discourses*, 26 vols. (London: Latter-day Saints Book Depot, 1854–82), 2:251.

[36] Brigham Young to Orson Pratt, August 30, 1855, Letterbooks.

[37] Brigham Young to Orson Pratt, October 30, 1856, Letterbooks.

with commenced the Reformation in these lands," Benson wrote, "and [we] were determined to trim off the dead branches that the work of our God might roll on and his Kingdom become purified."[38]

But the severe reduction in church membership in the British Isles suggests some of the missionaries exceeded the expectations of church leaders. Conceivably a few of the elders were more interested in trimming off dead wood than they were in reclaiming souls. In 1859 Mission President Asa Calkin warned traveling elders to be judicious in weeding out the wicked. Calkin was concerned that in preceding months hundreds of Saints had been unjustly cut off from the church.[39] In 1861, when Thomas Evans Jeremy was appointed to preside over the Welsh Mission, he was instructed to make himself familiar with the circumstances of the Saints and see to it that "they are not oppressed by the collection of tithing or donations." Jeremy was told that no one was to be cut off from the church without his permission.[40] In a letter to Brigham Young, Jeremy noted that several Saints had been excommunicated "for merely asking a question and they were not allowed to speak or defend themselves in a council." Jeremy related that excommunicated Saints would come to him in tears, and when asked why they had been cut off from the church, they responded that they were unable to meet the fiscal demands imposed on them by local presidents.[41]

That some church members might have been dealt with uncharitably is also given credence by the realization that both rebaptism and tithing were dropped as conditions of church fellowship within a short period. It would appear that rebaptism was not considered essential by 1858. Tithing was a requirement but a year or so longer. In a letter to Calkin in January 1860, Young instructed him to avoid oppressing the poor in any monetary concern, "nor make the non-payment of Tithing a matter of fellowship."[42]

---

[38] Ezra Taft Benson to Brigham Young, May 23, 1857, Incoming Correspondence.

[39] *Millennial Star* 21 (February 26, 1859): 139–40.

[40] Amasa Lyman, Charles C. Rich, and George Q. Cannon to Thomas Evans Jeremy, April 29, 1861, Correspondence and Papers of Thomas Evans Jeremy, LDS Church Archives.

[41] Thomas Evans Jeremy to Brigham Young, July 1, 1861, Jeremy Papers.

[42] Brigham Young to Asa Calkin, January 31, 1860, Letterbooks. In a second letter to Calkin, Young issued a slight qualification: "Do not oppress the people by requiring them to purchase any more books and papers than they freely wish to, nor except perhaps in certain cases, make tithing a matter of fellowship." See Young to Calkin, February 16, 1860, Letterbooks. Even before receiving Young's directive, Calkin had urged missionaries to be sensitive to nontithe payers. See *Millennial Star* 21 (January 29, 1859): 82 and 21 (February 26, 1859): 139–40. That excessive zealotry accompanied emphasis on tithing during the Reformation is also

Despite the larger than expected losses in church membership, mission leaders felt the Reformation was effectual. In their correspondence with Brigham Young both Pratt and Benson noted the vastly improved spiritual tone of Saints in the British Isles, and James Ure commented favorably on the effect of the Reformation in Scotland.[43] William Budge claimed that the Reformation had "caused a new spirit to take hold of the people." "The Saints are more diligent than heretofore," wrote Budge, "and understand that working is required as well as talking."[44] Asa Calkin, though concerned for a time with the improper use of the gift of tongues in meetings, observed in January 1858 that "there has never been a better feeling among the Saints in this country." There has been, he added, "a significant increase in union, peace, and zeal."[45]

And Brigham Young—what did he think? The Reformation did in fact affect the fortunes of British Latter-day Saints more than any other event in the 1850s, save, perhaps, the announcement of the practice of plural marriage. While hundreds of church members were spiritually rejuvenated, hundreds, or possibly thousands, were severed from the church.[46] But Young was probably satisfied with the course of reform in Great Britain. Naturally, he would have regretted the number of lost souls, but convinced that the vast majority of apostates were bickerers and not builders, he likely reasoned that both sides benefited. Indeed, it was always Young's contention that for a people entrusted with building the Kingdom of God, "one hundred good and faithful brethren" were better than "millions of half-hearted milk-and-water adherents who continually seek to serve both God and the devil."[47]

---

implied in the instruction to elders in 1861 to avoid, "terrorism, threats of disfellowshipping, or constraint . . . in enforcing it [tithing]." See *Millennial Star* 23 (January 26, 1861): 57.

[43] Orson Pratt to Brigham Young, October 2, 1857, Incoming Correspondence; Ezra Taft Benson to Brigham Young, May 23, 1857, Incoming Correspondence; James Ure to Orson Pratt, *Millennial Star* 19 (June 13, 1857): 379.

[44] William Budge to T. B. H. Stenhouse, *The Mormon*, July 25, 1857.

[45] Asa Calkin Diary, October 25, 1857, and January 30, 1858.

[46] Available membership records of the British Mission both provide helpful information and present intriguing questions. It would appear that membership dropped from 22,502 in mid-1856 to 15,682 in mid-1857, a reduction of roughly 7,000. Yet excommunications for the year 1857 totaled only 2,084. While considerable research needs to be done to get an accurate focus on membership statistics and procedures, a couple of educated guesses might be in order. I would surmise that: (1) it was decided during the Reformation to count as members only those who opted to be rebaptized; and (2) many of those that refused rebaptism were not formally excommunicated. They were simply not included as members.

[47] Brigham Young to Asa Calkin, *Millennial Star* 21 (February 19, 1859): 126.

14

The British Mission During the Utah War, 1857–58

RICHARD D. POLL

The Utah War of 1857–58 occurred because the president of the United States, James Buchanan, appointed a replacement for Territorial Governor Brigham Young, dispatched an army of 2,500 troops to protect the new governor, and gave Young no formal notification of what was afoot.[1] In the circumstances, the Great Basin Mormons wrapped themselves in a mantle of millennialist fervor and used guerrilla tactics to delay the army's advance, while probing for a nonviolent alternative and exploring for another refuge in case conflict proved unavoidable. Happily, the mediation of Colonel Thomas L. Kane, produced a peaceful settlement that gave Utah Territory a non-Mormon governor while leaving Brigham Young the de facto leader of its people.[2] The scenario unfolded in Utah between July 24, 1857, when word of Buchanan's program became public knowledge, and June 26, 1858, when Johnston's army marched through the deserted streets of Great Salt Lake City, evidencing by their peaceful behavior that the Saints were free to return to their homes. Given the state of communications, the Saints in Europe learned of Buchanan's project a little earlier and of its outcome a little later than their compatriots in Zion.

This confrontation had substantial effects on the Latter-day Saints in Great Britain, who were kept aware of its course through the *Millennial*

---

[1] This is a revised version of a paper presented at the annual meeting of the Mormon History Association in Oxford, England, July 6, 1987. All documents and journals cited in this paper, except as otherwise noted, were consulted in the Archives, Historical Department of The Church of Jesus Christ of Latter-day Saints, Salt Lake City.

[2] Useful on the Utah War are Norman F. Furniss, *The Mormon Conflict, 1850–1859* (New Haven: Yale University Press, 1960) and Richard D. Poll, *Quixotic Mediator: Thomas L. Kane and the Utah War* (Ogden, Utah: Weber State College, 1985).

Star.[3] It led to the recall of all but a handful of the American elders, who had borne the brunt of missionary labors and it left the direction of the mission in the hands of a Yankee businessman.[4] It affected the proselyting environment, the emigration and publication programs, and the morale of the members. It produced some new leaders, resolute followers, and impressive financial statistics. During the months of the Utah War, however, the mission lost both membership and recruiting momentum. To explain these effects, we must look first at the state of the British Mission early in 1857.[5]

The mission was by all odds the largest component of the European Mission, which had the same presidency and occupied the same headquarters at 42 Islington Street, Liverpool. The jurisdiction of the European Mission extended to South Africa, Australia, and the members and missionaries who occasionally turned up elsewhere in Asia, Africa, and the South Pacific. Within Europe proselyting was currently going on in Italy, Switzerland, France, Norway, Sweden, and Denmark, with meager results except in Denmark. Membership in all of these jurisdictions totaled almost 4,000. (See Table 9.)

The British Mission, with approximately 20,000 members, was divided into pastorates, conferences, districts, and branches, the boundaries and number of administrative units being under constant revision. The nine pastors in 1857 had supervisory responsibilities comparable to today's regional representatives, but they also had imprecisely defined line authority between

---

[3] Each issue of the *Millennial Star* carried a feature, "Passing Events," that reported news of possible interest to the Saints, drawn largely from the British and American press. Some U.S. press reports on Utah affairs were copied verbatim. Letters from Utah and from Latter-day Saint representatives in the eastern states appeared, as well as articles written by the editorial staff and mission personnel.

[4] Register of Missionaries, British Mission, Manuscript Histories of the Units of the Church, vol. I, contains lists of missionaries who arrived in England each year from 1837 through the nineteenth century. For 1855–58 it appears to have almost all of the names and arrival dates, but departure dates are missing for about 25 percent of these men. Of the eighty-eight elders apparently present in England when Samuel W. Richards arrived in October 1857, only five are shown with departure dates later than his, February 20, 1858. They are Asa S. Calkin, Jabez Woodard, James W. Taylor, Henry H. Harris, and George Rowley.

[5] The *Millennial Star* files, the large but uneven Manuscript History of the British Mission, and the extensive collection of manuscript conference and branch histories are full of unorganized information. Richard L. Evans, *A Century of Mormonism in Great Britain* (Salt Lake City: Deseret News Press, 1937), is detailed on the 1830s and early 1840s, but does not treat the rest of the nineteenth century except for some data on emigration. V. Ben Bloxham, James R. Moss, and Larry C. Porter, eds., *Truth Will Prevail: The Rise of The Church of Jesus Christ of Latter-day Saints in the British Isles 1837–1987* (Solihull, England: The Church of Jesus Christ of Latter-day Saints, 1987), is a more comprehensive, though somewhat uneven treatment; its coverage of the Utah War period is brief.

the mission president and the conference presidents.[6] The latter, who numbered about fifty, supervised traveling missionaries, and district and branch presidents. The mission president, almost all pastors, and some conference and district presidents were from the United States. Both Britain and America supplied the traveling elders who labored in the British Isles; some of the latter were English converts who had emigrated to Illinois or Utah earlier. Most district presidents and almost all branch presidents were locals. Orson Pratt presided over the European and British missions in 1856 and most of 1857, with Ezra Taft Benson as his first counselor.[7]

Table 9. Membership of the British Mission, 1855–61

| | (Membership totals as of December 31)[8] | | | | | | |
	1855	1856	1857	1858	1859	1860	1861
Membership, European Mission	29,249	26,307	19,238	18,623	17,610	18,843	21,155
Outside British Isles	3,248	3,805	4,018	4,437	4,583	4,990	6,262
Membership, British Mission	26,001	22,502	15,220	14,186	13,027	13,853	14,893
Baptized during year	2,426	3,820	4,223	2,564	2,132	3,222	4,132
Emigrated during year*	836	2,465	1,355	195	713	1,016	1,262
Died during year**	176	289	284	240	214	244	181
Excommunicated during year**	2,574	2,888	2,714	2,722	1,764	686	550

*Includes emigrants from the Continent emigrating under church auspices.
**Not clear whether these members outside the British Mission.

---

[6] *Millennial Star* 19 (August 22, 1857): 540–41, lists these pastorates: Sheffield, Glasgow, Manchester, Nottinghamshire, South, Southampton, London, Newcastle-on-Tyne, and Birmingham. Andrew Jenson, *Encyclopedic History of The Church* (Salt Lake City: Deseret News Publishing Co., 1941), 94, states that there were fifty-one conferences in 1852; P. A. M. Taylor, *Expectations Westward* (Ithaca, N.Y.: Cornell University Press, 1966), 249, lists thirty-six conferences in 1863.

[7] John Henry Evans and Minnie Egan Anderson, *Ezra T. Benson: Pioneer-Statesman-Saint* (Salt Lake City: Deseret News Press, 1947), 220–36, suggests that Benson spent much of his time on speaking tours of the British Isles and Scandinavia.

[8] Accurate membership statistics for this period do not exist. The data in this table, attributed to a December 31, 1863, entry in the journal of George Reynolds, then a British Mission clerk, are from a typescript in the file, "Church Membership, 1850–1945," in the Historical Department of The Church of Jesus Christ of Latter-day Saints, Salt Lake City. They are imprecise, as noted below. They do confirm that British Mission membership declined by 50 percent between 1855 and 1859, with emigration to America accounting for less than half of that decline and unexplained shrinkage during the Utah War period accounting for most of the rest. Membership in the other units of the European Mission, primarily in Scandinavia, increased almost one-third during the same period. In 1860 the declining trend in the British Mission was reversed.

Birmingham, Manchester, Liverpool, and London had multiple branches, with membership aggregates in the hundreds; elsewhere branches were small, their boundaries often determined by walking distances to meetings rather than size of membership. The traveling elders spent much of their time trudging from one Latter-day Saint household to another, exchanging gospel instruction, church news, and testimony for hospitality.[9] Where branches had sufficient will and numbers, their tract committees aided the full-time missionaries in distributing and gathering up tracts and *Millennial Stars*, and their priesthood members helped conduct public meetings.[10]

In compiling these numbers, George Reynolds presumably used past statistical reports from the conferences; no individual membership records were maintained by the mission. Transfers of membership were effected by letters of recommendation, which inactive members were unlikely to request when moving from one church jurisdiction to another in search of work or for other reasons. In the mid-1850s the conference reports reflected inputs from the branches that might be no more than estimates, with no effort to reconcile the numbers from one quarter to the next. Personnel changes around the end of 1857 may have resulted in more nonreporting and inaccurate reporting than usual.

Richard L. Jensen kindly shared his statistical findings with me. They agree with Reynolds on year-end numbers and general trends, but differ in many details. Two items from the available documents illustrate the problems: Between December 31, 1856, and December 31, 1858, the Birmingham Conference membership declined from 1,516 to 1,139, despite more than four hundred baptisms. The fragmentary data on emigration, excommunications, and deaths do not account for the net reduction. Manuscript History of Birmingham Conference. President Benjamin Evans gave a precise report on financial contributions from Wales at the European Mission conference in January 1859, but he could only estimate that Welsh membership was "between 1800 and 2000." *Millennial Star* 21 (January 29, 1859): 79.

It seems likely that President Calkin's insistence on more rigorous branch and conference record keeping produced a more accurate membership tally than those represented by the numbers for the two or three years previous. A plausible hypothesis is that knowledge of the identities of many inactive members left the mission with the American elders in the winter of 1857–58.

[9] The daily mileage faithfully recorded in many journals shows that twenty and even thirty miles were not uncommon. Useful on this and other aspects of missionary activity is Richard L. Jensen, "Without Purse or Scrip? Financing Latter-day Saint Missionary Work in Europe in the Nineteenth Century," *Journal of Mormon History* 12 (1985): 3–14.

[10] Charles W. Penrose, Journal, May 2–4, 1857. Penrose reports that eight tracts by Orson Pratt had been supplied in quantity to the conferences, "and societies were formed in each Branch to see them distributed." The tracts and other aspects of Pratt's missionary service are described in Breck England, *The Life and Thought of Orson Pratt* (Salt Lake City: University of Utah Press, 1985).

Trying to convert non-Mormons was, of course, the primary mission-ary calling. Open-air meetings were held regularly in the good weather months in towns where they were not prohibited, and advertised meetings were held in rented halls and the homes of members. Elders in the Chan-nel Islands showed ingenuity in following a cortege to the "strangers bury-ing ground," and, after the interment, speaking to a "large and attentive crowd."[11] Most audiences were small, however, and heckling was com-mon. When hostile opinion increased, open proselyting was sometimes curtailed; this was true during the months of the Utah War.

Missionaries and members alike looked forward to quarterly confer-ence meetings, where crowds in excess of 1,000 came together in the major population centers. A highlight of many such events was the social on the following Monday, described as a "tea party" in many of the journals. Music, recitations, dramatic presentations, and preaching augmented the food and informal fellowship. Charles Penrose and E. L. T. Harrison, members of a London branch, wrote a short farce, "The Mormons in the Family," that played to several appreciative audiences.[12]

Fund raising prompted many socials and was a part of others. Solici-tations were made to purchase tracts, assist missionaries, rent halls, pur-chase gifts for departing leaders, and for other special purposes. A day's or a week's wages was the customary pledge when a member wished to give more than the price of a ticket or pocket change. The hard times that followed the 1857 business panic led the leadership to urge contributions to the Poor Fund, a precursor of the Fast Offering Fund. The Penny Fund was a savings vehicle for Saints who could not accumulate emigrating money more rapidly. Tithing was preached in the British Isles, but not until the Reformation was it heavily stressed, and not until the fiscal reforms of 1858 was it brought under systematic management.[13]

Early in 1857 Pratt and Benson received instructions to launch a reform movement comparable to that which was still shaking up the Saints in Utah. This mission-wide revival was still going strong when the Utah War began. "The real saints take hold of it in earnest," Asa Calkin recorded in Liverpool. Charles Penrose described the effect of the Reformation in London. The priesthood leaders were rebaptized and then reconfirmed in

---

[11] William Thurgood, Journal, June 1, 1856.

[12] Penrose also played Dick Devilish in another production, "Priestcraft in Danger." Penrose, Journal, entries for May 1857.

[13] At a Birmingham priesthood meeting the call for a week's wages was made "to assist the Saints in the Valley," and "out of 60 brethern there, we obtained promises of £60." Samuel Francis, Journal, August 4, 1858. Francis earlier "was appointed treasurer for the subscription to be raised to purchase a watch for Elder William J. Noble." Ibid., June 27, 1858. The journal of Asa S. Calkin is parti-cularly informative on mission financial policies and activities.

a meeting at which "Pastor Ross spoke in tongues and Bro Benson instructed us [and] said he felt satisfied with London." This group was then charged to "baptize our districts beginning with the Presidents of Branches." Since a requirement for rebaptism was a commitment to tithe fully and regularly, some of the members refused; if they persisted in this stubbornness, they were cut off. Penrose recorded happily that "most of them in my district obeyed." In endorsing the policy that members refusing rebaptism should be denied fellowship, Benson told a group of branch presidents that "a new Church was being made."[14]

Outdoor preaching and tracting were assigned to the branches as spring weather permitted. Some baptisms resulted, but the scattered references to such events in the journals of the traveling missionaries suggest that most conversions occurred among the relatives and friends of active members. Handbills drew nonmembers to some special meetings; on the other hand, some advertised meetings drew no one at all. Special promotion was, of course, given to appearances by Pratt and Benson, and their tour of the mission drew audiences that numbered in the hundreds.[15] Such highly visible activities kindled both spiritual renewal and opposition.

The Saints in England were aware of the impending Utah troubles for several months before they received instructions on how to relate to them. Judge W. W. Drummond's letter of resignation from the Utah territorial supreme court generated newspaper comment in England; an April 22 editorial in the London *Daily Telegraph* reported Drummond's negative views on Mormonism and endorsed "any steps that may be taken by the American Government to break up this gigantic imposture." The *Millennial Star* carried a long editorial rebuttal of Drummond's charges, with a recommendation that conference presidents pass it on to newspapers. Responses to unfavorable articles in the British press appeared intermittently thereafter.[16] Despite the accessibility of this information, references to the conflict are relatively scarce in the missionary journals. The writers, both British and American, appear to have been confident that this formidable threat to Zion would not block the imminent triumph of the work of the Lord.

The reports from America were fuel for the anti-Mormon activists in Britain, already aroused by the Reformation. The summer of 1857 witnessed many acts of vandalism and harassment, from window breaking

---

[14] Calkin, Journal, April 24, 1857; Penrose, Journal, February 25 and March 2, 1857; Manuscript History of the London Conference, April 5, 1857.

[15] Eli Harvey, Journal, August-September 1857 reports several "no shows." Ezra T. Benson, Journal, June 2 and September 6, 1857, notes large crowds; about 2,000 people attended the September conference in London.

[16] *Millennial Star* 19 (May 16, 1857): 307; 19 (May 23, 1857): 328–33. Ibid., 19 (June 20, 1857): 392–96, rebuts a similar attack in the London *Times*, June 3, 1857.

and defacing of literature to heckling speakers and physically intimidating members on their way home from meetings. Crusading ministers, sometimes abetted by ex-Mormons, were particularly active in Liverpool, Bath, and Birmingham, where two meeting halls were seriously damaged. After a mob broke up a meeting, forcing participants to flee, "including some pregnant women," Conference President Charles Jones appealed to the lord mayor of Birmingham, and police protection was promised. A sympathetic editorial in the Birmingham *Journal* may have helped. Sporadic violence continued, however, until winter weather discouraged the troublemakers.[17]

Responses to requests for police protection were quite unpredictable; in Bath a vigorous police response ended harassment in July, while in October Benson was ordered out of a Bath police station after he had taken refuge there. In Alderney, the police constable broke up an open-air meeting and the local judge refused to permit future meetings, finding the Mormons to be "detrimental to public morals."[18]

On more than one occasion Pratt and Benson were badgered during and after meetings. The great-grandfather of today's church president described an occasion when, having been pursued to their lodgings on the Isle of Man, Pratt turned, removed his hat, bowed, and bade the rabble "good evening" before going indoors. He and his fellow apostle "preached the gospel during the remainder of the evening to a gent and his wife from London [who] paid good attention."[19]

Into this ferment came Samuel W. Richards with long-awaited instructions. He and George G. Snyder arrived in Liverpool on October 3, 1857, after a fifty-one day journey from Great Salt Lake City. The message from President Young was succinct: The Mormon emigration from Europe was to stop, except for Saints who might wish to go to Canada on their own and there wait until the way to Zion was open again. The American elders were to come home, "except one or two that would be required to take charge of the 'Star' " and other business in England. The returning elders were to "bring as many good faithful men with them" as they could, but not delay to recruit them. An apocalyptic tone reflected the strong antici-

---

[17] Charles F. Jones, Journal, June 30-September 20, 1857. In Liverpool, Mission Clerk William Henry Perkes was sent to two anti-Mormon lectures to look for members, "as they had been counseled not to go." He found none among the small audiences. Perkes, Journal, November 13 and 29, 1857.

[18] Edward Hanham to Orson Pratt, Bath, July 17, 1857, published in *Millennial Star* 19 (August 22, 1857): 542–43; Benson, Journal, October 4, 1857; William Thurgood, Journal, July 14–16, 1857.

[19] Benson, Journal, August 28, 1857.

pation of the millennium that the Mormon leader shared with most of the Saints in the 1850s.[20]

Action on several fronts followed quickly. Pratt issued "A Prophetic Warning to the Inhabitants of Great Britain," noting that the recent nation-wide day of fasting and prayer in behalf of the victims of the Sepoy muti-nies in India "will be a solemn mockery before God, if you receive not the message he has sent."[21] The mission presidency was reorganized, Richards replacing Pratt, with the mission business agent, Asa Calkin, as his first counselor and successor-designate, and George Snyder as his second.

The American elders, some eighty-eight in the British Isles and about a hundred in Europe as a whole, were alerted that they would be leaving as rapidly as passage and funding could be arranged. Pratt and Benson and a few others left immediately, but the rest did not go until January and February. Of the five who apparently remained, two were in presiding roles: Jabez Woodard directing the work in France and Italy, and Calkin heading the European and British missions.[22]

To aid the returnees, the local Saints were asked to give generously, and they did. A "tea party" in Birmingham, where the Odd Fellows Hall was festooned with flags, flowers, and banners bearing pictures and the names of Brigham Young, his counselors, and the mission presidency, was attended by about 500 Saints and raised a tidy sum. The total of donations reported to mission headquarters was £1,473, to which must be added items of apparel and gifts of many kinds. It was announced earlier that money collected from the several conferences "would be pooled and divided equally among the Elders, so that those from poor conferences would fare as well as those from rich ones."[23] Apparently collections went directly to

---

[20] Samuel W. Richards, Journal, August 12, 1857. Richards, who was thirty-three years old at the time, had served a mission in England earlier in the decade. On route to England he made an unsuccessful effort to contact Thomas L. Kane, but his journal is silent on his September activities in the eastern states. *Millennial Star* 19 (October 10, 1857): 651–53, quotes a New York *Times*, September 12, story of an interview with Richards in which he avowed the peaceful intentions of the Utah Mormons. On the other hand, he told Asa Calkin privately "that Brigham and his associates do not look for more than one more year of peace before there is an outbreak and war between the U.S. and the saints." Calkin, Journal, October 8, 1857.

[21] *Millennial Star* 19 (October 24, 1857): 680–81.

[22] See note 4 and Manuscript History of the British Mission, January 21 and February 9, 19, and 20, 1858. Norwegian Carl Widerborg remained in charge of the work in Scandinavia.

[23] Richards, Journal, January 4, 1858; Calkin to Brigham Young, July 6, 1858, excerpted in Calkin, Journal, same date; Manuscript History of the London Conference, November 22, 1857.

the mission office for use on ship bookings and other travel expense, with little or no funds going directly to individuals.

The emotional toll taken by this first war-related withdrawal of Mormon missionaries from Europe must have been substantial. At least one already polygamous elder had an all-night tryst with a female member, in which they pledged "that we wood be sealed to each other for Eturnity" as soon as circumstances permitted.[24]

Of profound consequence for all church members in Europe was the announcement in the *Star* on October 17: "In view of the difficulties which are now threatening the Saints, we deem it wisdom to stop all emigration to the States and Utah for the present."[25] The editorial expressed optimism that the way would soon be opened again, but a year elapsed before that happened. Since the large, subsidized emigration of 1856 had exhausted the Perpetual Emigrating Fund, only members who could pay their way or secure private help had been accepted into the emigrating companies of 1857 organized through the Liverpool office. This cut the emigration from 2,465 to 1,355 (Table 9) and may also have reduced the impetus for people to convert to Mormonism. In the absence of hard evidence, it seems fair to speculate that the prospect of no church emigration diminished activity among many nominal members during the following months.

To reduce Mormon visibility during this critical period, Richards instructed that outdoor preaching be discontinued. The full-time ministers were to encourage the individual Saints and put the branches in order, identifying and appointing local leaders to fill the leadership vacancies that were being created. The files of the *Star* show considerable shuffling of offices during the fall and winter, with men like Penrose, Harrison, Edward Tullidge, William Budge, and James Ross moving up in the mission hierarchy. Still, the daily routines described in the missionary journals were not radically different from those detailed during the previous winter. Even the elders from Zion wrote little about Utah affairs, or about their pending departures, until their sailing dates were near. Miles Romney received a letter from two of his sons, via California, asking that he bring home swords for them to wear with their Nauvoo Legion uniforms.[26]

When Asa Starkweather Calkin succeeded Richards as president of the British Mission on February 20, 1858, he was ready. A lawyer by

---

[24] William Pace, Journal, February 10, 1858. I participated in the 1939 withdrawal of missionaries from Germany and Denmark and witnessed the shedding of many tears.

[25] *Millennial Star* 19 (October 17, 1857): 668.

[26] Penrose, who became a conference president and a father during these hectic times, expressed a wish that he might be "in the mountains with the b'hoys." Journal, October 3, 1857. Romney, Journal, September 29, 1857.

Asa Calkin, president of the British Mission, 1858–60. Courtesy of Mrs. Agnes Pendleton.

training and a businessman by experience, he had been business manager in the Liverpool office since December 1855. He had supervised the large emigrations of 1856 and 1857, witnessed the successes and failures of the Reformation, and become well acquainted with the fiscal and bureaucratic aspects of the mission by the time the first Utah War news came to England.

On the night of July 22, 1857, according to his journal, he had a remarkable dream: "I saw myself here alone, that is all the American Elders had left for the Valley in a hurry upon a special call from the President. . . . But the strangest part of the dream was that I was the President of the Mission! And all the officers of the Mission were native Elders who had never been to Zion." Although he reported the experience to some of his office colleagues "as an instance of absurd dreaming . . . not at all likely to have a literal fulfillment," he did not forget it. The day after Samuel Richards arrived from Utah, he and Orson Pratt told Calkin that he was called to become mission president after a transition period. The mission's business responsibilities would be turned over to him immediately. He noted in his journal, "I think I shall pay more attention to my dreams in future." [27]

Asa Calkin was forty-eight years old when he entered this two-phased calling. By his own description, he was in good health, fatter than when he left Utah, and wore a beard all over his face except for the underlip, following the prevailing British fashion.[28] A native of upstate New York, he had become a Mormon in 1848 before going west to Great Salt Lake City. There he followed mercantile pursuits and acquired a plural wife, Eliza (Lizzie). Mariette, his wife since 1832, had borne nine children, only one of whom lived more than a few months.[29] Asa's letters to his wives and son Theodore, quoted frequently in his journal, throw interesting light on the man and his perception of his mission. In January 1858 he expressed regret that he was not coming home, confidence that the brethren would see that the family did not suffer more than others, and optimism that recent events "have infused new life, energy, faith and confidence in the saints in this country."[30]

As already noted, the four-month Richards-Calkin collaboration focused on reorganizing mission units, funding and arranging for the homeward journeys of the elders, gathering year-end reports for 1857, and publishing the *Millennial Star*. By the time Richards sailed, Calkin had already outlined a program. Excerpts from his "plan of operations" suggest that he may have chafed under the charismatic but inadequately systematic administrations of his predecessors:

---

[27] Calkin, Journal, July 23, September 25, and October 7, 1857. In his journal for September 25, he mentions the dream, now taking it seriously in view of the impending arrival of Samuel W. Richards.

[28] Ibid., January 30, 1858.

[29] See note 40 below.

[30] Long excerpts from the letter are in Calkin, Journal, January 21, 1858. He noted later that he was sending his family, by various missionaries, a gold ring, a pair of Colt revolvers, thirty yards of material, and $250 in cash. Ibid., February 1, 1858.

I am determined to control the Priesthood and establish an order and require the Priesthood to observe that order in all their ministrations.

I will control the funds of the church myself and set bounds to every man's use of it. They shall have enough to support them frugally while engaged in the ministry but not to exceed a certain amount to be determined by myself.[31]

I shall supply the Mission with Account books and require the Elders to keep a strict a/c of all monies received by them . . . shall require all church monies to be paid to the Pastors by the brethren under them, at least once a month.

The Pastors will be required to forward to this Office once in each month *all* money received by them except such as I shall authorize them to expend for the maintenance of the Cause.

All Conference houses shall be abolished and I will so arrange matters that every man in the Mission shall find as much to do as will employ his *whole time*. Every saint shall be visited as often as once in each week and the Tithing collected from them and paid over to the Branch President. Traveling Elders and Conference Presidents shall be required to visit every branch in the Conferences at the least in each month.

The Pastor is the President of the Pastorate . . . and the business with *this office must be* transacted by and through him.

With the help of the Lord and my brethren I will establish the above order in this Mission.[32]

With James D. Ross and William Budge as his counselors and the *Millennial Star* as his ubiquitous voice, Calkin launched his retrenchment program. Ross and Budge were both young, married converts who had served as conference presidents and pastors; they worked indefatigably in their new callings and then migrated to America about the time Calkin returned in 1860. As often as his administrative and editorial duties permitted, the president also visited the branches and conferences, being convinced that "one word of living counsel is worth a page of written." Through editorials in the *Star*, with such titles as "Reformation of Meetings," "Proper Officers," "Efficiency in Administration," "The Right Men in Their Right Places," and "Appropriation of Tithing," order and obedience were presented as hallmarks of testimony. Letters from Ross, Budge, and others in the full-time ministry acknowledged problems in some branches but were generally upbeat.[33]

---

[31] Months earlier, Pratt and Benson had written to Brigham Young about "how the means have been squandered" in the mission. Benson, Journal, August 27, 1857. This suggests that Calkin may have received a little encouragement in devising elements of his plan, and may also account for the encouragement that came from Young even before he learned about Calkin's reform program. One may only speculate on what prompted Young's request, in his letter of March 5, 1858, for a confidential report on the amount of tithing and other funds used by Samuel Richards while in England. Calkin, Journal, May 25, 1858.

[32] Ibid., February 13, 1858.

[33] Calkin to Brigham Young, July 6, 1858, copied in ibid., same date.

In addition to these business-oriented reforms, Calkin pursued the programs launched in 1857. New traveling elders were called; to settle debts before entering this calling, brickmaker Charles Turner withdrew all but £5 of his emigrating fund deposit, and by September only a few shillings of that remained.[34] Tithing was stressed and excommunication was still the penalty for willful noncompliance with this and other tenets of the gospel. Efforts to liquidate the publication debts involved appeals to the Saints as well as curtailment of publications. Hardly had the drive to help the returning missionaries come to a successful conclusion than one was launched to raise funds for the beleaguered Saints in Zion. The Penny Fund and other emigration savings programs were not forgotten, nor was the Poor Fund. With spontaneous dipping into tithing funds now restricted and conference house lodgings curtailed, the elders in full-time church service became more dependent upon the hospitality of the members.[35] To faithful Saints, the missionary visits were thus reminders that the gospel brought obligations as well as blessings.

With the spring came instructions from Brigham Young, dispatched via California. "It is wisdom that public preaching should measurably cease until the present excitement shall be over or wisdom shall otherwise direct," he wrote on February 4. A month later, while the outcome of Colonel Kane's mediation was still uncertain, Young gave the same kind of counsel he was following in Utah. The *Millennial Star* and other publications should be limited to what could be readily sold, "in case future events should compel a sudden closing up of the business of the office." The pragmatic prophet added, "Not that I am at all aware that such a step will ever be required, yet sound policy for us suggests to prepare for the worst while living and hoping for the best."[36]

After recovering from smallpox, Calkin wrote a long report to Young on July 6. He was pleased that some of his innovations had anticipated instructions from Utah, and he detailed some of the progress that had been made. Helping to pay off the emigration-related church debts in St. Louis had seriously depleted funds, but mission office tithing receipts in

---

Millennial Star 20 (June 5, 1858): 360–62; (June 19, 1858): 392–94; (September 4, 1858): 571; (October 9, 1858): 648–49; (October 30, 1858): 696–98.

[34] Charles Turner, Journal, April 16 and August 31, 1858.

[35] Pastor Charles F. Jones recorded that "Prest. Calkin decided what each [elder in full-time church service in the Sheffield conference] should receive weekly from Tithing for their support and traveling expenses, etc. The same was very satisfactory to the brethren." Jones, Journal, April 3, 1858.

[36] Excerpts in Calkin, Journal, April 25 and May 25, 1858. Another letter from Young, dated April 5, revealed the same uncertainty, although only Governor Cumming's ability to persuade Albert Sydney Johnston to bring his army into Utah peacefully was still untested. Ibid., June 26, 1858.

the first six months of 1858 had exceeded all of 1857. In addition, the members had donated handsomely to help the missionaries go home and reduced the £6,000 branch and conference publications debt by 10 percent. Three thousand pounds were now on hand, with a like sum in tithing expected before year end; £5,500 in individual emigration accounts and a printing bill of £300 were the only liabilities.[37]

Efforts "to allay the irritability" of the general populace had been generally successful; episodes of violence and vandalism were far less frequent than the year before. As for the spiritual condition of the members, Calkin understandably accented the positive: "Some few who are fearful . . . some who have not faith to live their religion, and cannot believe in the law of tithing . . . and some others still who make everything else, but the Kingdom of God, first, have left the Church and reduced our numbers a little, but we have a more healthy atmosphere and the faithful feel relieved by their absence. Some few are embracing the Gospel, and on the whole the Mission is in a healthy condition."[38]

Missionaries in the field, who met the members in handfuls except at quarterly conference meetings and who witnessed as many excommunications as baptisms, seem to have shared these perceptions. When he was transferred back to England after more than three years on the Continent, Samuel Francis wrote: "I was astonished to find that the Saints here have made such rapid progress. I found I was all behind, and thought I ought to be baptized into this Mission."[39]

While convalescing from smallpox in June, President Calkin married one of his nurses, Alice Elizabeth Perkes (Perks). The eighteen-year-old daughter of a Birmingham Latter-day Saint couple had been a housekeeper at 42 Islington for several months when she became one of the first in the mission family to come down with the disease and the first to recover. Her brother, William, a twenty-year-old office employee, escaped the disease. Neither his journal nor President Calkin's mentions the June 12 nuptials, but within a few weeks both refer to the new Mrs. Calkin without explanation. She accompanied her husband on a tour of the missions on the Continent in the fall, and in June 1859 she bore a daughter, Charlotte Mariett, the first of her six children.[40]

---

[37] Ibid., July 6, 1858. I found no comparable year-end summary, but scattered evidence argues that the financial condition of the mission continued to improve through the rest of the year.

[38] Ibid.

[39] Francis to Calkin, May 4, 1858, published in *Millennial Star*, 20 (June 5, 1858): 365. It seems clear that what pleased Francis was the more orderly handling of records, finances, and discipline; in Switzerland he had been involved in a bitter conflict among priesthood leaders.

[40] Calkin, Journal, July 16, 1858; Perkes, Journal, July 16 and November 6,

Calkin was certainly aware of the strictures against contracting plural marriages in England that applied to the mission.[41] He apparently construed the extension of his mission as warranting an exception, and he sent a request to President Young by Pratt. When approval came by Young's February letter, in the form of a postscript written in the Deseret alphabet, Calkin had already brought Agnes from Birmingham to Liverpool, along with a cousin who also lived in the mission home until July.[42] A postscript in Calkin's August 15 letter to Young, also in the Deseret alphabet, expressed thanks and reported that action had been taken.[43]

During the last half of 1858 the *Millennial Star* carried letters and press accounts on Utah affairs in almost every issue. The last three July issues were largely devoted to reports of the peacemaking success of Kane and Governor Cumming, and "we told you so" editorials. Sympathetic press comments on the "Move South" — the temporary abandonment of northern Utah settlements in the face of the oncoming U.S. Army — included this in the London *Times* from their New York correspondent: "these Western peasants seem to be a nation of heroes, ready to sacrifice everything rather than surrender one of their wives or a letter from Joe Smith's golden plates."[44]

The prospects for peace did not blunt the fund-raising drive on behalf of the Saints in Zion, which continued even after the peace commissioners proclaimed amnesty and Johnston's army took up residence at Camp Floyd, forty miles southwest of Salt Lake City. The proceeds were apparently applied to the liquidation of the British Mission indebtedness, as Brigham

---

1858; Family Group Record for Asa Starkweather Calkin, in the Church Family History Library, Salt Lake City; author's oral interview, February 9, 1987, with Caroline Stucki Addy, a descendant of Asa and Agnes. Asa's first wife, Mariette, came to Europe when he was released from his mission and the quartet returned to America in two staterooms on the *William Tapscott*, May 11, 1860. Emigrant Register, 1860, p. 193, Church Family History Library. According to other Family Group Records, the name of the child born in Liverpool was Amy Charlotte.

[41] "All the married men among the American and local Priesthood and all the single Elders from Zion were absolutely forbidden to court any women in the mission; this was an inflexible rule at that time." Compiler's note in Manuscript History of the London Conference, August 2, 1857.

[42] Neither Calkin's journal or other evidence known to the writer clarify whether Asa or Agnes had marriage in mind at the time she came to the mission headquarters.

[43] Calkin copied the postscripts in his journal, April 25 and August 15, 1858. The journal excerpts of Asa's letters to his Utah wives contain no mention of this marriage; when and how he advised Mariette and Lizzie is not known. They were in Provo as participants in the "Move South" when the marriage occurred.

[44] London *Times*, July 5, 1858, quoted in *Millennial Star* 20 (July 24, 1858): 472.

Young instructed Calkin to make that a top priority.[45]

The word from America understandably rekindled interest in emigration among the members in Europe. During the months of the Utah War, the returning missionaries and a single party of members, almost all Scandinavians, made up the total mission-supervised emigration — 181 souls.[46] Contributions to individual emigration accounts continued, encouraged by the mission leadership, but authority to resume preparations did not come from Salt Lake City until December. President Young acknowledged the anxiety of many poor members to emigrate, and would not "object to seeing about 10,000 Saints find their way to Utah" in 1859. However, the still-depleted Perpetual Emigrating Fund could not assist anyone. Those who wished to organize handcart companies might do so, and those who wished to come to the eastern states or Canada to earn funds for the rest of their travel were encouraged to do so. He added, "we would just as soon that the saints should be sifted and screened in the world a while as to have it all to do after they get here . . . it will save them the trouble of crossing the Plains twice."[47]

One company of 725 European saints was ready to sail from Liverpool in May 1859, but Mormon emigration did not move back into the thousands until a year later. (See Table 9.)

President Calkin returned from visiting the Scandinavian missions and Paris early in November 1858, just in time to greet the first of the eight missionaries who came from Utah late in the year.[48] They confirmed what the press had already reported about affairs in Zion but left him still uninformed about when his own mission might be expected to end. He went ahead, therefore, with plans for a European Mission leadership conference to be held in Birmingham early in January 1859. The proceedings of this conference, reported extensively in the *Millennial Star*, tell much about where the British Mission stood as the repercussions of the Utah War faded away.[49]

In a long year-end journal entry, Calkin made a generally favorable assessment of his stewardship. "I feel greatly blessed of the Lord," he

---

[45] Young to Calkin, September 10 and October 21, excerpted in Calkin, Journal, December 8 and 13, 1858.

[46] Conway B. Sonne, *Saints on the Seas: A Maritime History of Mormon Emigration* (Salt Lake City: University of Utah Press, 1983), 152, shows three companies, aggregating 178 persons, sailing early in 1858. Samuel W. Richards and two others returned on another vessel.

[47] Young to Calkin, October 21, 1858, published in *Millennial Star* 21 (January 8, 1859): 27; Young to Calkin, September 10, 1858, excerpted in Calkin, Journal, December 8, 1858.

[48] Register of Missionaries, British Mission, 1859.

[49] *Millennial Star* 21 (January 15–February 19, 1859).

wrote, "in having been able to bring about this great revolution and reformation in administration and in the faith, zeal and confidence of the saints." While the trials and test had proved "too severe for the faith of many," thousands of "really honest and faithful saints" had accepted the new administrative and financial discipline, including "the strict and rigid payment of tithing weekly." They also realized that "all hopes of assistance for emigration from the Perpetual Emigrating Fund" were gone, leaving "their emancipation from these lands" dependent "upon their own individual exertions."

He expressed gratitude for the good work of Ross and Budge, as well as the clerical and editorial staffs in the mission office, among whom the name of Edward Tullidge strikes a chord with historians. "On the whole," he concluded, "I am very well satisfied with the labours of the . . . closing year."[50]

In contrast with 1857, this evaluation has some legitimacy. As earlier noted, the spirit of the Utah Reformation generated baptisms, rebaptisms, excommunications, and persecutions early in that year. The net result was a rekindling of fervor among the Saints who met the requirements for rebaptism, but a reduction of total membership because new baptisms did not match losses to emigration, excommunication, and other causes. (See Table 9.) Then President Buchanan's political and military initiatives put the proselyting program on the defensive and depleted the leadership ranks. By December 31, if George Reynolds's later tabulations have any validity, the mission membership declined from 22,502 to 15,220 in a single year. Since the number of members who died, emigrated, or were cut off from the church exceeded the number of convert baptisms by only about 600, almost 7,000 erstwhile members were simply not counted in the reports. Conferences, districts, and branches also disappeared through consolidation or nonreporting. The process appears in microcosm in Samuel Francis's description of a scheduled meeting in a Midlands village: "There were only one saint there and three who had been Saints. I made the best I could of this small congregation, but I could not prevent myself from feeling that the saints were dying away there."[51]

The year 1858 witnessed some further reduction in the number of administrative units, priesthood holders, and members. The number of branches at the end of 1858 was 456, down from 531 in 1857 and 643 in 1856.[52] But after the 2,564 baptisms, 195 emigrations, 240 deaths, and

---

[50] Calkin, Journal, December 30, 1858.

[51] Francis, Journal, October 13, 1858; see also William H. Kelsey, Journal, May 21 and 30, 1858.

[52] Richard L. Jensen to author, December 3, 1987, shares data that he has gleaned from the *Millennial Star* and other sources in his extensive studies of European missionary work and emigration.

2,714 excommunications in Reynolds's tabulation are combined, less than 500 people have to be assigned to the "disappeared" category to reconcile the membership totals for the beginning and the end of the year. It is safe to say that the enumeration of 14,186 members more accurately represents the effective strength of the British Mission at the end of 1858 than do the much larger figures for two or three years before. Whether these Saints were made more faithful by their Utah War testing may be disputed, but that they contributed more money and kept better records may not.

That President Calkin measured his success in terms of records and finances is consistent with his business background and the emphasis on tithing and conformity that he inherited from the Reformation instituted by his immediate predecessors. His zeal produced more resistance than his journal, which ends in January 1859, implies. Letters from Brigham Young early in 1860 admonished him "to still so frequent and varied a cry for money . . . [so] as not to oppress, nor discourage the poor, nor afford to any a reasonable occasion for stumbling." By then he had apparently found tithing expenditures by the missionaries as difficult to control as had his predecessors, and even the conference houses that he disliked had not disappeared.[53] It is likely that the arrival of elders from America at the end of 1858 increased the pressure to use local funds for missionary travel and maintenance.

Neither the Reformation nor the Utah War reversed the membership decline that had already beset the British Mission as a result of the public advocacy of plural marriage by the church in America. The drop from 22,502 at the end of 1856 to 14,158 two years later should be attributed both to membership attrition and more accurate (or less optimistic) counting. It is not possible to say how much the withdrawal of American missionaries or the rigorous policies of President Calkin contributed to either.[54] The presidency that followed Calkin's in 1860 was marked by more emphasis on the voluntary nature of tithing, fewer excommunications, and a small net increase in membership, but the spectacular proselyting successes of 1837–52 were not repeated.

The most substantial impact of the Utah War upon British Mormons was to place greater leadership responsibilities on the local priesthood. However, the effect on the church in the British Isles was largely tempo-

---

[53] Young to Calkin, January 31, 1860. Richard Jensen called this letter to my attention, along with additional corroborating evidence. Jensen to author, December 3, 1987. Jensen, "Without Purse or Scrip?" 6–8.

[54] According to Brigham Young, Jr., who later referred to the Calkin era as a "reign of terror," a number of people who were excommunicated then returned to the church in the early 1860s. Brigham Young, Jr., Diary, December 15, 1862, quoted in Jensen to author, December 3, 1987.

rary. The importance of gathering was reemphasized in the postwar period by the first communications from Brigham Young and the first missionaries from Utah, and many of the new local leaders responded. James Ross, William Budge, Charles Penrose, Edward Tullidge, E. L. T. Harrison, and others went to America within a few years, some to lead the church and some to leave it there.[55]

A hundred years—and two world wars in which the American missionaries were again withdrawn—would elapse before a new approach to missionary work, a new concept of Zion, and new techniques of communication and direction from Salt Lake City would lead to the establishment and proliferation of locally led stakes and wards in the British Isles.

---

[55] Andrew Jenson, *Latter-day Saint Biographical Encyclopedia: A Compilation of Biographical Sketches of Prominent Men and Women in The Church*, 4 vols. (Salt Lake City: Andrew Jenson History Co., 1901–36), provides data on these and many other nineteenth-century British Mormons. Penrose became a counselor in the First Presidency; Harrison and Tullidge participated in the Godbeite schism.

15

Law and the Nineteenth-Century British Mormon Migration

RAY JAY DAVIS

Most migration of nineteenth-century Mormons from Great Britain to the United States took place between 1840 and 1891 — a time when there were few legal rules concerning leaving England, crossing the Atlantic, and entering the United States. This essay examines the relationship between law and the migration at four different milestone years: 1842, 1856, 1875, and 1891. These years illustrate the changing laws under which British converts embarked at Liverpool, crossed the Atlantic, and landed at New Orleans, New York, and other U.S. ports. Consideration will be given to British laws impacting emigration, laws of the United States and Great Britain regulating carriage of passengers by sea, and both state and federal U.S. immigration laws.

Although some converts had departed in earlier years for Zion, 1842 was the first year of numerically significant Mormon emigration from Great Britain. Consequently, it has been selected as the first milestone year. That year 1,600 Mormons left Liverpool by sailing ships, all bound for New Orleans. They composed about 2.5 percent of the nearly 64,000 emigrants departing the United Kingdom in 1842 for the United States.[1]

Unlike our century in which passports and visas are necessary for international travel, egress from Great Britain in 1842 was accomplished without legal documents. Earlier in English history the crown for political

---

[1] P. A. M. Taylor, *Expectations Westward: The Mormons and the Emigration of their British Converts in the Nineteenth Century* (Edinburgh and London: Oliver and Boyd, 1965), 145. For lists of ports of embarkation and disembarkation of Mormon-used emigrant vessels, see Conway B. Sonne, *Saints on the Seas: A Maritime History of Mormon Migration 1830–1890* (Salt Lake City: University of Utah Press, 1983), 148–59. Stanley C. Johnson, *A History of Emigration from the United Kingdom to North America 1763–1912* (London: Frank Cass and Company, 1966), 344.

reasons had power to bar persons from leaving the country through use of the prerogative writ of *ne exeat regno*. But by the eighteenth century the writ had evolved into a device to restrain debtors from fleeing financial obligations.[2] The Latter-day Saint converts who left in 1842 did not need to obtain any government permit or license to depart.

Various statutes enacted during the eighteenth century had banned artisans from leaving the country and prohibited export of certain types of machinery. These laws were repealed in 1824. Enforcement of this mercantilistic ban had been ineffective. According to a finding of a parliamentary inquiry, its main impact had been to keep from coming back artisans who had left the country but desired to return.[3] Mormon artisans who left in 1842 had no legal cloud upon any future return. Of course, they did not expect to come back, except perhaps as missionaries.

The Industrial Revolution, urbanization, and overpopulation brought England severe economic dislocation during the first half of the nineteenth century. Periodic agricultural depression and the population explosion complicated the problem of caring for the poor and distressed. Emigration of some persons assisted under the Poor Laws could reduce excess population and future relief costs. Hence an 1834 statute authorized property owners and rate payers to decide at public meetings to pledge up to half of future Poor Law tax income to defray expenses to help poor persons emigrate.[4] Although the Poor Law Amendment Act raised little money used for the Mormon exodus, it manifested a public policy favoring emigration.

Similarly, by 1842 the British government had taken steps to improve the lot of passengers sailing from the kingdom. As the emigration curve rose after the Napoleonic Wars, fortunes were made by using vessels which imported raw materials to carry passengers to foreign lands and English colonies. These ships, which were designed for cargo, were temporarily converted for passengers by constructing temporary bunks in the holds for steerage accommodations on the outward-bound journey. They were nei-

---

[2] Ray Jay Davis, "The Privilege-Right Distinction: Egress from the Country." (Thesis, Columbia Law School, 1956), 11–14.

[3] 5 Geo. IV, c. 97 (1824). Select Committee on Artizans and Machinery, *Sixth Report* (May 19, 1824), 590–91. Reprinted in British Sessional Papers 1824 (51) V, pp. 590–91. See also W. A. Carrothers, *Emigration from the British Isles* (London: Frank Cass and Company, 1966), 87–89.

[4] Milton Briggs and Percy Jordan, *Economic History of England*, 11th ed. (London: University Tutorial Press, 1964), 407–8. See also Johnson, *History of Emigration*, 288–89. 4 & 5 Geo. IV, c. 76 § 62 (1834). The 1834 Poor Law, however, was rather ineffective at least partly because of antipathy toward the Poor Law commissioners by the poor. Briggs and Jordan, *Economic History*, 408. See also Mark Brayshay, "Manpower for Britain's Empire," *History Today* 32 (August 1982): 43.

ther sanitary nor safe, but they were profitable.[5] Starting in 1803, a series of Passengers' Acts sought to regulate the laissez-faire emigrant carriage trade.[6] In 1816, 1817, and 1823 amendatory legislation added more detailed provisions concerning minimum space for passengers, provisioning, and placing a medical practitioner on vessels carrying more than fifty persons. But in 1827 the entire law was repealed, ostensibly because cheaper Atlantic fares would encourage needed emigration. The following year, however, at least partly because of disastrous epidemics and deaths on transoceanic crossings and in disembarkation ports, another Passengers' Act was enacted.[7]

By 1840 the agency to which Passengers' Acts enforcement had been delegated was known as the Colonial Land and Emigration Commission. It was part of the Colonial Office. In 1841 the commissioners issued a report stating the principal objects of English passengers' legislation. These objectives were: "1st. To regulate the number of emigrants conveyed in the different vessels, and to provide for their proper accommodations on board; 2ndly. To ensure a proper supply of provisions and water; 3rdly. To provide for the seaworthiness of the vessels; and, 4thly, to afford the poorer class of emigrants protection from the numerous frauds practiced upon them before they leave this country; to provide for their being carried to their stipulated destination; and to secure them a reasonable time for making arrangements before they are landed from the ship."[8] Attached to the commission's report were legislative recommendations to meet those objectives.

Parliament's response was passage of the Passengers' Act of 1842.[9] The law, which covered all ships leaving the United Kingdom, limited them to three passengers for every five tons and mandated six feet between decks and ten square feet space for every passenger on lower decks. Ships had to carry three quarts of fresh water per passenger per day and seven pounds of bread, biscuits, flour, oatmeal, or rice for each passenger each week. Babies under one year were not included in the head count and children under fourteen counted as half an adult. Only two tiers of bunks

---

[5] Helen I. Cowen, *British Emigration to British North America: The First Hundred Years* (Toronto: University of Toronto Press, 1961). See also Edwin C. Guillet, *The Great Migration: The Atlantic Crossing by Sailing Ship Since 1770*, 2d ed. (Toronto: University of Toronto Press, 1963), 10–11.

[6] The first such law was 43 Geo. III, c. 56 (1803).

[7] 7 & 8 Geo. IV, c. 19 (1827); 9 Geo. IV, c. 21 (1828). This last act affected only crossings to British North America. Conditions leading to reenactment of such are discussed in Cowen, *British Emigration*, 104–5.

[8] Colonial Land and Emigration Commissioners, *Report on Necessity of Amending the Passengers' Act* (July 22, 1841), 3.

[9] 5 & 6 Vic., c. 107 (1842).

were allowed and berths could not be less than six feet in length and eighteen inches in width for each passenger. Commission officers were given power to inspect ships for seaworthiness. Depending on the size of the ship, two to four lifeboats were necessary — about enough to accommodate cabin passengers. Although vessels headed elsewhere had to carry medical practitioners, those bound for North America did not. Passengers were entitled to passage money receipts, and passage brokers were required to be licensed by the commission.

Several observations can be made about the effectiveness of the legislation in achieving the commissioners' goals. The statutory space requirements were not very commodious. Required provisioning was monotonous and inadequate. Steerage passengers needed lifeboats in the event of trouble as much as did cabin passengers. Doctors could have helped in cases of injuries or disease. Nothing was said about personal security, light, or ventilation. And, without a sufficiently large corps of officers, enforcement would be uneven at best. In 1842 only one officer and an assistant staffed Liverpool and could not enforce the law adequately. Criminals preyed on emigrants in port; disease struck them on board.[10] Getting there definitely was not "half the fun."

Mormon emigrants fared better than did many others. By 1842 a pattern of guidance and supervision had been established. Church publications gave instructions about the trip and what food and supplies to bring.[11] Church agents smoothed the way past the swindlers and other criminals who infested ports at both ends of the oceanic crossing. Also, church representatives negotiated relatively inexpensive group fares for passage. On board church members were organized into groups with ecclesiastical leadership. Their routine was designed to minimize spiritual and physical losses during the crossing.[12] Later, Charles Dickens commented

---

[10] See Terry Coleman, *Passage to America: A History of Emigrants from Great Britain and Ireland to America in the Mid-Nineteenth Century* (London: Hutchinson and Company, 1972), 63-83, 205-12. One officer admitted upon inquiry by the commissioners that he and his assistant actually inspected only ships bound for British North America — one vessel in thirteen of those clearing Liverpool.

[11] See, e.g., *Millennial Star* 10 (August 15, 1848): 244-45.

[12] David H. Pratt and Paul F. Smart, "Life On Board A Mormon Emigrant Ship," *World Conference on Records: Preserving Our Heritage, August 12-15, 1980,* 13 vols. (Salt Lake City: The Church of Jesus Christ of Latter-day Saints, 1980), vol. 5, Series 418. Mormons believe that the migrants were protected and led by the hand of the Almighty. The thought is expressed in the hymn "For the Strength of the Hills."

> Thou hast led us here in safety
> Where the mountain bulwark stands
> As the guardian of the loved ones
> Thou hast brought from many lands.

favorably upon his inspection of Mormon shipboard arrangements, and the church system was applauded when Samuel W. Richards, mission president and shipping agent, gave testimony before a select committee of the House of Commons in 1854.[13] Mormon arrangements exceeded those mandated by the Passengers' Act.

The 1842 British Mormon migration crossed to New Orleans because it was cheaper and easier to travel up the Mississippi River by boat to Nauvoo than it was to reach there overland from east coast U.S. ports. At that time no federal legislation regulated immigration into the United States. Consequently, the only restriction upon entrance into the country was one enacted by the Louisiana legislature. An 1842 law assessed a head tax of $2 each upon passengers coming from foreign ports. The proceeds supported operations of the charity hospital of the City of New Orleans. Ships' masters were either to collect cash for the tax or to sell enough baggage of nonpaying passengers to raise the money. They then paid the hospital collectors.[14]

Subsequent versions of the Louisiana law made it clear that the tax was intended to defray city costs for hospital operation and that immigrants would receive gratuitous medical care.[15] The city provided the immigrants a service in return for the head tax. And the Louisiana taxpayers did not have to bear all the burden of hospital operation. However, shipowners and foreigners disliked the discrimination in the law which did not tax travelers coming from American ports. But entrance of 1842 British Mormon migrants into the United States was relatively inexpensive and quite simple.

After the church moved to Utah and as railroads extended westward, beginning in 1855 British converts disembarked at Atlantic coast ports rather than New Orleans.[16] The peak year was 1856, the second milestone year. Over 3,500 British converts immigrated, which was 3 percent of departures that year from the United Kingdom to the United States.[17] The

---

Text by Felicia D. Hemans, adapted by Edward L. Sloan, *Hymns of the Church of Jesus Christ of Latter-day Saints* (Salt Lake City: The Church of Jesus Christ of Latter-day Saints, 1985), No. 35.

[13] Charles Dickens, *The Uncommercial Traveler* (New York: Oxford University Press, 1958), 220–32. Select Committee on Emigrant Ships, *Second Report, Minutes of Evidence* (May 23, 1854), 108–17. See also Samuel Richards, "Missionary Experience," *Contributor* 11 (1890): 155–59. This is Samuel Richards's account of his appearance before the committee.

[14] La. Acts c. 81 (1842).

[15] La. Acts c. 295 (1850).

[16] Sonne, *Saints on the Seas,* 151. Mormon travelers also landed at such other Atlantic coast ports as Philadelphia and Boston, but New York came to be the main port of entry for European Mormons after they switched from New Orleans.

[17] Taylor, *Expectations Westward,* 145.

overall emigration total was only 112,000, a drop from the average of the prior ten years. Probably this was due to the shipping shortage which had developed during the Crimean War and to earlier cresting of the wave of Irish Potato Famine emigrants.[18]

Although Americans generally supported unfettered immigration during the mid-nineteenth century, as early as colonial times several jurisdictions had imposed legislative and administrative regulations on landing immigrants upon their shores.[19] Governmental concerns focused upon criminals, paupers, and the diseased.[20] By 1856 New York City had a fairly comprehensive regulatory system. Mormons landing there that year first underwent quarantine on board ship off Staten Island and then were delivered ashore at Castle Garden on the southern tip of Manhattan Island. The quarantine was intended to protect New Yorkers from contagion. Persons with contagious diseases were put ashore at a hospital on Staten Island; other people who were sick were sent to Wards Island for hospitalization.[21]

Castle Garden, the other facility maintained by New York, was meant to protect immigrants. This official depot was a large former music hall and opera house. It was a place for processing new arrivals. They could obtain information about lodging, employment, and further transportation needs. There also newcomers could rest, take meals, and send and receive letters. No unlicensed persons were supposed to be on the premises; no officials were allowed to make recommendations about any particular onward route as contrasted with others. Within its walls Castle Garden functioned effectively. Some ship captains, however, put passengers ashore in New Jersey or Long Island where the system's benefits were unavailable. And once immigrants left Castle Garden they frequently emerged into the hands of criminals who sought to exploit them. Fortunately for Mormon travelers in New York, as had been the case in Liverpool, church agents were avail-

---

[18] Johnson, *History of Emigration*, 344. For an account of the Irish migration, see Kerby Miller, *Emigrants and Exiles: Ireland and the Irish Exodus to North America* (New York: Oxford University Press, 1895).

[19] The Democratic Party catered to immigrants, and the Whigs took no stand. A nativist party, the "Know-Nothings," existed for a short time as a third party. John Hicks, *The Federal Union* (Boston: Houghton Mifflin Company, 1937), 562–65.

[20] For a survey of colonial and state immigration policy, see Edward P. Hutchinson, *Legislative History of American Immigration Policy, 1788–1965* (Philadelphia: University of Pennsylvania Press, 1981), 388–404.

[21] The New York City immigration facilities are discussed in Taylor, *Expectations Westward*, 212. Taylor refers to Friedrich Kapp, *Immigration and the Commissioners of Emigration of the State of New York* (New York: The Nation Press, 1870), as a leading authority on New York efforts to deal with immigration. For an example of a quarantine provision, see 1846 N.Y. Laws, c. 300 § 1.

able to help them organize for the trip to Utah and to keep them out of the malefactors' clutches.[22]

New York's quarantine and immigration facilities were the product of state law. A series of enactments stretching back to colonial days built the New York immigration law. It was administered by commissioners of emigration, among whom were by designation the presidents of the German Society and the Irish Emigrant Society and the mayors of New York City and Brooklyn. The commission had authority to appoint doctors and other immigration officials. Title to the Marine Hospital on Staten Island was transferred to it from the health department and it was authorized to buy facilities, such as Castle Garden. Ships were barred from landing immigrants at any facilities other than those under control of the commission. There was a manifesting requirement. For example, in a May 5, 1847, law, the masters of vessels coming from outside the state were required to make a report about their passengers' former place of residence, age, and occupation. A bonding requirement initially was used to finance the law's operation. Captains had to post a $300 bond for each passenger. If the city needed to expend money for ill or destitute persons, it could recoup against the bond. This was followed by an alternative head tax on each passenger landed in lieu of the bond. Subsequently there was merely a head tax. [23]

The New York head tax, as well as those of Louisiana and Massachusetts, was challenged in court. The Constitution of the United States on which the challenges were based said little about immigration. Clause 1 in Section 9 of Article 1 on legislative powers of the national government provided that "[t]he Migration or Importation of such Persons as any of the States now existing shall think proper to admit, shall not be prohibited by the Congress" before 1808, but a head tax up to $10 per person could be imposed. This provision, however, probably was inserted to prevent the new national government from banning the slave trade until 1808. It was the Commerce Clause to which the Supreme Court turned in its consideration of the state head taxes. That provision delegated Congress power to "regulate commerce with foreign Nations." According to the 1849 decision in the so-called *Passenger Cases*, the New York and Massachusetts head taxes were unconstitutional violations of the international commerce provision. Such state laws trespassed upon ground reserved for the national

---

[22] The Castle Garden establishment is described in James M. Burns, *The Vineyard of Liberty* (New York: Alfred Knopf, 1982), 406. See also Johnson, *History of Emigration*, 118, and Taylor, *Expectations Westward*, 213, 214. John Taylor was there in 1855, T. B. H. Stenhouse in 1858–59, and George Q. Cannon in 1860.

[23] 1847 N.Y. Laws, c. 195 § 4; 1847 N.Y. Laws, c. 483; 1848 N.Y. Laws, c. 219 § 1-2; 1847 N.Y. Laws, c. 195 § 1. New York immigration restrictions are described in Johnson, *History of Emigration*, 132–36.

government. It should be noted, however, that in *City of New York v. Miln*, which was decided in 1837 over a decade before the *Passenger Cases*, New York's reporting rules had been upheld.[24]

The uncertain status of immigration law authority in the United States was one factor delaying enactment of federal immigration legislation. The precursor to U.S. immigration law came in 1819 with passage of the first U.S. Passenger Act.[25] That law required a manifest or list of all passengers on board ships entering the United States. It also copied the provision of the then current British Passengers' Act respecting overcrowding — a limit of two passengers for every five tons of vessel burden. And it made some provisioning requirements of passenger ships leaving the country.

The U.S. law under which the 1856 British Mormon immigrants entered the country was the Passenger Act of 1855.[26] It set an allowance of one passenger for every two tons of vessel burden, two children between one and eight counted as one passenger, and children under one were not counted. It made requirements for deck space per passenger, the amount of headroom, construction of berths, ventilation, cooking equipment, food supplies, and sanitation. This U.S. act which applied to the British Mormon 1856 immigration was easier to administer than was its British counterpart. Prosecutions for violation would take place in U.S. courts where the witnesses were, rather than in British courts which had a difficult time getting witnesses most of whom would be overseas.

By 1856 the British Passengers' Act also had evolved to provide more protection for persons leaving the United Kingdom. For example, the Act of 1855 limited sailing ships to carriage of one "statute adult" to every two tons of registered tonnage, required seven feet of space between decks, separated unmarried males into a compartment separate from females, had requirements as to light, ventilation, privies, and medical facilities, demanded lifeboats, and banned carriage of dangerous cargo and ballast on passenger ships. Food and water requirements were adequate. Passengers could do better than merely subsist on provisions supplied by the vessels.[27]

In their 1855 report, the Colonial Land and Emigration Commission called attention to the fact that British and U.S. laws were inconsistent. They noted that assimilation of the acts would be useful. But they also

---

[24] U.S. Const. art. 1, § 9, cl. 1; U.S. Const. art. 1, § 8, cl. 3; 48 U.S. 283 (1849); 36 U.S. 102 (1837).

[25] Cf. Hutchinson, *Legislative History*, 83; 3 Stat. 492 (1819).

[26] 10 Stat. 715 (1855).

[27] 18 & 19 Vic., c. 119 (1855). One study of Mormon transoceanic crossings notes that on at least twelve ships used between 1846 and 1866 "the fare was poor or ran short." Pratt and Smart, "Mormon Immigrant Ship," 8–10.

admitted that, even though most immigrants to the United States were coming from Britain, many came from other European nations which also had laws, each differing from the other and from that of the United Kingdom. They saw difficulty framing a law in the United States which would embrace the provisions of all European laws, "without making it so vague as to be practically worthless."[28] Ships carrying Mormon and other European immigrants to the United States in 1856 were subject to multiple regulation.

The next milestone year was 1875, the year Congress first regulated immigration as such. Ironically, in the mid-1870s, annual emigration from the United Kingdom to the United States was the least of any period between the American Civil War and the twentieth century. British Mormon emigration also was down. According to one study, between 1871 and 1885 there were no more than 1,500 British converts annually leaving for the United States and no fewer than 600. This overall decrease, however, cannot be attributed to tighter legal requirements. Rather, it was the significantly smaller British LDS Church membership than during the prior three decades. Emigration, apostasy, and lower conversion rates resulted in membership reduction.[29] Hence, although the 1875 legal regime was different from that of 1856, the legal difference did not account for the decrease in either the general or the Mormon emigration to the United States.

The most striking legal distinction between the 1875 legal situation and that of earlier years was enactment of the first national law in the United States to deal with immigration as such. Earlier laws had dealt with naturalization of immigrants and their transportation to the United States; but proposals for specific immigration restrictions failed until 1875. At least until the Supreme Court spoke in the *Passenger Cases* in 1849 there was uncertainty over federal power; thereafter there was question about policy issues in passage of uniform national immigration regulation.[30] Nativist political groups advocated severe restrictions, but Congress demonstrated resistance to their blandishments. It was not until the 1870s that officeholders from the major political parties began to favor restrictions.[31]

---

[28] Colonial Land and Emigration Commissioners, *Fifteenth General Report* (1855), 27.

[29] Johnson, *History of Emigration*, 344; Taylor, *Expectations Westward*, 145; Richard L. Jensen, "Whether, When, and How to Gather Zion? A Close Look at Emigration of Latter-day Saints from the British Isles," presentation given at a Symposium Celebrating the 150th Anniversary of The Church of Jesus Christ of Latter-day Saints in the British Isles (Provo, Utah, 1987), figure 3.

[30] See Hutchinson, *Legislative History*, 11–63; 48 U.S. 283 (1849).

[31] See Kirk H. Porter and Donald B. Johnson, *National Party Platforms, 1840–1968* (Urbana: University of Illinois Press, 1970), 101–2, 126.

The vision of the United States as a land of opportunity for all oppressed, downtrodden, and poor blurred very slowly.

The Immigration Act of 1875 consisted of five sections.[32] Three dealt with prostitutes who under that law were excluded from immigration. The statute also barred entry by convicts, excepting those guilty only of political crimes. Additionally, the 1875 act prohibited bringing in Oriental persons without their consent and declared that contracting to supply so-called coolie labor was a felony.

The current massive immigration code grew from this limited start. In 1875 there was political pressure to do something about importing prostitutes, criminals, and cheap laborers. In addition the time was ripe for passage of a federal law. The Supreme Court's invalidation of state efforts created a situation in which even usual advocates of states' rights appealed to Congress to act.[33]

The nineteenth-century British Mormon immigrants were not impacted by the 1875 immigration law. But it demonstrated that Congress had and could use the power to deal with immigration. Congressional hostility toward Mormons already had surfaced.[34] It also pointed the way toward future legislative drafting techniques. Exclusion, which in 1875 struck criminals and prostitutes, was to become a major feature of immigration legislation. Tying exclusion to "immorality" was to surface later as an anti-Mormon device.

By 1875 the need for passenger acts to protect travelers was diminished. Enforcement of existing laws had become more effective. Also, the advent of steam between 1840 and 1860 changed the nature of the shipping industry. Sailing boats had been owned by individuals and small groups; steam vessels were more expensive and beyond the economic reach of all except well-financed corporations.[35] With steam power, crossing was faster and easier; exposure to the elements was reduced; schedules could be established.

Mormon migrants were slower than other transatlantic voyagers to change to steam. British converts, even with assistance of the Utah-based Perpetual Emigrating Fund, lacked financial means to pay higher fares

---

[32] 18 Stat. 477 (1875).

[33] Hutchinson, *Legislative History*, 66.

[34] For example, in 1862 Congress had enacted a law prohibiting bigamous marriages in territories of the United States. 12 Stat. 501 (1862). It was aimed at the Mormons. Its constitutionality was upheld in *Reynolds v. United States*, 98 U.S. 145 (1878). For a discussion of the contribution of the *Reynolds* case to U.S. constitutional thought, see Ray Jay Davis, "Plural Marriage and Religious Freedom: The Impact of Reynolds v. United States," *Arizona Law Review* 15 (1973): 287.

[35] Johnson, *History of Emigration*, 120–22.

than the old sailing ship prices.[36] Steam cost slightly more.[37] But during the 1860s, the Mormons switched to steam. They also discovered Guion and Company, a steamship operator which carried the organized Mormon migration from Europe for the next quarter of a century. Guion was willing to charge Mormon groups about one-third under the going fare when transatlantic crossing tickets were high and no more than regular passengers when fares were low.[38] Guion and the Mormons successfully bucked the shipping cartel efforts to keep up prices. The 1870s saw the opening rounds of the struggle between shipping lines, working through so-called shipping "conferences," and shippers over monopolistic pricing. Without the aid of antitrust legislation which came later in the United States, the Mormons got a price break.[39]

The last of the four years for which legal regulation of the British Mormon migration will be considered is 1891. The 1880s saw a continued decline in crossings by British Mormon converts. After 1886, in no year during the nineteenth century were there as many as 500. The harvest of souls in the United Kingdom largely had been completed at least for the time being. Also, it was toward the end of the nineteenth century that immigration to the United States shifted from its earlier heavy concentration upon the passage of northern and western Europeans to its next phase of southern and eastern European dominance.[40] The legal situation for the 1891 Mormon British converts was less favorable than it had been during the earlier years. Perhaps it was just as well the crest had come earlier.

---

[36] The Perpetual Emigrating Fund was a corporation established by the Mormons which solicited donations from church membership to help defray immigration expenses of impecunious members. Persons assisted had at least a moral obligation to reimburse the fund for such help. The history of the P.E.F. and of its operations are discussed in Leonard Arrington, *Great Basin Kingdom: An Economic History of the Latter-day Saints, 1830–1900* (Cambridge: Harvard University Press, 1958), 77–79; Gustive Larson, *Prelude to the Kingdom: Mormon Desert Conquest* (Francestown, N.H.: Marshall Jones Co., 1947), 106–15; Wallace Stegner, *The Gathering of Zion: The Story of the Mormon Trail* (Salt Lake City: Westwater Press, 1981), 223–24.

[37] Johnson, *History of Emigration*, 121.

[38] Richard L. Jensen, "Steaming Through: Arrangements for Mormon Emigration from Europe," *Journal of Mormon History* 9 (1982): 4.

[39] The British courts took a fairly relaxed view of cartels and boycotts. See, e.g., *The Mogul Steamship Co., Ltd. v. McGregor, Gow and Co.*, House of Lords [1892] A.C. 25. For a discussion of the distinction in U.S. antitrust law between conduct of combinations and individual conduct, see James Rahl, "Conspiracy and the Antitrust Laws," *Illinois Law Review* 44 (1950): 743.

[40] Taylor, *Expectations Westward*, 145–46. Avery Craven and Walter Johnson, *The United States: Experiment in Democracy* (Boston: Ginn and Company, 1947), 462. See also James Burns, *The Workshop of Democracy* (New York: Alfred Knopf, 1985), 147.

The year 1882 was a banner one for enactment of laws having potential impact upon the Mormon migration. First, there was a strengthened
U.S. Passenger Act.[41] It increased the space requirements to 100 cubic
feet per passenger on the two upper decks and allowed 120 on the lowest
deck. Also the act set the food allowance per passenger as "equal in value
to one and a half navy rations of the United States, and of fresh water not
less than four quarts per day shall be furnished each of such passengers."
Then there was the Edmunds Act making bigamous cohabitation (something easier to prove than the act of marrying bigamously) a crime.[42] It
was a prelude to the Edmunds-Tucker Act which disincorporated the Latter-
day Saint Church and the Perpetual Emigrating Fund.[43] Enforcement of
that law left the church fighting for existence rather than building the
kingdom by bringing people from the British Isles. Finally in 1882 there
was another federal immigration law. The Immigration Act of 1882 imposed
a head tax on immigrants in response to requests from maritime states for
financial assistance in dealing with the immigration.[44] It also expanded
the list of excludable categories by adding mental defectives and persons
likely to become public charges to the earlier convict and immoral clauses.

The Immigration Act of 1882 was made politically feasible because
the Supreme Court in 1876 in *Henderson v. Mayor of New York* struck down a
New York alternative head tax or bonding arrangement. (A companion
case struck down the similar Louisiana law.) Also, in 1883 the Court, in
People v. Compagnie Generale Transatlantique, ruled that the New York immigration legislation could not pass constitutional muster as an inspection
law. Continuing its line of immigration tax cases, in 1884 the Supreme
Court upheld the federal head tax on the ground that Congress could regulate immigration "as part of commerce with foreign nations."[45] These
Head Money Cases assured federal primacy.

While the 1880s migration of British and other European converts was
taking place, a final act of official hostility was unfolding in the House of
Representatives. House Bill 12291, a proposal to add polygamists to the

---

[41] 22 Stat. 186 (1882).

[42] 22 Stat. 31 (1882). For statutory interpretation of the law, see, e.g., *Cannon
v. United States*, 116 U.S. 44 (1885); *Clawson v. United States*, 114 U.S. 477 (1885).

[43] 24 Stat. 635 (1887). The constitutional validity of the law was confirmed in
Late Corporation of the Church of Jesus Christ of Latter-day Saints v. United States, 136 U.S.
1 (1890).

[44] 22 Stat. 214 (1882). The legislative history of the federal head tax is related
in Maldwyn Jones, *American Immigration* (Chicago: University of Chicago Press,
1960), 250–51. In 1882 Congress also enacted a ban on Chinese naturalization. 22
Stat. 58 (1882). This was a preliminary to the Chinese Exclusion Act of 1888. 25
Stat. 476 (1888).

[45] 92 U.S. 259 (1875); 107 U.S. 59 (1882); 112 U.S. 580 (1882).

exclusion list, was under consideration.[46] Although it was and is hard to enforce that sort of exclusion, its discussion by the House manifested an anti-Mormon tendency in congressional immigration policy. The ban became a permanent part of the U.S. Immigration and Naturalization Code in 1891[47] —after the official Mormon renunciation of polygamy.[48]

Sometimes law may be susceptible to selective enforcement and to use for other administrative discrimination. As American public attitudes became more anti-Mormon, some government officials leveled their authority against Mormon immigration. In 1879 Secretary of State William Evarts sent a circular to U.S. diplomats in England and other northern European countries advising them of federal antibigamy legislation and Mormon prose-lyting. He suggested that U.S. consular representatives inform foreign governments that Mormons might experience difficulty being admitted to the United States and that U.S. consular officials seek foreign help in dissuading Mormons from leaving for America. The Guion Line rebuffed a British police effort to have a poster placed with it stating there might be troubles at disembarkation by Mormons in the United States. The British press reacted angrily to the official meddling and nothing else came of the Evarts circular.[49] But official antipathy had been registered.

In 1886 Edmund Stephenson, a New York emigration commissioner, claimed that Mormons were likely to become financially dependent upon the state, a rather unusual assertion in view of the fact that the church regularly smoothed the way for Mormon travelers to leave for the West as soon as possible. During the year, nevertheless, all Mormons on three ships were questioned on the matter, some were detained, and a few were deported. The last company of Saints that year to sail were sent to Phila-delphia to avoid further harassment. After inquiry by the Treasury Depart-ment, Customs Bureau officials were directed to refrain from discrimina-

---

[46] 50th Cong., 2d Sess., H.R. 12291 (1889).

[47] 26 Stat. 1084 (1891). Between 1907 and 1952 the statute included a ban on immigration of persons who "believe in polygamy." Edward Hutchinson, *Legislative History*, 482. The current provision does not. 8 U.S.C. § 1182 (a) 11 (1982). It excludes polygamists, persons who practice polygamy, and persons who advocate the practice of polygamy. The latter is a disability for exercise of speech. Perhaps it is not as offensive to a sense of civil liberties as barring persons for belief, but certainly it is not sensitive to American ideals.

[48] Official Declaration 1, *Doctrine and Covenants*.

[49] For accounts of the Evarts circular, see Brigham H. Roberts, *A Comprehen-sive History of the Church of Jesus Christ of Latter-day Saints* (Salt Lake City: Deseret News Press: 1930) 1: 550-55. Jensen, "Steaming Through," 7. The British press reaction is chronicled in Richard L. Evans, *A Century of "Mormonism" in Great Brit-ain: A Brief Summary of the Activities of the Church of Jesus Christ of Latter-day Saints in the United Kingdom* (Salt Lake City: Deseret News Press, 1937), 206-9.

tion against Mormons because of their religion. There was only one incident the following season.[50]

In addition to polygamist exclusion, which was specifically aimed at Mormons, other provisions of the immigration code adopted by 1891 also could be the basis for exclusion of Latter-day Saint British immigrants: the pauperism provisions in the 1882 and 1891 acts, the contract labor provision of the 1885 and 1891 laws, and the loathsome or contagious disease exclusion of the 1891 law. The pauperism exclusion was the result of concern in Congress that impecunious immigrants might become a financial burden on the community. The 1882 act spoke of "persons unable to take care of himself or herself without becoming a public charge." A dollar figure by which immigrant inspectors could measure such pauperism was not inserted into the immigration code until 1907. The contract labor provisions were intended to keep out unwanted competition for American jobs from persons hired abroad to work for cheap wages and whose transportation to the United States was paid for by someone else. It first appeared in the 1885 law. In the 1891 act persons whose tickets or passage was paid for by money of another or who were assisted by others to come were excluded. Exceptions were made for persons helped by friends or relatives and for ministers or professors. Help from Utah conceivably could disqualify a British Saint from entry. The 1891 law also had a contagious disease provision. Two years later the president was given authority to exclude aliens if a serious threat of disease should arise.[51] The power never was exercised.[52]

Exclusion, the technique selected by Congress to implement its various policy decisions on immigration, was a rather ineffective means for carrying out such policy determinations. Polygamists, paupers, contract laborers, and even some sick persons were not visibly different from other would-be immigrants. Mormon groups could be identified because of their shipboard conduct, but U.S. officials could not readily determine which, if any, of them fell into the banned classes. Screening abroad through an entry permit or visa requirement was not instituted by the United States until 1918.[53] Application forms and documentation before departure can keep out persons ineligible for entry better than inquiry upon their arrival.

The British Mormon migration between 1842 and 1891 took place when generally the law either was favorable or at least neutral toward persons leaving Great Britain, crossing the Atlantic, and entering the United

---

[50] Jensen, "Steaming Through," 7–8.
[51] 22 Stat. 214 (1882); 34 Stat. 898 (1907); 23 Stat. 732 (1885); 26 Stat. 1084, § 1, 5 (1891); 27 Stat. 449 (1893).
[52] Hutchinson, *Legislative History*, 417.
[53] 40 Stat. 559 (1918).

States. After the bulk of the migration, the law on the American end turned less supportive. Perhaps it was mere historical accident that such was the case. But at least the benign legal regime during the Victorian era eliminated one source of trouble in what was already a difficult undertaking. It can be said, paraphrasing Daniel, "And none did stay their way."[54]

---

[54] Daniel 4:35.

16

Mormonism in Victorian Britain:
A Bibliographic Essay

DAVID J. WHITTAKER

July 19, 1987, marked the 150th anniversary of the arrival of the first Mormon missionaries to Liverpool harbor. The following day, the missionary contingent disembarked; shortly thereafter they headed north to Preston, where a brother of one of the missionaries lived. From Preston the missionary work spread up the Ribble Valley, north toward Scotland, and south toward the Manchester area. In the spring of 1840 a second wave of missionaries arrived in Liverpool. Consisting mainly of members of the Quorum of the Twelve Apostles, this group added much-needed organizational and leadership skills to the effort. By 1842 missionaries had visited all the key locations in England, and had established branches in Scotland, Ireland, the Isle of Man, in addition to the eastern edges of Wales. By the time they departed (1841–42) the British Mission was well organized and supported by an effective publishing and emigration program. Together, these early missions laid the foundations for the most successful LDS foreign mission in the nineteenth century. And once a successful beachhead was established in Great Britain, Mormon missionaries fanned out into Europe, and then, following the routes of the British Empire, into many other areas of the world.

The purpose of this essay is to suggest bibliographical material for the student interested in the history of the LDS Church in the British Isles. The focus will be on the nineteenth century, the period coinciding with the reign of Victoria.

THE HISTORICAL/CULTURAL SETTING

The Industrial Revolution began in England. By the 1830s canals and rails spider-webbed the land. The economic upheaval that industrialization brought would forever change not only England, but the world. Good histories of England describe in detail these changes and their implications for British religious history. The standard textbook by David Harris Willson and Stuart E. Prall, *A History of England*, 3d ed. (New York: Holt, Rinehart and Winston, 1984) is an excellent place to begin. Two recent histories, both with good illustrations, are Kenneth O. Morgan, ed., *The Oxford Illustrated History of Britain* (New York: Oxford University Press, 1984) and Asa Briggs, *A Social History of England* (New York: Viking Press, 1984). Histories of England covering the nineteenth century include Ernest L. Woodward, *The Age of Reform, 1815–1870*, 2d ed. (Oxford: The Clarendon Press, 1962); Asa Briggs, *The Making of Modern England, 1784–1867, The Age of Improvement* (New York: Harper and Row, 1965), originally published in 1959; Walter L. Arnstein, *Britain, Yesterday and Today, 1830 to the Present*, 5th ed. (Lexington, Mass.: D.C. Heath, 1987); J. F. C. Harrison, *The Early Victorians, 1832–51* (London: Weidenfeld and Nicolson, 1971), published in America as *Early Victorian Britain*; Geoffrey Best, *Mid-Victorian Britain, 1851–1875* (London: Weidenfeld and Nicolson, 1971); William L. Burn, *The Age of Equipoise, A Study of the Mid-Victorian Generation* (New York: Norton, 1965); Walter E. Houghton, *The Victorian Frame of Mind, 1830–1870* (New Haven: Yale University Press, 1957); Norman Gash, *Aristocracy and People, Britain, 1815–1865* (London: Edward Arnold Publishers, 1979), a volume in the "New History of England" series, published by Harvard University Press in the U.S.; R. K. Webb, *Modern England*, 2d ed. (New York: Harper and Row, 1980); Anthony Wood, *Nineteenth Century Britain, 1815–1914*, 2d ed. (New York: Longman, 1982); Edward P. Thompson, *The Making of the English Working Class* (New York: Random House, 1963); Dorothy Marshall, *Industrial England, 1776–1851*, 2d ed. (London: Routledge and Kegan Paul, 1982); F. M. L. Thompson, *The Rise of Respectable Society, A Social History of Victorian Britian, 1830–1900* (Cambridge: Harvard University Press, 1988); and Edward Royle, *Modern Britain: A Social History, 1750–1985* (London: Edward Arnold, 1988). Probably the best biography of Queen Victoria is Stanley Weintraub, *Victoria: An Intimate Biography* (New York: Dutton, 1987). Also valuable is G. Kitson Clark, *The Making of Victorian England* (Cambridge: Harvard University Press, 1962). The story of the Empire is told in John Bowle, *The Imperial Achievement, The Rise and Transformation of the British Empire* (Harmondsworth: Penguin Books, 1977); Walter Phelps Hall et al., *A History of England and the Empire-Commonwealth*, 4th ed. (Waltham, Mass.: Blaisdell Publishing Co., 1961); and T. O. Lloyd, *The British Empire, 1558–1983* (Oxford: Oxford University Press, 1984).

The most useful atlas from a historical perspective is Malcolm Falkus and John Gillingham, eds., *Historical Atlas of Britain* (London: Granada Publishing, 1981). Also valuable are W. G. Hoskins, *The Making of the English Landscape* (Harmondsworth, England: Penguin Books, 1970), first published in 1955; and Paul Coones and John Patten, *The Penguin Guide to the Landscape of England and Wales* (New York: Viking Penguin, Inc., 1986). An important source of historical, statistical, and demographic information, also containing detailed maps, is Samuel Lewis, *A Topographical Dictionary of England . . . ,* 4 vols. (London: S. Lewis and Co., 1831). The Religious Census of 1851 has much information on the Mormons, including meeting locations. See *Census of Great Britain, 1851, Religious Worship, England and Wales, Report and Tables* (London: George E. Eyer and William Spottiswood for Her Majesty's Stationery Office, 1853). A good study of this census is Kenneth S. Inglis, "Patterns of Religious Worship in 1851," *Journal of Ecclesiastical History* 11 (April 1960): 74–86.

Bibliographic guides to the Victorian era include Josef Lewis Altholz, *Victorian England, 1837–1901* (Cambridge: Cambridge University Press for the Conference on British Studies, 1970); Lionel Madden, *How to Find Out About the Victorian Period, A Guide to Sources of Information* (Oxford: Pergamon Press, 1970); and more comprehensively, the following two volumes: Lucy M. Brown and Ian R. Christie, eds., *Bibliography of British History, 1789–1851* (Oxford: The Clarendon Press, 1977); and H. J. Hanham, comp. and ed., *Bibliography of British History, 1851–1914* (Oxford: The Clarendon Press, 1976). A valuable scholarly periodical is *Victorian Studies*; the same journal has issued Brahma Chaudhuri, ed., *Annual Bibliography of Victorian Studies* (Edmonton, Alberta: LITIR Database) since 1981.

Students of local history are well served by the following: William B. Stephens, *Sources for English Local History*, 2d ed. (Cambridge: Cambridge University Press, 1981); W. G. Hoskins, *Local History in England*, 3d ed. (London: Longman, 1984); Alan Rogers, *Approaches to Local History*, 2d ed. (London: Longman, 1977); and John Richardson et al., *The Local Historian's Encyclopedia*, 2d ed. (New Barnet, Hertsfordshire: Historical Publications, 1986). For those seeking historical aids for their genealogical research in the British Isles, see vols. 5–6 ("British Family and Local History") in *World Conference on Records, Preserving Our Heritage, 12–15 August 1980* (Salt Lake City: The Church of Jesus Christ of Latter-day Saints, 1980).

The student of Mormon history will be interested in the history of religion in Britain, and while there is no one complete work which covers all of the essential topics, the following studies will be useful. The general reader will find David L. Edwards, *Christian England*, 3 vols. (Grand Rapids, Mich.: Eerdmans Publishing Co., 1980–1984) useful and very readable. Horton Davies, *Worship and Theology in England*, 5 vols. (Princeton, N.J.: Princeton University Press, 1961–75) treats theology in much more detail. J. R. H. Moorman, *A History of the Church in England*, 3d ed. (London: Adam and Charles Black, 1973) is an excellent one-volume survey. W. R. Ward, *Religion and Society in England, 1790–1850* (London: B. T. Batsford, Ltd., 1972) is an excellent but complicated study of Methodism, with relevance to many early Mormon themes. Studies which provide the details of the context for Mormonism in nineteenth-century Britain include Ernest E. Best, *Religion and Society in Transition: The Church and Social Change in England, 1560-1850* (New York: Edwin Mellen Press, 1982); A. D. Gilbert, *Religion and Society in Industrial England, Church, Chapel and Social Change, 1740-1914* (New York: Longman, 1976); Thomas Walter Laqueur, *Religion and Respectability: Sunday Schools and Working Class Culture, 1780-1850* (New Haven: Yale University Press, 1976); Hugh McLeod, *Religion and the Working Class in Nineteenth-Century Britain* (London: Macmillan, 1984); Paul T. Phillips, *The Sectarian Spirit: Sectarianism, Society and Politics in the Victorian Cotton Towns* (Toronto: University of Toronto Press, 1982); Kenneth S. Inglis, *Churches and the Working Classes in Victorian England* (London: Routledge and Kegan Paul, 1963); George Kitson Clark, *Churchmen and the Condition of England, 1832-1885* (London: Methuen, 1973); J. F. C. Harrison, *The Second Coming, Popular Millenarianism, 1780-1850* (Brunswick, N.J.: Rutgers University Press, 1979); Owen Chadwick, *The Victorian Church*, 2 vols., 3d ed. (London: SCM Press, 1987); Desmond Bowen, *The Idea of the Victorian Church: A Study of the Church of England, 1833-1889* (Montreal: McGill University Press, 1968); and Robert Curie, Alan D. Gilbert, and Lee Horsley, *Churches and Churchgoers: Patterns of Church Growth in the British Isles since 1700* (Oxford: Clarendon Press, 1977).

David Hempton, *Methodism and Politics in British Society, 1750-1850* (London: Hutchinson, 1984) suggests useful categories for approaching the major themes of the period. Another important study is Julia Stewart Werner, *The Primitive Methodist Connexion: Its Background and Early History* (Madison: University of Wisconsin Press, 1984). See also Rupert E. Davies and Gordon Rupp, eds., *A History of the Methodist Church in Great Britain*, 3 vols. (London: Epworth Press, 1965-83). A related study is Brian H. Harrison, *Drink and the Victorians: The Temperance Question in England, 1815-1872* (London: Faber and Faber, 1971).

James Obelkevich, *Religion and Rural Society, South Lindsay, 1825-1875* (Oxford: Clarendon Press, 1976) is an excellent study of the broad spectrum of religious experience, from folk religion to the established church, in its social context. This study suggests the increasing attention that scholars are giving to the lives and activities of common people. A valuable history from this perspective in J. F. C. Harrison, *The Common People of Great Britain* (Bloomington: Indiana University Press, 1985). The same author takes a closer look at the Mormons in "The Popular History of Early Victorian Britain: A Mormon Contribution," *Journal of Mormon History* 14 (1988): 3-15, reprinted in the present volume. The history of Mormonism in Great Britain is but one example of the Anglo-American religious connection; a good study emphasizing a major aspect of this relationship is Richard Carwardine, *Transatlantic Revivalism, Popular Evan-*

gelicalism in Britain and America, 1790–1865 (Westport, Conn.: Greenwood Press, 1978).

British attempts to understand the Mormons can be traced through histories and travel accounts in the nineteenth century. Perhaps the most popular history was Charles Mackay, The Mormons; or the Latter-Day Saints, which went through five London editions between 1851 and 1857. A good discussion of this work is in Leonard J. Arrington, "Charles Mackay and His 'True and Impartial History' of the Mormons," Utah Historical Quarterly 36 (Winter 1968): 24–40. Richard F. Burton, The City of the Saints (London, 1862) is discussed in Fawn M. Brodie, "Sir Richard Burton: Exceptional Observer of the Mormon Scene," Utah Historical Quarterly, 38 (Fall 1963): 295–311. The larger picture is presented in Edwina Jo Snow, "Singular Saints: The Image of the Mormons in Book-Length Travel Accounts, 1847–1857" (MA thesis, George Washington University, 1972); and more specifically in her two essays: "William Chandless: British Overlander, Mormon Observer, Amazon Explorer," Utah Historical Quarterly 54 (Spring 1986): 116–36; and "British Travelers View the Mormons, 1847–1877," forthcoming in BYU Studies.

THE BRITISH MISSION, 1837–1900

There is no adequate one-volume history of Mormonism in Great Britain. Richard L. Evans, A Century of "Mormonism" in Great Britain (Salt Lake City: Deseret News Press, 1937), reprinted by Bookcraft, 1986, was for many years the only survey. It is heavily dependent upon the Millennial Star for its historical substance, although the author did consult several "Manuscript Histories" of various British units of the church. In general, however, the volume is inadequate for the contemporary student of LDS British history. The availability of many documentary sources today reveals errors of both fact and judgment in this pioneering effort. A one-volume multiauthored comprehensive history of the church in Great Britain has recently appeared: V. Ben Bloxham, James R. Moss, and Larry C. Porter, eds., Truth Will Prevail: The Rise of the Church of Jesus Christ of Latter-day Saints in the British Isles, 1837–1987 (Solihull, England: The Church of Jesus Christ of Latter-day Saints, 1987). While the volume is a welcome addition to the literature, it is seriously marred by the uneven scholarship of the essays as well as by the serious flaw of a last-minute editorial decision to eliminate the bibliographical references for the entire volume, thus preventing the serious student from being able to follow up on the sources used in the various essays. Those references are, however, available on request from the Religious Studies Center at Brigham Young University.

A valuable guide to the diaries and journals of Mormon history is Davis Bitton, comp., A Guide to Mormon Diaries and Autobiographies (Provo,

Utah: Brigham Young University Press, 1976). A useful index arranged by topic can help the researcher quickly locate the relevant records for Britain. This volume is a good guide to the holdings of various repositories to about 1973, but the serious student must check with the respective library or archive for more recent acquistions. An excellent guide to the printed matter relating to the first 100 years of Mormon history is Chad Flake, comp., *A Mormon Bibliography, 1830–1930* (Salt Lake City: University of Utah Press, 1978). A ten-year update will soon be released by the same press. The most important repository of Mormon material, particularly as it relates to the British experience, is the Archives/Library of the Historical Department, The Church of Jesus Christ of Latter-day Saints, Salt Lake City. Particularly valuable are the various "Manuscript Histories" of the various units of the church throughout the British Isles. A day-by-day history is available in the "Manuscript History of the British Mission." Also valuable are the European Mission Statistics, 1855–76, covering a period not reported in the *Millennial Star*, but available only by special permission. A guide to the various American repositories holding significant Mormon material in all areas will appear as a specical issue of *BYU Studies* being edited by David J. Whittaker.

In addition to the documentary sources, the student must spend many hours in the *Millennial Star*. Published in England from 1840 to 1970, in its pages are essays (historical and doctrinal), editorials on all aspects of Mormonism, letters from missionaries, reports of conferences on all levels of church units (general to branch), and counsel from church leaders in America. It is not possible to overemphasize the importance of this publication for a fuller understanding of the Mormon experience in Great Britain.

The first published history was *Journal of Heber C. Kimball . . . Giving an Account of His Mission to Great Britain, and the Commencement of the Work of the Lord in that Land . . .* (Nauvoo: Robinson and Smith, 1840). This sixty-page pamphlet remains a classic in Mormon literature, still conveying the dramatic story of the initial missionary work in England. But it was prepared without Kimball's journals and ought to be used in conjunction with the actual diaries, which are now conveniently available in Stanley B. Kimball, ed., *On the Potter's Wheel: The Diaries of Heber C. Kimball* (Salt Lake City: Signature Books and Smith Research Associates, 1987). A shorter account by Heber C. Kimball, Orson Hyde, and Willard Richards appears in *Millennial Star* 1 (April 1841): 289–96. Several important early letters have been edited for publication: see Ronald W. Walker, ed., "The Willard Richards and Brigham Young 5 September 1840 Letter from England to Nauvoo," *BYU Studies* 18 (Spring 1978): 466–75; and David H. Pratt, "Oh! Brother Joseph [letter of Parley P. Pratt to Joseph Smith, dated Manchester, 4 December 1841]," *BYU Studies* 27 (Winter 1987): 127–31. A history of the first missions (1837–41) which makes extensive use of the large manuscript holdings of the Historical Department of the LDS Church is James B. Allen, Ronald K. Esplin, and David J. Whittaker, "Young Men with a Mission" (tentative title of forthcoming volume). A survey of the early Mormon letters and diaries in Britain with an eye to their literary quality is Eugene England, "A Modern Acts of the Apostles, 1840: Mormon Literature in the Making," *BYU Studies* 27 (Spring 1987): 79–95. Photographic essays include "A Pictorial Story of the Founding of the Church in the British Isles," *The New Era* 1 (November 1971): 20–27; and "The Way it Looks Today: A Camera Tour of Church History Sites in Great Britain," *The Ensign* 9 (December 1979): 32–45. A useful pocket guide to the early Mormon historic sites in the British Isles is James R. and Lavelle Moss, *Historic Sites of The Church of Jesus Christ of Latter-day Saints in the British Isles* (Salt Lake City: Publishers Press for The Church of Jesus Christ of Latter-day Saints, 1987). While this work is a good beginning, much more work needs to be done on local site identification and history.

The most scholarly study of the nineteenth-century Mormon experience in Great Britain is P. A. M. Taylor, *Expectations Westward: The Mormons and the Emigration of Their British Converts in the Nineteenth Century* (Ithaca: Cornell University Press, 1966), first published in Edinburgh in 1965. Based on his dissertation at Cambridge University in 1950, Taylor carefully examines both the British setting and the subsequent gathering to church headquarters in America. The American setting of the church at the time of the first British Mission is given in Milton V. Backman, Jr., *The Heavens Resound: A History of the Latter-day Saints in Ohio, 1830–1838* (Salt Lake City: Deseret Book Co., 1983), esp. 107–24; and James B. Allen and Glen M. Leonard, *The Story of the Latter-day Saints* (Salt Lake City: Deseret Book Co., 1976). Shorter treatments of the first missions include Stanley B. Kimball, "First Mission to Britain," *The Improvement Era* 64 (October 1961): 720–21, 744, 746; Norman Hill, "The Trumpet of Zion: Mormon Conversion and Emigration in Britain," *Tangents* 3 (Spring 1975): 56–69; James B. Allen and Malcolm R. Thorp, "The Mission of the Twelve to England, 1840–1841: Mormon Apostles and the Working Classes," *BYU Studies* 15 (Summer 1975): 489–526; Malcolm R. Thorp, "The Religious Backgrounds of Mormon Converts in Britain, 1837–52," *Journal of Mormon History* 4 (1977): 51–66; Thorp, "The Setting for the Restoration in Britain: Political, Social and Economic Conditions," *Truth Will Prevail*, 44–70; Thorp, "Social and Religious Origins of Early English Mormons," *World Conference on Records, Preserving Our Heritage, 12–15 August 1980*, 13 vols. (Salt Lake City: The Church of Jesus Christ of Latter-day Saints, 1980), vol. 6, Series 444; Thorp, "Sectarian Violence in Early Victorian Britain: The Mormon Experience, 1837–1860," forthcoming in *Bulletin of the John Rylands Library*; Lavina Fielding Anderson, "In the Crucible: Early British Saints," *The Ensign* 9 (December 1979): 50-55; John E. Thompson, "A History of the British Mission of the Latter Day Saints (1837-1841)," *Restoration Studies I* (Independence, Mo.: Temple School of the Reorganized Church of Jesus Christ of Latter Day Saints, 1980), 42-57; closely following Joseph Smith's *History of the Church*; James R. Moss, "Laying the Foundations in Britain," in *The International Church*, ed. Moss et al. (Provo, Utah: Brigham Young University Press, 1982), 13-28; and Alice Kimball Smith, "The Opening of the British Mission," *Utah Genealogical and Historical Magazine* 3 (1912): 53-64. A popular survey of the history of the LDS Church through the Victorian period is Richard O. Cowan, "Church Growth in England, 1841-1914," *Truth Will Prevail*, 199-235.

Good treatments of these formative years are found in the various biographies of the key individuals who were involved. Thus the serious student will want to consult the appropriate chapters in the following works: James B. Allen and Thomas G. Alexander, eds., *Manchester Mormons: The Journal of William Clayton, 1840-1842* (Salt Lake City: Peregrine Smith, 1974); James B. Allen, *Trials of Discipleship: The Life of William Clayton* (Urbana: University of Illinois Press, 1987); Orson F. Whitney, *Life of Heber C. Kimball* (Salt Lake City: Kimball Family, 1888), 3d ed., 1967; Stanley B. Kimball, *Heber C. Kimball* (Urbana: University of Illinois Press, 1981); Eugene England, *Brother Brigham* (Salt Lake City: Bookcraft, 1980); Leonard J. Arrington, *Brigham Young, American Moses* (New York: Alfred A. Knopf, 1985); Ronald K. Esplin, "Brigham Young in England," *The Ensign* 17 (June 1987): 28-33; Breck England, *The Life and Thought of Orson Pratt* (Salt Lake City: University of Utah Press, l985); Richard H. Cracroft, "Liverpool, 1856: Nathaniel Hawthorne Meets Orson Pratt," *BYU Studies* 8 (Spring 1968): 270-72; Matthias F. Cowley, *Wilford Woodruff, History of His Life and Labors* (Salt Lake City: Bookcraft, 1964), originally published in 1909; Scott Kenney, ed., *Wilford Woodruff's Journal*, 9 vols. (Midvale, Utah: Signature Books, 1983-85), vols. 1-2; David J. Whittaker, "Harvest in Herefordshire'" *The Ensign* 17 (January 1987): 46-51; Arthur B. Erekson, *A History of John Benbow* (Provo, Utah: by the author, 1987); Howard H. Barron, *Orson Hyde, Missionary, Apostle, Colonizer* (Bountiful, Utah: Horizon Publishers, 1977); B. H. Roberts, *The Life of John Taylor* (Salt Lake City: Bookcraft, 1963) originally published in 1892; Samuel W. Taylor, *The Kingdom or Nothing: The Life of John Taylor, Militant Mormon* (New York: Macmillan, 1976); Eliza R. Snow, *Biography and Family Record of Lorenzo Snow* (Salt Lake City: Deseret News Co., 1884); Parley Parker Pratt, ed., *Autobiography of Parley P. Pratt* (Salt Lake City: Deseret News Press, l985), Utah: original ed. 1874; Merlo J. Pusey, *Builders of the Kingdom* . . . (Provo, Utah: Brigham Young University Press, 1981), 36-44 (George A. Smith) and 139-46 (John Henry Smith); Richard W. Sadler,

"Franklin D. Richards and the British Mission," *Journal of Mormon History* 14 (1988): 81–95; Lawrence R. Flake, "George Q. Cannon: His Missionary Years," (D.R.E. dissertation, Brigham Young University, 1970); Leonard J. Arrington, *Charles C. Rich* (Provo, Utah: Brigham Young University Press, 1974), 225–46; John R. Talmage, *The Talmage Story; Life of James E. Talmage — Educator, Scientist, Apostle* (Salt Lake City: Bookcraft, 1972), 1–12, 203–18; T. Edgar Lyon, Jr., "In Praise of Babylon: Church Leadership at the 1851 Great Exhibition in London," *Journal of Mormon History* 14 (1988): 49–61; Donald Q. Cannon, "George Q. Cannon and the British Mission," *BYU Studies* 27 (Winter 1987): 97–112; and Kenneth W. Godfrey, "Charles W. Penrose: The English Mission Years," *BYU Studies* 27 (Winter 1987): 113–25. The lives of Mormon women in Britain have generally been ignored by historians; a limited corrective is Leonard J. Arrington, "Mormon Women in Nineteenth-Century Britain," *BYU Studies* 27 (Winter 1987): 67–83.

Important unpublished graduate studies are Sam Hamerman, "The Mormon Missionaries in England, 1837–1852" (MA thesis, University of California, Berkeley, 1937); Robert L. Lively, "The Catholic Apostolic Church and the Church of Jesus Christ of Latter-day Saints: A Comparative Study of Two Minority Millenarian Groups in Nineteenth-Century England" (D.Phil. thesis, Mansfield College, Oxford University, 1972); Susan L. Fales, "The Nonconformists of Leeds in the Early Victorian Era: A Study in Social Composition" (MA thesis, Brigham Young University, 1984); John Cotterill, "Midland Saints: The Mormon Mission in the West Midlands, 1837–77" (Ph.D. thesis, University of Keele, 1985); and Jan Harris, "The Mormons in Victorian England" (MA thesis, Brigham Young University, 1987), some of which is presented in "Mormons in Victorian Manchester," *BYU Studies* 27 (Winter 1987): 47–56. A valuable study of early Latter-day Saints in London is Lynone W. Jorgensen, " 'What Am I and My Brethren Here For?': The First London Mormons, 1840–1845" (MA thesis, Brigham Young Univeristy, 1988).

For a look at anti-Mormon polemics in the early Victorian period, see Craig L. Foster, "Anti-Mormon Pamphleteering in Great Britain, 1837–1860" (MA thesis, Brigham Young University, 1989).

The gathering of British converts to America has been the subject of a variety of studies. Accounting for about 20 percent of Utah's population between 1860 and 1880, this emigration had, and continues to have, a tremendous impact on the church. The first immigrants gathered to Nauvoo: see the short essay by Stanley B. Kimball, "The First Immigrants to Nauvoo," *The Improvement Era* 66 (March 1963): 178–80, 209–10. The first group of emigrating members is the subject of James B. Allen, ed., " 'We Had a Very Hard Voyage for the Season': John Moon's Account of the First Emigrant Company of British Saints," *BYU Studies* 17 (Spring 1977): 339–41.

Scholarly examinations of various aspects of Mormon emigration include W. H. G. Armytage, "Liverpool, Gateway to Zion," *Pacific Northwest Quarterly* 58 (April 1957): 39–43; Gustive O. Larson, "Story of the Perpetual Emigrating Fund Co.," *Mississippi Valley Historical Review* 18 (September 1931): 184–94 (based on his MA thesis, University of Utah, 1926); Larson, *Prelude to the Kingdom* (Francistown, N.H.: Marshall Jones Co., 1947); Larson, "The Mormon Gathering," in *Utah's History*, ed. Richard D. Poll et al. (Provo, Utah: Brigham Young University Press, 1978), 175–91; M. Hamlin Cannon, "The 'Gathering' of British Mormons to Western America: A Study in Religious Migration," (Ph.D. dissertation, American University, 1950); Cannon, "Migration of English Mormons to America," *American Historical Review* 52 (April 1947): 436–55; Taylor, *Expectations Westward*; Taylor, "Why Did British Mormons Emigrate?" *Utah Historical Quarterly* 22 (July 1954): 249–70; Taylor, "Mormons and Gentiles on the Atlantic," *Utah Historical Quarterly* 24 (July 1956): 195–214; Taylor, "The Mormon Crossing of the United States, 1840–1870," *Utah Historical Quarterly* 25 (October 1957): 319–38; William Mulder, "Mormonism's 'Gathering': An American Doctrine with a Difference," *Church History* 23 (September 1954): 248–68; Wilbur S. Shepperson, "The Place of the Mormons in the Religious Emigration of Britain," *Church History* 20 (July 1952): 207–18; Glenn M. Leonard, "Westward the Saints: The Nineteenth-Century Mormon Migration," *The Ensign* 10 (January 1980): 6–13; Conway B. Sonne, *Saints on the Seas: A Maritime History of Mormon Migration, 1830–1890* (Salt Lake City: University of Utah Press, 1983); Sonne, *Ships, Saints, and Mariners: A Maritime Encyclopedia of Mormon Migration, 1830–1890* (Salt Lake City: University of Utah Press, 1987); David H. Pratt and Paul F. Richards, "Life on Board a Mormon Emigrant Ship," *World Conference on Records, Preserving Our Heritage, 12–15 August 1980* (Salt Lake City: Corporation of the President, The Church of Jesus Christ of Latter-day Saints, 1980), Series 418 (Volume 5), 1–34; Richard L. Jensen and Gordon Irving, "The Voyage of the Amazon: A Close View of One Immigrant Company," *The Ensign* 10 (March 1980): 16–19; William G. Hartley, "'Down and Back' Wagon Trains," *The Ensign* 15 (September 1985): 26–31; Hartley, "The Great Florence Fitout of 1861," *BYU Studies* 24 (Summer 1984): 341–71; Hartley, "Coming to Zion: Saga of the Gathering," *The Ensign* 5 (July 1975): 14–18; Richard L. Jensen, "The British Gathering to Zion," *Truth Will Prevail*, 165–98; and James B. Allen, ed., "To the Saints in England: Impressions of a Mormon Immigrant," *BYU Studies* 18 (Spring 1978): 475–82. Not to be forgotten is James Linforth, *Route from Liverpool to Great Salt Lake Valley, Illustrated . . . From Sketches Made by Frederick Piercy . . .* (Liverpool: F. D. Richards, 1855), reprinted in 1962 with an introduction by Fawn M. Brodie. Two valuable studies of the larger story of Britons in the American West are Clark C. Spence, *British Investments and the American Mining Frontier, 1860–1901* (Ithaca: Cornell University Press for the American Historical Association, 1958); and Oscar Osburn Winther, "English Migration to the American West," *Huntington Library Quarterly* 27 (February 1964): 159–73. See also W. Turrentine Jackson, "British Impact on the Utah Mining Industry," *Utah Historical Quarterly* 31 (Fall 1963): 347–75.

Studies of missionary work in Scotland include Breck England, "Gospel Seeds in Scottish Soil," *The Ensign* 17 (February 1987): 26–31; Frederick S. Buchanan, "The Emigration of Scottish Mormons to Utah, 1849–1900" (MS thesis, University of Utah, 1961); Buchanan, "Scots Among the Mormons," *Utah Historical Quarterly* 36 (Fall 1968): 328–52; Buchanan, "The Ebb and Flow of the Church in Scotland," in *Truth Will Prevail*, 268–98; and Buchanan, "The Ebb and Flow of Mormonism in Scotland, 1840–1900," *BYU Studies* 27 (Spring 1987): 27–52. An important series of nineteenth-century letters dealing with the Mormon-Scottish experience (1853–72) appears in Frederick Stewart Buchanan, ed., *A Good Time Coming: Mormon Letters to Scotland* (Salt Lake City: University of Utah Press, 1988). A look at one area of impact is Linda L. Bonar, "The Influence of the Scots Stonemasons in Beaver, Utah," *Utah Preservation/Restoration* 3 (1981): 54–60.

The first scholarly study of Mormonism in Wales was T. H. Lewis, *Y Mormoniaid Yng Nghymru* (Caerdydd: Gwasg Prifysgol Cymru, 1956). More accessible studies are Douglas James Davies, "The Mormons at Merthyr-Tydfil" (B.Litt. thesis, Oxford University, 1972); and Davies, *Mormon Spirituality: Latter-day Saints in Wales and Zion* (Nottingham: University of Nottingham, 1987; Logan, Utah: distributed by Utah State University Press, 1987). See also T. H. Lewis, "Letters from Welsh Pioneers," *The Ensign* 1 (September 1971): 35–37; and Thomas J. Griffiths, "Out of Darkness Came Light," *The New Era* 11 (June 1981): 8–11. Ronald D. Dennis, with command of the Welsh language, has prepared two book-length studies. One is an immigration study: *The Call of Zion: The Story of the First Welsh Mormon Emigration* (Provo, Utah: Brigham Young University, 1987); the second is a bibliographical study of the more than one hundred Welsh Mormon imprints, *Welsh Mormon Writings from 1844 to 1862: A Historical Bibliography* (Provo, Utah: Brigham Young University, 1988). Dennis's overview of the Welsh Mission is "The Welsh and the Gospel," *Truth Shall Prevail*, 236–67; his study of the activities of early Welsh anti-Mormonism is in "The Reverend W. R. Davies vs. Captain Dan Jones," *BYU Studies* 27 (Spring 1987): 53–65. Ronald Dennis has also edited the published Welsh letters of Dan Jones, *Captain Dan Jones, The Millennial Star Letters, 1845–1856* (Provo, Utah: published by the editor, 1971). See also Rex LeRoy Christensen, "The Life and Contributions of Captain Dan Jones" (MA thesis, Utah State University, 1977).

The beginning work on the church in Ireland (though somewhat sketchy and impressionistic) is Brent A. Barlow, "History of the Church . . . in Ireland since 1840" (MA thesis, Brigham Young University, 1968); see also Barlow, "The Mormons and the Irish," *The Improvement Era* 72 (April 1969): 36–40; and Barlow, "The Irish Experience," in *Truth Will Prevail*, 299–331. John Taylor recalled in 1870 the opening of the Irish Mission: see *Juvenile Instructor* 5 (October 15, 1870): 166–67.

Early missionary work on the Isle of Man by John Taylor is discussed in his letter of February 3, 1841, in *Times and Seasons* 2 (May 1, 1841): 400–402; in his letter of February 27, 1841, in *Millennial Star* 1 (March 1841): 276–80; in his undated letter to Parley P. Pratt in *Millennial Star* 2 (May 1841): 12–16; and in the letter of James Blakeslee to Joseph Smith, dated June 11, 1841, in *Times and Seasons* 2 (July 15, 1841): 483–85. The papers of an early convert and later plural wife of John Taylor, Ann Pitchforth, are in the Brigham Young University archives. See also Paul Thomas Smith, "Among Family and Friends: John Taylor's Mission to the British Isles," *The Ensign* 17 (March 1987): 36–41.

THE EMPIRE AND BEYOND

The movement of Mormonism into Europe and beyond is too large a topic to be dealt with here. However, the expansion of the church through the British Empire needs to be mentioned. Early Mormon missionaries followed the routes of the British Empire much like Paul moved throughout the Roman Empire centuries earlier. No study traces this in detail, but a useful place to begin is with David J. Whittaker, "Pamphleteering in an International Setting," in "Early Mormon Pamphleteering" (Ph.D. dissertation, Brigham Young University, 1982), 236–320, which traces the movement of Mormon missionaries in the Mediterranean, then to South Africa, India, and Australia. This study cites most of the relevant literature. See also Peter Crawley and David J. Whittaker, *Mormon Imprints in Great Britain and the Empire* (Provo, Utah: Friends of the Brigham Young University Library, 1987).

By the end of the 1840s, with the closing down of Mormon presses in Nauvoo and New York, Liverpool took on more importance in the publishing affairs of the church. For the next fifty years Liverpool was *the* Book Supply Depot for church literature. An essay on these developments is David J. Whittaker's, "Early Mormon Pamphleteering," *Journal of Mormon History* 4 (1977): 35–49, and more fully in Whittaker's dissertation by the same title, and in Whittaker, "To 'Hurl Truth Through the Land': Publications of the Twelve [in the British Isles], 1837–1842," (forthcoming). Thus Liverpool supplied LDS missionaries all over the world with tracts and various published items. From England came important tracts of Parley P. Pratt and his brother Orson. In 1851 *The Pearl of Great Price* first appeared, compiled initially as a useful collection of early historical and scriptural items for new converts. It was added to the the the Mormon canon in a general conference in 1880, with many in the conference audience being British converts who had "grown up" with the work. In 1853 the first biography in the church, Lucy Mack Smith's *Biographical Sketches of Joseph Smith the Prophet and His Progenitors for Many Generations*, was published in England. The first compilation of general conference addresses was issued in England: *The Journal of Discourses* appeared from 1854 to 1886. Because of the lower costs of printing and binding, many editions of the LDS scriptures were printed in England in the nineteenth century. In fact, the current editions of the LDS Hymnal and the Book of Mormon trace their roots to early British editions. Additional perspectives are provided in Gordon K. Thomas, "The Book of Mormon in the English Literary Context of 1837," *BYU Studies* 27 (Winter 1987): 37–45; and Thomas E. Lyon, "Publishing a Book of Mormon Poetry: *The Harp of Zion* [by John Lyon]," *BYU Studies* 27 (Winter 1987): 85–95.

The impact of the British Mission on the church is suggested in Ronald K. Esplin, "A Preparation for Ascendency: Brigham Young and the Quorum Experience in England, 1840–1841," in Esplin, "The Emergence of Brigham Young and the Twelve to Mormon Leadership, 1830–1841" (Ph.D. dissertation, Brigham Young University, 1981), 427–98. See also the perceptive essay by Ronald W. Walker, "Cradling Mormonism: The Rise of the Gospel in Early Victorian England," *BYU Studies* 27 (Winter 1987): 25–36. The "decline" is the subject of Bruce A. Van Orden, "The Decline in Convert Baptisms and Member Emigration from the British Mission after 1870," *BYU Studies* 27 (Spring 1987): 97–105, although this study is impressionistic and lacks a sociological perspective. Other studies include Roger J. Kendle, "The British Legacy in the Church—Preston's Proud Saints," *The Ensign* 9 (December 1979): 46–49; James R. Moss, "The British Legacy in the Church—The Kingdom Builders," *The Ensign* 9 (December 1979): 26–31; Frederick S. Buchanan, "Imperial Zion: The British Occupation of Utah," in *The Peoples of Utah*, ed. Helen Z. Papanikolas (Salt Lake City: Utah State Historical Society, 1976), 61–113; Kate B. Carter, ed., "British Contributions to Utah," *Heart Throbs of the West*, vol. 20 (Salt Lake City: Daughters of Utah Pioneers, 1941), 73–112; Ronald W. Walker, "The Godbeite Protest in the Making of Modern Utah" (Ph.D. dissertation, University of Utah, 1977)—many of the key Godbeites were British converts; Walker, "Heber J. Grant's European Mission, 1903–1906," *Journal of Mormon History* 14 (1988): 17–33; William Mulder, "Immigration and the 'Mormon Question': An International Episode," *Western Political Quarterly* 9 (June 1956): 416–33; Malcolm R. Thorp, "The British Government and the Mormon Question, 1910–1922," *Journal of Church and State* 21 (Spring 1979): 305–23; Thorp, "The Mormon Peril': The Crusade Against the Saints in Britain, 1910–1914," *Journal of Mormon History* 2 (1975): 69–88; and Thorp, "Winifred Graham and the Mormon Image in England," *Journal of Mormon History* 6 (1979): 107–21. Important material on the early anti-Mormon films, many of which first appeared in England, is in Richard Alan Nelson, "A History of Latter-day Saint Screen Portrayals in the Anti-Mormon Film Era, 1905–1936" (MA thesis, Brigham Young University, 1975). Malcolm Thorp, "James E. Talmage and the Tradition of the Victorian Lives of Jesus," *Sunstone* 12 (January 1988): 8–13, suggests how influential some British religious writings have been on Mormon thought. Two valuable essays by John S. Tanner reveal the impact Milton had on Mormon thought: "Making a Mormon of Milton," *BYU Studies* 24 (Spring 1984): 191–206; and "Milton and the Early Mormon Defense of Polygamy," *Milton Quarterly* 21 (May 1987): 41–46. See also Richard J. Dunn, "Dickens and the Mormons," *BYU Studies* 8 (Spring 1968): 325–34.

Some studies concerned largely with more recent topics help place the Victorian period and its legacy for British Mormons in perspective. A useful place to start is David J. Whittaker, "Mormonism in Great Britain, 1837–1987," a short bibliographical essay in Mormon History Association *Newsletter*, 66 (July 1987): 1–4. More academic studies include Derek Cuthbert, "Church Growth in the British Isles, 1937–1987," *BYU Studies* 27 (Spring 1987): 13–26, which includes statistical information and charts; Madison H. Thomas, "The Influence of Traditional British Social Patterns on LDS Church Growth in Southwest Britain," *BYU Studies*, 27 (Spring 1987): 107–17; Tim B. Heaton, Stan L. Albrecht, and J. Randal Johnson, "The Making of British Saints in Historical Perspective," *BYU Studies*, 27 (Spring 1987): 119–35. Robert Buckle, "Mormons in Britain: A Survey," in *A Sociological Yearbook of Religion in Britain*, ed. Michael Hill, 7 vols. (London: SCM Press, 1971), vol.4, 122–79, presents valuable information on demography and statistics. Some comparative material is found in John Gray, "Some Aspects of the Social Geography of Religion in England: The Roman Catholics and the Mormons," in *A Sociological Yearbook of Religion in Britain*, vol. 1, 47–76.

Index

Harries, Thomas, 135, 140
Harris, George Henry, writing of, 9
Harris, Jan, 168, 170
Harrison, E. L. T., 228, 232, 242, 242n55
Harrison, John F. C., 159, 172
Harvis, Henry John, 176
Hay, Richard Constantine, 163
Hazen, Robert, writing of, 10
Headingley-cum-Burley, 158
Head Money Cases, 254
Head tax, 247, 249, 254
Hedlock, Reuben, 17, 96
Hemel Hempstead Branch, 206
Henderson v. Mayor of New York, 254
Henshaw, William, 119
Herefordshire, 93
Herrick, Joseph, 145
"High church" movement, 33, 34
Higinbotham, Jane, 8
Hobson, Jesse, 219
Holbeck, 158, 172–74, 176
Holland, John, 150
Holt, Robert, 207
Hope Street Chapel, 43, 64–65
Horton, Joseph, 162
House of Commons, 247
Howells, Llewelyn, 131
Howells, William, 119
Hunslet, 158, 172, 173, 176
Hutchinson, Robert, 111
Hyde, Orson, 17, 35–36, 51, 70, 71, 73, 75, 75n16, 75n18, 76, 77, 77n24, 88, 90
Hyde Branch, 205, 208

Immigration, 251; polygamy and, 252, 254–56, 255n47; regulation of, 243, 247–51, 254, 256; taxes on, 247, 249, 254. *See also* Emigration
Immigration Act of 1875, 252
Immigration Act of 1882, 254
Immigration and Naturalization Code, 255
Independents, 19, 22, 35, 145, 161–62n17, 166n26, 167
Industrial Revolution, 109, 164, 244, 258
Inglis, K. S., 23
Ipswich, 142, 146, 148, 150

Irish Potato Famine, 248
Irving, Edward, 46, 47, 113
Irvingites, 65, 66; Mormonism and, 45–47. *See also* Catholic Apostolic Church

Jarvis, Henry John, 177, 199
Jefferies, William, 218
Jehovah's Witnesses, 16, 29
Jeremy, Thomas Evans, 196, 196n8, 196n9, 222
Jews, 27n28, 41
John, Philip, 131
Johnston, Albert Sidney, 224, 236n36, 238
Jones, Abednego L., 133
Jones, Aneurin L., 121, 133
Jones, Anna, 121
Jones, Charles, 230
Jones, Dan, 119, 133n52, 134, 135, 139–41; photo of, 197
Jones, David Bevan. *See* Elfed, Dewi
Jones, Eleanor, 139
Jones, William, 121
Journal of Discourses, 204

Kane, Thomas L., 224, 231n20, 236, 238
Kent, Samuel, 41
Kilmarnock, 115, 185, 186n21
Kimball, Heber C., 17, 32, 35–36, 43, 49, 56, 67, 68, 70, 73–79, 75n16, 75n19, 76n23, 82–85, 84n52, 92, 94
Kimball, William H., 196n9; photo of, 197
Kingdom of God, 16, 27, 187, 189, 212, 223, 237
Kirkgate, 172, 174
Kirtland, 70–74, 76, 79n31, 89n67, 180
Kirtland High Council, 72, 72n8

Lancashire, 145, 168, 170
Land's End Conference, 203
Lang, John Dunmore, 112
Larkin, Elijah, 217
Latter-day Saints' Millennial Star, 17, 25–27, 27n28, 38, 45, 83, 83n44, 87, 88n65, 100, 127, 138, 151, 196, 200, 204, 221, 224–25, 225n3,